Penguin Education U P S 17

Leadership

Penguin Modern Psychology Readings

General Editor
B. M. Foss

Advisory Board
P. C. Dodwell
Marie Jahoda
S. G. Lee
W. M. O'Neil
R. L. Reid
Roger Russell
P. E. Vernon
George Westby

Leadership

Selected Readings

Edited by C. A. Gibb

Penguin Books

Penguin Books Ltd, Harmondsworth,
Middlesex, England
Penguin Books Inc., 7110 Ambassador Road,
Baltimore, Maryland 21207, U.S.A.
Penguin Books Ltd, Ringwood,
Victoria, Australia

First published by Penguin Books, 1969

Made and printed in Great Britain by
Richard Clay (The Chaucer Press), Ltd.,
Bungay, Suffolk
Set in Linotype Times

Contents

Part One **Introduction**

Part Two **A Beginning**

Part Three **Personality**

Part Four Interaction Theory

Part Five Emergence of Leaders

Part Six Followers

Part Seven A Contemporary View

Part Eight Leadership in Complex Situations

Part One **Introduction**

Leadership is a matter that concerns every member of society. Its study is the study of influence of one's behaviour by that of another. So much is every man involved in influence relationships with friends, colleagues, wife, and children as well as with group leaders, bosses, and political leadership, that it may seem superfluous for psychologists to devote time and other resources to the scientific study of the many relationships of which all men have first-hand experience. However, the very ubiquity of leadership and its far-reaching effects have directed a great deal of thoughtful attention to the nature and conditions of the power one man has over others. Men and children are fascinated by the inexplicable power of the hypnotist, historians by the great political power of national leaders, workers by the growth to power of business tycoons, and all of us by the extent to which the power of others infiltrates even the most intimate corners of our lives. It was natural and inevitable that at every stage of the development of psychology some psychologists should have applied their newly developed techniques and insights to the leadership process. This has not only given formal strength and scientific status to much that astute observers had known all along but it has refined knowledge of relationships and has contributed new insights, as this volume demonstrates.

Any attempt at disciplined thinking about leadership and leading immediately reveals the great variety of different concepts to which this term is applied. The leading yacht in a race, a nation's leading jockey or its leading poet, the leader of a political party or of a gang of thieves, the manager of a large industrial enterprise and a prime minister, all are leading by virtue of very different considerations. In general, psychological interest in this area has been restricted to relationships between people in which influence is exerted by one individual upon another or by one or a few individuals upon a larger number and this has become for psychology the definition of leadership. But even this requires refinement. One may be influenced by the disapproved behaviour of another to act in a way that otherwise he would not. In common parlance it is said he is driven rather than led to this action, and in general such an influence would not be included in the concept of leadership; it may, however, require consideration in the study of influence processes as the differentiation of 'push' and 'pull' leadership by Cooper and McGaugh (1963) suggests. (See Reading 14, page 243.) Leading implies a shared direction and common group membership which, in turn, implies common, or at least compatible, goals so related that each member in achieving his goals assists others to the achievement of their group-related objectives.

The study of leadership is essentially one aspect of the study of the mechanisms devised by groups for the efficient pursuit of their goals and for the satisfaction by members of those needs which have been group-invested. By a mechanism of role differentiation, groups use the differential characteristics of members to the advantage of all by assigning group tasks to those best qualified to perform them. Leadership is an aspect of this process. Role differentiation is clearly more detailed than the broad concept of leadership implies and leadership is now understood to have a role structure which varies somewhat from one situation to another.

In order to understand leadership it is necessary also to understand the nature of the *group*. While this volume unavoidably has much to say about groups as, for example, in Stogdill, Reading 3, page 39, Hemphill, Reading 12, page 223, and Gibb, Reading 11, page 214, it does not attempt even an introduction to the psychology of groups, which may be found in Homans (1950), Sprott (1958), and Kemp (1964). Leadership occurs in groups whose members satisfy individual needs through interaction with others. Leadership exists for a group whenever its norms and structure allow the special abilities and resources of one member to be used in the interests of all. It is to groups rather than to individuals that the concept of leadership is applicable. The individual fulfils a role prescription and so provides leadership for a group. This is perhaps a novel point which is well discussed in this introduction by Bavelas, Reading 1, page 17, and more fully by Gibb, Reading 11, page 214. A leader is not a person characterized by any particular and consistent set of personality traits as Stogdill, Reading 5, page 91 shows, but is simply a group member who is more frequently or persistently perceived to perform acts of influence. Almost all members of a group will under some circumstances exercise influence over others; the identification of leaders, therefore, is not an all-or-none affair and the differentiation of leaders from other active participants, the followers, is not complete. See page 293, and Hollander (1961).

Another consideration of particular interest to the student of leadership is that the power to influence the behaviour of others is differently derived in different groups and situations. Under some circumstances influence may be voluntarily accepted, and indeed exists, because group members value the act as a perceived contribution to their achievement of satisfaction. But under other circumstances, most clearly illustrated by a group within an hierarchical organization, power derives not from perceived contribution but rather from a delegation from the organization to which the members acquiesce in order to preserve their membership which satisfies important needs. In the one case (leadership) authority is spontaneously accorded by fellow group members who become followers. In the other (headship) the authority derives from an extra-group power and the acquiescent subordinates cannot properly be called followers. There is a sensitivity to the interaction between leader and followers which is not necessarily present between head and subordinates. This is a valuable concept for the understanding of differential qualities of leadership found in complex organizations. It is discussed in greater detail by Cooper and McGaugh in Reading 14, page 248, and by Gibb (1954).

Followers may be considered the creators of leadership in at least two distinct senses. First and most simply, there can be no leaders without followers. There is no influence unless the behaviour of another has been affected. Interaction implies two poles both of which must be active. In this sense, receipt of influence defines influence and establishes leadership; leaders and followers are collaborators. It is not surprising therefore that leaders and followers frequently exchange roles (Hollander, 1961). The second sense is rather more subtle but equally basic. Leadership is given by the perception of group members that an act of one of their number contributes positively to group progress and the attainment of distributed satisfactions. It is this valuation which determines that there will be influence. In addition, the expectations of the follower and the acceptance he accords the leader may be as influential in the production of the act of leading as are the resources of the leader himself. It is for this reason that it is often observed that responsibility generates leadership. The explicit existence of a role in the culture means that there are widely shared expectations of behaviour appropriate to the role and as a result the role incumbent finds it easier to perform acts in which he might otherwise hesitate and fumble. This is particularly true where the acts required are those of influence in a culture which otherwise tends to frown upon unjustified influence or manipulation.

Observers of leadership whether among animals, primitive peoples, neonate or highly organized groups have repeatedly noted the relativity of leadership to the changing situation. Individuals clearly perceived to have a major contribution to make in one set of circumstances and so to lead are just as clearly often not leaders in changed circumstances. The more different the situations the less likely it is that the same individuals will be leaders (Carter and Nixon, 1949). The significance of the situation has been stated by Gibb (1968) in the following terms:

The elements of the situation are: (i) the structure of interpersonal elations within a group; (ii) characteristics of the group as a group and taken as a unit; (iii) characteristics of the larger culture in which the group is and from which group members have been drawn; (iv) the physical conditions within which the group finds itself constrained to act; and (v) the perceptual representation within the group and its members of these elements and the attitudes and values engendered by them. The situation is especially liable to modification through changes in interpersonal relations, the entrance of new members and departure of others, changes in physical conditions and the like, which alter possibilities and consequently the perceived probabilities of goal attainment or assessments of costs. Research [Stogdill, Reading 5; Gibb, 1954] has shown that a person does not become a leader solely by virtue of any particular pattern of personality traits, but rather by possession of any attribute which by virtue of its relevance to the situation, and its situationally determined evaluation by other group members, establishes a relation of leading-following.

The important fact is that as groups confront different situations and tasks, group needs and leadership roles change. Whether this means that different individuals become leaders depends both upon the extent of the changes in role requirements and upon characteristics of role incumbents. Work by Carter (1953) and Hemphill (1961) indicates a need for a taxonomy of tasks and situations as an early step in understanding fully the distribution of leadership among group members.

It is implied by what has been said above that leadership is a group function; it is the performance of those acts which help the group achieve its preferred outcomes. Such acts may be performed by one or many members of the group and there is nothing in the nature of the leadership relation itself requiring either 'focused' or 'distributed' leadership. Empirical evidence suggests that the effectiveness of groups is increased when leadership is distributed in such a way that maximum advantage is taken of the differential skills of each group member. However, there are in groups two clearly discernible 'needs': to achieve 'valued states' or goals and to maintain group cohesion; and Bales' (1953) early observation that small instrumental discussion groups generated both 'instrumental' and 'social-emotional' leaders has been often confirmed both in empirical research and theoretical analysis (Bales and Slater, 1955; Hollander and Webb, 1955; Halpin and Winer, 1952; Fleishman and Harris, Reading 22; Collins and Guetzkow, 1964; Secord and Backman, 1964). Other terms by which this same distinction has been recognized are 'task' – 'human relations' orientation, directive – permissive and 'structuring' – 'consideration' behaviour. Definitions of the latter terms will be found in Fleishman and Harris (Reading 22). Work by Fiedler (1964; and Reading 13, page 231) and his associates has established a relation between these two basic role patterns and personality attributes to the extent that it seems possible to use personality measures as indices of the extent to which leadership is 'task oriented' or 'considerate'. The principal contribution of Fiedler's work, however, has been that it led him to an analysis of group situations, to ordering them in terms of their favourableness to the leader and to a recognition that 'the type of leader attitude required for effective group performance depends upon the degree to which the group situation is favourable or unfavourable to the leader' (1964, p. 164). In general, the nature of the relation between personality and leadership is, at this time, very open as the articles and excerpts of Part Three will indicate. More refined analysis of the kind begun by Fiedler, and by Cattell and Stice (Reading 6) is undoubtedly needed to clarify this important area.

Implicit in the recognition that leadership is situation-contingent is the understanding that leader behaviour varies with such group factors as organization structure and pattern of communication. Probably the most prominent determinant of variation in these structural aspects is the duration of the group. The work of Sherif and Sherif (1956) has established the fact that enduring groups develop organization and structure and these form a very influential part of the situation to which leadership must be related as Stogdill (Reading 3, page 42) indicates. So much is this so that the complex hierarchical organizations in which most human endeavour is made, present a very different picture of leadership from that obtained in the small laboratory group. At the present time only a few tentative and suggestive investigations are available to point the way to a psychology of influence and control in such organizations. Such work, however, as that of Etzioni (1961), Bass (1965), and Katz and Kahn (1966) suggests that this gap may soon be filled.

The articles and excerpts in this collection represent the stuff of which the psychology of leadership is at present made. The development of a research area is a slow and step-wise process to which very many scholars and students contribute in ways that can never be fully recognized. Certainly it has not been possible to include here every paper which by virtue of its small contribution deserves mention. It has been necessary often to be content with a later paper which, in turn, gives credit to an earlier contributor. That the papers selected belong to a particular psychological tradition, in which the editor participates, there is no doubt. However, an effort has been made to extend the coverage at some points particularly to include comment on and criticism of this core material of the psychology of leadership.

References

BALES, R. F. (1953), 'The equilibrium problem in small groups', in T. Parsons, R. F. Bales and E. A. Shils, *Working Papers in the Theory of Action*, The Free Press.

BALES, R. F., and SLATER, P. E. (1955), 'Role differentiation in small decision-making groups', in T. Parsons, R. F. Bales *et al.*, *The Family, Socialization and Interaction Processes*, The Free Press.

BASS, B. M. (1965), *Organizational Psychology*, Allyn and Bacon.

CARTER, L. (1953), 'Leadership and small group behavior', in M. Sherif and M. O. Wilson, *Group Relations at the Crossroads*, Harper.

CARTER, L., and NIXON, Mary (1949), 'Ability, perceptual, personality and interest factors associated with different criteria of leadership', *Journal of Psychology*, vol. 27, pp. 377–88.

COLLINS, B. E., and GUETZKOW, H. (1964), *A Social Psychology of Group Processes for Decision Making*, Wiley.

COOPER, J. B., and MCGAUGH, J. L. (1963), *Integrating Principles of Social Psychology*, Schenkman.

ETZIONI, A. (1961), *A Comparative Analysis of Complex Organizations*, The Free Press.

FIEDLER, F. E. (1964), 'A contingency model of leadership effectiveness', in L. Berkowitz (ed.), *Advances in Experimental Social Psychology*, vol. 1, Academic Press.

FIEDLER, F. E. (1965), 'Leadership: A new model', *Discovery*, April.

GIBB, C. A. (1954), 'Leadership', in G. Lindzey (ed.), *Handbook of Social Psychology*, Addison-Wesley.

GIBB, C. A. (1968), 'Leadership', in *International Encyclopedia of the Social Sciences*, Collier-Macmillan.

HALPIN, A. W., and WINER, B. J. (1952), *The Leadership Behavior of the Airplane Commander*, Ohio State University Research Foundation.

HEMPHILL, J. K. (1949), *Situational Factors in Leadership*, Ohio State University Personnel Research Board.

HEMPHILL, J. K. (1961), 'Why people attempt to lead', in L. Petrullo and B. M. Bass (eds.), *Leadership and Interpersonal Behavior*, Holt, Rinehart and Winston.

HOLLANDER, E. P. (1961), 'Emergent leadership and social influence', in L. Petrullo and B. M. Bass (eds.), *Leadership and Interpersonal Behavior*, Holt, Rinehart and Winston.

HOLLANDER, E. P., and WEBB, W. B. (1955), 'Leadership, followership and friendship: An analysis of peer nominations', *Journal of Abnormal and Social Psychology*, vol. 50, pp. 163–7.

HOMANS, G. C. (1950), *The Human Group*, Harcourt, Brace.

KATZ, D., and KAHN, R. L. (1966), *The Social Psychology of Organizations*, Wiley.

Introduction

KEMP, C. G. (1964), *Perspectives on the Group Process*, Houghton Mifflin.

SECORD, P. F., and BACKMAN, C. W. (1964), *Social Psychology*, McGraw-Hill.

SHERIF, M., and SHERIF, C. (1956), *An Outline of Social Psychology*, rev. edition, Harper.

SPROTT, W. J. H. (1958), *Human Groups*, Penguin.

1 A. Bavelas

Leadership: Man and Function

A. Bavelas, 'Leadership: man and function', *Administrative Science Quarterly*, vol. 5 (1960), pp. 491–8.

There is a useful distinction to be made between the idea of leadership as a personal quality and the idea of leadership as an organizational function. The first refers to a special combination of personal characteristics; the second refers to the distribution throughout an organization of decision-making powers. The first leads us to look at the qualities and abilities of individuals; the second leads us to look at the patterns of power and authority in organizations. Both of these ideas or definitions of leadership are useful, but it is important to know which one is being talked about, and to know under what conditions the two must be considered together in order to understand a specific organizational situation.

Early notions about leadership dealt with it almost entirely in terms of personal abilities. Leadership was explicitly associated with special powers. An outstanding leader was credited not only with extensions of the normal abilities possessed by most men but with extraordinary powers such as the ability to read men's minds, to tell the future, to compel obedience hypnotically. These powers were often thought of as gifts from a god, as conditional loans from a devil, or as the result of some accidental supernatural circumstance attending conception, birth, or early childhood. Today, claims of supernatural powers are made more rarely, but they are not entirely unknown. Of course, milder claims – tirelessness, infallibility of intuition, lightning-quick powers of decision – are made in one form or another by many outstandingly successful men. And when they do not make them for themselves, such claims are made for them by others who, for their own reasons, prefer such explanations of success to other more homely ones.

Introduction

Outright supernatural explanations of leadership have, in recent times, given way to more rational explanations. Leadership is still generally thought of in terms of personal abilities, but now the assumption is made that the abilities in question are the same as those possessed by all normal persons: individuals who become leaders are merely presumed to have them to a greater degree.

For many years, attempts to define these abilities and to measure them failed. This was not only because the early techniques of measurement were primitive and unreliable but for a more important reason. The traits that were defined as important for leadership were often nothing more than purely verbal expressions of what the researcher felt leaders *ought* to be like. Few of the many lists of traits that were developed had very much in common. Typical of the items that frequently appeared on such lists were piety, honesty, courage, perseverance, intelligence, reliability, imagination, industriousness. This way of thinking about leadership is still very common. It persists, not because it is helpful in analysing and understanding the phenomenon of leadership, but because it expresses a deep and popular wish about what leaders *should* be like.

Modern trait research proceeds in a very different way. Leadership traits are no longer selected arbitrarily. They are, instead, largely derived from the results of tests that are carefully designed, administered, and interpreted. And the techniques of measurement and analysis which are applied to the data that are gathered have been extensively developed and refined. Numerous trait studies have been made of the physical, intellectual, and social characteristics of leaders. On various tests, persons who are leaders tend to be brighter, tend to be better adjusted psychologically, and tend to display better judgment. Studies that have concentrated on the social behavior of leaders show that they 'interact' more than nonleaders. They tend to give more information, ask for more information, and to take the lead in summing up or interpreting a situation.

Despite these accomplishments, the trait approach has in recent years been subjected to increasing criticism. A common objection is that the results are obtained by a method that requires an initial separation of people into 'leaders' and 'nonleaders' or 'good leaders' and 'not-so-good leaders'. The validity of the distinguishing traits that come out of such work, the argument goes, can only be as good as the validity of the preliminary grouping of the persons being studied. All of this leads to the question, 'On what basis is the initial separation of subjects made, and how is it justified?'

At first glance, this may appear a trivial and carping question. In fact, however, it is one of the most serious obstacles in the way of all leadership research. It is obviously impossible to define 'good leaders' without reference to a system of values. To say that a man is a 'good leader' means that his behavior and its consequences are held to be of greater worth than other behaviors and results.

What system of values shall the researcher adopt that is both scientifically acceptable and socially useful in distinguishing good or successful leaders from others? Many attempts have been made to find a suitable criterion, but the results have been generally unsatisfactory – not that it is difficult to find standards which are desirable and inspiring, but that such standards tend to be based, just as the early lists of traits were, on qualities that are difficult or impossible to measure. And often they just do not seem to 'work'. For example, there have been attempts to distinguish leaders from nonleaders in terms that rest essentially on moral and ethical considerations. It may be a significant commentary on our society that there appears to be no particular correlation between a man's ethics and morals and his power to attract followers.

It has been suggested that many of the philosophical difficulties that attend the definition of 'good leader' can be avoided if one accepts the more limited task of defining 'good executive'. In business and industry, one would like to think, there should be practical, quantitative ways of making the distinction. Many attempts have been made in this direction. Reputation, financial success, hierarchical position, influence, and many other criteria have been tried without much satisfaction. The inadequacies of such standards are obvious to any experienced executive.

There is a second and more interesting objection that has been made to the trait approach. It is based not on the question of the accuracy or the validity of the assumptions that are made but upon the nature of the 'traits' themselves. Traits are, after all, statements about personal characteristics. The objection to this is that the degree to which an individual exhibits leadership depends not only on *his characteristics*, but, also, on the *characteristics of the situation* in which he finds himself. For example, a man who shows all the signs of leadership when he acts as the officer of a well-structured authoritarian organization may give no indication of leadership ability in a less-structured, democratic situation. A man may become influential in a situation requiring deliberation and planning but show little evidence of leadership if the situation demands immediate action with no opportunity for weighing alternatives or thinking things out. Or, to take still another instance, a man may function effectively and comfortably in a group whose climate is friendly and co-operative but retreat and become ineffective if he perceives the atmosphere as hostile.

The case for the situational approach to leadership derives its strength from this fact: while organizations in general may exhibit broad similarities of structure and function, they also, in particular, show strong elements of uniqueness.

It is a matter of common observation that within any normal industrial organization, providing there has been a sufficient past, there will be found patterns of relationships and interaction that are highly predictable and highly repetitive. Some of these re-occurring situations will be unique to that organization. It is this uniqueness that is referred to when one speaks of the 'personality' of a company. This is what a management has in mind when it selects a new member with an eye to how he will 'fit in'. The argument of the researcher who stresses the situational aspects of leadership is that these unique characteristics of an organization are often crucial in determining which of two equally competent and gifted men will become a 'leader', and further that in the very same organization these unique patterns may change significantly at different levels of the hierarchy. The very same 'leadership abilities' that helped a man rise to the top may, once he is there, prove a positive detriment.

The status of trait and situational leadership research can be summed up in this way: (1) the broad similarities which hold for a great number of organizations make it possible to say useful things about the kind of person who is likely to become a leader in any of those organizations, and (2) the unique characteristics of a particular organization make it necessary to analyse the situational factors that determine who is likely to become a leader *in one particular organization*. To put it another way, when specific situational patterns are different from organization to organization, one cannot say what personal traits will lead to acknowledged leadership. Instead, one must try to define the leadership functions that must be performed in those situations and regard as leadership those acts which perform them. This point of view suggests that almost any member of a group may become its leader under circumstances that enable him to perform the required functions of leadership and that different persons may contribute in different ways to the leadership of the group.

In these terms we come close to the notion of leadership, not as a personal quality, but as an *organizational function*. Under this concept it is not sensible to ask of an organization 'who is the leader?' Rather we ask 'how are the leadership functions distributed in this organization?' The distribution may be wide or narrow. It may be so narrow – so many of the leadership functions may be vested in a single person – that he is the leader in the popular sense. But in modern organizations this is becoming more and more rare.

What are these 'leadership functions'? Many have been proposed: planning, giving information, evaluating, arbitrating, controlling, rewarding, punishing, and the like. All of these stem from the underlying idea that leadership acts are those which help the group achieve its objectives, or, as it is also put, to satisfy its 'needs'. In most face-to-face groups, the emergence of a leader can well be accounted for on this basis. That person who can assist or facilitate the group most in reaching a satisfactory state is most likely to be regarded as the leader. If one looks closely at what constitutes assistance or facilitation in this sense, it turns out to be the making of choices or the helping of the group to make choices – 'better' choices, of course.

But can the function of leadership be reduced simply to decision making or the facilitation of decision making? The objection can be raised that such a definition is much too wide to be useful. Every action, even every physical movement one makes, is after all 'chosen' out of a number of possible alternatives. If when I am at my workbench I pick up a screwdriver in preference to a hammer, I am clearly making a choice; am I, by virtue of that choice, displaying leadership? Something is obviously wrong with a definition of leadership which imputes it to any act that can be shown to have involved a choice. Common sense would argue that customary, habitual, and 'unconscious' actions, although they may logically contain elements of choice, should be separated from actions that are subjectively viewed by the person taking them as requiring a decision. Common sense would also argue that questions of choice that can be settled on the basis of complete information should be considered differently from questions of choice in which decisions must be taken in the face of uncertainty. And common sense would argue that some distinction should be made between decisions that, although made on equally uncertain grounds, involve very different orders of risk.

This is, of course, the implicit view of the practicing manager, and although it may contain very knotty problems of logic it is the view that will be taken here. Stated in general terms, the position that will be taken is that organizational leadership consists of *uncertainty reduction*. The actual behavior through which this reduction is accomplished is the making of choices.

We saw above that not all choices are equally difficult or equally important. Some choices are considered unimportant or irrelevant and are ignored, and of course whole areas may be seen as so peripheral to the interests of the organization that they are not perceived as areas of choice at all. Other choices that *must* be made are so well understood that they become habitual and automatic. Some of these are grouped into more or less coherent bundles and given a job name. The employee learns to make them correctly as he becomes skilled in the job. In most job evaluation plans, additional credit is given if the job requires judgment. This is a way of saying that there are choices remaining in the job that cannot be completely taken care of by instructions but must be made by the employee as they come along.

There are other choices which, although they are equally clear and habitual, are of a more general nature and do not apply just to a specific job but apply to all. These are customarily embodied in rules and procedures. Rules and procedures are, in this sense, decisions made in advance of the events to which they are to be applied. Obviously, this is possible and practical only to the extent that the events to which the rules and procedures apply can be foreseen, and the practical limit of their completeness and specificity depends on how these future events can be predicted.

Following this line of analysis, it is theoretically possible to arrange all the logically inherent choices that must be made in operating an industrial organization along scales of increasing uncertainty and importance. At some level in this hierarchy of choices, it is customary for management to draw a line, reserving for itself from that point on the duty and the privilege of making the required decisions.

Precisely where a management draws this line defines its scope. The way in which a management distributes the responsibility for making the set of choices it has thus claimed to itself defines its structure. What organizational leadership *is* and what kinds of acts constitute it are questions that can be answered only within this framework of scope and structure. In these terms leadership consists of the continuous choice-making process that permits the organization as a whole to proceed toward its objectives despite all sorts of internal and external perturbations.

But as every practicing manager knows, problems occasionally arise that are not amenable to the available and customary methods of analysis and solution. Although uncertain about which choice to make, a management may nevertheless have to make a decision. It is in situations of this kind that many of the popular traits attributed to leaders find their justification: quickness of decision, the courage to take risks, coolness under stress, intuition, and, even, luck. There is no doubt that quick, effective, and daring decisions are a highly prized commodity in a crisis, but just as precious a commodity is the art of planning and organizing so that such crises do not occur. The trend of management has been to remove as many of its decisions as possible from the area of hunch and intuition to that of rational calculation. More and more, organizations are choosing to depend less on the peculiar abilities of rare individuals and to depend instead on the orderly processes of research and analysis. The occasions and opportunities for personal leadership in the old sense still exist, but they are becoming increasingly rare and circumscribed.

This new emphasis has not eliminated the role of personal leadership, but it has significantly redefined it. Under normal conditions of operation, leadership in the modern organization consists not so much in the making of decisions personally as it does of maintaining the operational effectiveness of the decision-making systems which comprise the management of the organization. The picture of the leader who keeps his own counsel and in the nick of time pulls the rabbit out of the hat is out of date. The popular stereotype now is the thoughtful executive discussing in committee the information supplied by a staff of experts. In fact it may be that the brilliant innovator, in the role of manager, is rapidly becoming as much an organizational embarrassment as he is an asset.

This trend, reasonable though it may appear on the surface, conceals two serious dangers. First, we may be systematically giving up the opportunity of utilizing the highest expressions of personal leadership in favor of managerial arrangements which, although safer and more reliable, can yield at best only a high level of mediocrity. And second, having committed ourselves to a system that thrives on the ordinary, we may, in the interests of maintaining and improving its efficiency, tend to shun the extra-ordinary.

It is no accident that daring and innovation wane as an organization grows large and successful. On different levels this appears to have been the history of men, of industries, of nations, and even of societies and cultures. Success leads to 'obligations' – not the least of which is the obligation to hold what has been won. Therefore, the energies of a man or administration may be absorbed in simply maintaining vested interests. Similarly, great size requires 'system', and system, once established, may easily become an end in itself.

This is a gloomy picture, because it is a picture of decay. It has been claimed, usually with appeals to biological analogies, that this is an inevitable cycle, but this view is, very probably, incorrect. Human organizations are not biological organisms; they are social inventions.

2   I. Knickerbocker

Leadership: A Conception and some Implications

Excerpt from I. Knickerbocker, 'Leadership: a conception and some implications', *Journal of Social Issues*, vol. 4 (1948), pp. 23–40.

During several years of working with the problems of human relations which arise in organizations of people, my colleagues and I have sought a satisfactory conceptualization of the phenomena of leadership. We have gradually crystallized some ideas which have been helpful both theoretically and practically. However, a recent survey of the literature on leadership suggests that we have wandered from the paths customarily followed by students of the subject.

Motivated by the conviction that some systematic frame of reference, however rough, is better than none, we offer the following analysis of leadership for what it may suggest to those who are interested. While these are in part speculative considerations, they have been tested for usefulness through some years of practice.

Much of the literature on leadership represents an attempt to study the leader as an entity possessed of characteristic traits and occupying rather inertly a status position relative to other individuals who are not too clearly related to him.[1] Actually, the leader emerges as a consequence of the needs of a group of people and of the nature of the situation within which that group is attempting to operate. Stogdill (see Reading 5), after an exhaustive survey of the literature, concludes that:

leadership is not a matter of passive status, or of the mere possession of some combination of traits. It appears rather to be a working relationship among members of a group, in which the leader acquires status through active participation and demonstration of his capacity for carrying cooperative tasks through to completion.

1. A notable exception is Barnard (1938).

Jenkins (1947, p. 75), reviewing the literature dealing with the problem of the selection of leaders in various fields, finds that:

The situation does not appear to be a particularly happy one with regard to the deriving of general principles or of setting up a systematic theory of leadership from the available information. A few statements may be set forth, however, that appear to hold for the findings of a number of the investigations reviewed; this list should be thought of as a series of hypotheses for further investigation.

His first statement is as follows:

1 Leadership is specific to the particular situation under investigation. Who becomes the leader of a given group engaging in a particular activity and what leadership characteristics are, in a given case, are a function of the specific situation including the measuring instruments employed. Related to this conclusion is the general finding of wide variations in the characteristics of individuals who become leaders in similar situations, and even greater divergence in leadership behavior in different situations.

These authors, and a few others, have apparently recognized some of the inadequacies of the literature of leadership and of traditional research approaches to the subject. However, we are left standing on the threshold of a house which has not yet been erected. It is the purpose of this article to draw a tentative architect's sketch of the house which is so badly needed.

Although the evidence does not support the romantic conception of the leader endowed with magic attributes, this conception is widely held. One wonders why it persists with such vitality. Perhaps the fact that each of us commenced his life under the guidance of a leader – a big man, of tremendous endowment, with almost limitless power – would help to explain the prevalence and tenacity with which this Leader concept is held.

Each of us had a father, a prestige figure, magically endowed. Many of us found security in that figure. Since we continue to need security, perhaps we continue to carry with us out of childhood the father symbol, the Leader. If such an assumption may be accepted, then we can readily see that the leader, or the man whom we conceptualize as a leader, should be larger, more intelligent, more mature, more cultured, more impressive than we. (See Reading 5.)

Individuals so endowed relative to the group with which they are associated statistically would be seen more often as potential leaders and statistically be placed more often in a position where they might practice leadership, and finally, statistically more often might become leaders. All this could happen frequently enough to give us the feeling that leaders somehow are different and permit us to make the misleading research finding that the leader is an entity who can be considered apart from his functional relationship to his followers.

Following our assumptions further, we should not be surprised to find that men who have achieved through function a position of leadership have usually possessed many of the mythical attributes of the leader. They serve as ink blots onto which people project their desires for security and dependence. To be sure, the degree of such endowment may be expected to vary with the closeness of the association between leader and followers. It is more difficult for their immediate associates to see them as leaders magically endowed. A consideration of Hitler and Roosevelt as seen by remote followers and immediate associates may lend some reality to this hypothesis.

It is interesting to speculate upon the possibility of the leader created by concerted action through various media of publicity in the absence of any true functional relationship between leader and followers. It doesn't seem impossible that such a leader might exist as an entity devoid of functional followers, but becoming for people the symbol, Leader. Certainly for most people the great leaders of history have been only a symbol. Any functional relationship between the people and the leader has been remote, if it existed at all. *Yet the leader in each case has arisen through performing certain functions relative to some group somewhere, sometime.* It would be interesting to compare the attitudes toward the leader of individuals from two groups, one composed of those functionally related to him as leader, the other composed of those for whom he existed as the symbol, Leader. From the historical literature there would appear to be sharp differences between the man and Leader to his functional followers and the same leader to those people who were not functionally related to him.

There is no reason to assume that the two concepts, leader and

27

functional leadership, may not be fused in many cases. Certainly the former would appear to grow out of the latter. If some people are in search of the former, some of them at least may try to see in each functional leader, a Leader. It would appear that those leaders with sufficient sense of the dramatic to lend themselves readily to conforming to the outward appearance of being a leader may more readily become one. Lincoln was rather a disappointment to many people in this respect. Hitler and Mussolini took to the role more readily. The functional leader always earns respect and prestige to the extent that he fulfils his function, but immediate contact is apt to inhibit the growth of the extremes of the leader concept. Hence the many cynical proverbs concerning the prophet in his own country.

It would appear then that the usual notion of the leader serves to cover two quite separate concepts (Van Dusen, 1948, p. 68). The first is an emotionally held conviction that some men are leaders and as such are set apart from the common horde. These leaders do not owe their position to their functional relationship to followers, but to an almost magical aura which surrounds them. They have god-like attributes which they have not earned but rather with which they have been endowed.

Our hypothesis is that this concept arises in our culture out of the relationship of the very young child with his father. An examination of the leader concept in other cultures or an analysis of differences between leader concepts among male and female in our own culture should help test this hypothesis. If the hypothesis be granted, then the statistical appearance of certain traits ascribed to the leader, and the statistical appearance of leaders with these traits is not surprising. Nor is it surprising that experimentally devised but functional tests of leaders do not bear out the coincidence of the specific traits and the function of leadership.

The other concept – functional leadership – places emphasis not on a fixed set of personal characteristics nor on particular kinds of leadership behavior, but upon the circumstances under which groups of people integrate and organize their activities toward objectives, and upon the way in which that integration and organization is achieved. Thus the leadership function is analysed and understood in terms of a dynamic relationship. A leader may acquire followers, or a group of people may create a leader, but the significant aspects of the process can only be understood in dynamic, relationship terms. Evidence and speculation to date make it appear that this functional or operational conception of leadership provides the more useful approach (Ordway, 1935, p. 20, p. 61; Jenkins, 1947; Reading 5; Whitehead, 1936, p. 68; Stogdill and Shartle, 1948).

We need some schema which will emphasize this relationship between leader and led as a dynamic pattern. As an aid to thinking about such relationships, we have developed the following simple schema:[2]

1. *Existence for each individual may be seen as a continual struggle to satisfy needs, relieve tensions, maintain an equilibrium.*

Each of us uses many different *means* for the satisfaction of his needs. We use muscular skills, personal appearance, intelligence, knowledge. We use tools, food, money. The means we habitually use may become needs themselves. In each specific case, however, some *means* is used for the satisfaction of a need or of a pattern of needs.

2. *Most needs in our culture are satisfied through relationships with other individuals or groups of individuals.*

This assumption points up the fact that people and our relationship with people constitute the *means* upon which we rely most heavily for the satisfaction of our needs. Other people as it were possess the means which we would use to satisfy our needs. We do not grow our own food, make our own clothes, provide our own transportation, educate ourselves, or even provide our own recreation. We satisfy such needs, and many others, through means controlled and provided by others. When we are lonely, another person appears to us as means and controls; in a sense the means we would like to use. When we are insecure, a closer relationship with someone is the means we seek and that someone controls the means. Often another person may possess the means

2. In the interests of brevity, only three of a half dozen or more interrelated generalizations are here mentioned. The reader will discover that they are closely integrated with others outlined by McGregor (1948).

in the form of money, skill, knowledge, or tools which we need as means for the satisfaction of our needs. We attempt then to establish a relationship which will be a means to gain the use of something which in turn will be a means to need satisfaction. To the manager the worker possesses the means of skill or hands. Through relationship with the worker as means, the manager hopes to obtain the further means he requires to satisfy his needs. To the worker, the manager controls the means of job and pay. So all of us seek through relationships with others the means, or the means to the means, for satisfying needs.

3. *For any individual the process of employing his relationship with other individuals as means for the satisfaction of his needs is an active rather than a passive process.*

He does not wait passively for the occurrence of such relationships as will provide means for need satisfactions. He institutes appropriate relationships or utilizes those which already exist toward the end of satisfying his needs. The relationship is thus an active, striving one, through which each party is operating to augment his means for need satisfaction (or to protect the means already at hand). Since each individual possesses some quantum of means small or large which some other individual might utilize for need satisfaction, each individual through his control of those means has some bargaining power relative to others. The control of means ('scarce means', the economists call them), which others desire for the satisfaction of needs, constitutes what we ordinarily call power. The use of power (or 'means control') to gain the means for need satisfaction from others appears to be the essential aspect of all human relationships. The individual who controls many or scarce means which other people seek to utilize for need satisfaction is in a position of power. Such power may be used by an individual either to reduce the means of other individuals (punishment), or to augment their means (reward) toward the ultimate end of inducing these other individuals to provide him with means for the satisfaction of his own needs.

This approach furnishes us with the bare essentials of a schema for considering the dynamic aspect of the relationship between people. That relationship appears to consist essentially in an active striving to procure through other people the means for need satisfaction. The relationship is of course bilateral, each party seeking means through the other. We should expect an individual to attempt to establish a relationship only when it appears to promise means and to maintain it only so long as it continues to do so. We might also predict that the greatest number of individuals would attempt to establish a relationship with that individual who in their perceptual field gave greatest promise of providing means (Jennings, 1947, p. 412). Finally, we might predict that individuals would attempt to break off relationships with and avoid those individuals who threaten to reduce their means, and if they could not do so would react protectively and possibly aggressively.

Let us consider a group of people including one who would be designated by the others as the leader if we asked. Let us make a general application of our schema to such a situation. We have a leader attempting to find a means through the activities of the group members for the satisfaction of *his* needs. At the same time the group members are in the relationship with him simply because he appears to them the best means available for the satisfaction of such of *their* needs as can be satisfied through this group.

Let us ask some questions concerning the individuals in the group.

Question 1

Why are the individuals in the group?

Because through it or through the leader they anticipate finding means for satisfying needs (or means for protecting themselves against a threatened loss of need satisfaction). If we run over groups that we know well; such as a labor union, a church, a business association, a social club, etc., we seem to find that we joined such groups because they appeared to offer means. We leave them when they no longer seem to do so.

Question 2

Why do the individuals accept direction of their activities?

Because this behavior appears to them to provide means for the satisfaction of their needs. The leader is seen as a means;

31

through the relationship with him, needs are satisfied (or a reduction in need satisfaction is prevented). The leader may promise a chicken in every pot, a glorious future, or more money for less work. If the group member sees satisfaction of needs in the direction the leader indicates, if he believes the leader will serve as a means for getting those satisfactions, the group member follows. On the other hand, the leader may say 'follow me, or disaster may befall you', 'follow me, or I'll see to it that you rue the day you refuse', 'follow me or else . . .'. Again, if the group member believes that the leader controls the relevant means, if the group member sees a threat to his available means in failing to go in the directions the leader indicates, the group member follows. The individual then is related to the leader as a means to need satisfaction or as a means to protect available means from reduction. He follows and permits his activities to be directed because he believes that to do so will get him what he wants.

Question 3

Why does the leader arise?

Even in the simplest situation, such as when a group embarks on discussion which will eventuate in a decision of some sort, a leader seems to be essential. Operationally, it is difficult for a group to speak or act except through an individual member. If everyone talks at once, no one can hear or attend. If everyone plans at once, or acts at once without a plan, there is no group but rather a collection of individuals planning or acting. For the group to act as a unit or to show organization, it is necessary that individual members speak for it. The necessity for an ordering of discussion is readily apparent as a means to a group. Such ordering must come through the action of an individual. Someone must verbalize the necessity for order, the methods of ordering, the final agreement on methods, and, the agent. Some individual must order and in doing so he provides simple but necessary means for the group. Even at this very simple level, the necessity for a leader is real and apparent to most groups. To the extent that the objectives of the group require greater diversity of effort and greater coordination, the need for a leader will increase.

Now let us look at the leader and ask some questions about his behavior. Let us again answer the questions in terms of our frame of reference and examine the answers for the sense they make.

Question 4

How is the leader to be characterized?

The leader is not a disembodied entity endowed with unique characteristics. He is the leader of a group and is the leader only in terms of his functional relationship to the group. Therefore the part he plays in the total dynamic pattern of the behavior of the group defines him as leader. He is a leader not because he is intelligent, skilful or original, but because his intelligence, skill, or originality is seen as a means by the group members. He is a leader not because he is relatively imposing of stature, well-dressed, fluent of speech, or from a higher socio-economic background, but because these factors tend to predispose group members to expect better means from their possessor.

The leader is followed because he promises to get, or actually gets his followers more nearly what they want than anyone else. If he does so, he will be followed, be he small, insignificant looking, and relatively speechless. In our culture we have some predisposition to expect people with certain characteristics to provide better means. Also certain characteristics such as intelligence may by and large in fact enable certain individuals to provide better means. However, the leader is a product not of his characteristics, but of his functional relationship to specific individuals in a specific situation. As a result, the variability of leaders' characteristics upsets all but the broadest statistical efforts at analysis.

Question 5

How does the leader arise?

The leader appears to arise in one of two ways. First, as a result of agreement among members of a group that some individual serves as better means than any other. Such agreement may be wholly predictive, a matter of guess-work, or may be the result of experience among various members. The agreement of the members of a group may be verbalized or tacit. The member of a group who suggests 'let's go get a cup of coffee' may collect a following and for a minute or so be a leader simply because he has voiced at an instant an operation which appears as a means to other members. The member of a group who is known to possess some special skill which is at the moment a necessity may be turned to and be expected to function as a leader because of his possession. In our culture it is not unusual for any group to make it first a business to choose a leader.

The second way in which a leader may arise is as a result of objectives which require a group of people for their achievement. An individual, for example, wants to accomplish something which can only be accomplished if he can direct the activities of a number of other people. He seeks then to find a group, or an assortment of individuals, who will accept his direction of their activities. If our basic assumptions above are correct, he will acquire 'followers' only if, *in their eyes*, following him promises to result in increased need satisfaction (or in avoidance of reduction of need satisfaction).

Question 6

Why does the leader lead?

Through leading, the leader obtains means of satisfying his needs. Perhaps he finds satisfaction in the operation of leading, in manipulating people or in helping them. Perhaps the prestige and recognition accorded the leader are important sources of satisfaction. Or, to take the most obvious aspect, perhaps the result of the activities he directs is itself the means he seeks.

Consider, for example, the industrial manager. He may obtain satisfaction from his leadership role in a variety of ways. He may obtain satisfaction simply from being 'the boss', from being able to tell people what to do, to control their activities and their satisfactions. He may find satisfaction, in being regarded as their benefactor, in their gratitude for his favors, or their fear of his punishments. He may enjoy the way he is treated by those outside the organization who are impressed with his title and position. Finally, he may obtain a higher salary, promotion, and recognition from the achievements of the group whose activities he directs.

The motivation of the individual certainly plays a part in the likelihood of his leading. Many adults seem to dislike to lead. Others lead occasionally when, by reason of some special skill or knowledge they possess, it seems to them or to the group reasonable that they should do so. Some lead when only through the concerted activities of a group of people can they find a means to some need satisfaction. Still others enjoy leading. The actual operation of leading is a means to need satisfaction for them. Such individuals are apt to seek situations in which whatever means they have will be in demand. They attempt to acquire the skills which will be means, and a manner which will indicate their possession of means. If there are 'born leaders', they arise from this group. Due to the many objectives in our culture which can only be achieved through group effort, many organizations arise. A great many people find leading – that is the job of a superior in an organization – to be the means through which they satisfy important needs.

Question 7

What is the function of the leader?

The function of the leader is to organize the activities of the members of the group toward the accomplishment of some end through controlling means for the satisfaction of the relevant needs of the members of the group. When the leader has been chosen by a group of people who have decided upon an objective to be attained, the leader's function is obvious and his job is relatively simple. When the leader, however, is not chosen by the group, but appointed and given means control by someone outside the group, or appoints himself because he requires a group to achieve his purposes (as in business or military organizations), his job is considerably more difficult. In such circumstances the objective to be attained through the activities of the group is the objective of those who appointed him leader. This may not be the objective of the group he is to lead. Nevertheless, he must appear to the people he is to lead as a means for *their* need satisfaction or they will not accept his direction.

Sometimes, as a consequence, the appointed leader is an individual who would never have been chosen by the group he leads, but one who cannot be rejected because he controls important means for need satisfaction. He is 'accepted' as the lesser evil. He appears to the group as a means only in the negative sense. Nevertheless, even in such extreme cases, the leadership function remains the same.

Question 8

Can all of the various kinds of leaders be accounted for by this same frame of reference?

The term leader is certainly used to designate many different positions and functions. It may be used to indicate a figurehead, a position in an organization, a self-appointed dictator possessed of sufficient 'or else' power to force a following, or an individual who has been designated as leader by voluntary action of the group. To cut through the diverse usage which has been made of the term leader, we might say that to the extent that any individual succeeds in collecting an actual following, he does so because he controls means. The dictator may be followed because he has created or made use of a situation in which all alternatives to following him are less desirable as means. The superior in the formal organization, for instance in industry, may often occupy a position similar to that of dictator without being particularly aware of it. The man who can control means available to other people can use his control to force that alternative behavior which appears a better means within the restricted choice although a worser one within a larger but forbidden frame of reference. To the extent that the means controlled are scarce means, to that extent the possibility of limiting alternatives as a means of control is possible. The leader chosen by voluntary action of a group is seen as the best means rather than the lesser evil. But all leaders, whatever their personal objectives, must serve as means for their followers, or they will not be leaders (i.e. they will have no followers).

Our conclusions from the above discussion of the nature of leadership may be summarized as follows:

1. The symbolic or romantic conception of the leader, although widely prevalent, does not explain the phenomena of leadership. It exists, I have suggested, as a consequence of the nature of the individual's relationship with his father in early childhood. It represents a magical, perhaps wishful, attempt to find security through surrogate relationships resembling that early one. The

leader, realistically and factually, is not a person endowed with a list of characteristics which make him what he is.

2. When conceived in terms of the dynamics of human social behavior, leadership is a function of needs existing in a given situation, and consists of a relationship between an individual and a group.

3. The functional relationship which is leadership exists when a leader is perceived by a group as controlling means for the satisfaction of their needs. Following him may be seen either as a means to increased need satisfaction or as a means to prevent decreased need satisfaction.

4. The leader may 'emerge' as a means to the achievement of objectives desired by a group. He may be selected, elected, or spontaneously accepted by the group because he possesses or controls means (skill, knowledge, money, associations, property, etc.) which the group desires to utilize to attain their objectives – to obtain increased need satisfaction.

5. On the other hand, the leader may appoint himself or be appointed by someone outside the group to be led. In this instance leadership is a means to the achievement of the leader's objectives (or the objectives of those who appoint him). However, there will be no relationship with the group – no followers – except in terms of the leader's control of means for the satisfaction of the needs of the followers. Either the leader's objectives must also be those of the group (and he himself be seen by the group as a means to their attainment), or else accepting the leader's direction must be seen by the group members as the best available means to prevent reduced need satisfaction.

References

BARNARD, C. (1938), *Functions of the Executive*, Harvard University Press.
JENKINS, W. O. (1947), 'A review of leadership studies with particular reference to military problems', *Psychological Bulletin*, vol. 44.
JENNINGS, H. H. (1947), in Newcomb and Hartley (eds.), *Readings in Social Psychology*, Henry Holt.
MCGREGOR, D. (1948), 'The staff function in human relations', *Journal of Social Issues*, vol. 4.
ORDWAY, T. (1935), *The Art of Leadership*, McGraw-Hill.

Introduction

STOGDILL, R. M., and SHARTLE, C. L. (1948), 'Methods of determining patterns of leadership behavior in relation to organization structure and objectives', *Journal of Applied Psychology*, vol. 32, pp. 286–91.

VAN DUSEN, A. C. (1948), 'Measuring leadership ability', *Personnel Psychology*, vol. 1.

WHITEHEAD, T. N. (1936), *Leadership in a Free Society*, Harvard University Press.

3 R. M. Stogdill

Leadership, Membership, Organization

R. M. Stogdill, 'Leadership, membership and organization', *Psychological Bulletin*, vol. 47 (1950), pp. 1–14.

The present paper is concerned with a point of view regarding the relation of leadership to group organization. It represents one attempt within the Ohio State Leadership Studies staff to clarify and systematize certain aspects of the leadership problem. Such clarification appears to be necessary as a preliminary step toward the development of an integrated program of research on leadership problems in formal organizations.

The pioneering work of Lewin [9], Moreno [10], and their followers has resulted in marked progress in the development of methods for studying leadership as a phenomenon of *groups*. However, comparable progress remains to be made in the development of methods for the study of leadership as an aspect of *organization*. Several factors appear to have operated as barriers to the development of scientific theory and method in this area. One is the lack of an adequate definition of leadership. A second is the fact that much of the literature on leadership, the terms 'group' and 'organization' are used interchangeably or are defined in exactly the same terms. A third derives from two opposed theoretical approaches represented, on the one hand, by those theories of organization in which the leader is conceived as a symbol of authority or as an embodiment of superior personal traits, and on the other hand, by a type of group-oriented theory in which leadership appears to be regarded as a manifestation of social pathology. A fourth, and related obstacle, results from a reaction of social scientists against the authoritarian principles advanced in many discussions of organization. Some social theorists appear to reject all concepts of organization as authoritarian; and some researchers appear reluctant to deal experimentally with such concepts as responsibility, authority, stratification, and similar phenomena related to organization. It is beyond the scope or purpose of this paper to portray the magnitude of the latter two difficulties. Nevertheless, it seems relevant to recognize the fact that they are present and act to the detriment of scientific work in the field.

The Ohio State Leadership Studies are being conducted on the basis of these assumptions: (1) that group organization is a recognizable social phenomenon in our culture; (2) that as such it is a legitimate subject for scientific study; and (3) that the variables of organization can be isolated and defined so as to permit their scientific study. It is the purpose of the present paper to examine various concepts relevant to leadership and organization, and to develop a formulation of the problem which will suggest hypotheses that can be subjected to experimental test.

Groups and Organizations

Wilson [17] has reviewed the important sociological literature relating to concepts of the social group. He reports that in 'current sociological literature one finds no consensus as to the meaning of the *group*', and concludes that much experimental work is yet to be done in order to delimit the group concept in any satisfactory manner. An important step in this direction has been made by Hemphill [5], who has devised scales for the measurement of such group dimensions as size, permeability, stability, viscidity, homogeneity of membership, and the like.

The most satisfactory definition available at the present time appears to be that of Smith [15] who defines a *social group* as 'a unit consisting of a plural number of organisms (agents) who have collective perception of their unity and who have the ability to act/or are acting in a unitary manner toward the environment'. Krech and Crutchfield [8] present a similar view. They state that

the criteria for establishing whether or not a given set of individuals constitutes a psychological group are mainly two: (1) all the members must exist as a group in the psychological field of each individual, i.e. be perceived and reacted to as a group; (2) the various members must be in dynamic interaction with one another.

A special kind of group is the *organization*. An organization may be defined as a social group in which the members are differentiated as to their responsibilities for the task of achieving a common goal.

Znaniecki [18] has reviewed the sociological literature relating to various concepts of organization. He stresses the fact that the terms *group* and *organization* are rather tenuous concepts, in that it is often difficult to determine whether a particular aggregate of persons constitutes a group, and that it may also be difficult at times to determine whether a particular group can be regarded as an organization. He points out that social organization –

. . . can be realized only in a lasting 'social group' or 'association'. Individuals belonging to such a group are aware that they will be regularly expected to perform certain actions, and some of them act as organizers, leaders, coordinators of the regular activities of others with reference to the common purpose. Not all of these individuals need be continuously active; indeed, in many groups a considerable proportion remain passive, acting only in reaction to the actions of others. The common purpose of the organized actions may be simple or complex.

Some of the consequences of distinguishing between the terms 'group' and 'organization' are the following: First, there is nothing in the term 'group' which gives any clue as to the nature of leadership. Second, there is nothing in the group definition which provides any foundation for integrating leadership with group phenomena, except at a superficial level of social perception or interaction. Third, the group orientation can suggest research methods relating to leadership only in so far as the social group is defined in terms of organization. The concept of organization, however, with its implications for the differentiation of responsibility roles, does permit the study of leadership as an aspect of the relationships between members who are coordinating their efforts for the achievement of common goals.

A group may or may not have leaders. If it does have leaders, it is an organization, for at least some of the members are thereby differentiated from the others as to responsibility, or role expectation in relation to some common purpose. The members of a group may or may not have mutual responsibilities for a common task. If the members do have differentiated responsibilities in relation to common goals then the group is an organization – a particular kind of group. The continued presence of leaders and of responsibility differentiations in relation to group goals are indicative of organization. It may not always be easy to determine the exact point at which a group emerges into an organization.

Leadership as an Aspect of Organization

The following definition of leadership may serve as a starting point for discussion. Leadership may be considered as the process (act) of influencing the activities of an organized group in its efforts toward goal setting and goal achievement. The definition of leadership relates it directly to the organized group and its goal. It would appear that the minimal social conditions which permit the existence of leadership are the following:

1. A group (of two or more persons).
2. A common task (or goal oriented activities).
3. Differentiation of responsibility (some of the members have different duties).

There are innumerable other group and situational factors which may influence leadership in varying degrees, but these appear to be the minimal conditions which will permit the emergence of leadership. There must be a group with a common task or objective, and at least one member must have responsibilities which differ from those of the other members. If all members perform exactly the same duties in exactly the same way there is no leadership. A leader then is a person who becomes differentiated from other members in terms of the influence he exerts upon the goal setting and goal achievement activities of the organization.

The foregoing discussion suggests that leadership cannot emerge unless the members of a group assume different responsibilities. It has been suggested that group organization also is founded upon differentiation of responsibility. It would then appear that leadership and organization are derived from a common factor or, viewed from a different light, that leadership is an aspect of group organization. This view has been expressed in various forms by writers in the field of business organization. Davis [3], for example, states that the –

. . . development of organization structure is largely a problem in the division of responsibility, and involves two important problems: (1) the grouping of similar functions to form the various organization elements in a manner that will promote effective cooperation, and (2) the determination of the proper relationships between functional groups and organization elements, with a view to promoting both cooperation and effective executive leadership.

The definition of leadership does not specify how many leaders an organization shall have, nor whether the leadership influence of an individual is continuous or intermittent, nor whether the influence of the leader shall be for the welfare or detriment of the organization and its members. It merely specifies that leaders may be differentiated from other members in terms of the extent to which they influence the activities of the organization in its efforts toward the achievement of goals. The definition of effective and ineffective leadership is an additional problem.

Aspects of Responsibility

Brown [2] in a challenging analysis of organization maintains that 'an enterprise is a mosaic of its individual responsibilities. The sum of them must exactly equal the whole requirement of administration.' He continues, 'responsibility is that part in administration which is assigned to a particular member of an enterprise. Its definition is an act of organization.'

Responsibility cannot be regarded as a simple or uncomplicated variable. Jucius [7] writes,

By responsibility is meant, first, the obligation to do an assigned task, and, second, the obligation to someone for the assignment. But what is meant by obligation and how far does it extend? This implies a willingness to accept, for whatever rewards one may see in the situation, the burden of a given task and the risks which attend in the event of failure. Because of the rewards and penalties involved, it is highly essential to specify the limits of responsibility.

Formal organization can seldom define all the possible variations of responsibility and personal interaction to be expected of all members in all situations. Nevertheless, organization appears to be founded upon a basic system of stable expectations regarding differential responsibilities and relationships among the members. This is not a one-way process. That is, it is not the organization alone which sets up role expectations for its members. The members set up expectations for each other and for the organization as a whole. It is assumed for purposes of the present discussion that this principle applies not only to stratified organizations, such as military and industrial establishments. It applies as well to membership in any organized group, whether it be a business, political, educational, religious, fraternal, or social organization and regardless of size, stratification, purpose, or member characteristics. The essential relationship which makes possible the conduct of organized group activities is a differentiation of responsibility roles among the members. Without this there is no possibility of coordination or of leadership toward goal achievement. The very process of organization defines the responsibilities of the members and thereby the formal leadership of the group. It is true that in some organized groups, such as recreational groups, the responsibilities of members may appear to be vaguely defined. However, this is not equivalent to saying that no responsibilities exist.

Responsibility, in its broadest scope, defines not only the duties for which a member is accountable; it defines also the persons to whom and for whom he is accountable in the discharge of his duties. In doing so, it also defines a member's formal status, or location in the organization hierarchy. Authority and formal status systems in organization are but aspects of the division of responsibility.

Responsibilities in a systematic organization are determined by the assignment of persons to particular positions, the duties of which are outlined in an organization manual or organization chart. In less systematic organizations the responsibilities of a particular job or position may be determined by on-the-spot instructions, by general hints or by unverbalized assumptions. In a systematic organization an individual's *work patterns* (the tasks he *actually* performs) will correspond fairly close with his *responsibility patterns* (the tasks he *is supposed* to perform). However, as the mission and activities of the organization change there will be found in many instances an increasing discrepancy between the tasks being performed and the responsibilities originally outlined and defined.

Attributes of Organization

The studies of Roethlisberger and Dickson [12] and others have directed attention to the factor of informal groups within formal organization. Informal organization, as usually defined, refers to the friendship groups and cliques – based upon close association, mutual interests or antagonisms, and the like – which develop within formal organization. It has been pointed out by Homans [6] that this conception is too narrow, since what is informal in a factory may be formal in a primitive society. Firey [4], who defines informal organization in terms of schism, presents a more useful approach to the problem. He maintains that 'if we regard behavioral conformity, in which interactional processes are highly repetitive and synchronized, as the overt counterpart of a social system, then behavioral nonconformity may be taken as the overt counterpart of schism within a system'.

An organization in operation seldom corresponds exactly with the organization model as charted. The intervention of human social factors and other influences result in the emergence of informal organization, that is, in the development of work patterns and interaction patterns which do not correspond with responsibility patterns.

It would appear then that there are two fundamental sets of variables which define the operations of an organized group. These are:

1. *Variables which define formal organization*
(*a*) Responsibility variables (the work one is expected to do).
(*b*) Formal interaction variables (the persons with whom one is expected to work).

2. *Variables which define informal organization*
(*a*) Work performance variables (the tasks one actually performs).
(*b*) Informal interaction variables (the persons with whom one actually works).

45

If we regard the variables listed above as basic variables of organization, we can also regard them as variables of membership and of leadership. In other words, an organization can be studied in terms of these four types of variables: responsibilities, work performances, formal interactions, and informal interactions. Leadership can also be studied in terms of the same variables.

Responsibility variables define the duties that the members are expected to perform. The responsibilities of a given position may remain the same, whether A or B occupies the position.

Work performance variables are defined by the tasks performed and by the methods of their performance. Individual A may accept a position previously occupied by B. The responsibilities as defined by organization charts and manuals may remain the same, but the tasks actually performed by A may differ somewhat from those performed by B, and the methods of performance may vary markedly.

Formal interaction variables define the persons to whom and for whom the members are accountable, as well as others with whom they are expected to cooperate, in the discharge of their responsibilities.

Informal interaction variables are defined by the persons with whom the members actually work and cooperate in the performance of their tasks.

Informal organization comes about as a result of the development of discrepancies (*a*) between work performance and responsibilities as defined and (*b*) between informal interactions and formally defined interactions. Thus leadership is ever confronted with the task of reconciling discrepancies – discrepancies between what ought to be done and what is being done, between goals and achievements, between organizational needs and available resources, between the needs of individual members and the requirements of organization, between formal lines of cooperation and informal patterns of cooperation.

An organization in action comprises a complex of many variables in interaction. In making a pictorial representation of a business organization, the usual procedure is to plot the division of formal responsibility on a two-dimensional chart. The horizontal dimension of the chart shows the division of responsibility for various kinds of work. The vertical dimension of the chart shows the division of responsibility for different levels of decision making, and indicates the persons to whom one is accountable and those for whose performance one is accountable in the discharge of duties. This dimension defines the formal authority and status systems of the organization. Level (position in the organization hierarchy) and function (kind of work performed) are not independent dimensions. Although functions tend to differ from level to level, there is considerable overlap. Results from the Ohio State Leadership Studies [13, 16] have shown that the functions of top leadership tend to be supported at each lower level in the leadership structure by increasingly more detailed and routine work in the same functions.

Personal interaction can also be conceived as varying in both horizontal and vertical directions. The horizontal dimension is defined by the range (number) of members with whom an individual interacts. Some persons tend to work alone or with single individuals, while others are observed to work with large numbers of persons. The vertical aspect of personal interaction is defined by the number of strata (*echelons*) above and below his own in which a member works with others. Some persons may be observed to work only with others at the same level in the organization. Others tend to work only with subordinates, and still others tend to work only with superiors. These tendencies may or may not represent expression of individual differences in social interaction patterns. Results obtained thus far in the Ohio State Leadership Studies suggest that these patterns of interaction may be determined in part by the functions served by various types of positions. Technical consultants and staff aids tend to spend more time with superiors. Members in supervisory positions are observed, as would be expected, to spend more of their time with assistants, and subordinates. Members in coordinative positions tend to spend time with superiors and subordinates, as well as with associates at the same level in the organization. A member's function or duties may determine to a considerable degree which persons in the organization he may influence, as well as the nature of the influence that he can exert.

Group Organization Defines and Delimits Leadership

The very process of defining responsibility serves to structure and delimit the role that the leader may play in the organization. He cannot perform all the duties of all the members. His own accomplishment is therefore dependent upon the performance of others. His responsibilities are circumscribed by the outlined procedures and delegated responsibilities necessary for the achievement of stated goals.

Each member must work within the organizational framework which defines the limits of his participation (how far he ought to go and beyond which he ought not to go) in performance of duties. It also sets the requirements for his cooperation with others and defines his relationships with his superiors and subordinates. This organizational structuring is not viewed alike by all persons. To some it appears as a barrier to participation or recognition. To others it appears as a prod and stimulus to greater effort and participation. For still others it provides a secure and comfortable sphere of activities and working relationships. Organization, therefore, in defining the responsibilities and working relationships of its members, sets up barriers to participation, as well as facilitating it.

Even as the organization sets boundaries by providing a framework within which members discharge their responsibilities, so the individual presents various barriers to the influence of the organization upon his own behavior and reactions. Some members may be limited in capacity to discharge their responsibilities, while others who are highly skilled in the techniques of their responsibilities are limited in capacity to interact with others. Each member carries into the organization his past experiences, his needs, ideals, personal goals, and commitments to other organizations, which may modify and determine his capacity for participation. It would appear that the extent to which the behavior of different members is determined by the characteristics of the group represents a continuum from little to great, and also, that the extent to which the behavior of the different individuals determines the behavior of groups may be conceived as representing a similar continuum.

It becomes apparent that a study in leadership represents a

study of relationships, of variables in interaction. According to Pigors [11], a study of leadership must consider: (1) the leader, (2) the members as individuals, (3) the group as a functioning organization, and (4) the situation.

All organizations operate within a larger cultural and environmental framework. No organization can escape entirely the influence of the external situation. The organization may be influenced by the availability of resources, by changes in the social order of which it is a part, by competition of other organizations for the participation, resources or loyalty of its members, and by innumerable other factors outside the control of the organization itself. These factors also influence the leadership of the group.

Leadership and Effectiveness of Organization

According to Barnard [1] the persistence of cooperation depends upon two conditions: (*a*) effectiveness, the accomplishment of cooperative purpose, and (*b*) efficiency, the satisfaction of individual motives. Thus, although in many situations it may appear desirable to effect a maximum of goal achievement with a minimum of organizational expenditure, such a procedure might jeopardize the welfare or morale of the members. It then becomes evident that there are many situations in which organization is confronted by a complex of contradictory factors which must be considered in arriving at a decision. It also becomes apparent that the effectiveness of an organization cannot always be evaluated in terms of the degree to which it has attained its objectives. It may be necessary first to evaluate the goals and objectives themselves or the cost of their attainment. A carefully thought out discussion of factors to be considered in setting organizational goals, arriving at decisions, and evaluating the success of an organization has been presented by Simon [14]. He states: 'The accomplishment by an administrative program of its organizational goals can be measured in terms of *adequacy* (the degree to which its goals have been reached) or of *efficiency* (the degree to which the goals have been reached relative to the available resources).' Simon, in agreement with Barnard, maintains that the criterion of adequacy alone is not valid as a measure of group accomplishment. He observes that 'the fundamental criterion of administrative decision must be a criterion of *efficiency* rather than a criterion of *adequacy*. The task of administration is to maximize social values relative to limited resources.'

If organizational goals are employed as reference points in evaluating effectiveness, then the goals themselves must be subject to evaluation. In addition, the cost (human or material) of goal attainment must be considered as a factor in evaluation. Both Barnard and Simon imply that organization cannot be regarded as a unit in isolation – or as a law unto itself. The motive of organization is the creation of social value or goods for its members, and these values bear some significant relation to the values of society in general.

Since leadership is related to the determination of group goals, it becomes apparent that the leader is seldom a free agent. In influencing the activities of the organization in its striving toward goal achievement he must consider certain social values, not only in relation to the members, but in relation to society as well. If he ignores the welfare of the members he is likely to lose their following. If he ignores the welfare of society he is likely to lead his group into difficulty. Thus leadership is subject to determination by factors which are external to the organization, as well as by internal group factors.

The Definition of Leadership

The definition of leadership as a process of influencing the activities of an organized group in its task of goal setting and goal achievement should perhaps be re-examined. Does it define leadership? What are its implications? Admittedly, it defines only at a high level of generality. Certainly it does not include all social acts and influences, but it is nevertheless, an inclusive rather than a restrictive definition of leadership. Even so, it is more restrictive than most of those attempted in the recent literature. The definition restricts leadership to influence within the organized group. It does not imply domination or direction of others, nor any technique of influence; nor does it specify any particular member who should be regarded as a leader. The definition permits the study of any member of an organization to determine the extent of his leadership influence, and permits consideration of the possibility that every member may contribute towards determining the leadership of the organization.

The definition carries the implication that leadership may be not so much an attribute of individuals as an aspect of organization. In this respect it parallels the concept of authority. It is generally recognized that an executive in a business concern has authority in relation to his employees only during the time they are working as members of the organization. His authority does not extend outward into the direction of their personal or social lives. Nor does his position as an executive give him authority over other persons who are not members of his organization. In other words, authority is a relationship that exists between persons who are mutually participating as members of an organized enterprise. Authority is not an attribute of one or a few persons. Authority is an interactional process by means of which the organization defines for each individual the scope for action he has in making decisions, carrying out responsibilities, and enlisting the cooperation of others. The authority of any single individual will be largely circumscribed and defined by the authority of others, and at the same time, his own degree of authority will in part determine the authority of others.

Leadership appears also to be determined by a system of interrelationships. As such it must be regarded as an aspect of organization, just as authority is a derivative of organization. If leadership is determined by a system of interacting variables, then each of the several dimensions of responsibility and personal interaction might be conceived as representing a gradient of influence. If so, then it should be possible to measure leadership influences in terms of these dimensions.

Some members may be regarded as rating higher than others in leadership by virtue of the fact that they have responsibility for making decisions which exert a marked influence upon the activities of the organization. Some members may influence the activities of the organization as a result of personal interaction with other members, even though they do not hold positions of high-level responsibility. Some members may rate high in both types of influence. It would not be expected that any organization could be found in which all influence is exerted by a single

51

member. It would rather be expected that all the members of the organization could be ordered or ranked to some degree in terms of the influence they exert in various dimensions. The proposal to measure leadership in terms of the influence exerted by individuals may appear to contradict the statement that leadership is an aspect of organization rather than an attribute of individuals. But this is not a necessary conclusion. It was pointed out that authority is generally understood to be an aspect of organization. However, it can be observed that some members exercise more authority than others. The judgment can also be made that some persons have 'too much' or 'too little' authority. Such observations indicate an evaluation of conditions relative to various factors in the organization. In the same way it can be observed that member A exerts more leadership influence in some situations; while members B, C, and D exert more influence in determining activities of the organization in other instances. It may be that the leadership of A is circumscribed by the leadership of B, C, and D who are in competition with him; or it may be that the leadership of A is dependent upon the supporting leadership of B, C, and D. In either event, the leadership influence of any one member is determined in part by the leadership exerted by others, and the balance may change from time to time.

Summary

An organization is composed of individuals. Its existence is dependent upon the cooperation and performance of individuals who play different roles. Measures of authority, leadership, and the like, are but measures of aspects of organization, even though the measurements are made in terms of members and the relationships among members. Leadership exists only in so far as individuals, as members of organizations, are differentiated as to the influence they exert upon the organization; and the leadership influence of any one member will be determined to a large degree by the total leadership structure of the organization. It is for this reason that leadership has been here defined in terms of influence upon the activities of the organization, rather than in terms of influence upon persons.

The advantages of this formulation of the leadership problem are as follows: First, it removes leadership from the broad, vaguely defined realm of social interaction in general, and integrates it with the basic variables which describe an organized group. Second, and more important, is the fact that it suggests the development of methods for studying leadership as an aspect of work performance, work methods, and working relationships.

An attempt is being made to develop such methods for the Ohio State Leadership Studies. For example, the goals and structure of organization and the responsibility patterns of members are determined by examining organization charts and manuals and by interviews with members of the organization. Work patterns are determined by modified job analysis procedures. Sociometric methods are employed to determine working relationships between the members and to chart the informal organization. The social values and role concepts of leaders and members are studied by means of attitude scales. These methods are supplemented by various check lists and rating scales.

In conclusion, a word of caution may be in order. The present paper has been concerned with a search for the minimal factors which will permit a functional integration of the concepts: leader, member, and organization. In attempting to isolate these minimal common elements, many other important factors associated with leadership and group functioning have been excluded as not contributing to this central purpose. The present formulation represents merely one segment of a set of hypotheses to be subjected to experimental test.

References
1. BARNARD, C. I. (1938), *The Functions of the Executive*, Harvard University Press.
2. BROWN, A. (1947), *Organization of Industry*, Prentice-Hall.
3. DAVIS, R. C. (1940), *Industrial Organization and Management*, Harper.
4. FIREY, W. (1948), 'Informal organization and the theory of schism', *American Sociological Review*, vol. 13, pp. 15–24.
5. HEMPHILL, J. K. (1949), *Situational Factors in Leadership*, Bureau of Educational Research, Ohio State University.
6. HOMANS, G. C. (1947), 'A conceptual scheme for the study of social organization', *American Sociological Review*, vol. 12, pp. 13–26.
7. JUCIUS, M. J. (1947), *Personnel Management*, Irwin.

8. KRECH, D. and CRUTCHFIELD, R. S. (1948), *Theory and Problems of Social Psychology*, McGraw-Hill.

9. LEWIN, K., LIPPITT, R., and ESCALONA, S. K. (1940), *Studies in Topological and Vector Psychology. I.*, University of Iowa Studies on Child Welfare, vol. 16, no. 3.

10. MORENO, J. L. (1934), *Who Shall Survive?*, Nervous and Mental Diseases Publishing Co.

11. PIGORS, P. (1935), *Leadership or Domination*, Houghton-Mifflin.

12. ROETHLISBERGER, F. J., and DICKSON, W. J. (1939), *Management and the Worker*, Harvard University Press.

13. SHARTLE, C. L. (1949), 'Leadership and executive performance', *Personnel*, vol. 25, pp. 370–88.

14. SIMON, H. A. (1947), *Administrative Behavior*, Macmillan.

15. SMITH, M. (1945), 'Social situation, social behavior, social group', *Psychological Review*, vol. 52, pp. 224–9.

16. STOGDILL, R. M., and SHARTLE, C. L. (1948), 'Methods for determining patterns of leadership behavior in relation to organization structure and objectives', *Journal of Applied Psychology*, vol. 32, pp. 286–91.

17. WILSON, L. (1945), 'Sociography of groups', in G. Gurvitch, and W. E. Moore, eds., *Twentieth Century Sociology*, Philosophical Library, pp. 139–71.

18. ZNANIECKI, F. (1945), 'Social organization and institutions', in G. Gurvitch, and W. E. Moore, eds., *Twentieth Century Sociology*, Philosophical Library, pp. 172–217.

Part Two **A Beginning**

The history of the study of leadership is very much older than its investigation by psychologists. Men have always been interested in the power one has to influence the behaviour of another. Serious writing on the subject can, as with most things, be found at least among the early Greeks. Plato's *Republic* was largely a treatise on power and leadership, and in almost all literary periods there have been political philosophers especially who have attempted analyses of power and how to achieve it or maintain it. With exploration and world expansion came an intense interest in new and different cultures and particularly in the forms of leadership and of accession to leadership encountered among previously unknown peoples. Naturalist observers of animal behaviour too have shown an interest in the study of leadership and organization of animal groups which is much older than psychological study as such. The paper by Lewis M. Terman (Reading 4) which has been selected to represent a 'beginning' position for psychologists, indicates well the nature of much of this naturalist and anthropological work. The early date of Terman's paper and his reference to a paper by Alfred Binet and N. Vaschide which was also published in 1904 indicates that psychological interest in this topic is about as old as psychology itself. Other indications of an early interest in the more scientific approach to leadership may be seen in Webb (1915) and Gowin (1915).

From Terman, however, we have both a careful account of much that was known and suggested in 1904 that was relevant to the scientific study of leadership and an *experiment* designed to identify 'leaders' and to assess those qualities by virtue of which they were leaders. It is of more than passing interest that looking back now over almost 65 years of experimental work in this area, it is clear that some of the most 'sophisticated' understandings of leadership were already available to Terman.

He observed that strength and clarity of leadership increased as 'group spirit' increased and group goals had greater clarity. 'Leadership is intensified in times of emergency' (p. 73). He recognized too that the criteria of leadership must be carefully defined and that different criteria identify different group members as leaders. In addition, he noted, significantly with some surprise, that the same members do not necessarily appear as leaders when groupings are changed.

From his survey of animal studies Terman concluded that leadership must be viewed in its biological setting and suggested that the survival processes of evolution have favoured the gregarious and that this implies a tendency not to be independent and self-reliant but rather to 'follow' and to seek leadership. The necessary relation between leading and the needs of followers did not escape him.

Anthropological studies gave him three very 'modern' propositions. With respect to the selection of leaders, different groups value different activities and states and leaders are so chosen that they make a major contribution to the group's achievement of valued states. Secondly, it is observed that many groups choose leaders for special purposes, such as war, and that effective power changes hands as these purposes change. Thirdly, Terman noted observations that the power of the chief was greatly strengthened by alliance with the priesthood, which bears a similarity to Bales' discovery (page 264) which cannot fail to surprise and please.

There can be little doubt but that the experimental study of leadership was given a very good start in 1904, but the significance of much that Terman suggested was not immediately apparent and it was his effort to discover distinguishing attributes of leaders that most appealed to a psychological profession just becoming possessed of mental tests and other means of assessing ability and personality. Indeed, even in later post World War Two years when the dynamic approach to interpersonal relations had prepared both psychologists and sociologists to make use of their insights, it was not Terman's paper which gave psychologists and sociologists the lead so much as new approaches by Stogdill (Reading 5) and Gibb (Reading 10) to the literature as it then was, much in the manner of Terman's own review of 1904.

References

GOWIN, E. B. (1915), *The Executive and his Control of Men*, Macmillan.
WEBB, E. (1915), 'Character and intelligence', *British Journal of Psychology Monographs*.

4   L. M. Terman

A Preliminary Study of the Psychology and Pedagogy of Leadership

Excerpts from L. M. Terman, 'A preliminary study of the psychology and pedagogy of leadership', *Journal of Genetic Psychology*, vol. 11 (1904), pp. 413–51.

Scope of the Subject

Leadership is interesting from many points of view. In the first place there are two opposite poles of thought with regard to what it counts for in the progress from savagery to civilization. Some credit only the leaders as a factor in race progress, others only the masses.

The former tendency, of which Carlyle is a good exponent, has been most common in the past. Until recently, histories were little more than chronicles of wars and court intrigues. In reading such histories we forget that there were in those days other people than generals, kings, and nobles, with here and there a philosopher or religious reformer. Emerson viewed all institutions as 'the lengthened shadows of one man'. Carlyle defines history as 'nothing but the biographies of a few great men'.[1]

In a different form, the question of leadership is the crucial question of economics. We are infinitely better provided with material comforts than was primitive man. The task here is to decide what factors have contributed most to this advance. Thereon depends the justness or oppression of the distributive process. If the masses are powerless in themselves to accomplish anything, then we should welcome any evidence in favor of the 'Subsistence Theory'. On the other hand, Karl Marx and his followers assert that the *laborers* create everything, and that the captain of industry is truly a captain of exploitation.

Again, to express our thoughts, we use an intricately complicated set of symbols which none of us could have invented. We employ them without serious or sudden alteration. We

1. Mallock, *Aristocracy and Evolution*, 1902.

fashion our clothes, our houses, and even our politics and religion after patterns which are already given. On such consideration, it is evident why Tarde, having asked the question, what is society, should have answered it thus, briefly, '*c'est l'imitation*'. On the other hand it must be remembered that without something original to imitate, there can be no advance. As James puts it, there are two legs on which society walks: invention and imitation.

Though this study cannot concern itself with the details of the psychology of imitation or invention, and much less with their broader historical, economical, and sociological relations, it may yet be of value to take a bird's-eye view of some of the larger aspects of the subject.

If Tarde's claim for an 'inter-psychology' is warranted,[2] a large share of the work devoted to it must, either nearly or remotely, concern leadership. Broadly conceived, so as to include every form of attraction and repulsion, it is the chief fact of social life. Each member of society is both a leader and a follower, though predominantly, either one or the other. It comes, consciously or unconsciously, into every case of human relation.

At the beginning of every such relation there is an incipient duel, fought silently, but none the less decisive. It may be the remnant of an old instinct once of vital importance to the life of the anthropoid, namely, the tendency to evaluate instantly and accurately as regards possible injury or service every other animal happened upon. Does not this very thing survive in our relations with one another? We 'take the measure' of every man we meet. We 'size him up', or 'plot his curve', and whether or not we like to own it, to a certain extent we regulate our actions toward that one accordingly. If we judge ourselves superior, conduct takes on characteristic forms according to the occasion and our own nature: for example, haughtiness, imperiousness, condescension, the air of self importance, the instructive tone, etc. On the other hand, if we judge ourselves inferior there is present a feeling of timidity, a less confident heartbeat and less steady gaze. The voice becomes hollow instead of commanding or assuring. Spoken sentences are given a rising and questioning inflection.

2. Tarde, *International Quarterly*, 1903. Inter-Psychology.

It would seem that such data as this study deals with ought to be the beginning place for the study of sociology. In these days of evolution and genetic methods of study generally, sociology ought not to lag behind. The biologist no longer confines himself to the morphology of adult forms. He studies germination, embryology, growth, sports, and rudimentary organs. Like the historian, he must interpret the present and foretell the future through a study of the past. The political economist draws illustrations freely from the facts of savage society. The psychologist, in order to interpret the adult mind with its multiplicity of instincts, reflexes, feelings and ideational elements, watches their development from childhood and even calls to his aid the mental unfolding in the phylogenetic series. The same is true in psychological detail. If we are concerned with a so-called double personality, the important thing is to get a snap shot of the incipient bisection. If with a fixed idea, the primary shock is of more interest and importance than many later details. The same must be true, if possibly to a less degree, of the facts with which sociology deals. [. . .]

In government, unlike religion, we have passed, or rather are passing, through an important transformation. In primitive society *qualitative* values, that is *personal* elements, were predominant. At present the hereditary limited monarchy and democracy have undermined the hero and his qualitative value. The ideal of democracy is to bestow upon its leaders a purely quantitative value.[3] The effects and counter-effects of this momentous change would make interesting and legitimate subject matter for psychology.

In brief, there is room for many concrete studies in leadership, such as will concern the educator, the philosopher of religion, the historian and political scientist, as well as the psychologist. Every kind of political organization from the primitive to the modern, every sort of dominance, intrigue, revolution, abdication, war, and what not, that we find in the adult world, is paralleled in the personal and social relations of school children. It is not only probable that much light would be thrown on the former by the latter, but such cross-sections of child society as are pictured in our returns are of importance in themselves. They are the foreshadowing of the political and religious organizations

3. Binet and Vaschide, *Monist*, March, 1904.

that will hold forth a generation or so hence. They are the *alpha* of which a future government, or religion, or revolution, will be the *omega*.

At the very outset, however, we meet a very great difficulty. Leadership resolves itself into many questions. It may be treated from the standpoint of the child, the savage, or civilized man. But if we thus once begin to break up the subject where are we to end? Shall we not have to regard as fairly distinct from each other, political leadership, military, religious, ethical, musical, scientific, etc.? Will not the problem depend on whether we have in mind the poor or the rich, the ignorant or the learned, the emotional or the deliberate, the good or the degraded, the self-reliant or suggestible, and so on forever?

To an extent the implication is legitimate. The qualities of persons no doubt affect us a little as do colors or forms. This need not mean, however, that it will be useless to try to make out the qualities of leadership. Perhaps a last analysis will sometime reveal that above and beyond these species of leadership there is a genus; or, to change the figure, that a least common multiple of the many types exists.

Leadership Among Animals

Very little is known about leadership among animals. Most of the observations so far made are by persons of little scientific training. No one has employed experimentation or even careful observation. There are several difficulties in the way of such a study. In the first place, the observations would have to be of long duration in proportion to the results gained. In the second place, it is doubtful if the artificial environment of captivity would call forth whatever phenomena might be frequent in the normal state. Moreover, the activities involved in leadership are not simple, and the component factors must first be studied separately before much light can be thrown on the psychical complex as a whole. These related and preliminary facts are not yet fully determined. To illustrate, it is evident that the question of animal leadership is largely coincident with that of imitation. But it is not certain just how much and what sort of imitation exists among animals.

Keeping this in mind, we may use the term leadership in a broad sense, so as to include most of the facts of imitation, suggestion, sentinel posting, and group chieftainship. The following are a few of the observations, of varying degrees of reliability, coming under these headings.

1. *So-called imitation and suggestion*

Morgan[4] states: 'If one of a group of chicks learns by casual experience to drink from a tin of water, others will come up and peck at the water and will themselves drink. A hen teaches her little ones to pick up grain and other food by pecking on the ground and dropping suitable material before them, the chicks seeming to imitate her actions.' 'A little pheasant and guinea fowl followed two ducklings . . . and seemed to wait upon their bills, to peck where they pecked and to be guided by their actions.' 'If a group of chicks have learned to avoid cinnabar caterpillars, and if one or two from another group are introduced and begin to pick up the caterpillars, the others will sometimes seize them though they would otherwise have taken no notice of them.' Morgan also cites a quotation to the effect that if pigeons are reared exclusively on small grain they will starve before eating beans. But when they are thus starving, if a bean-eating pigeon is put among them, they follow its example, and thereafter adopt the habit. Again, 'I have often observed that in broods of chicks brought up under experimental conditions by themselves, and without opportunity of imitating older birds, there are one or two more active, vigorous, intelligent, and mischievous birds. They are the leaders of the brood; the others are their imitators. Their presence raises the general level of intelligent activity. Remove them, and the others show a less active, less inquisitive, less adventurous life, if one may so put it. They seem to lack initiative.' In agreement with this, Dr Wesley Mills found that when he introduced his mongrel pup to the society of the other dogs, its progress was extraordinarily rapid.

Dr Kinnaman, in experimenting with his two rhesus monkeys, found very many examples of imitation similar to those mentioned by Morgan, and in addition to the cases that might be classed as instinctive imitation, at least two cases which he would

4. Morgan, *Habit and Instinct*, pp. 166–82.

class as intelligent imitation. These were both imitations of the male by the female.[5] In one case the female had several times completely failed at removing a plug fastening and had quit 'in disgust'. 'At this juncture the male was turned out of his cage. He went immediately to the box, she following some four feet away. Knowing the trick perfectly, he seized the end of the plug with his teeth and removed it. I set the box again. This time the female rushed to it, seized the plug by the end as the male did, and procured the food. This she repeated immediately eight times in exactly the same way.' The other case was similar. There were also numerous cases where one monkey followed the other when it jumped onto the table or into the window.

Mill[6] states that suggestive action began with his puppy from the fortieth day. He thinks that suggestive action accounts for a large part of the dog's activity, such as sheep worrying, etc. Morgan noticed that when he approached the bars with his three puppies, one went through at once and the two others followed apparently through imitation. Hobhouse quotes a similar case of three stags trying to get over a fence.

We need not enter into the much disputed question as to whether such activities are really imitative. Whether we adopt the liberal interpretation of Hobhouse and Mills, or, on the other hand, agree with Thorndike in altogether denying intelligent imitation to animals below the primates, the objective results are the same. We have an animal doing a thing which it would not have done but for perceiving its performance by another. The above examples are given as representing leadership and suggestion reduced to their lowest terms. It may be that such activities can be denominated 'leading' and 'following' only in an objective sense. It is an undoubted fact, however, that many animals act from the stimulus of a like or similar activity in another.

2. *Sentinel posting and allied phenomena*

Rocky Mountain sheep live together in small bands, posting sentinels wherever they are feeding or resting, who watch for and[7]

5. *The American Journal of Psychology*, vol. 13, pp. 121 ff.
6. Mill, *Animal Intelligence*, p. 163.
7. David Starr Jordan, *Animal Life*, p. 165.

give warning of the approach of enemies. Hobhouse[8] quotes from Mr Cornish, describing the maneuvers of wild geese when they alight on a field of grain. 'They post a sentry who either stands on some elevated part of the field, or walks slowly with the rest, never, however, venturing to pick up a grain, his whole energies being employed in watching.' Espinas[9] and Brehm[10] cite many similar instances as regards antelopes, termites, and many species of birds.

What are the mental activities involved in these well-known habits of sentinel posting? The response given by the individuals to a sentinel call is easy enough to explain, being only a special case of instinctive reaction. But the conduct of the sentinel is harder to understand without crediting the animals concerned with a knowledge of the purpose they are fulfilling. The older observers did not hesitate to make this assumption. Perhaps no single explanation will suffice. As a special adjustment to the needs of gregarious life, the activity may be partly instinctive, partly traditional, and partly intelligent. We certainly cannot speak of a 'social system' among the animals, or regard the functions of the sentinel as especially set apart and delegated with human forethought to one member of the group.

3. Group chieftainship and dominance

Some observations indicate that among certain of the higher animals there is a more genuine form of leadership than we have so far discussed. It may rather vaguely be denominated chieftainship or dominance over a group. For example, 'Birds in their long flights keep together, often with definite leaders who seem to discover and to decide on the course of flight for the whole of the flock.'[11] Espinas[12] says that llamas used in South America to carry heavy burdens over the mountains are allowed to go loose in groups, each group led by a single male richly caparisoned. Brehm says that among elephants a male usually leads the herd. When the leader is shot down, the rest usually flee at once. Darwin, speaking of the semi-wild cattle of the La Platte, says they

8. Hobhouse, *Mind in Evolution*, p. 272.
9. Espinas, *Les Sociétés Animals*.
10. Brehm, *Thierleben*.
11. D. S. Jordan, loc. cit., p. 166.
12. Espinas, op. cit., p. 499.

are easily counted, since they group themselves in bunches of 40 to 100. The owner has only to see if the leader of each group is present.

Brehm states that among monkeys, the strongest or oldest, that is, the most capable member of the group, puts himself up as leader. 'This respect is not accorded to him by common consent, but only after obstinate struggle with other ambitious ones. The longest teeth and strongest arms decide. The ones that will not willingly submit are brought to time by bites and slaps.'[. . .]

Every farmer boy has observed the fights and quarrels of domestic horses and cows for individual and group supremacy. Several incidents of this sort have been related to me. Also as a boy on a farm where 15 to 20 horses and 30 to 50 cattle were kept, I witnessed many of these contests for supremacy. Among either the cattle or horses there was usually one whom the others allowed to have his own way in every respect. He drank first at the trough, grazed where he pleased, and ate from whatever box he took a fancy for. The dominance was generally settled once for all in a few lively encounters. After that the subdued ones showed only mild protests or none at all. If the make-up of the group remained unchanged the dominant member usually retained his superiority. When a strange individual was admitted his relative rank in the group was pretty definitely fixed before many days.

On the other hand, there were certain ones that might be designated as outcasts. These had to stand aside for all the others. They seemed timid, lacked spirit, and showed no inclination to try to better their condition. Their lot was sometimes a hard one. In going to and from the pasture, they were chased and horned by all the others. At the trough they were the last to drink. Sometimes another who had drank his fill would still stand guard over the water and prevent the outcast from drinking for some minutes.

There were all degrees between these two extremes of rank. Each individual had his position relative to all the others and only in rare cases did he try to better it. If attacked by a superior he gave way, with little show of fight. Now and then, however, bitter encounters took place, a reversal of rank sometimes resulting. Neither with the cattle nor the horses did the dominance seem to depend much on size, and not altogether on actual fighting ability. A quick show of courage, and readiness to attack seemed more essential. In some cases I was quite sure that certain members could easily have improved their group rank if they had only tried. As a specific instance, one peppery little mare of only 4 or 5 years was 'boss' over about a dozen other horses most of whom were both older and larger. She attacked quickly and delivered her blows or bites in such rapid succession that opposition was soon scattered. Among animals, as will be seen also among children, the very consciousness of superiority or inferiority goes far to make the superiority or inferiority real. The bluff is perhaps even more effective with them than with human beings.

Among the most reliable observations reported, bearing on this study, are those of Francis Galton on the wild ox of South Africa.[13] They cover an extended period of time, and the report is based altogether on Mr Galton's own experience. The herds were found very hard to manage, as no individual could be persuaded to go first in any desired move, each one backing to give place to his neighbor. For this reason, fore-oxen were highly prized, and there was great difficulty in securing good ones. 'The ordinary member of the herd is wholly unfitted by nature to move in so prominent and isolated a position.' Breakers watch assiduously for those who show self-reliant nature by grazing apart or ahead of the rest. 'The born leaders are far too rare to be used for any less distinguished service than that which they alone are capable of filling. The mass are essentially slavish and seek no better lot than to be led by one of their number who has enough self-reliance to accept the position.'

It must be supposed that leadership among animals is an off shoot, or example, of the traits denominated by the term 'gregarious instincts'. The whole question must be viewed in its biological setting. Leadership in certain individuals implies a want of self reliance in the others. This want is fostered by the very fact of gregarious living. The conditions of life have made a want of self reliance a necessity to most of the herd. If each animal had the qualities of a leader they would graze apart, defenseless, and easily surprised. As Galton states, 'The wild

13. *Human Faculty*, p. 68 ff.

beasts trim and prune every herd into compactness, and reduce it to a closely united body with a single leader.' A member of the troop tends to acquire a certain supremacy for the simple reason of his greater independence, activity, and capability. A very little intelligence operating on the hereditary tendency to follow and imitate will suffice to fix the habits in question.

But the full extent and significance of animal leadership will only be determined by studies made under rigid experimental conditions.

Leadership Among Primitive Races

Among most primitive races the chief has to be brave, strong, cunning, and enduring. As Carlyle reminds us the king is literally the *man who can*, the *könning man*. The office is not generally hereditary, but goes as a prize to the deserving, either through common consent or formal election.

Ordinarily he must prove that he has useful qualities before he can become chief. If he has proved his valor and skill in exploits of war and in dangerous hunts, well and good. But if his metal is yet untried, initiations are sometimes resorted to as a test.[14] The Columbian Indian tribes impose a long fast, and later the older ones apply vigorous lashes with a whip till the candidate is covered with stripes. If he allows the least complaint to escape during this rude preliminary test he is dishonored and rejected. If he courageously persists, he is then covered with stinging ants. As a final test, he is suspended in a hammock over a fire of leaves so that he feels the heat and is suffocated by the smoke. Tyler states that among certain savage tribes he is chosen as chief who can lift the largest beam and carry it longest. For the work that savages have to do, the immediate usefulness of the qualities thus brought out is evident, though wisdom and moral courage tend gradually to replace cunning and physical endurance.

The following quotations give an idea of a few of the qualities sought for in chiefs: Schoolcraft[15] says Indian chiefs are as a rule a manly, intelligent body of men, with a bold and independent

14. Letourneau, *Political Evolution*, p. 16.
15. Schoolcraft, *Archives of Aboriginal Knowledge*, vol. 5, p. 152.

air and gait, and with good powers of oratory. 'Their repose of character and ease of manners cannot fail to strike one; but what is still more remarkable is to hear one of them, when he rises to speak, fall into a train of elevated remarks which would often do honor to a philosopher.'

Among the Iroquois[16] the rank of chief was personal. It was gained by the character and achievements of the individual and died with him. Among the Omahas[17] the chief must enjoy a good reputation and have given feasts to the poor and orphans. The leaders of the Columbian Indians 'are always men of commanding influence and often of great intelligence. They take the lead in haranguing the council of wise men, who meet to debate on matters of public moment.' The head man among the Indians of Guiana[18] is generally the most successful hunter, who without having any formal authority obtains a certain amount of preference. His order to go anywhere or to do anything is implicitly obeyed. Among other Indian tribes[19] the hunters union comes to possess more power than the chief and his council. They are the tribe's stomach. If the chief does not show special hunting ability he may be left at home to manage the affairs of the women and children and weaklings, or in some cases his power reduced to that of determining the time of the hunt. Among the Australian tribes[20] there is no recognized head, whether king or chief, but men of preponderating influence are those distinguished for courage, strength, and force of character. These, in connection with the elders, generally advise as to public actions, settle internal disputes, and enforce obedience to traditional law. Among certain African tribes[21] the most wealthy and liberal chief is reckoned the best. In most cases, however, it is the one with greatest knowledge and skill, especially in matters of war. 'The family stock also has a leader, usually the eldest, but apart from warfare, his influence is little. Moreover, the chief's nearest relatives have a certain ascendency, and thus we find them already

16. Hale, *Iroquois Book of Rites*, p. 68.
17. Letourneau, op. cit., p. 46.
18. Thurn, *Indians of Guiana*, p. 211.
19. Ratzel, *History of Mankind*, vol. II, p. 135.
20. John Matthew, *Australian Aborigines*, p. 93.
21. Ratzel, loc. cit.

striving to give a more oligarchical character to their government.' The Polynesian chieftain[22] derives his power from his
age, personal influence, and yet more from his wealth. As with
the Indians, pecuniary inequality engenders political inequality.
It is said that among the Esquimos, the most successful weather
prophet is often chosen leader.

It is an oft noted fact that the power of the chief is greatly
strengthened in many cases by alliance with the priesthood.
Ratzel states that conversion to Christianity has almost always
destroyed the power of native chiefs, by killing the influence of
their magic. Morris emphasizes[23] this point. 'In fact, it seems to
have been through the influence of religious ideas that men first
rose to power and became supreme over their fellows.' There is a
tendency to regard the chief who leads in acts of public worship
as the representative of the divine ancestor, and as such a tribe
develops into a nation, its chief adds to himself the power and
position of high priest. In America it was true everywhere that
the head of the established religion became the head of the
nation. Thus, Montezuma was high priest and derived his power
largely from that position. Such rulers become autocrats in a
double sense, supreme lords of body and soul. The powerful
monarchs of Assyria led their armies to conquest in the name of
the national deity, whose vice-regents they claimed to be. The
autocratic emperors of Rome went so far as to claim in some cases
to be themselves gods. The emperor of China still holds the
position of father of his people, the representative of the original
ancestor and high priest of the nation. Even in modern Russia,
the emperor derives some of his dignity from his position as head
of the national church.

War, as well as religion, has played a great part in the leadership of primitive men. Among many tribes it gives rise to a special
leader whose office is separate from that of peace chieftain. In
some cases, the tribe is divided into two separate divisions, a
war group and a peace group, each with its own head. Other
tribes have usually only a peace chieftain and elect a war captain
only as occasion requires. Not infrequently the peace chieftain
simply adds the duties of war captain to his own, making himself

22. Letourneau, op. cit., p. 71.
23. Morris, *Man and his Ancestor*, pp. 191 ff.

supreme. When the tribe habitually has separate leaders for peace and war, the former generally inherits his office while the latter seldom does. The position of war captain is so vitally important that it comes only as the reward of highest merit.

The following quotations illustrate the practices among a few primitive races. When the Patagonians form a confederation against an enemy,[24] they choose a chief from among the most renowned warriors. But always the power of the war chiefs is transitory. It expires with the occasion that gave it birth. In New Zealand,[25] if a war or other enterprise is about to be launched, a man is chosen chief who has already proved his bravery and prudence. But the expedition over, the improvised chief is again lost in the crowd. Among the Pueblos, each tribe or village has a chief to whom a certain degree of respect is conceded. His influence is maintained chiefly by his oratorical powers or military skill. In war, his authority is recognized, but in time of peace his rule is nominal.

Bancroft also states that the Comanches of New Mexico vest little authority in the chief during peace, but on the war path his commands are implicitly obeyed. It also happens that chiefs are sometimes chosen to lead some particular war or marauding expedition, their authority expiring immediately on their return home.

According to Schurtz,[26] the contrast between the war and peace groups shows plainest with the American tribes. The sachem was the peace ruler and his office was hereditary. His duties were limited entirely to affairs of peace. His relations touched chiefly the gens whose official head he was. The war chief was chosen for his bravery in war, his wisdom in matters of diplomacy, or his talkativeness in council. His relations touched chiefly the tribe. The head of the clan had to do with the narrow self-satisfying ways of the clan; the war chief, with the tribal union and the state building powers. Among the Delawares, for example, the peace captain had very little power. Imperial manners did not become him. He had rather to seek the submission of his subjects through liberality. The war chiefs were not exactly elected, but

24. Letourneau, op. cit., p. 56.
25. Cook's Voyages, vol. 8, p. 103.
26. Schurtz, Altersklassen u. Männerbünde, Chapters 2 and 4.

gathered a following through personal influence. Small wars were sometimes undertaken by the war chief independently, but important ones with the consent of the peace chieftain. The inhabitants of New Pommeronia have a hereditary peace ruler, and also a war captain, whose influence rests strictly on personal qualities. Between these two heads there is continual strife, which, strange to say, is usually unfavorable to the war chief. The La Platte tribes, the Cherokee, the Iroquois, the South Sea peoples, the Maori, the New Guineans, and, as Miss Kingsly thinks, all the true Negroes offer close parallels to the above described forms. However, among some, as for example the inhabitants of Tonga, the war chief has succeeded in pressing the king entirely into the background. This recalls the *Hausmeier* of the Frankish kings, or the overshadowing of the Mikado by the Shogun. On the other hand, the opposite tendency has usually prevailed in Africa, the war chief taking a back place or being chosen in case of necessity only. The shepherd tribes of Messai in peace are ruled by patriarchs, but in war a common leader is chosen to take charge till peace is re-established. Likewise among the Arabs, the *scheich*, or peace patriarch, gives way in war to the *Argyd*, who is chosen from the ranks of the bravest men.

As Schurtz points out, the same general facts hold with the ancient peoples of Europe. The Germans during the migration period were under the double leadership. The *Fürst* was originally the head of a family, or family group. Opposed to him was the *Herzog*, or war chief. The activity of the former was directed within, and rested on patriarchal authority. The latter represented the spirit of aggressiveness. Sometimes one, sometimes the other, had the upper hand in the same people. The Franks during their migration were under the Herzogen, but after they had won permanent homes, the kingdom was handed over to the Merowingian family.[27]

We see, therefore, that the institution of war chiefs, though temporary in the beginning, tends in the long run to the organization of a régime more or less monarchical, and the tendency is greater the more frequent are the wars. Morris[28] says: 'The head

27. Schurtz, loc. cit.
28. Morris, loc. cit., p. 199.

man became a war chief and the war chief a king. Success made him a hero to his people. He grew to be the lord of conquered tribes; into his hands fell the bulk of the spoils. . . . War was the great agent in this evolution. It might have emerged slowly in peace, it came with startling rapidity in war.' We may say, in short, it happens universally that leadership is intensified in times of emergency. War, conflict, and adventure are its fertile soil. It grows directly with the need of concerted action, this point coming out time and again in the questionnaire returns.

The club-like organizations described by Schurtz and others also give occasion for the phenomena of leadership among primitive races. Though existing in many parts of the world, they are perhaps most numerous among the Malay tribes. To reach highest rank in the clubs one must have money, means of life, and wine. 'One who has reached highest rank is really a great man and bears the title of *Wetuka* as though he had attained heaven.' Without his permission no one can be advanced a single rank.[29] The clubs have 3 or 4 to as high as 18 grades, or degrees. The members of each grade wear an insignia. Some of the clubs are democratic and embrace nearly all the people, while others are aristocratic and admit only a few of the leading persons.

It is noteworthy that few clubs of this kind among primitive races are conducted by women, and such as they do have are only weak imitations of those found among men.[30] We thus have the strange paradox that woman, regarded as the founder of society, has less of the purely social tendency than man. The solution, of course, lies in the fact that we must distinguish between the purely social instincts and the sexual instincts. Schurtz takes the view that the former are not an outcropping of the latter, and that therefore the family may not be the primary social grouping. Woman's weakness in the purely social relations, coupled with her devotion to family life, makes it seem reasonable that the two instincts are not interdependent, and that they may not even have a common origin. As will be seen later, the questionnaire returns also bring out strongly both quantitative and qualitative sex differences in leadership.

29. Schurtz, loc. cit.
30. Schurtz, op. cit., p. 48.

Leadership Among Children

1. *Experimental*

The following experimental study was made. It is in part a repetition of some work done by Binet.[31] It seemed, however, that the study should embrace a much larger number of pupils[32] and should also be made more intensive. That is, facts concerning the pupils should be gained from other sources than the tests.

One hundred pupils of the Bloomington, Indiana, public schools acted as subjects. They were distributed as follows:

Grade 2,   12 boys and 12 girls.
„   4,   12 „   „   12 „
„   6,   8 „   „   12 „
„   8,   8 „   „   8 „

In addition, 8 boys and 8 girls, in the colored school, ranging from the 5th to the 8th grade, were tested separately.

The general aim was to discover those pupils who might be termed 'leaders' of their fellows, and to ascertain the qualities whereby they held this ascendency. It is evident that without long personal acquaintance with each pupil, and without opportunity for long and careful observations of their actions during work and play, the outcome of the study must be meagre enough. The results are not claimed to have a high degree of absolute value.

The tests were as follows: On a heavy cardboard about 16 × 24 inches were fastened pictures and objects, to the number of ten. The pupils were withdrawn, four at a time, to an unoccupied and quiet room. To throw them off their guard they were told that they were to engage in a memory test. It was further explained that the cardboard would be turned so that they could view for ten seconds the objects and pictures pasted on the other side. After the removal of the cardboard from sight they were to answer a number of questions concerning what they had seen. They were given to understand that we would record the

31. Binet, *La Suggestibilité*, p. 330 ff.
32. Binet used only 24.

reply of each pupil and the order in which it was given. They were therefore urged to reply both quickly and correctly. The answers were given with loud voice. The instructions were always repeated till they were clearly understood.

Binet used only three pupils in each group. On consideration, it seemed best to have more. Groups of five were first tried but the order of the replies being too difficult to get, the number was reluctantly reduced to four. Binet also chose one member of each group to act as chairman of that group, allowing him to read the questions, to record the answers, and at the same time to act as subject himself. To say nothing of the relative disadvantage thus thrown on such a pupil, it appeared that even so slight an exhibition of preference on the part of the experimenter would likely affect the group spirit. Accordingly all were allowed to stand on equal footing, either myself or an assistant asking the questions while the other kept the records. The girls and the boys were tested separately. Moreover, except in the colored school, the pupils of any group were chosen from a single grade.

Twenty-three questions were asked concerning the objects and pictures, 11 of which were catch questions; that is, they asked about things which were not on the cardboard. These were intended to serve as a test of the pupils' suggestibility. It was found somewhat difficult to hit upon the right sort of catch questions and to locate them properly in the series. Two extremes were to be avoided. The traps must not be too glaring, else the suspicions of the subject would be aroused. Neither must they be so easily led up to that none would escape them. Usually they were separated by fair questions, and the more obvious ones were placed toward the latter part of the list, since we hoped by that time to have won the confidence of the pupils.

When all the 100 subjects had been thus tested in groups of 4, a second series was begun in an exactly analogous way, with a new set of objects on the cardboard and a new set of 23 questions, 9 of which were catches. 80 of the former 100 pupils participated. For this series of experiments the former groups were broken up and new ones formed. In the latter, the pupils were intentionally so chosen that each group would contain at least one pupil who had shown himself a leader, and one who had appeared to be an automaton in the previous tests. It could thus be determined whether the rank of a pupil in any group of the first series had wholly a relative, or to some extent an absolute meaning.

In elaborating the results the following points were noted for each pupil:

1. The number of times his reply was first, second, third, or fourth.

2. Originality.

3. The number of times each pupil of a group imitated each of the others.

4. Total number of imitations made by each.

5. Total number of times each pupil was imitated, by all the others.

6. Suggestibility, as measured by the number of times the subject fell into the trap.

The arbitrary use of some of the above terms must be explained. 'Originality' means that the answer could not have been influenced by the answer of any other pupil. This does not, however, preclude its being suggested by a trap question. The 'originality' can be shown in two ways: First, by answering before all the others; second, by giving an answer which, though not first, differed from the preceding answers in such a way that it could not have been influenced by them. Here, it must be acknowledged, there was often room for doubt, since it was not always possible to calculate just how far contrary suggestion was at work. 'Suggestibility' was computed in per cent. If the pupil fell into all the traps his 'suggestibility' was reckoned 100%. If into 4 out of a total of 8, 50%, etc. The other items will be made clear by the following illustration: Suppose that in answer to a question the same reply was given by all, A, B, C, and D, in a group. If A answers first, he is 'original'. B answers second, and since his answer is the same as A's, he is credited with one 'imitation'. C answers third and therefore 'imitates' A and B once each. D answers fourth and therefore 'imitates' A, B, and C once each. That is, A makes no 'imitation', B makes one, C makes two, and D makes three. A was 'imitated' three times, B twice, and C once.

As expected, certain of the pupils answered first nearly always, while others were generally last and were content to repeat exactly or with slight variation the answer of another. For example, in one group,

	First	Second	Third	Fourth
A answered	1	4	8	10
C ,,	9	6	5	2

It soon became evident that not always could those who answered first be called 'leaders'. Fifteen times it occurred that the group rank of pupils in quickness and in number of times 'imitated' differed radically, i.e. by as much as two places. Here, we have an unmistakable exhibition of personal preference. Those who have not the initiative for framing an answer of their own, will prefer to repeat the answer of one pupil rather than that of another. The first reply is a stimulus which always tends to result in an activity of the other pupils suggested by it or imitative of it, but in the above fifteen cases the tendency was generally overcome by some inhibition. It likewise happened several times that the quickest were not the most 'original'. With twelve pupils there was a wide divergence between the group rank in 'originality', and that in number of times 'imitated'. Another, and perhaps more significant result was the fact that low 'originality' often accompanied low 'suggestibility', and *vice versa*. In fact the average 'suggestibility' of the *leaders* was slightly greater than that of the *automatons*, the percentage being 62 and 59 respectively. Their comparative 'originality', however, was 13·4 and 5·6, out of a total of 23 questions answered. This fact may have been due to the intense desire of the leaders to answer first, though the subjects were repeatedly reminded that it was as important to answer correctly as to answer quickly.

A greater number than expected, namely, 19 out of 80, obtained in the second series of tests a radically different rank from what they had gained in the first series. Of 22 leaders in the second series, 12 had been leaders in the first series, and five had occupied very low rank. Out of 32 automatons in the second series, 18 had been so in the first series, and 7 had occupied very high rank.

The following table shows the grade and sex differences for

'originality'. Each number represents the number of original answers out of the total set of 23.

Grade	2	4	6	8	Colored	Average for each sex	
Boys	8·50	8·33	9·25	10·12	9·50	9·14	} Series I
Girls	7·16	6·91	8	10·62	9·62	8·50	
Boys	9·85	7·25	8	10	7·12	8·44	} Series II
Girls	6·37	5·87	8	9·62	8·87	7·75	
Average for each grade	7·97	7·09	8·31	10·09	8·78	8·45	

The following table shows the percentage of 'suggestibility'.

Grade	2	4	6	8	Colored	Average for each sex	
Boys	50	77	77	45	73	64 +	} Series I
Girls	66	76	77	52	77	60 +	
Boys	72	76	91	45	78	72 +	} Series II
Girls	86	97	90	55	61	78 −	
Average for each grade	68·5	81·5	83·7	49·2	72·2	68 +	

The second part of our task was to get further facts about the pupils that would throw light on the cases of leadership among them. This the teachers were kind enough to furnish by answering 22 questions in regard to each pupil. They are as follows:

1. Age? 2. Size, in relation to grade? 3. Dress? 4. Is dress gaudy? 5. Any physical peculiarity or deformity? 6. Health? 7. Are parents wealthy or otherwise prominent? 8. Is it an only child? 9. Quality of school work? 10. Notable for boldness or daring? 11. A leader in games or pranks? 12. If so, is it by forcing others or by natural attraction? 13. Liked or disliked by other pupils? 14. Why? 15. Fluent of speech in conversation? 16. Any dramatic qualities? 17. Looks? 18. Reads much or little? 19. Timid or forward? 20. High tempered or amiable? 21. Selfish or considerate? 22. Emotional or deliberate in temperament?

Questions like 2, 3, and 9 were graded on a scale of five. To illustrate, 1 = very large, 2 = large, 3 = average, 4 = small, 5 = very small. Questions like 16, 18, 19, and 20 were graded similarly on a scale of three. Some of the most important results are summed up in the following table.

	Grade	2	4	6	8	Colored	Average
Age in years	Leaders	$7\frac{2}{3}$	$10\frac{3}{7}$	$13\frac{1}{5}$	14·75	14	
	Automatons	$7\frac{2}{3}$	$10\frac{1}{2}$	12·60	14·80	14·60	
Size, on scale of five	Leaders	2·16	2·62	2·33	3·20	2	2·48
	Automatons	3·11	3	2·80	3	3	2·98
Dress, on scale of five	Leaders	2·50	3·28	1·83	1·80	2·50	2·38
	Automatons	2·70	3·25	2·40	2	2·60	2·59
Quality of work, scale of five	Leaders	2·40	2·14	2·50	2·20	3	2·41
	Automatons	2·50	3·50	2·60	3	2·60	2·84
Looks, scale of three	Leaders	2·25	1·62	1·50	1·20	2	1·72
	Automatons	2·11	2·12	2·20	1·75	2·20	2·09
Selfishness, scale of three	Leaders	2·20	1·56	2	1·20	2·25	1·84
	Automatons	2	2	2	2·25	2	2·05

Several of the questions do not furnish data to show anything clearly. To sum up the chief results, the pupils who were leaders in the tests are larger, better dressed, of more prominent parentage, brighter in their school work, more daring, more fluent of speech, better looking, greater readers, and less selfish than the automatons. It was found that a surprising number of times the leaders were graded on size, dress, and school work either as 5 or 1. To illustrate, in grade 4 the leaders are graded on school work as 1, 1, 5, 1, 1, 5, 1. The automatons of the same grade received the following ranks on the same question: 3, 4, 3, 3, 4, 3, 5, 3. This indicates that possibly there is a tendency for children to be influenced by what is unusual; that they are on the lookout for striking qualities of whatever sort; anything to get clear of tiresome mediocrity.

Finally, the same pupils, excepting those in grade 2, were allowed to answer the following questions:

What one of your schoolmates would you rather be like if you were not yourself? Why? Several other questions were asked calling for ideals, but the answers were so scattered that no well defined tendency could be made out. Above all it was desired to find out how much oftener, if any, those pupils stamped as leaders by the experiments would be chosen consciously as ideals by their mates, than would the automatons. The results show that they were chosen $4\frac{1}{2}$ times as often. The fact is important as indicating the validity of the method of experimentation and the great importance of suggestion and imitation as elements in leadership.

Summary of experimental results. 1. A large number maintain a well defined rank either as first or last in the groups.

2. The leaders in the tests were twice as often mentioned by the teachers as being leaders, and further were chosen $4\frac{1}{2}$ times as often by their mates as ideals.

3. Suggestibility, as measured by these tests, rises from the second to the fourth grade and then falls rapidly in the succeeding grades. The naïveté with which the smallest children gave correct answers to the catch questions was remarkable. It reminds one of the old story of the king who thought to appear in procession before his people in a magic garment, visible to all except the wicked, and whose nakedness was denounced only by a little child.

4. The pupils show marked choice in imitating the answers of others. Circumstances favor the quickest, but not always are these the most imitated.

5. The leaders have a high average suggestibility. This may indicate that there is some truth in the assertion, often made, that to be a leader it is more important to lead the way than to be right.

6. The group rank of many pupils in the second series was radically different from what it had been in the first. This does not seem to be due to a wide divergence between the average reaction time or 'originality' of the second group as compared to the first. It is the group spirit as mirrored in the consciousness of each pupil. In one group a certain pupil *feels* himself inferior; he follows, therefore, the answers of the others. In another group the same pupil may *feel* himself superior, and be so regarded by the

others. This recalls Emerson's words: 'Who has more soul than I, masters me, though he should not raise his finger. . . . Who has less, I rule with like facility.'

7. The leaders in the tests, according to the testimony of their teachers, are on the average larger, better dressed, of more prominent parentage, brighter, more noted for daring, more fluent of speech, better looking, greater readers, less emotional, and less selfish than the automatons.

8. As regards the reasons given by the pupils for choosing certain of their schoolmates for ideals, intelligence increases in importance rapidly from the second to the eighth grade and goodness as rapidly falls.

9. According to the opinion of the teachers, such pupils are preferred most often for the following qualities, given in order of their importance: intelligence, congeniality, liveliness, and goodness.

10. The data were not suited to bring out race differences in the qualities of leadership.

2. *Questionnaire returns*

The following questionnaire was sent out.

1. What are the causes and reasons of strong likes and dislikes among children, or for great respect and contempt?

2. Describe cases of excessive dominance of one boy or girl over one or more others or over a group, always giving sex and age. Give concrete cases with details and illustrations. Describe the leader.

3. How much is due to (*a*) size, (*b*) strength, (*c*) skill or feats and what, (*d*) good looks, (*e*) good disposition, (*f*) good and kindly manners, (*g*) mental superiority and rank in studies, (*h*) natural kindness and helpfulness, (*i*) wealth and social station, (*j*) dress, (*k*) superior age or maturity?

4. Give cases of boys and girls generally disliked or neglected or even outcast, and state causes, whether the opposite of the above.

5. Is unpopularity the obverse of popularity? Does this differ at different ages? Can you intimate any differences between the age from 7 to 12, 12 to 16, and from 16 to 20 or 25?

(a) Can you describe a case of great influence by a young person who desired not to have this power?

(b) How far is it unconscious and how far striven for, and if the latter by what devices?

(c) Can you give cases of failure or exposure on the part of those striving for leadership?

(d) Can you give cases where a leader has grown weary of power, and abdicated? Lost prestige by taking too much, or sought to transfer it?

6. Can you describe individual or collective revolts against a leader?

7. Give cases where dominance has benefited the followers, fag, or henchmen, and state how.

(a) Cases of moral, mental, or physical injury resulting from such dominance.

(b) Cases of the good or evil effects of mashes, friendships, cronyisms between those equal or unequal in independence or influence.

8. (a) How can leadership be utilized in the school? (b) How can persecution or unpopularity be mitigated? (c) Does this differ in boys and girls?

9. Describe briefly a bluffer, as to scholarship, courage, honesty, frankness. Must bluffing have spectators? Describe bluffing as a form of ostentatious intimacy; effect of it on other children and their reactions to it, imitation, criticism, sympathy, etc.; how far was it genuine and how far affected?

Questions 2, 3, 4, 5, and 9 were the most fruitful. The others will not be taken up for treatment here. 305 returns were received. In addition to these about 100 had previously been collected from a questionnaire slightly different from the one given above. In all about 600 leaders were reported and described more or less fully. Almost exactly two-thirds of these were girls. This is due to the fact that the returns were from normal school students in the eastern states, most of whom were females. For this reason the cases of leadership among the girls are no doubt more accurately described than those among the boys. The same fact also necessarily distorts the sex differences.

Unfortunately a large number of those answering failed to state the age either of the leader or the followers. This study can

Leadership qualities		Girls%	Boys%
Group 1	Good looks	19·5	17
	Neatness and dress	13·5	8
	Politeness, good manners, etc.	10·8	8
Group 2	Wealth and social station	13·5	16
Group 3	Age	10	17
	Size	10	19
Group 4	Strength	5	20
	Activity, quickness, skill in devising and playing games, etc.	21·5	39
Group 5	Kindness	7	5
	Helpfulness	4	3
	Generous, considerate, unselfish	9	2
	Peaceful, peacemaker, etc.	2·5	
	Sympathetic	2	
	Protected the younger	0·5	
Group 6	Loyalty		2
	Honest, frank, just, etc.	2	6
Group 7	Jolly, lively, ready for fun, etc.	8·5	4
Group 8	Courage, boldness	4·5	5
Group 9	Brightness, scholarship, etc.	10·5	18
	Good judgment	1	
	Tact	1·5	2
	Cunning	1·5	
	Originality	2	
	Musical ability	2	1
Group 10	Bribery, flattery, and coaxing	3	1
Group 11	An 'only' child	2·5	1
	Used to having own way at home	3·5	
Group 12	Strong willed	4·5	1
	Self confident, decided manner	4	6
	Boastful, conceited, etc.		2
Group 13	Domineering, bossy, a bully, etc.	5·5	6
	Inspires fear	2	2
	Sharp tongued, sarcastic, etc.	5	2
	Haughty	1·5	
Group 14	Good disposition and temper	13·5	8
	Friendly, pleasant, gentle, attractive, amiable	4	1
	Unaffected, natural, unobtrusive, meek	2·5	1
Group 15	Strange		1
	Greater experience	1·5	7
	Coarse	1	2
	Uses slang	0·5	
	Mischievous	1	2
	Smoked		1
	Wit		3

therefore throw little light on the development of leadership and its age differences, though this phase of the subject is of the utmost importance.

We may glance first at the qualities most often mentioned as elements of leadership. The numeral represents the percentage of cases in which the particular quality was mentioned.

It seems therefore that girls, in order to be leaders, stand more in need of such qualities as are mentioned in groups, 1, 7, 10, 11, and 14 than do boys. The boy leaders on the other hand are more likely than girls to have the qualities of groups 3, 4, 6, 8, 15, and brightness of group 9. The other qualities are not very unequally divided. Their values may readily be seen from the table.

The returns are not adapted to bring out the relative frequency of leadership with boys and girls. The fact, however, that one-third of the leaders described are boys, although almost all the returns were written by young women, would indicate that it is probably more common with boys. Several of those answering state this as their opinion. From the returns it appears also that leadership is more intensive with the boys. The group spirit is stronger with them and they are less likely to revolt against their leader. The girls show more of a tendency to divide up into small groups. Jealousy more often comes in as a disturbing element than with the boys. Personal resentment is aroused more readily and is not so easily allayed. They show less of the give and take spirit than do boys. If it be objected that the phenomena of leadership are more common among the boys only because of the group games and rough out-door sports in which boys engage, it may be replied that this very fact is only an additional proof that girls do not have the inherent social tendencies that boys have. The differences here mentioned are in line with the differences in social tendencies already noted between the males and females of primitive races. They are also paralleled by the common observation of men and women in civilized life. On the other hand, it must be acknowledged that there is no sure means of ascertaining just to what extent the observed differences everywhere are a mere artifact produced by social environment. If any one is so radical as to claim that all the apparent differences can be thus explained away, there is no way utterly to refute him. The conclusive experiment cannot be made. [. . .]

The bulk of the returns show that in the first three or four years of school life there is little real leadership. The relationships are personal and not of the group kind. Several may play together, but when they do, they act independently of each other. Whatever phenomena of leadership are found at this period are less permanent and more partial than later. A marked change comes in the pre-adolescent stage of 10 to 12 years. Friends are chosen on account of personal attraction and admiration rather than for purely accidental reasons. Concerted action begins to replace individual play. These tendencies become more and more accentuated until by 15 to 18 years the group spirit becomes strong, personal attachments are made in accordance with subjective ideals, and a large proportion of the total number of boys and girls could instantly be classed either as popular or unpopular among their fellows. There is also plainly evident a tendency to evaluate themselves as inferior or superior to others. Domineering acts are now due to conscious self-assertion and no longer to childish egoism. A new diffidence appears, very different from the bashfulness of childhood. [. . .]

Part Three **Personality**

Long before psychologists took an active part in the study of
leadership two different approaches to its understanding were
well established. These have often been called the 'great man'
and 'times' theories. (See Reading 14 by Cooper and
McGaugh.) The one has argued that history has been made by
the qualities of leaders and is to be understood by a close
examination of their characteristics, the other has seen the
leader as made, or at any rate selected, by history, by the
spirit and needs of the times. As in many other areas where
theories have been opposed, continuing research seems to
suggest some truth in each and to give rise to a concept of
interacting forces in the determination of leadership and group
progress. This development is elaborated in Part Four.

Psychology came to this interactionist position earlier and
with greater conviction, however, than did historians and
politicians who, many of them, still adhere to a 'great man'
view. Among the consequences of such a view are repeated
attempts to describe the ways in which leaders differ from
others, to specify and even to measure the personality
characteristics which mark off the leaders and perhaps even
guarantee their success. Psychologists and sociologists, whether
by conviction that this was right or in order to be helpful by
testing the theories of their social science colleagues, devoted
much energy and resources to the search for leadership traits
especially in the period of the twenties and thirties.
Terman's 'preliminary study' of 1904 (Reading 4) seemed to
have set a course of recognition that personality characteristics
relevant to leadership would vary with the nature of the group
to be led and of the task it was to perform. Nevertheless, as

Stogdill's survey of the literature (Reading 5) shows, many investigators sought to describe the characteristics of leaders and differentiate these from those of other group members. While individually they met with little success and one study was often seen, if not to contradict, at any rate to fail to confirm another – these studies organized and seen in perspective by Stogdill did provide a firm basis for an interaction theory and a big step ahead.

Stogdill's thorough review of the literature to 1947 has become a classic in social psychology. Its basic conclusion is that the 'qualities, characteristics, and skills required in a leader are determined to a large extent by the demands of the situation in which he is to function as a leader'.

This review of Stogdill's and the contemporary and independent work of Gibb (1947; see also Reading 10) did move thinking about leadership strongly towards an emphasis upon the 'times' or the situation as a major determinant, though in neither case was such a strong shift intended. Stogdill did not entirely discard the view that some personality characteristics were more likely to be found in leaders than in others. Gibb offered evidence that in military groups at least leaders had superior intelligence and were judged more self-confident, sociable, aggressive, and adjustable.

From within an intensive research programme designed to study the emergence of leaders in small temporary groups of men, Raymond Cattell and Glen Stice derived Reading 6. While not explicitly denying the force of the situation in selecting or 'casting up' leaders these authors emphasize the extent to which personality variables come through. They have also added a further interactive element to the theoretical position by showing that personality is differently related to leadership depending upon the procedures used to identify leaders in the same situation and task. One could not overlook the fact that if the Cattell and Stice suggestion of a multiple correlation of 0·91 between personality and elected leadership were confirmed, little room would remain for situational determinants. But there is, at least, informal work which suggests that such a high coefficient cannot be replicated though the basic truth of their proposition undoubtedly remains.

In an excellent review of the relationships between personality and performance in small groups, Richard Mann (1959; see also Reading 7) included an examination of the relationships between personality and leadership. Mann too accepts that there is sufficient evidence to justify a belief that leadership 'is a joint function of personality and the particular group setting'. Again, he finds that in a sufficient number and proportion of studies, personality comes through to enable him to conclude that a relationship between some aspects of personality and leadership is well established. In particular intelligence, adjustment, and extraversion characterize leaders in a variety of situations and identified by a variety of techniques.

Clare Clifford and Thomas Cohn in Reading 8 perform an important function in giving clarity to much of the preceding work. They point to the fact that earlier workers had not been sufficiently explicit in recognizing that often they talked of the attributes of leaders not *per se* but *as perceived* by other group members. Their wide-ranging approach has led them to conclude that 'leadership is – in part at least – a function of personal attributes perceived by the followers', and to accept the proposition that personality variables do have a part in the understanding of leadership.

The sociological perspective of Arnold Rose (Reading 9) offers another view of the 'trait' approach to leadership by suggesting that leaders can be expected to differ from others in some characteristics *because* of the requirements of the leader roles they fill. Rose concludes after studying a number of leaders of community organizations, that 'group leaders differ only in degree and proportion, not in kind or absolutely, from the general population, and that what differences there are are due to the more active social participation of the leaders'. Rose himself points out that his investigation has not been definitive but when seen in association with the point clearly made by Clifford and Cohn it must be taken as a possibility that leaders may be perceived to have different attributes from those of others *because* they are leaders. Such an hypothesis must be fully covered in future research though it is clear that it could not explain the results reported by Cattell and Stice.

For the time being at least it would seem more likely that personality which is laid down early by both hereditary and learning processes is a forceful determinant of an individual's chances to be a leader.

References

GIBB, C. A. (1947), 'The principles and traits of leadership', *Journal of Abnormal and Social Psychology*, vol. 42, pp. 267–84.

MANN, R. (1959), 'A review of the relationships between personality and leadership and popularity', *Psychological Bulletin*, vol. 56, pp. 241–70.

5   R. M. Stogdill

Personal Factors Associated with Leadership: a Survey of
the Literature

R. M. Stogdill, 'Personal factors associated with leadership: a survey of the
literature', *Journal of Psychology*, vol. 25 (1948), pp. 35–71.

Smith and Krueger [100] have surveyed the literature on leadership to 1933. Recent developments in leadership methodology, as
related especially to military situations, were reviewed in 1947 by
Jenkins [54]. The present survey is concerned only with those
studies in which some attempt has been made to determine the
traits and characteristics of leaders. In many of the studies surveyed leadership was not defined. In others the methods used in
the investigation appeared to have little relationship to the problem as stated. An attempt has been made to include all studies
bearing on the problem of traits and personal factors associated
with leadership. In all except four cases the original book or
article has been read and abstracted in detail. The data from one
American and three German publications have been derived
from competent abstracts.

The present survey lists only those factors which were studied
by three or more investigators. Evidence reported by fewer investigators has not been regarded as providing a satisfactory basis
for evaluation. It is realized that the number of investigations in
which a factor was studied is not necessarily indicative of the
importance of the factor. However, the frequency with which a
factor was found to be significant appears to be the most satisfactory single criterion for evaluating the data accumulated in
this survey, but other criteria, such as the competency of the
experimental methods employed and the adequacy of the
statistical treatment of data have also been regarded in evaluating
the results of a particular study.

In analysing data obtained from various groups and by various
methods the question arises as to the extent to which results may
be influenced by differences in social composition of the groups,

differences in methodology, and differences in leadership criteria. There is no assurance, for example, that the investigator who analyzes the biographies of great men is studying the same kind of leadership behavior that is revealed through observation of children's leadership activities in group situations. It is of interest, however, that some of the studies employing the two different methods yield remarkably similar results. On the other hand, there are some factors that appear only in certain age and social groups or only when certain methods are employed.

A. Methods

The primary methods which have been employed for the identification and study of the personal characteristics of leaders have been the following: observation of behavior in group situations; choice of associates (voting); nomination or rating by qualified observers; selection (and rating or testing) of persons occupying positions of leadership; and analysis of biographical and case history data. The various studies employing these methods are listed, and the salient details of the methods are briefly described below.

1. *Observation and time sampling of behavior in group situations*
   [21, 22, 40, 47, 49, 50, 55, 63, 73, 78, 81, 89, 112, 115, 118]

In these studies the behavior of two or more individuals is observed in situations which permit the emergence of leadership activities. The situation may be highly structured in advance, as in the studies of children's groups by Henning [49], Luithlen [63], Miller and Dollard [73], and Terman [112]; or the situation may be natural and uncontrolled, as in some of the boys' gangs studied by Thrasher [115]. The periods of observation may range from five-second periods at definitely spaced intervals to an hour or more of continuous observation. The relative merits of the various time sampling methods have been evaluated by Arrington [2]. Chapple and Donald [21] have devised a method for recording the frequency and duration of observed social contacts by executives on a polygraph.

The observational studies which have yielded the most relevant data on leadership are those of Chevaleva-Ianovskaia and Sylla [22] and the pioneering investigation of Terman [112]. Henning [49] has devised a number of ingenious experimental situations for the study of leadership in pairs of children, but the investigations in which these methods are employed have proved disappointingly unproductive.

2. *Choice of associates* (*voting, naming, ranking, sociometrics*) [4, 7, 10, 15, 16, 31, 32, 33, 34, 35, 39, 52, 53, 55, 60, 66, 68, 74, 77, 78, 79, 82, 86, 101, 106, 108, 117, 124]

The usual procedure in these studies, most of which use children or students as subjects, is to ask the members of a group to name the persons whom they would prefer as leaders, and, in some cases, to describe the characteristics of each nominee which make him desirable as a leader. Sociometrics is an extension of this method which involves the construction of a 'sociogram' or chart showing graphically the preference relationship of each member to every other member of the group. The outstanding investigation of this group is that of Jennings [55], who has combined observational with sociometric methods to produce a study of unusual human insight. Another study which is characterized by insight into human behavior is that of Buttgereit [15]. Other studies which are outstanding as to methodology and statistical treatment of data are those of Dunkerley [33], Partridge [82] and Tryon [117].

3. *Nomination by qualified observer* [3, 14, 23, 25, 26, 57, 80, 88, 95, 96, 102]

In these studies, leaders are named by teachers, club leaders, or other adult observers who are regarded as being in a position to identify the leaders in the groups selected for study. The leaders are compared with the members of control groups. None of the studies employing this method are in any way outstanding.

4. *Selection of persons occupying positions of leadership* [5, 8, 11, 12, 17, 18, 20, 24, 37, 38, 41, 42, 44, 45, 46, 51, 61, 67, 72, 75, 76, 85, 90, 91, 92, 93, 94, 99, 109, 111, 116, 120, 121]

Leadership in these studies is regarded as synonymous with holding office or some position of responsibility. The majority of the studies use high school or college subjects, and define leadership as holding some office such as president of student body, president of a fraternity or sorority, captain of athletic or debating team, chairman of a club, and the like. However, a number of the studies deal with adults in rural communities and small cities. The study of Carlson and Harrell [18] is concerned with congressmen. Thurstone [116] studied government administrators. The most competent of the studies from the point of view of methodology and treatment of data are those of Bellingrath [5], Caldwell and Wellman [17], Flemming [38], Sward [109] and Thurstone [116].

5. *Analysis of biographical and case history data* [1, 6, 13, 27, 30, 58, 59, 69, 70, 71, 83, 104, 105, 114, 122, 123]

Ackerson [1] and Brown [13] base their studies on the analysis of case histories of delinquent children. The remaining studies are based on the analysis of biographical data. The works of Merriam [69, 70], and Michels [71] might be classified with this group. Outstanding contributions based on these methods are those of Ackerson [1] and Cox [27].

6. *The listing of traits considered essential to leadership* [29, 41, 48, 56, 107, 110]

In all of these studies except that of Jones [56] the authors have asked different groups of persons, usually business executives and members of the professions, to list the traits which they believe to be essential to leadership. Little uniformity is found among the items contained in such lists. Only intelligence, initiative, and responsibility are mentioned twice each among the top five items in the lists reported by Gowin [41], Heath and Gregory [48], Jones [56] and Starch [107].

7. *Supplementary aspects of methodology*

Various supplementary measures have been employed in an effort to determine the traits associated with leadership. The most frequently used are tests of intelligence and personality; but questionnaires, rating scales, and interviews have been utilized in some cases. For purposes of reference, the various studies employing these methods are listed below.

(*a*) Standardized tests.

(i) Intelligence tests [1, 8, 12, 28, 37, 50, 66, 67, 68, 78, 82, 88, 90, 91, 118].

(ii) Personality tests [7, 14, 25, 26, 45, 46, 62, 75, 92, 93, 94].

(iii) Intelligence and personality tests [9, 17, 33, 34, 52, 53, 65, 98, 109, 116].

(*b*) Questionnaires [5, 11, 23, 24, 29, 41, 42, 48, 60, 102, 111].

(*c*) Rating scales [3, 4, 27, 32, 34, 35, 36, 38, 40, 42, 57, 72, 80, 82, 91, 95, 97, 113, 117, 119, 120, 124].

(*d*) Interviews [11, 13, 20, 51, 76, 78, 88, 96, 106, 109].

(*e*) Factor analysis [9, 18, 26, 33, 38, 43, 116, 117].

8. *Age groups studied*

For purposes of reference and evaluation the various investigations are classified below according to age groups studied.

(*a*) Preschool age [40, 47, 81].

(*b*) Elementary school age [1, 7, 15, 50, 61, 64, 66, 68, 73, 78, 79, 82, 85, 89, 112, 117, 118].

(*c*) High school age [1, 3, 5, 11, 12, 13, 15, 16, 17, 23, 24, 34, 35, 37, 38, 39, 55, 61, 64, 78, 82, 85, 86, 88, 90, 91, 94, 95, 96, 101, 102, 108, 117, 120].

(*d*) College students [4, 8, 14, 32, 33, 36, 44, 45, 48, 52, 53, 57, 65, 67, 72, 74, 75, 77, 80, 92, 97, 98, 106, 109, 119, 124].

(*e*) Adults [6, 18, 20, 21, 25, 26, 29, 30, 41, 42, 46, 51, 52, 58, 59, 69, 70, 71, 76, 83, 93, 99, 103, 104, 105, 107, 110, 111, 114, 116, 122, 123].

B. Results

The results of this survey are presented in the form of discussions of the evidence accumulated on those factors which were studied by three or more investigators. When contradictory evidence is presented, the bibliographic references are listed to show separately those studied presenting positive, negative, and neutral data respectively.

1. *Chronological age*

(*a*) Leaders found to be younger [3, 5, 37, 39, 53, 90].
(*b*) Leaders found to be older [5, 15, 40, 41, 75, 78, 79, 81, 82, 124].
(*c*) No differences found [1, 11].
(*d*) Differs with situation [17].

The evidence as to the relation of age to leadership is quite contradictory. Pigors [84] observes that leadership does not appear in children before the age of two or three years, and even then usually takes the form of overt domination. Active leadership of a group seldom appears before the age of nine or ten, at which age the formation of groups and gangs may become a noticeable feature in the social development of children. According to Pigors the four following stages are necessary for the appearance of leadership in children, development of determination and self control; grasp of abstractions and social ideals; awareness of personalities; and sufficient memory span to pursue remote goals rather than immediate objectives. Arrington [2], however, finds no evidence from a survey of time sampling experiments to support the proposition that leadership increases with age in preschool children.

Baldwin [3], Finch and Carroll [37], Garrison [39], Hunter and Jordan [53] and Remmelin [90] find leaders to be younger than their followers. In the latter two studies these differences are statistically reliable. Bellingrath [5] finds girl leaders to be younger than non-leaders, but boy leaders to be older. Leaders are found to be older than followers by Buttgereit [15], Goodenough [40], Gowin [41], Moore [75], Newstetter [78], Nutting [79], Parten [81], Partridge [82], and Zeleny [124]. Gowin found outstanding executives to be 12·2 years older on the average than the average of lesser executives. Ackerson [1] and Brown [11] do not find leaders and followers to be differentiated on the basis of age. The correlation coefficients reported by a number of these authors are shown in Table 1. These correlation coefficients range from −0·32 to 0·71, with the average coefficient being approximately 0·21.

According to Caldwell and Wellman [17], the relationship of age to leadership differs in various situations. Leaders in athletics are found to be close to the class average in age, while boy editors and student council members are younger than average, as are girl club leaders and student council and citizenship representatives. In view of these various findings, chronological age cannot be regarded as a factor which is correlated with leadership in any uniform direction or degree.

Table 1

Correlation of Variables with Leadership

Author	I.Q.	Grades	Age	Height	Weight
Ackerson (boys)	0·18		−0·01		
(girls)	0·32		−0·11		
Bellingrath (boys)	−0·139*	0·05*	0·27	0·17	0·25
(girls)			−0·32	0·44	0·42
Drake	0·47				
Eichler	0·0614	0·1155	0·2067		
Flemming	0·44				
Garrison (School 1)		0·30	−0·12	−0·02	−0·02
(School 2)		0·36	−0·25	−0·13	−0·04
Goodenough	0·10		0·71	0·71	0·52
Howell	0·08	0·39			
Levi (Elem.)	0·259	−0·274			
(Jr. H. S.)	0·255	−0·0005			
Newstetter	0·17		0·45		
Nutting	0·90	0·11	0·20		
Parten	0·34		0·67	0·67	
Partridge	0·54		0·55	0·43	0·46
Reynolds	0·22	0·27			
Sheldon	0·060	0·190		0·049	0·024
Zeleny	0·44		0·487	0·346	0·204

* Total scores of boys and girls combined.

2. *Height*

(a) Leaders found to be taller [5, 34, 40, 41, 75, 81, 82, 97, 124].
(b) Leaders found to be shorter [39, 53].
(c) No differences found [3, 91].
(d) Depends upon situation [17].

Inspection of Table 1 reveals correlations between height and leadership ranging from −0·13 to 0·71. The general trend of these studies is to indicate a low positive relationship between height and leadership, the average correlation being about 0·30. Hunter and Jordan [53] and Garrison [39] find student leaders to be somewhat shorter than nonleaders, and Baldwin [3] and Reynolds [91] find no relation between height and leadership in students.

3. *Weight*

(a) Leaders found to be heavier [3, 5, 40, 41, 82, 97, 124].
(b) Leaders found to be lighter [53, 75].
(c) No differences found [39, 97].

The correlation coefficients shown in Table 1 suggest a low positive relationship between weight and leadership. The average correlation coefficient is about 0·23. Hunter and Jordan [53] find leaders to be significantly lighter than nonleaders. Garrison [39] and Moore [75] also report leaders to be somewhat lighter than followers, although the differences are not significant.

4. *Physique, energy, health*

(a) Physique [6, 57, 79, 97, 119].
(b) Athletic ability, physical prowess [15, 38, 82, 87, 106, 115, 119].
(c) Energy [5, 13, 27, 108, 120].
(d) Health [3, 5, 88, 108].
(e) Health and physical condition not a factor [1, 3, 8, 53].

Bernard [6], Kohs and Irle [57], Nutting [79], Sheldon [97], and Webb [119] report that superior physique is a characteristic of leaders. However, the correlation coefficients of 0·28, 0·18, 0·114, and 0·23 reported by Kohs and Irle [57], Nutting [79], Sheldon [97], and Webb [119] respectively suggest that this relationship is very slight. Bowden [8] concludes from the results of his study of college students that leadership is not the result of a dominating physique. Baldwin [3] finds that high school leaders do not differ from followers in freedom from physical defects.

Leaders, according to Baldwin [3], Bellingrath [5], Reals [88], and Stray [108] appear to have some advantage over non-leaders in possessing better health, although Ackerson [1] and Hunter and Jordan [53] do not find health to be a differentiating factor.

Athletic ability and physical prowess do appear to be associated with leadership status in boys' gangs and groups. Evidence to this effect is presented by Buttgereit [15], Flemming [38], Partridge [82], Puffer [87], Spaulding [106], Thrasher [115], and Webb [119]. Coefficients of correlation of 0·38, 0·62, and 0·40 between athletic ability and leadership are reported by Flemming, Partridge, and Webb respectively.

According to Bellingrath [5], Brown [13], Cox [27], Stray [108], and Wetzel [120], leaders are also characterized by a high rate of energy output. Cox [27] finds various groups of great leaders to differ markedly in physique, energy output, and athletic prowess, with only the military leaders being outstanding in these traits.

5. *Appearance*

(*a*) Leaders present a better appearance [3, 4, 6, 11, 33, 38, 80, 82, 88, 112, 117].
(*b*) Leaders are better dressed [33, 112].
(*c*) No relationship found [124].
(*d*) Appearance negatively correlated with leadership [1, 40].

The evidence presented in these studies suggests a possible relationship between appearance and leadership. Dunkerley [33] found that students chosen as leaders in social activities differed significantly from nonleaders in appearance and dress, but students chosen as leaders in intellectual and religious activities did not differ markedly from nonleaders in these respects. Partridge [82] found a correlation of 0·81 between appearance ratings and leadership status. A correlation of 0·21 between attractive appearance and leadership is reported by Flemming [38], but the correlation between beautiful and leadership is 0·05. Tryon's [117] study suggests that appearance is more closely associated with leadership in boys than in girls. She reports correlation coefficients of 0·49 and 0·06 respectively for 15-year-old boys and girls, while the correlation coefficients for 12-year-old boys and girls are 0·31 and 0·08 respectively. In Goodenough's [40] study, beauty was found to be negatively correlated with leadership in pre-school children, the correlation coefficient being −0·20. Ackerson [1] reports correlation coefficients of 0·12 and −0·06 between slovenly appearance and leadership for boys and girls respectively, while slovenly appearance and leading others into misconduct are correlated 0·32 and 0·31 for delinquent boys and girls.

6. *Fluency of speech* [6, 14, 22, 40, 45, 60, 65, 70, 98, 112, 116, 117, 124]

Baldwin [3] reports a definite trend for leaders to be rated by their teachers as confident in tone of voice, while nonleaders tend to be rated as lacking in confidence as to tone of voice. A factor analysis [38] of teachers' ratings of high school leaders reveals 'pleasant voice' as one of the four factors found to be associated with leadership. Flemming [38] reports a correlation of 0·28 between 'pleasing voice' and leadership in high school students. Partridge [82] reports that boy leaders can be reliably distinguished from nonleaders when taken into the presence of strange boys, but hidden from view so that judgments must be made on speech alone. However, Fay and Middleton [36], in repeating this experiment under somewhat similar conditions, found a correlation of only 0·08 between leadership ratings and degree of leadership as estimated by voice alone. Eichler [34] also reports a correlation of −0·112 between voice and leadership.

Talkativeness and leadership are reported by Tryon [117] to be correlated to the extent of 0·41 and 0·31 for 12-year-old boys and girls respectively, while the correlation coefficients for 15-year-old boys and girls are 0·15 and 0·44 respectively. In Goodenough's [40] study a correlation of 0·61 between talkativeness and leadership is found. Thurstone [116] did not find highly paid administrators to surpass their less well paid associates in word fluency test scores, but he did find a significant difference in linguistic ability test scores. Simpson [98] also reports verbal ability to be correlated with capacity to influence others. The correlation coefficient is 0·45.

Chevaleva-Ianovskaia and Sylla [22] find that child leaders are characterized by longer duration of verbal excitation. Terman [112] reports that leaders are more fluent of speech, and Leib [60] finds leaders to excel in speaking ability. The same skills are reported in adult leaders by Bernard [6] and Merriam and Gosnell [70]. Zeleny [124] reports a correlation of 0·59 between leadership ratings and total remarks made in class. Interesting conversation and leadership are correlated 0·28 in Flemming's [38] study. Further evidence is found in the studies of Burks [14] and Malloy [65], who report that vividness and originality of expression and facility of conversation are associated with successful social relationships. Considering the size of the experimental groups, the competence of the experimental methods employed, and the positive nature of the evidence presented, it would appear that fluency of speech, if not tone of voice, is a factor to be considered in the study of leadership. It has long been recognized that effective leadership cannot be maintained in an organization without an adequate system of intercommunication. Thus it does not seem surprising that some of the most searching studies of leadership should reveal the capacity for ready communication as one of the skills associated with leadership status.

7. *Intelligence*

(a) Leaders brighter [1, 11, 12, 27, 33, 38, 40, 50, 53, 57, 67, 78, 79, 81, 82, 91, 97, 101, 109, 112, 113, 119, 124].

(b) No difference [5, 11, 34, 52, 98].

(c) Too great differences militate against leadership [37, 50, 64, 67, 118].

All except four of these studies present evidence which indicates that the average child or student leader surpasses the average member of his group in intelligence. Statistically reliable differences are reported by Hunter and Jordan [53], Remmelin [90], and Sward [109]. In most of these studies there is considerable overlapping of intelligence test scores, indicating that superior intelligence is not an absolute requirement for leadership. Nevertheless, the general trend of the findings indicate that leadership status is more often than not associated with superiority in intelligence. The correlation coefficients shown in Table 1 reveal a consistently positive relationship. The average of these coefficients is approximately 0·28.

Recent factorial studies reveal a number of points which may be of considerable significance for the future study of leadership. Cattell [19], for example, reports that the intelligence factor is heavily weighted with such character elements as wise, emotionally mature, persevering, mentally alert, vigorous, conscientious, etc. These items correspond fairly closely to the factors which are found in the present survey to be supported by an excess of positive over negative evidence. Thorndike [114] reports a correlation of 0·60 between intellectual ability and estimability of character in 305 male members of European royal families. Thus it appears that high intelligence may be associated with other characteristics which contribute toward a person's value as a leader.

One of the most significant findings concerning the relation of intelligence to leadership is that extreme discrepancies between the intelligence of potential leaders and their followers militate against the exercise of leadership. Hollingworth [50] found that 'among children with a mean I.Q. of 100, the I.Q. of the leader is likely to fall between 115 and 130 I.Q. That is, the leader is likely to be more intelligent, but *not too much more* intelligent than the average of the group led.' Observation further showed that a child of 160 I.Q. has very little chance of being a popular leader in a group of children of average intelligence, but may become a leader in a group of children with a mean I.Q. of 130. One of the difficulties in this connection seems to be concerned with communication. The average child cannot comprehend a large part of the vocabulary employed by a child of unusually superior intelligence to express exact meanings in relation to his more mature and complicated interests. Differences in interests, goals, and activity patterns also act as barriers to joint participation, which is a necessary condition for group leadership. Hollingworth's findings are confirmed by a number of investigations. Finch and Carroll [37], studying groups of 66 gifted, 66 superior, and 66 average children, arrive at the conclusions that 'given a superior group of children to lead, the leading will tend to be done by the gifted children', even though the leaders as a group tend to be younger than the group led. In an early study of the formation of boys' gangs, Warner [118] found that leaders and followers differ much more in chronological age than in mental age. She observed that older boys with mentalities below normal tend to group with younger boys who have a mental age near their own and slightly higher, and that when groups of retarded delinquent boys contact groups of brighter delinquents the contacts are 'so short and non-social that no noticeable event takes place'. Maller [64], studying cooperation and competition among children, found that homogeneity of intelligence rather than level of intelligence is important in cooperative behavior. McCuen [67] studied leadership in 58 college student organizations. He found that 'there is a tendency to select leaders with scores slightly above the average of their respective groups'. He concludes that 'the crowd seems to desire to be led by the average person. Evidently in a democratic society the leader must not be too far detached from the group.'

Two studies by Lehman [58, 59] are of interest in this connection. In the earlier study he determined the age intervals at which outstanding men in various professions made their best contributions. In the second study he determined the optimal age intervals for eminent leadership. Chemists, for example, were found to make their best contributions during the age intervals 28–32 years, while the optimal ages for eminent leadership in chemistry are 45–49 years. Thus it appears that even in science, a man's contributions and communications must be understood by, and in accord with the thinking of, his contemporaries in order for him to rise to a position of leadership in his profession.

8. *Scholarship*

(*a*) Leaders make better scholastic records [1, 3, 5, 15, 17, 28, 33, 39, 52, 53, 75, 80, 90, 91, 97, 98, 109, 112, 119, 120, 121, 123].
(*b*) Leaders make poorer scholastic records [79].
(*c*) No differences found [5, 24, 34, 57].

Leaders are found, with a high degree of uniformity, to make better average scholastic grades than do nonleaders. These results are not surprising in light of the fact that leaders are found to be more intelligent on the average than their followers. The findings by such investigators as Buttgereit [15], Caldwell [17], and others suggest that superior scholarship may not be a mere byproduct of superior intelligence, but may possess direct value for leadership status when it comprises one aspect of a general ability to get things done. There is also a suggestion that superior accomplishment along lines that are valued by the group carries prestige value which may also contribute toward leadership status. But there is an abundance of evidence which indicates that a position of leadership is ordinarily not founded upon superior intelligence and accomplishment alone since these two factors may be present to a high degree in many persons who do not occupy positions of leadership. The magnitude of the correlation coefficients shown in Table 1 suggest that intelligence and scholarship account for only a fraction of the total complex of factors associated with leadership status.

9. *Knowledge* [10, 14, 15, 16, 31, 38, 71, 79, 89, 108, 124]

The results of these studies suggest that persons chosen as leaders tend to be those who know how to get things done. Of particular interest is Caldwell's [16] experiment in which he asked 282 high school pupils to nominate boy and girl leaders for three different situations: a trip to the wharf, the production and presentation of a program before a neighboring school and, the reorganization of a program for administering athletics in the school. There was revealed 'a clear judgment on the part of these pupils as to the members of the group best fitted to lead them'. The most important abilities ascribed to these leaders were intelligence and practical knowledge relative to the situations for which they were chosen as leaders. In this connection it seems worth while to consider the findings of Baldwin [3] and Burks [14] relative to the association between leadership and the ability to make constructive and creative suggestions. Burks, for example, finds that ability to present constructive ideas relative to difficult situations is closely associated with successful social relationships. Also in this connection should be considered the studies of Cox [27], Drake [32], Flemming [38], Stray [108], and Thrasher [115], who find that originality and constructive imagination are characteristics of leaders. Additional evidence relative to the ability to get things done is presented by Bellingrath [5] and Dunkerley [33]. Cox [27] and Peck [83] report that great leaders are characterized, and differentiated from the average by greater intensity of application and industry. In summarizing the results of these various studies, it appears that specialized knowledge and ability to get things done are factors which contribute toward leadership status.

10. *Judgment and decision*

(*a*) Soundness and finality of judgment [5, 32, 33, 38, 119].

(*b*) Speed and accuracy of thought and decision [26, 33, 45, 119].

In view of the positive correlations found between intelligence and leadership, it is not surprising to find a similar relationship between judgment and leadership. Bellingrath [5], Drake [32], and Webb [119] report correlations ranging from 0·34 to 0·69 between common sense and leadership, while Bellingrath [5], Drake [32], Flemming [38], and Webb [119] report correlations of 0·60, 0·34, 0·28, and 0·69 respectively between judgment and leadership. Farsightedness and leadership are found to be correlated to the extent of 0·55, 0·25, and 0·33 in the studies of Bellingrath, Drake, and Webb. Two of the factor analysis studies, those of Cowley [26] and Dunkerley [33], reveal soundness and finality of judgment as a factor common to leaders. In addition to the judgment factor, Cowley [26] also found three factors which appeared to represent speed of decision. In spite of the small number of studies bearing on judgment and decision, the general competence of the methods employed lends confidence to the results obtained. Hanawalt, Richardson, and Hamilton [45] find that leaders use the ' ?', or 'undecided', response on the Bernreuter test significantly less frequently than nonleaders, and this tendency is especially noticeable on the most differentiating items.

11. *Insight*

(a) Keenly alive to environment, alert [13, 15, 17, 27, 33, 35].
(b) Ability to evaluate situations [8, 15, 22, 70, 116].
(c) Social insight [8, 47, 55, 84, 124].
(d) Self insight [27, 77].
(e) Sympathetic understanding [10, 14, 38, 47, 55, 74, 119].

Traditionally, insight has been regarded as one aspect of general intelligence. However, the discussion of Jennings [55] and others suggests that insight may be socially conditioned to a high degree. Some of the most competent investigators of the leadership problem have contributed evidence which suggests that insight and awareness are factors associated with leadership ability. Brown [13], Buttgereit [15], Caldwell and Wellman [17], Cox [27], Dunkerley [33], and Fauquier and Gilchrist [35] find that leaders are characterized by alertness and keen awareness of environment. Ability to evaluate situations is found to be a factor in the studies of Bowden [8], Buttgereit [15], Chevaleva-Ianov-skaia and Sylla [22], Merriam and Gosnell [70], and Thurstone [116]. Less clearly defined, is social insight, reported to be a factor associated with leadership in the studies of Bowden [8], Hanf-mann [47], Jennings [55], Pigors [84], and Zeleny [124]. 'Studies the motives of others', is an item found by Brogden [9] and Guilford and Guilford [43] to measure Guilford's *T* factor, which is described as intellectual leadership or thinking introversion. The results of these various studies suggest that alertness to the surrounding environment and understanding of situations are intimately associated with leadership ability, yet very little is understood regarding the nature of these processes. No worker who is responsible for improving the social effectiveness of in-dividuals can fail to be impressed by the persistent blindness of maladapted individuals to the social situations in which they are attempting to adjust. From the point of view of understanding personal qualifications for leadership, it would appear that one question which is in need of thorough investigation is that con-cerning the fundamental nature of awareness and social insight.

12. *Originality* [5, 14, 27, 32, 38, 108, 119]

Although the number of studies containing data on this trait is rather small, the magnitude of the correlations found suggests that the relationship between originality and leadership is worthy of further investigation. The correlation coefficients reported by Bellingrath [5], Drake [32], Flemming [38], and Webb [119] range from 0·38 to 0·70, and are higher on the average than those for any other trait except popularity. Cox [27] finds great leaders to rate unusually high in originality.

13. *Adaptability* [8, 14, 17, 21, 22, 34, 38, 47, 70, 85]

These studies suggest that ready adaptability to changing situa-tions is a factor which may be associated with leadership capacity, although the correlation coefficients of 0·13 and 0·21 reported by Eichler [34] and Flemming [38] are not impressive. Ability to adjust to situations has also been regarded traditionally as an aspect of general intelligence but, as described in the ref-erences considered here, this factor appears to contain a large social component. This fact has long been recognized by clinical observers, who have repeatedly pointed out that persons of high intelligence may be rendered ineffectual in their vocational, social, and other adjustments through extreme self-preoccupation and inhibition to action, the latter of which is found to be negatively correlated with leadership.

14. *Introversion–Extroversion*

(*a*) Leaders found to be more extroverted [17, 40, 75, 92, 109].

(*b*) Leaders found to be more introverted [27, 72].

(*c*) No differences found [5, 32, 53, 90].

The only studies which report a marked relationship between extroversion and leadership are those of Goodenough [40] and Sward [109]. Goodenough reports a correlation of 0·46 between extroversion and leadership in children. Sward finds that leaders rate reliably higher than nonleaders in extroversion as rated on the Heidbreder scale. Richardson and Hanawalt [92] find that college leaders rate reliably lower in introversion than the Bernreuter norms and also lower than nonleaders, although the difference between leaders and nonleaders is not significant. Hunter and Jordan [53] and Remmelin [90], also report that Bernreuter introversion scores do not differentiate leaders from nonleaders. Middleton [72] finds leaders rating low in extroversion, while Bellingrath [5] and Drake [32] find no significant correlations between introversion–extroversion scores and leadership.

All the groups of great leaders except soldier–statesmen in Cox's [27] study are rated as introverted, with soldier–fighters rating very high in introversion. Thurstone's [116] study of Washington administrators revealed successful administrators as rating higher than less successful administrators in Guilford and Guilford's [43] T factor, which is measured by such items as, 'introspective, analyses himself', 'often in a meditative state', 'analyses the motives of others', and 'not more interested in athletics than in intellectual pursuits'. Brogden and Thomas [9] add to this last such items as, 'he does not want anyone to be with him when he receives bad news', 'he does not try to find someone to cheer him up when in low spirits', 'prefers to make hurried decisions alone'. These items are of interest when considered in relation to the findings on mood control. In view of the diversity of findings it appears very doubtful that leaders can be described with any degree of uniformity in terms of introversion–extroversion.

Much the same situation exists in regard to self-sufficiency. Hunter and Jordan [53] and Richardson and Hanawalt [93] find that leaders make high self-sufficiency scores on the Bernreuter test, but Dunkerley [33], Remmelin [90], and Richardson and Hanawalt [92] find no significant differences.

15. *Dominance*

(*a*) Leaders found to be more dominant, ascendant [1, 8, 21, 27, 32, 53, 75, 90, 92, 93, 117].
(*b*) Bossy, domineering persons rejected as leaders [10, 16, 47, 55].
(*c*) No differences found [34, 119].

The evidence concerning the relationship of dominance to leadership is contradictory. Cox [27] and Drake [32] find 'desire to impose will' to be associated with leadership, but Webb [119] reports a zero order correlation between those two factors. Ackerson [1] reports a correlation of approximately 0·20 between bossiness and leadership in problem children. Leadership and bossiness are related to some extent in the children studied by Tryon [117], who reports correlations of 0·28 and 0·29 between these two factors for 15-year-old boys and girls respectively. Chapple and Donald [21], Richardson and Hanawalt [92, 93], and Hunter and Jordan [53] find leaders to be significantly more dominant than nonleaders. Small but positive differences in ascendance are reported by Bowden [8] and Moore [75]. Eichler [34], however, find that leaders and nonleaders do not differ in dominance. Still stronger contradictory evidence is presented by Broich [10], Jennings [55], and Hanfmann [47] who find that bossy, domineering persons are rejected as leaders. Caldwell [16] reports that high school pupils express preference for leaders who can keep order without being bossy. These findings indicate that leadership cannot be defined in terms of personal dominance.

16. *Initiative, persistence, ambition*

(*a*) Initiative and willingness to assume responsibility [1, 5, 14, 15, 18, 32, 33, 45, 74, 97, 108, 120].

(b) Persistence in the face of obstacles [5, 15, 27, 32, 71, 72, 74, 84, 85, 97, 119, 124].

(c) Ambition, desire to excel [3, 5, 6, 27, 32, 44, 119].

(d) Application and industry [5, 18, 27, 33, 38, 83].

All except one of the studies in which initiative was found to be a trait ascribed to leaders were investigations in which student leaders were nominated by their associates and the traits which were thought to make them desirable as leaders were described. The study of Carlson and Harrell [18] represents some departure from this method, in that 53 Washington correspondents were asked to name the 10 ablest senators and 10 ablest representatives in rank order, and to rate them from 1 to 10 on integrity, intelligence, industry, and influence. A factor analysis of these ratings revealed Factor 1 to be heavily loaded with industry and influence, and might be called push or aggressiveness. Industry and leadership are correlated 0·55 and 0·16 in the studies of Bellingrath [5] and Flemming [38]. Dunkerley's [33] factor analysis also reveals a trait cluster identified as initiative which is descriptive of intellectual and social leaders, but not religious leaders. Drake [32] and Sheldon [97] report correlations of 0·56 and 0·52 between aggressiveness and leadership.

Cox [27] finds that great face to face leaders are characterized to an outstanding degree by 'persistence in the face of obstacles', 'capacity to work with distant objects in view', 'degree of strength of will or perseverance', and 'tendency not to abandon tasks from mere changeability'. Pigors [84] finds that the development of determination, and sufficient memory span to pursue remote goals rather than immediate objectives are necessary conditions for the appearance of leadership in children. The remainder of the studies which present evidence on this point represent a variety of points of view. Pinard [85], in an experimental study of perseveration in 194 'difficult' children, ages 8 to 15, found that of 24 leaders, 17 belonging to the moderate nonperseverator group were rated as more reliable, self controlled and persistent, and as the most constructive leaders. Drake [32] and Webb [119] find correlations of 0·23 and 0·59 between leadership and strength of will. Webb [119] reports a correlation of 0·70 between leadership and 'persistence in overcoming

109

obstacles', and of 0·53 between leadership and persistence. In Bellingrath's [5] study of high school students, persistence is found to be correlated with leadership to the extent of 0·68, while Eichler [34] and Sheldon [97] report correlations of 0·23 and 0·339 between leadership and persistence. An interesting sidelight is presented in Ackerson's [1] study of problem children, among whom stubbornness was correlated with leadership to the extent of 0·15 for boys and 0·12 for girls.

Cox [27] also presents evidence which indicates that great face to face leaders, such as soldiers, religious leaders, and statesmen, are characterized to an outstanding degree by 'desire to excel at performances'. Hanawalt, Hamilton and Morris [44], in a study of 20 college leaders and 20 nonleaders, found that level of aspiration of leaders is significantly higher than that of nonleaders. Coefficients of correlation of 0·47, 0·29, and 0·64 between leadership and desire to excel are reported by Webb [119], Drake [32], and Bellingrath [5] respectively.

That leadership is related to work, rather than to passive status or position, is suggested by the fact that a number of investigators have found leaders to rate high in application and industry. Cox [27] finds great leaders to rank unusually high in this respect. The correlation coefficients reported by Bellingrath [5], Flemming [38], and Webb [119] range from 0·16 to 0·55.

17. *Responsibility* [1, 3, 5, 14, 16, 27, 32, 33, 38, 55, 74, 79, 82, 85, 108, 119, 120]

Student leaders are found to rate somewhat higher than followers in dependability, trustworthiness, and reliability in carrying out responsibilities in the studies of Baldwin [3], Bellingrath [5], Burks [14], Caldwell [16], Dunkerley [33], Moore [74], Nutting [79], Pinnard [85], and Wetzel [120]. Trustworthiness and leadership are correlated 0·64 in Webb's [119] study, 0·37 in Drake's [32] study, and 0·10 in Flemming's [38] study. Correlations of 0·42, 0·21, and 0·53 between conscientiousness and leadership are reported by Webb [119], Drake [32], and Bellingrath [5] respectively. Partridge [82] reports a correlation of 0·87 between dependability and leadership. Jennings [55] finds that the girls chosen as leaders tend to be those who inspire confidence. Cox [27] finds all groups of great face to face leaders rating high in trustworthiness and conscientiousness, with religious leaders rating outstandingly high in these traits.

18. *Integrity and conviction*

(*a*) Integrity, fortitude [6, 18, 27, 70, 72, 83].
(*b*) Strength of convictions [17, 20, 27, 71, 74, 98, 119].

Intellectual fortitude and integrity of character represent traits which are apparently associated with eminent leadership in maturity. All the studies which contribute evidence on this point are concerned with outstanding adult leaders, except that of Middleton [72], who found that 'character' is one of the traits associated with leadership in college students.

Michels [71] reports that strength of convictions is also a characteristic of successful political leaders. Cox [27] finds that the great face to face leader is characterized to an outstanding degree by 'absence of readiness to accept the sentiments of his associates'. This trait is especially conspicuous in revolutionary statesmen. Webb [119] reports a correlation of −0·32 between leadership and acceptance of sentiments of others. Caldwell and Wellman [17] find that one of the characteristics of high school leaders is insistence upon acceptance of their ideas and plans.

Adult leaders, in a community studied by Chapin [20], appeared to hold opinions similar in general to those of the group but they 'expressed the trends of opinion of the rank and file more sharply, more decisively, and more consistently'. Simpson [98], in a study of those who influence and those who are influenced in discussion, found that influence score correlated −0·41 with influenceability score. It appears that persons in various types of groups may be valued as leaders because they know what they want to accomplish and are not likely to be swayed from their convictions.

The evidence on liberalism–conservatism suggests that the attitudes which will be regarded as acceptable in leaders are largely determined by the nature of the situation. Hunter and Jordan [53] found college student leaders to be somewhat more liberal than nonleaders in attitudes toward social questions. Newcomb [77] reports that in a college where liberalism is a tradition and ideal those women students having the most

111

prestige are regarded as most liberal. Middleton [72], on the other hand, reports campus leaders to be rated low in radicalism. In Thurstone's [116] study of Washington administrators the Allport-Vernon Social Values scale was found to be the most effective of a battery of 75 tests in differentiating higher salaried from lower salaried administrators. Successful administrators rated significantly higher in social and theoretical values and significantly lower in economic and religious values. Drake [32] and Webb [119] have found low positive correlations between leadership and interest in religion.

19. Self confidence

(a) Self assurance [5, 15, 26, 27, 32, 74, 92, 93, 117, 119, 124].
(b) Absence of modesty [1, 27, 38, 72, 117, 119].

The authors reporting data on the relationship of self confidence to leadership are uniform in the positive direction of their findings. The following correlation coefficients are reported: 0·58 by Bellingrath [5], 0·59 by Drake [32], and 0·12 by Webb [119]. Cowley [26] found self confidence to be one of six factors possessed in common by three widely different types of leaders. Cox [27] finds great leaders to be characterized to an unusual degree by such traits as self confidence, esteem of own special talents, and tendency to rate them correctly. Buttgereit [15], Moore [74], and Zeleny [124] also report leaders to rate high in self confidence. Richardson and Hanawalt [92, 93] find college and adult leaders to make higher self-confidence scores on the Bernreuter test than nonleaders. Hunter and Jordan [53] and Remmelin [90] do not find Bernreuter self-confidence scores to differentiate between leaders and nonleaders. Tryon [117] describes leaders as assured in class and as assured with adults.

Sward [109] finds that inferiority scores on the Heidbreder rating scale do not differentiate leaders from nonleaders, although women leaders rate themselves higher in inferiority attitudes than do their associates. Ackerson [1] reports correlations of −0·02 and 0·08 between inferiority feelings and leadership in boys and girls.

The following findings suggest that leaders tend to be persons who are not handicapped by an excessive degree of modesty.

Cox [27] reports that great military leaders and statesmen are characterized to a greater than average degree by eagerness for the admiration of the crowd, and desire for the limelight, although they exhibit offensive manifestations of self esteem to a lesser degree than average. Middleton [72] also finds leaders to rate low in modesty. A correlation of −0·09 between leadership and modesty is reported by Flemming [38]. Eagerness for admiration is correlated −0·16 with leadership in Webb's [119] study, while Drake [32] reports a correlation of −0·11 between conceit and leadership. Both Ackerson [1] and Tryon [117] report positive correlations between leadership and attention-getting or show-off tendencies. These correlation coefficients range from 0·15 to 0·30. The general trend of these findings suggests that leaders rate higher than their followers in self confidence and self esteem.

20. *Mood control, mood optimism*

(a) Controlled in mood, seldom gloomy [17, 55, 65, 119].
(b) Moods not controlled [1, 27].
(c) Happy, cheerful disposition [32, 40, 117, 119].
(d) Happiness not a factor [1, 3].
(e) Sense of humor [14, 32, 38, 108, 117, 119].

Jennings [55] states that one of the characteristics of girl eaders in an institution is the ability to control their own moods so as not to impose their negative feelings, depressions, and anxieties on others. Caldwell and Wellman [17] and Malloy [65] also find leaders to be characterized by constancy of mood. Webb [119] reports a correlation of −0·45 between depression and leadership. Ackerson [1] and Cox [27], however, report some association between leadership and moods of depression, although not to a significant degree, and the extent differs with different groups.

Drake [32], Tryon [117], and Webb [119] find that a cheerful, happy disposition is associated with leadership. These authors report correlation coefficients ranging from 0·29 to 0·60 between leadership and cheerfulness. Ackerson [1] and Baldwin [3] do not find cheerfulness to be a distinguishing factor in leadership. Ackerson [1] finds that 'unhappy' and 'leadership' are correlated −0·03 for boys and 0·06 for girls. Drake [32], Flemming

[38], Tryon [117], and Webb [119] report correlation coefficients ranging from 0·34 to 0·64 between leadership and sense of humor. Stray [108] also finds leaders to be characterized by a sense of humor. Goodenough's [40] finding of a correlation of 0·53 between leadership and laughter is also relevant to this subject.

The scarcity of evidence concerning the relation of mood control to leadership cannot be regarded as confirmation of its unimportance. The evidence available suggests that mood control may be significantly related to leadership effectiveness. The question appears to warrant thorough investigation.

21. *Emotional control*

(*a*) Leaders found to be more stable and emotionally controlled [3, 5, 8, 17, 32, 34, 72, 84, 112, 119, 120].
(*b*) Leaders found to be less well controlled [1, 27, 35, 97, 117].
(*c*) No differences found [32, 38, 124].

A number of manuals which outline the practical techniques for gaining friends and becoming a leader regard self-control as a very important prerequisite for attaining these goals. The evidence relating to this contention is divided. Eichler [34] reports a correlation of 0·18 between leadership and self-control. Baldwin [3], Pigors [84], and Wetzel [120] also find self-control to be a factor related to leadership. Bellingrath [5] and Drake [32] report correlation coefficients of 0·70 and 0·38 respectively between leadership and stability. Leaders are found by Middleton [72] and Terman [112] to rate low in emotionality, while Bowden [8] and Caldwell and Wellman [17] find leaders to be well balanced and self composed in comparison with their followers. Webb [119] reports correlations of −0·25 between irritability and leadership, and −0·36 between readiness for anger and leadership.

Cox [27], however, finds great face to face leaders to rate high in degree of excitability. This trait is present to an unusual degree in revolutionary statesmen. Ackerson [1] reports correlation coefficients of 0·12 for boys and 0·36 for girls between irritability and leadership in problem children. A correlation of 0·158 between leadership and excitability was found by Sheldon. Fauquier and Gilchrist [35] also report leaders to be more excitable than nonleaders. Zeleny [124] finds no difference between leaders and nonleaders in degree of emotional control. Drake [32] and Flemming [38] report zero order coefficients of correlation between leadership and excitability.

The data relating to anger and fighting throw further light on this subject. Cox [27] finds great face to face leaders, except statesmen, to be characterized by a tendency toward liability to anger, and 'a tendency to flare up on slight provocation'. Ackerson [1] reports that 'temper tantrums' and 'leader' are positively correlated, while 'temper tantrums' and 'follower' are negatively correlated. Webb [119], however, finds a correlation of -0.12 between leadership and occasional extreme anger. Tryon [117] reports correlation coefficients of 0.59, 0.48, 0.25, and 0.40 between fighting and leadership for 12-year-old boys, 15-year-old boys, 12-year-old girls, and 15-year-old girls respectively. Ackerson [1] finds fighting and leadership to be correlated 0.13 for boys and -0.17 for girls, but fighting and leading others into bad conduct are correlated 0.20 for boys and 0.36 for girls. Incorrigibility and defiance are also positively correlated with leadership, and to a still higher degree with leadership in misconduct, while these traits are correlated negatively with 'followers'.

These studies do not lend convincing support to the view that leaders are necessarily persons who are characterized by a high degree of self control or by lack of capacity for emotional expression.

22. Social and economic status

(a) Leaders come from higher socio-economic background [5, 11, 12, 20, 30, 39, 51, 53, 88, 90, 99, 104, 109, 111, 123].
(b) No difference [3, 40].

Evidence presented in studies representing a wide variety of leadership situations indicates that leaders tend to come from a socio-economic background superior to that of the average of their followers. Only two investigators, Baldwin [3] and Goodenough [40], report negligible differences. On the other hand the differences in social and economic status between leaders and nonleaders are usually not extreme. Only Remmelin [90] finds differences which are statistically reliable.

23. *Social activity and mobility*

(*a*) Leaders participate in more group activities [1, 3, 5, 11, 12, 20, 24, 45, 53, 62, 70, 77, 88, 90, 91, 92, 94, 102, 103, 124].
(*b*) Leaders exhibit a higher rate of social mobility [104, 105, 115, 118, 123].

Baldwin [3], Brown [11], Chapin [20], Courtenay [24], Link [62], Merriam and Gosnell [70], Reals [88], Richardson and Hanawalt [92], Roslow [94], Smith and Nystrom [102], Sorokin [103], and Zeleny [124] find that leaders surpass followers in the number, extent, and variety of group activities in which they participate. Zeleny [124] reports correlations ranging from 0·17 to 0·682 between leadership and participation in extra-curricular activities. Leadership has been defined by a number of authors as 'occupying one or more positions of responsibility in group activities'.

Physical and social mobility is found by Sorokin [103], Sorokin and Zimmerman [105], and Winston [122] to be a factor associated with adult leadership. Sorokin and Zimmerman report that farmer leaders are characterized to a high degree by a tendency to shift from place to place, and from one occupational or economic position to another. The same tendency in inventors is observed by Winston [123]. Social mobility, or perhaps more properly, social detachment, appears to be a factor in the formation of boys' gangs studied by Thrasher [115] and Warner [118].

24. *Bio-social activity*

(*a*) Active in games [10, 13, 15, 31, 89, 117].
(*b*) Lively, active, restless [1, 13, 21, 22, 38, 60, 65, 74, 117].
(*c*) Daring, adventurous [112, 115, 117].

This list of traits is difficult to classify, since in few cases is the behavior clearly defined. The majority of investigators appear to emphasize the social aspects of these behaviors, although in some cases emphasis seems to be placed on an underlying physical component of energy or vitality. This is merely one example of the difficulty, and perhaps futility, mentioned by a number of investigators, of attempting to analyse human behavior into distinct and separate traits.

Broich [10], Brown [13], Buttgereit [15], and Reininger [89], find that child leaders are more active in games than nonleaders. In Tryon's [117] study leadership and 'active in games' are correlated 0·52 to 0·74 for groups of 12- and 15-year-old boys and girls. Terman [112], Thrasher [115], and Tryon [117] find leaders to be more daring and adventurous than followers. Correlations of 0·57 to 0·78 between daring and leadership are reported by Tryon [117]. Cowley [26] finds motor impulsion to be a factor common to different types of leaders. According to Chevaleva-Ianovskaia and Sylla [22], leaders are characterized by a predominance of excitation over inhibition. Liveliness is reported by Leib [60] and Brown [13] to characterize leaders. Flemming [38] finds a correlation of 0·47 between leadership and liveliness, while Goodenough [40] reports a correlation of 0·29 between physical activity and leadership. Ackerson [1] and Tryon [117] report correlation coefficients of the order of approximately 0·20 between 'restlessness' and leadership. These findings suggest that physical activity and mobility are factors associated with leadership.

25. Social skills

(a) Sociability [1, 7, 14, 34, 38, 40, 55, 65, 72, 74, 77, 86, 97, 117].
(b) Diplomacy, tact [6, 32, 38, 47, 81, 108, 119, 120].

Fairly high positive correlations between sociability and leadership are reported by Bonney [7], Drake [32], Flemming [38], Eichler [34], Goodenough [40], Sheldon [97], Tryon [117], and Webb [119]. These correlation coefficients are shown in Table 2.

Burks [14], Malloy [65], Middleton [72], and Prosh [86] also find student leaders to rate higher than non-leaders in sociability. Ackerson [1] finds that belonging to a gang is correlated 0·26 with leader and 0·21 with follower. Leader and intimate circle are correlated 0·39 in Webb's [119] study. Moore [74] and Newcomb [77] report friendliness and social skills respectively as factors which distinguish leaders from followers. Cox [27] also finds great leaders to rate above average, but not to an outstanding degree in fondness for companionship and social gatherings.

Courtesy, tact, and diplomacy are found by Bernard [6], Wetzel [120], Drake [32], Flemming [38], Hanfmann [47], Parten

[81], Stray [108], and Webb [119] to be traits which distinguish leaders from nonleaders. Drake, Flemming, and Webb report correlations of 0·08, 0·27, and 0·73 respectively between tact and leadership. Flemming [38], however, finds a correlation of −0·03 between courtesy and leadership. Ackerson reports correlations

Table 2

Correlation between Social Traits and Leadership

Investigator	Variable	Correlation with leadership
Bonney	Social skills	0·53
Drake	Sociability	0·52
Flemming	Sociability	0·33
Eichler	Social intelligence	0·098
Goodenough	Sociability	0·98
Sheldon	Sociability	0·471
Tryon	Friendly	0·44 to 0·74
Webb	Sociability	0·39

of 0·10 and 0·07 between rudeness and leadership for boys and girls respectively, while the correlations between rudeness and leading others into bad conduct are 0·24 and 0·40 for boys and girls respectively. Ackerson also finds that both bashfulness and seclusiveness are negatively correlated with leadership.

Ackerson [1], Goodenough [40], and Webb [119] find correlations ranging from −0·29 to 0·21 between offensive manifestations and leadership. Ackerson's [1] findings suggest that misconduct is not necessarily a bar to leadership. Stealing, for example, is correlated 0·12 and 0·21 with leadership, while stealing and leading others into misconduct are correlated 0·46 and 0·16 for boys and girls respectively.

26. *Popularity, prestige* [1, 5, 18, 27, 39, 71, 73, 79, 117, 124]

Evidence from a diversity of studies indicates that leaders are persons who tend to rate higher than average in popularity. The correlation coefficients shown in Table 3 reveal a fairly high relationship between popularity and leadership. Nutting [79] points out, however, that popularity cannot be regarded as synonymous with leadership. The evidence presented by Ackerson [1], Bellingrath [5], Carlson and Harrell [18], Cox [27], Garrison [39], Michels [71], Miller and Dollard [73], Nutting [79], Tryon

Table 3

Correlation between Popularity and Leadership

Investigator	Variable	Correlation with leadership
Ackerson (boys)	Popularity	0·32
(girls)		0·40
Bellingrath	Popularity	0·80
Garrison (School 1)	Admiration	0·82
(School 2)		0·58
Nutting	Popularity	0·60
Tryon (boys, age 12)	Popularity	0·47
(boys, age 15)		0·64
(girls, age 12)		0·23
(girls, age 15)		0·68

[117], and Zeleny [124] indicate that popularity and prestige are rather closely associated with leadership status.

27. Cooperation

(a) Cooperativeness [3, 10, 16, 32, 33, 35, 47, 65, 77, 119, 120].
(b) Work for the group, corporate responsibility [10, 15, 27, 55, 60, 79, 84, 119].
(c) Ability to enlist cooperation [3, 16, 47, 55, 69, 70, 79].

Leaders are found by Baldwin [3], Dunkerley [33], Fauquier and Gilchrist [35], Newcomb [77], and Wetzel [120] to rate higher in cooperativeness than followers. Drake [32] and Webb [119] report correlations of 0·44 and 0·69 between cooperativeness and leadership. Ability to enlist cooperation and to control others in a group enterprise are found by Baldwin [3], Caldwell [16], Hanfmann [47], Merriam [69, 70], and Nutting [79] to be characteristics associated with leadership ability. Broich [10], Jennings

119

[55], Leib [60], Nutting [79], and Pigors [84] find that leaders tend to be persons who are able to work for the group welfare. A sense of social responsibility is found by Buttgereit [15] to be a characteristic of leaders. Webb [119] reports a correlation of 0·69 between leadership and corporate spirit. Cox [27] also reports that great leaders rate outstandingly high in sense of corporate spirit.

28. *Patterns of leadership traits differ with the situation* [1, 5, 16, 17, 23, 25, 27, 29, 33, 45, 46, 55, 76, 77, 82, 95, 96, 109, 112] There is a preponderance of evidence from a wide variety of studies which indicates that patterns of leadership traits differ with the situation. Ackerson's study [1] reveals marked differences in the conduct and personality patterns of children who are regarded as leaders in general and children who are regarded as leaders in misconduct. Boys and girls in these two groups also differ somewhat. Bellingrath [5] finds marked differences in the extent to which leaders in athletics, student government, publications, and clubs participate in extra-curricular activities and are chosen as leaders under varying circumstances. The investigation of Caldwell and Wellman [17] reveals athletic leaders to be tallest among the leaders and to excel in physical achievements, while editors are younger, and shorter than average, but rank higher in scholarship than other groups of leaders studied. Cowley's [25] studies reveal marked differences in the traits of criminal leaders, Army leaders, and student leaders. The profiles of average trait ratings of groups of great leaders studied by Cox [27] differ markedly from one group to another, especially in physical and emotional traits, but much less so in traits which might be classified as intellectual, self regard, and persistence. Dunkerley's [33] factor analysis of the intercorrelations of 15 variables representing trait ratings of 167 women college students, reveals a factor identified as social leadership, and two factors identified as religious leadership.

Hanfmann [47] observes three types of leadership among preschool children: the objective leader who engages in constructive play and gets what he wants by saying why he needs it; the social leader whose goal is play with another rather than play in itself;

and the gangster who gets his way by force and complete disregard for others. Schuler [95] concludes that as age increases, dominant–submissive behavior in adolescent boys may be ascertained with increasing reliability by teachers in one situation, such as the school, but at the same time it becomes less possible to predict those tendencies in another environment, such as the home.

Superior socio-economic status as well as higher intelligence and scholastic attainment are found by Sward [109] to differentiate 125 campus leaders from 125 followers. However, a classification of the leaders into subgroups reveals the following distinguishing differences: bright, relatively unmotivated, unsocial, self confident campus editors; rather insecure, intellectualistic and very intelligent debaters; strongly socialized and intellectually mediocre campus politicians; and extroverted women leaders.

Terman [112] finds that children who are leaders in one experimental situation may not be leaders when matched against different children in other situations. Children who are 'automatons', or nonleaders, in most situations, may achieve leadership in some situations. Those children who are leaders in most situations are said by their teachers to be characterized by intelligence, congeniality, liveliness, and goodness.

In Tryon's study [117], the trait clusters found to characterize boys and girls at 12 years of age differ from those found at 15 years of age. This is especially true for girls, who appear to mature somewhat more rapidly in social interests than do boys. The leadership cluster for 12-year-old boys is composed of the items: daring, leader, active in games, friendly; while that for 15-year-old boys contains the items: daring, leader, active in games, fights. The leadership trait cluster for 12-year-old girls contains the items: daring, leader, humor about jokes; while for 15-year-old girls the following items appear: popular, friendly, enthusiastic, happy, humor about jokes, daring, leader.

The total weight of evidence presented in this group of studies suggests that if there are general traits which characterize leaders, the patterns of such traits are likely to vary with the leadership requirements of different situations.

121

29. *Transferability and persistence of leadership* [23, 24, 57, 61, 80, 96]

Follow up studies, although yielding somewhat variable results, suggest a certain degree of persistence or transferability of leadership. Levi [61] studied 230 leaders in elementary and junior high school, 206 of whom were studied again in senior high school. The correlation between leadership in elementary school and eadership in senior high school is 0·188, while the correlation between junior high school leadership and leadership in senior high school is 0·515. There is a low negative correlation between athletic leadership in elementary school and in high school, but a correlation of 0·442 was found between athletic leadership in the junior and senior high school situations.

Kohs and Irle [57] made a follow-up study of the military careers of 116 college students. Three faculty members rated these students on various traits. Correlations between army rank and various ratings ranged from 0·108 to 0·39. The best criteria for predicting military success were found to be judges' estimates of potential value to the service and judges' estimates of intelligence. Judges' estimates of leadership were correlated 0·108 with Army rank. Scholarship was not predictive of Army rank. Page [80], studying cadets at West Point, found first-year leadership rank to be correlated 0·667 with fourth-year leadership rank. Rank in bearing and appearance was most highly correlated with rank in leadership; while rank in athletic activities, tactics, and academic standing were correlated with leadership rank in progressively lesser degrees.

Clem and Dodge [23] made a comparative study of the post school success of 27 leaders, 36 high ranking scholars, and 38 random pupils from six successive high school graduating classes. Leaders rank highest in outstanding achievements, number of honors received, and quantity of publications. The random group ranks highest in community leadership and amount of money accumulated. In general, the leaders tended to be more successful than scholars and the random group, although the differences are not impressive. Courtenay [24] studied 100 women leaders and 100 nonleaders from 13 successive high school graduating classes. The two groups were matched as to socio-economic background, ethnic heritage, scholarship, and age at graduation. It was found that 72 leaders went to college, while only 29 nonleaders went to college. Twice as many leaders as nonleaders were engaged in professional work. The average salary of leaders exceeded that of nonleaders. The leaders were more active in community work. Shannon [96] compared leaders, scholars [honor roll members], and a random group from five high school graduating classes. It was found that graduates who were on the honor roll were but little more successful than the random group. It was concluded that 'whatever is required to excel in the extra-curricular life of the high school, seems to be the same thing that contributes most to success later'.

These findings suggest rather strongly that high scholarship alone may not be predictive of success after graduation from high school. Leadership in school activities is somewhat more predictive of later success, but the extent to which leadership persists and transfers is not clearly determined.

Summary

1. The following conclusions are supported by uniformly positive evidence from 15 or more of the studies surveyed:

(*a*) The average person who occupies a position of leadership exceeds the average member of his group in the following respects: (1) intelligence, (2) scholarship, (3) dependability in exercising responsibilities, (4) activity and social participation, and (5) socio-economic status.

(*b*) The qualities, characteristics, and skills required in a leader are determined to a large extent by the demands of the situation in which he is to function as a leader.

2. The following conclusions are supported by uniformly positive evidence from 10 or more of the studies surveyed:

The average person who occupies a position of leadership exceeds the average member of his group to some degree in the following respects: (i) sociability, (ii) initiative, (iii) persistence, (iv) knowing how to get things done, (v) self confidence, (vi) alertness to, and insight into, situations, (vii) cooperativeness, (viii) popularity, (ix), adaptability, and (x) verbal facility.

3. In addition to the above, a number of factors have been found which are specific to well defined groups. For example, athletic ability and physical prowess have been found to be characteristics of leaders in boys' gangs and play groups. Intellectual fortitude and integrity are traits found to be associated with eminent leadership in maturity.

4. The items with the highest overall correlation with leadership are originality, popularity, sociability, judgment, aggressiveness, desire to excel, humor, cooperativeness, liveliness, and athletic ability, in approximate order of magnitude of average correlation coefficient.

5. In spite of considerable negative evidence, the general trend of results suggests a low positive correlation between leadership and such variables as chronological age, height, weight, physique, energy, appearance, dominance, and mood control. The evidence is about evenly divided concerning the relation to leadership of such traits as introversion–extroversion, self sufficiency, and emotional control.

6. The evidence available suggests that leadership exhibited in various school situations may persist into college and into later vocational and community life. However, knowledge of the facts relating to the transferability of leadership is very meagre and obscure.

7. The most fruitful studies, from the point of view of understanding leadership, have been those in which leadership behavior was described and analysed on the basis of direct observation or analysis of biographical and case history data.

Discussion

The factors which have been found to be associated with leadership could probably all be classified under the general headings of *capacity*, *achievement*, *responsibility*, *participation*, and *status:*

1. *Capacity* (intelligence, alertness, verbal facility, originality, judgment).

2. *Achievement* (scholarship, knowledge, athletic accomplishments).

124

3. *Responsibility* (dependability, initiative, persistence, aggressiveness, self confidence, desire to excel).

4. *Participation* (activity, sociability, cooperation, adaptability, humor).

5. *Status* (socio-economic position, popularity).

These findings are not surprising. It is primarily by virtue of participating in group activities and demonstrating his capacity for expediting the work of the group that a person becomes endowed with leadership status. A number of investigators have been careful to distinguish between the leader and the figurehead, and to point out that leadership is always associated with the attainment of group objectives. Leadership implies activity, movement, getting work done. The leader is a person who occupies a position of responsibility in coordinating the activities of the members of the group in their task of attaining a common goal. This leads to consideration of another significant factor.

6. *Situation* (mental level, status, skills, needs and interests of followers, objectives to be achieved, etc.).

A person does not become a leader by virtue of the possession of some combination of traits, but the pattern of personal characteristics of the leader must bear some relevant relationship to the characteristics, activities, and goals of the followers. Thus, leadership must be conceived in terms of the interaction of variables which are in constant flux and change. The factor of change is especially characteristic of the situation, which may be radically altered by the addition or loss of members, changes in interpersonal relationships, changes in goals, competition of extragroup influences, and the like. The personal characteristics of leader and of the followers are, in comparison, highly stable. The persistence of individual patterns of human behavior in the face of constant situational change appears to be a primary obstacle encountered not only in the practice of leadership, but in the selection and placement of leaders. It is not especially difficult to find persons who are leaders. It is quite another matter to place these persons in different situations where they will be able to function as leaders. It becomes clear that an adequate analysis of leadership involves not only a study of leaders, but also of situations.

The evidence suggests that leadership is a relation that exists between persons in a social situation, and that persons who are leaders in one situation may not necessarily be leaders in other situations. Must it then be assumed that leadership is entirely incidental, haphazard, and unpredictable? Not at all. The very studies which provide the strongest arguments for the situational nature of leadership also supply the strongest evidence indicating that leadership patterns as well as non-leadership patterns of behavior are persistent and relatively stable. Jennings [55] observes that 'the individual's choice behavior, in contrast to his social expansiveness, appears as an expression of needs which are, so to speak, so "central" to his personality that he must strive to fulfill them whether or not the possibility of fulfilling them is at hand.' A somewhat similar observation is made by Newstetter, Feldstein, and Newcomb [78], who report that:

Being accepted or rejected is not determined by the cordiality or antagonism of the individual's treatment of his fellows, nor evidently, is the individual's treatment of his fellows much affected by the degree to which he is already being accepted or rejected by them. Their treatment of him is related to their acceptance or rejection of him. Their treatment of him is, of course, a reaction to some or all of his behaviors, but we have been completely unsuccessful in attempting to measure what these behaviors are.

The authors conclude that these findings provide 'devastating evidence' against the concept of the operation of measurable traits in determining social interactions. The findings of Newstetter and his associates do not appear to provide direct evidence either for or against a theory of traits, but they do indicate that the complex of factors that determines an individual's status in a group is most difficult to isolate and evaluate.

The findings of Jennings and Newstetter suggest that the problem of selecting leaders should be much less difficult than that of training nonleaders to become leaders. The clinician or group worker who has observed the fruitless efforts of socially isolated individuals to gain group acceptance or leadership status is aware of the real nature of the phenomena described by Jennings and Newstetter. Some individuals are isolates in almost any group in which they find themselves, while others are readily accepted in most of their social contacts.

A most pertinent observation on this point is made by Ackerson [1], who reports that 'the correlation for "leaders" and "followers" are not of opposite sign and similar magnitude as would be expected of traits supposed to be antithetical'. These may not be the opposite poles of a single underlying trait. 'It may be that the true antithesis of "leader" is not "follower", but "indifference", i.e. the incapacity or unwillingness either to lead or to follow. Thus it may be that some individuals who under one situation are leaders may under other conditions take the rôle of follower, while the true "opposite" is represented by the child who neither leads nor follows.'

The findings suggest that leadership is not a matter of passive status, or of the mere possession of some combination of traits. It appears rather to be a working relationship among members of a group, in which the leader acquires status through active participation and demonstration of his capacity for carrying cooperative tasks through to completion. Significant aspects of this capacity for organizing and expediting cooperative effort appear to be intelligence, alertness to the needs and motives of others, and insight into situations, further reinforced by such habits as responsibility, initiative, persistence, and self confidence. The studies surveyed offer little information as to the basic nature of these personal qualifications. Cattell's [19] studies suggest that they may be founded to some degree on basic intelligence, but Cattell and others also suggest that they are socially conditioned to a high degree. Problems which appear to be in need of thorough investigation are those relating to factors which condition social participation, insight into situations, mood control, responsibility, and transferability of leadership from one situation to another. Answers to these questions seem basic not only to any adequate understanding of the personal qualifications of leaders, but also to any effective training for leadership.

References

1. ACKERSON, L. (1942), *Children's Behavior Problems: Relative Importance and Inter-correlation among Traits*, Univ. Chicago Press.
2. ARRINGTON, R. E. (1943), 'Time sampling in studies of social behavior: A critical review of techniques and results with research suggestions', *Psychol. Bull.*, vol. 40, 81–124.

3. BALDWIN, L. E. (1932), *A Study of Factors usually Associated with High School Male Leadership*, Unpublished Master's thesis, Ohio State Univ.

4. BARKER, R. G. (1942), 'The social interrelations of strangers and acquaintances, *Sociometry*, vol. 5, 169–79.

5. BELLINGRATH, G. C. (1930), 'Qualities associated with leadership in extra-curricular activities of the high school', *Teach. Coll. Contr. Educ.*, no. 399.

6. BERNARD, J. (1928), 'Political leadership among North American Indians', *Amer. J. Sociol.*, vol. 34, 296–315.

7. BONNEY, M. E. (1943), 'The constancy of sociometric scores and their relationship to teacher judgments of social success and to personality self-ratings', *Sociometry*, vol. 6, 409–24.

8. BOWDEN, A. O. (1926), A study of the personality of student leaders in colleges in the United States', *J. Abn. and Soc. Psychol.*, vol. 21, 149–60.

9. BROGDEN, H. E., and THOMAS, W. F. (1943), 'The primary traits in personality items purporting to measure sociability', *J. of Psychol.*, vol. 16, 85–97.

10. BROICH, K. (1929), 'Führeranforderungen in der Kindergruppe', *Z. angew. Psychol.*, vol. 32, 164–212.

11. BROWN, M. (1933), 'Leadership among high school pupils', *Teach. Coll. Contr. Educ.*, no. 559.

12. BROWN, M. (1934), 'Leadership among high school pupils', *Teach. Coll. Rec.*, vol. 35, 324–6.

13. BROWN, S. C. (1931), 'Some case studies of delinquent girls described as leaders', *Brit. J. Educ. Psychol.*, vol. 1, 162–79.

14. BURKS, F. W. (1938), 'Some factors related to social success in college', *J. Soc. Psychol.*, vol. 9, 125–40.

15. BUTTGEREIT, H. (1932), 'Führergestalten in der Schulklass', *Z. angew. Psychol.*, vol. 43, 369–413.

16. CALDWELL, O. W. (1920) 'Some factors in training for leadership', *Nat. Ass. Sec. Sch. Prin., Fourth Yearb.*, 2–13.

17. CALDWELL, O. W., and WELLMAN, B. (1926), 'Characteristics of school leaders', *J. Educ. Res.*, vol. 14, 1–15.

18. CARLSON, H. B., and HARRELL, W. (1942), 'An analysis of Life's "Ablest Congressman" poll', *J. Soc. Psychol.*, vol. 15, 153–8.

19. CATTELL, R. B. (1946), *Description and Measurement of Personality*. World Book.

20. CHAPIN, F. S. (1945), *Community Leadership and Opinion in Red Wing*, Univ. Minnesota Press.

21. CHAPPLE, E. D., and DONALD, G., Jr. (1946), 'A method of evaluating supervisory personnel', *Harvard Bus. Rev.*, vol. 24, 197–214.

22. CHEVALEVA-IANOVSKAIA, E., and SYLLA, D. (1929), 'Essai d'une étude sur les enfants meneurs', *J. de Psychol.*, vol. 26, 604–12.

23. CLEM, O. M., and DODGE, S. B. (1933), 'The relation of high school leadership and scholarship to post-school success', *Peabody J. Educ.*, vol. 10, 321–9.

24. COURTENAY, M. E. (1938), 'Persistence of leadership', *Sch. Rev.*, vol. 46, 97–107.

25. COWLEY, W. H. (1928), 'Three distinctions in the study of leaders', *J. Abn. and Soc. Psychol.*, vol. 23, 144–57.

26. COWLEY, W. H. (1931), 'Traits of face-to-face leaders', *J. Abn. and Soc. Psychol.*, vol. 26, 304–13.

27. COX, C. M. (1926), *The Early Mental Traits of Three Hundred Geniuses*, Stanford Univ. Press.

28. CRAWFORD, A. B. (1928), 'Extra-curriculum activities and academic work', *Person. J.*, vol. 7, 121–9.

29. DASHIELL, J. F. (1930), 'Personality traits and the different professions', *J. Appl. Psychol.*, vol. 14, 197–201.

30. DAVIS, J. (1930), 'A study of one hundred sixty-three outstanding communist leaders', *Publ. Amer. Sociol. Soc.*, vol. 24, 42–55.

31. DETROIT TEACHERS COLLEGE. (1929), *How Children Choose Friends*, Detroit Teachers College.

32. DRAKE, R. M. (1944), 'A study of leadership', *Charac. and Pers.*, vol. 12, 285–9.

33. DUNKERLEY, M. D. (1940), 'A statistical study of leadership among college women', *Stud. Psychol. and Psychiat.*, vol. 4, 1–65.

34. EICHLER, G. A. (1934), 'Studies in student leadership', *Penn. St. Coll. Stud. Educ.*, no. 10.

35. FAUQUIER, W., and GILCRIST, T. (1942), 'Some aspects of leadership in an institution', *Child. Devel.*, vol. 13, 55–64.

36. FAY, P. J., and MIDDLETON, W. C. (1943), 'Judgment of leadership from the transmitted voice', *J. Soc. Psychol.*, vol. 17, 99–102.

37. FINCH, F. H., and CARROLL, H. A. (1932), 'Gifted children as high school leaders', *J. Genet. Psychol.*, vol. 41, 476–81.

38. FLEMMING, E. G. (1935), 'A factor analysis of the personality of high school leaders', *J. Appl. Psychol.*, vol. 19, 596–605.

39. GARRISON, K. C. (1935), 'A study of some factors related to leadership in high school', *Peabody J. Educ.*, vol. 11, 11–17.

40. GOODENOUGH, F. L. (1930), 'Inter-relationships in the behavior of young children', *Child Devel.*, vol. 1, 29–48.

41. GOWIN, E. B. (1915), *The Executive and His Control of Men*, Macmillan.

42. GOWIN, E. B. (1918), *The Selection and Training of the Business Executive*, Macmillan.

43. GUILFORD, J. P., and GUILFORD, R. B. (1939), 'Personality factors, *D*, *R*, *T*, and *A*', *J. Abn. and Soc. Psychol.*, vol. 34, 21–36.

44. HANAWALT, N. G., HAMILTON, C. E., and MORRIS, M. L. (1934), 'Level of aspiration in college leaders and non-leaders', *J. Abn. and Soc. Psychol.*, vol. 38, 545–8.

45. HANAWALT, N. G., RICHARDSON, H. M., and HAMILTON, R. J. (1943),'Leadership as related to Bernreuter personality measures: II. An item analysis of responses of college leaders and non-leaders', *J. Soc. Psychol.*, vol. 17, 251–67.

46. HANAWALT, N. G., and RICHARDSON, H. M. (1944), 'Leadership as related to the Bernreuter personality measures: IV. An item analysis of responses of adult leaders and non-leaders', *J. Appl. Psychol.*, vol. 28, 397–411.

47. HANFMANN, E. (1935), 'Social structure of a group of kindergarten children', *Amer. J. Orthopsychiat.*, vol. 5, 407–10.

48. HEATH, C. W., and GREGORY, L. W. (1946), 'What it takes to be an officer', *Infantry J.*, vol. 58, 44–5.

49. HENNING, H. (1929), 'Ziele und Möglichkeiten der experimentellen charakterprüfung', *Jahrbuch d. Charakterol.*, vol. 6, 213–73.

50. HOLLINGWORTH, L. S. (1926), *Gifted Children*, Macmillan.

51. HOOKER, E. R. (1928), 'Leaders in village communities', *Soc. For.*, vol. 6, 605–14.

52. HOWELL, C. E. (1942), 'Measurement of leadership', *Sociometry*, vol. 5, 163–8.

53. HUNTER, E. C., and JORDAN, A. M. (1939), 'An analysis of qualities associated with leadership among college students', *J. Educ. Psychol.*, vol. 30, 497–509.

54. JENKINS, W. O. (1947), 'A review of leadership studies with particular reference to military problems', *Psychol. Bull.*, vol. 44, 54–79.

55. JENNINGS, H. H. (1943), *Leadership and Isolation*, Longmans Green.

56. JONES, A. J. (1938), *The Education of Youth for Leadership*, McGraw-Hill.

57. KOHS, S. C., and IRLE, K. W. (1920), 'Prophesying army promotion', *J. Appl. Psychol.*, vol. 4, 73–87.

58. LEHMAN, H. C. (1937), 'The creative years in science and literature', *Sci. Mon.*, vol. 45, 65–75.

59. LEHMAN, H. C. (1942), 'Optimum ages for eminent leadership', *Sci. Mon.*, vol. 54, 162–75.

60. LEIB, A. (1928), 'Vorstellungen und Urteile von Schülern über Führer in der Schulklasse', *Z. angew. Psychol.*, vol. 30, 241–346.

61. LEVI, I. J. (1930), 'Student leadership in elementary and junior high school, and its transfer into senior high school', *J. Educ. Res.*, vol. 22, 135–9.

62. LINK, H. C. (1944), 'The definition of social effectiveness and leadership through measurement', *Educ. and Psychol. Meas.*, vol. 4, 57–67.

63. LUITHLEN, W. F. (1931), 'Zur Psychologie der Initiative und der Führereigenschaften', *Z. angew. Psychol.*, vol. 39, 56–122.

64. MALLER, J. B. (1925), 'Cooperation and competition: An experimental study in motivation', *Teach. Coll. Contr. Educ.*, no. 384.

65. MALLOY, H. (1936), 'Study of some of the factors underlying the establishment of successful social contacts at the college level', *J. Soc. Psychol.*, vol. 7, 205–28.

66. McCANDLESS, B. R. (1942), 'Changing relationships between dominance and social acceptability during group democratization', *Amer. J. Orthopsychiat.*, vol. 12, 529–35.

67. McCUEN, T. L. (1929), 'Leadership and intelligence', *Education*, vol. 50, 89–95.

68. McGAHAN, F. E. (1941), 'Factors associated with leadership ability', *Texas Outlook*, vol. 25, 37–8.

69. MERRIAM, C. E., (1926), *Four American Party Leaders*, Macmillan.

70. MERRIAM, C. E., and GOSNELL, H. E. (1929), *The American Party System*, Macmillan.

71. MICHELS, R. (1915), *Political Parties*, Macmillan.

72. MIDDLETON, W. C. (1941), 'Personality qualities predominant in campus leaders,' *J. Soc. Psychol.*, vol. 13, 199–201.

73. MILLER, N. E., and DOLLARD, J. (1941), *Social Learning and Imitation*, Yale Univ. Press.

74. MOORE, L. H. (1932), 'Leadership traits of college women', *Sociol. and Soc. Res.*, vol. 17, 44–54.

75. MOORE, L. H. (1935), 'Leadership traits of college women', *Sociol. and Soc. Res.*, vol. 20, 136–9.

76. NAFE, R. W. (1930), 'A psychological description of leadership', *J. Soc. Psychol.*, vol. 1, 248–66.

77. NEWCOMB, T. M. (1943), *Personality and Social Change*, Dryden Press.

78. NEWSTETTER, W. I., FELDSTEIN, M. J., and NEWCOMB, T. M. (1938), *Group Adjustment: A Study in Experimental Sociology*, Western Reserve Univ.

79. NUTTING, R. L. (1923), 'Some characteristics of leadership', *Sch. and Soc.*, vol. 18, 387–90.

80. PAGE, D. P. (1935), 'Measurement and prediction of leadership', *Amer. J. Sociol.*, vol. 41, 31–43.

81. PARTEN, M. B. (1933), 'Leadership among preschool children', *J. Abn. and Soc. Psychol.*, vol. 37, 430–40.

82. PARTRIDGE, E. D. (1934), 'Leadership among adolescent boys', *Teach. Coll. Contr. Educ.*, No. 608.

83. PECK, E. M. (1931), 'A study of the personalities of five eminent men', *J. Abn. and Soc. Psychol.*, vol. 26, 37–57.

84. PIGORS, P. (1933), 'Leadership and domination among children', *Sociologus*, vol. 9, 140–57.

85. PINARD, J. W. (1932), 'Tests of perseveration', *Brit. J. Psychol.*, vol. 32, 5–19.

86. PROSH, F. (1928), 'The basis on which students choose their leaders', *Amer. Phys. Educ. Rev.*, vol. 33, 265–7.

87. PUFFER, J. A. (1905), 'Boys gangs', *Ped. Sem.*, vol. 12, 175–213.

88. REALS, W. H. (1938), 'Leadership in the high school', *Sch. Rev.*, vol. 46, 523–31.

89. REININGER, K. (1927), 'Das soziale Verhalten von Schulneulingen', *Wien Arb. pädag. Psychol.*, vol. 7, 14.

90. REMMELIN, M. K. (1938), 'Analysis of leaders among high school seniors', *J. Exp. Educ.*, vol. 6, 413–22.

91. REYNOLDS, F. J. (1944), 'Factors of leadership among seniors of Central High School, Tulsa, Oklahoma', *J. Educ. Res.*, vol. 37, 356–61.

92. RICHARDSON, H. M., and HANAWALT, N. G. (1943), 'Leadership as related to Bernreuter personality measures: I. College leadership in extra-curricular activities', *J. Soc. Psychol.*, vol. 17, 237–49.

93. RICHARDSON, H. M., and HANAWALT, N. G. (1944), 'Leadership as related to the Bernreuter personality measures: III. Leadership among adult men in vocational and social activities', *J. Appl. Psychol.*, vol. 28, 308–17.

94. ROSLOW, S. (1940), 'Nation-wide and local validation of the *PQ* or Personality Quotient test', *J. Appl. Psychol.*, vol. 24, 529–39.

95. SCHULER, E. A. (1935), 'A study of the consistency of dominant and submissive behavior in adolescent boys', *J. Genet. Psychol.*, vol. 46, 403–32.

96. SHANNON, J. R. (1929), 'The post-school careers of high school leaders and high school scholars', *Sch. Rev.*, vol. 37, 656–65.

97. SHELDON, W. H. (1927), 'Social traits and morphologic type', *Person. J.*, vol. 6, 47–55.

98. SIMPSON, R. H. (1938), 'A study of those who influence and of those who are influenced in discussion', *Teach. Coll. Contr. Educ.*, no. 748.

99. SMITH, C. (1937), 'Social selection in community leadership', *Soc. For.*, vol. 15, 530–45.

100. SMITH, H. L., and KRUEGER, L. M. (1933), 'A brief summary of literature on leadership', *Bull. Sch. Educ., Indiana Univ.*, vol. 9, no. 4.

101. SMITH, M. (1935), 'Comparative study of Indian student leaders and followers', *Soc. For.*, vol. 13, 418–26.

102. SMITH, M., and NYSTROM, W. C. (1937), 'A study of social participation and of leisure time of leaders and non-leaders', *J. Appl. Psychol.*, vol. 21, 251–9.

103. SOROKIN, P. A. (1927), *Social Mobility*. Harper.

104. SOROKIN, P. A. (1927), 'Leaders of labor and radical movements in the United States and foreign countries', *Amer. J. Sociol.*, vol. 33, 382–411.

105. SOROKIN, P. A., and ZIMMERMAN, C. C. (1928), 'Farmer leaders in the United States', *Soc. For.*, vol. 7, 33–46.

106. SPAULDING, C. B. (1934), 'Types of junior college leaders', *Sociol. and Soc. Res.*, vol. 18, 164–8.

107. STARCH, D. (1943), *How to Develop Your Executive Ability*, Harper.

108. STRAY, H. F. (1934), 'Leadership traits of girls in girls' camps', *Sociol. and Soc. Res.*, vol. 18, 241–50.

109. SWARD, K. (1933), 'Temperament and direction of achievement', *J. Soc. Psychol.*, vol. 4, 406–29.

110. SWIGART. J. S. (1936), *A Study of the Qualities of Leadership and Administrative Qualifications of Thirty-eight Women Executives*, Master's thesis, Ohio State Univ.

111. TAUSSIG, F. W., and JOSLYN, C. S. (1932), *American Business Leaders*, Macmillan.

112. TERMAN, L. M. (1904), 'A preliminary study in the psychology and pedagogy of leadership', *Ped. Sem.*, vol. 11, 413–51. [Reading 4, this edition.]

113. TERMAN, L. M., et al. (1925), *Genetic Studies of Genius: I. Mental and Physical Traits of a Thousand Gifted Children*, Stanford Univ. Press.

114. THORNDIKE, E. L. (1936), 'The relation between intellect and morality in rulers', *Amer. J. Sociol.*, vol. 42, 321–34.

115. THRASHER, F. (1927), *The Gang: A Study of 1,313 Gangs in Chicago*, Univ. Chicago Press.

116. THURSTONE, L. L. (1944), *A Factorial Study of Perception*, Univ. Chicago Press.

117. TRYON, C. M. (1939), 'Evaluations of adolescent personality by adolescents', *Monog. Soc. Res. Child Devel.*, vol. 4, no. 4.

118. WARNER, M. L. (1923), 'Influence of mental level in the formation of boys' gangs', *J. Appl. Psychol.*, vol. 7, 224–36.

119. WEBB, E. (1915), 'Character and intelligence', *Brit. J. Psychol. Monog.*, no. 20.

120. WETZEL, W. A. (1932), 'Characteristics of pupil leaders', *Sch. Rev.* vol. 40, 532–4.

121. WILKINS, E. H. (1940), 'On the distribution of extra-curricular activities', *Sch. and Soc.*, vol. 51, 651–6.

122. WINSTON, S. 'Studies in negro leadership: Age and occupational distribution of 1,608 negro leaders', *Amer. J. Sociol.*, vol. 37, 595–602.

123. WINSTON, S. (1937), 'Bio-social characteristics of American inventors', *Amer. Soc. Rev.*, vol. 2, 837–49.

124. ZELENY, L. (1939), 'Characteristics of group leaders', *Sociol. and Soc. Res.*, vol. 24, 140–9.

6 R. B. Cattell and G. F. Stice

Four Formulae for Selecting Leaders on the Basis of Personality

R. B. Cattell and G. F. Stice, 'Four formulae for selecting leaders on the basis of personality', *Human Relations*, vol. 7 (1954), pp. 493–507.

I. Two Concepts of Leadership and Leadership Measurement

Although the literature on leadership measurement and selection is considerable [1, 12, 13, 14, 15, 16, 17] it cannot be denied that psychologists and administrators charged with selecting people to fill pre-established positions of leadership are currently disappointed with the results. As a consequence, the psychologists are turning toward other conceptualizations, or are emphasizing situational determinants, as in the work of Gibb [12], while the selection of leaders continues to be based largely upon such things as school marks, experience, and other vaguely defined rules of thumb.

The failure of research to lead to either good theoretical generalizations or to effective applied work arises, in the opinion of the present writers, from the lack of meaningfulness, validity, and relevance *in the personality measurements themselves*; from failure to use sound operational definitions of a leader, and perhaps from a tendency to ignore low, but sometimes suggestive, relationships where they have been found. However, the problem now seems to be ripe for more fruitful investigation; first, because the advance of personality research has made it possible to use measures of meaningful, factorially independent, personality traits where previously personality has been measured only by *ad hoc* tests of unknown composition and validity; and second, by virtue of the growth of new concepts, as a result of broader experimental work, in group dynamics.

The recent theoretical developments and empirical test results in regard to the definition of unitary personality traits seem to be well known [5, 18]. It is necessary therefore to indicate advances only in the second matter, namely, the revised concept of leadership measurement in the group dynamics setting. In a theoretical treatment we have suggested that there are always two distinct areas from which leadership measurements can be obtained: measures of the internal group process, and measures of the total group performance or product. The former, by far the most common basis in past research reports, includes direct observations of the kind of interaction and its channels, and also, less satisfactorily, retrospective and introspective sociometric reports. By contrast the 'group performance' criterion of leadership, perhaps more frequently used in the hard realm of international politics, asks the question, 'How well did this group perform under this leader?', and takes as a measure of leadership adequacy, a measure of group performances – usually corrected in practice by intuitive allowances for situational factors which are believed to be important.

The reluctance of some leadership researches to shift to this second, 'behavioristic' definition of leadership seems to be based largely on a theoretical or practical inability to separate the effectiveness of the group population from the effectiveness of the leader, as they contribute to the given performance. This difficulty vanishes completely in theory and largely in practice as we develop methods of measuring the *syntality* of the group with reference to which the leadership occurs.

If the characteristics of a group are measured along independent dimensions, as suggested in a recent research [2, 9], we obtain a profile of what may be called the group syntality – the dimensions of group behavior. This measurement of syntality permits a precise statement – in terms of change on syntality dimensions – of the way in which a group changes under the impact of a new situation, internal organization, or leader. It is proposed then that the proper 'behavioristic' definition of a leader should be in terms of *the extent of his influence upon each of the relevant dimensions of the group syntality* [7].

With regard to the *designation* as apart from the *measurement* of leadership, there appear, correspondingly, to be two criteria, not always consciously distinguished. On the one hand the leader is taken as the person who occupies a given status in the group. He may occupy this either through election by the group or appointment from outside the group, but in either case he is

135

presumed to be the person who performs certain acts including, generally, giving directions to the group and serving as its spokesman. On the other hand the leader is taken as the person, whatever his formal status, whose behavior has significant influence upon what the group does or how it does it. Too often, it would seem, studies of leadership have failed to recognize this distinction clearly. Much of the mere consistency (as distinct from validity) and some of the resulting prestige enjoyed by sociometric ratings of leadership resides circularly in a single simple fact: while group members can agree upon which members hold the position of 'leader', the inconsistencies between such agreement and the attempts to evaluate leadership in terms of group productivity is evidently due to a low correlation between actually influential behavior and formal leadership status.

In the present paper it is proposed to examine leadership in a way which has not been done before, namely, by considering it in the content of many diverse measures of group performance, resolved into syntality dimensions. This was made possible by an Office of Naval Research study on 100 groups of 10 men each, the results of which, as far as the group measurements are concerned, have already been presented in more detail elsewhere [8, 9].

The findings to be described here are those based, on the one hand, on the measurement of individuals in terms of well-defined personality factors and, on the other, upon defined groups performing in standardized situations. In this way it is possible to obtain a number of measurements of leadership with a degree of uniformity and objectivity which has perhaps seldom been possible in the past. The theoretical analysis of leadership *designation* and *measurement* along the lines indicated above, has been set out in detail elsewhere [6, 7]. Here we shall deal with a particular experiment exemplifying the principles there discussed.

II. Design of the Experiment

It was our aim to take a moderate size face-to-face group concerned with a variety of activities typical of those which such groups are commonly called upon to face. A greater degree of control over the selection of the populations and over the experimental conditions of group behavior was exercised than has generally been possible in leadership observations. Thus the populations were composed of persons of the same sex (men), of a fairly narrow age range (18–30), and chosen as having no previous acquaintance of one another in such group life. Each of the 80 groups (20 of the 100 were dropped because of incomplete data) was in competition with the other groups for a considerable monetary prize ($100.00 to be given to the best group in each set of 10 groups). After the testing, by the personality tests, of the individual members who were to be in the group, each group met for three sessions of three hours each. During these sessions it was called upon to perform a wide variety of activities, such as a construction task, a committee meeting, a jury-like decision-reaching situation, a code problem-solving situation, a discussion – designed to arrive at the common attitude and interest of the group on certain questions – and so on. The forty-four distinct performance measurements so obtained have been described fully elsewhere [8, 9]. The measures when intercorrelated and factor-analysed yielded about 16 group dimensions – 13 of them sufficiently stable for measurement – on each of which each group had a measurable value.

The observations made on the group during its performances covered not only the measurements of time and errors in the various total group activities, but also observations by two observers in a great variety of interactions within the group, sociometric reports by members of the group on their relations with other members, and records of who had been the designated (elected) leaders, together with the circumstances under which they were elected. Owing to a shortage of computational resources it has not yet been possible to classify the groups according to their standing on the 13 syntality dimensions. Thus, no direct measures of leadership in terms of influence on these dimensions are available, though the observers' rating and interaction data on the influence exerted by an individual on the group are available to be used as a short cut to the same principle. These observers, working under standardized, repeated conditions, observed the effects of the various members of the group upon the behavior and performance of the group, and they recorded each group-influencing act, marking it with the number of the person who made it. Secondly, after the first session of three hours, in which no formal leader was specified, the group were invited to select a leader from among their members. In every case they chose to do so. Three times during the course of the second meeting, and again at the end of the meeting, they were asked to hold elections to decide who would serve as leader for the next activities. In all cases they were permitted to re-elect their contemporary leader or to select a new one.

These represent two extremes, as it were, of the possible leadership observation. But the full rostra of experimentally independent leadership evaluations, made in the course of these experiments, admit intermediate grades. Those to be reported in this paper are:

1. 'Problem-solving leader' (252)[1]

Immediately after each situation each observer (there were generally two) checked, in a mimeographed form, the code name for each group member who, at any time in the course of the situation, had been observed to have had a significant influence upon the group. The total number of checks (44 was the largest possible number) was computed for each member, and, finally, the members were ranked in the group in terms of the number of checks they received. Those with the most checks were ranked high in amount of leadership shown.

2. 'Salient leader' (253)

To be scored a leader in this category two observers had independently, and for the same situation, to star the subject as being the *most important* leader in at least one of the twenty-two situations presented in the course of the three meetings. All subjects upon whom two observers had agreed at least once were taken as leaders. Since only one observer was used for the Great Lakes groups this measure could not be computed for them.

3. 'Sociometric or popular leader' (112)

At the end of the final meeting all group members were asked to recall which of them had shown leadership in the course of the

1. The number in parentheses following each heading refers to the index number of the measurement in the master list of variables (9, pp. 20–39) from which the score was computed.

group meetings and to record their numbers in the order of importance of their leadership. Six blanks were provided.

In computing 'leadership scores' by this criteria, the first blank was weighted 4 points, the second 3, the third 2, and all remaining ones 1. The distribution of scores was then broken into 'leaders' and 'nonleaders' at what appeared to be the point of inflection between two modes in this distribution.

4. *'Elected leader'* (413)

Any person who was elected leader on one or more occasions was taken as a 'leader' using this criteria.

To complete the description of the experimental work it is necessary only to describe how the individual personality measurements were made. Since the measurements could be made on cooperative subjects, and could be made before the creation of the group situations in which they might become rivals for leadership, it seemed reasonably safe to depend upon a pencil and paper questionnaire, especially because no behavioral measures of the primary personality factors were available at the time the work began in 1947. Each subject was accordingly given both the A and the B form of the *16 Personality Factor Questionnaire* [4]. This questionnaire is based upon a large scale factorization of items chosen to represent a wide range of personality responses and many areas of behavior [4, 5]. It has been developed by various item-analytic purification technics and now measures 16 factors by either 20 or 26 questions each. These factors have been correlated with ratings and also with a number of other tests, such as the Humor Test [10], and the Music Preference Test [11]. The factors, which are symbolized by letters of the alphabet, represent such dimensions as emotional maturity versus neuroticism, cyclothymia versus schizothymia, surgency versus desurgency, high intelligence versus low intelligence, dominance versus submissiveness, and so on. Although these factors are practically orthogonal in the original factorization, they have some moderate intercorrelations, ranging from 0.0 through $+0.4$ in the questions by which they are now measured. The fact that this test was given to subjects in a slightly abbreviated form, compared with the item total in the present standard test, creates some slight difficulties in equating the raw scores with the norms for the standard published 16 P.F. [Personality Factor], but these difficulties can be overcome by suitable corrections, and in any case they do not affect the main findings. The subjects were exhorted to respond frankly and were assured that the responses would be kept private and would not influence their occupational or student standing.

III. The Experimental Population

Although 80 groups, involving 800 men, were used for the principal study, the present analysis of leadership behavior was worked out in only 34 of these groups, including a total of 334 men. The discrepancy between the number of men and of groups was caused by a few cases where the personality questionnaire was not filled out. Fourteen of the groups were composed of subjects who had just arrived (within 72 hours) at San Antonio, Texas, to begin Officer Candidate School in the Air Force, and twenty of the groups were of subjects who had arrived (within 12 hours) to begin Boot Training at Great Lakes, Illinois.

IV. *Analysis of the Results*

The plan of analysis is a very simple one. First we will compare the profiles of leaders with nonleaders, where leaders are chosen separately for each of the criteria described above. In this way we hope to discover which of the measured personality factors are significant, how far each is significant for leadership, and how it may be possible to weigh the significant factors in order to produce a pattern measurement distinguishing leaders from nonleaders.

We will then compare the four profiles of leaders in order to discover what if any relation exists between the method of selection and the personality characteristics of the resulting selectees.

The results in terms of mean scores for all criteria of leadership are shown in Table 1, the actual critical ratios for differences that were found to be significant in Table 2, and the size of the differences in terms of standard score units are plotted on Figure 1.

It will be seen at once that a number of differences exist which

Table 1   Mean 16 P.F. Scores for Leaders and Nonleaders

	Criterion 1: 'Problem Solvers'				Criterion 2: 'Salient Leaders'			Criterion 3: 'Sociometric Leaders'			Criterion 4: 'Elected Leaders'		
	High	Middle	Low	d	L	NL	d	L	NL	d	L	NL	d
A	17·8	17·9	17·5	0·3	18·3	19·7	−1·4	17·1	17·9	−0·8	18·6	17·4	1·2
B	11·4	10·4	9·7	1·7	12·5	11·7	0·8	10·4	10·5	−0·1	10·9	10·3	0·6
C	35·1	34·1	33·6	1·5	36·1	34·2	1·9	34·6	32·9	1·7	34·8	34·0	0·8
E	25·6	24·4	24·0	1·6	27·0	26·0	1·0	26·8	24·5	2·3	25·2	24·4	0·8
F	26·9	25·6	25·0	1·9	26·1	26·2	−0·1	25·6	25·9	−0·3	26·4	22·5	3·9
G	22·1	21·0	20·6	1·5	22·4	21·3	1·1	21·7	21·1	0·6	22·4	20·8	1·6
H	36·7	33·3	32·9	3·8	39·8	35·8	4·0	36·2	34·1	2·1	36·6	32·2	3·4
I	9·8	10·7	10·7	−0·9	9·8	10·6	−0·8	10·4	10·4	0·0	10·0	10·6	−0·6
L	18·1	18·6	18·4	−0·3	16·8	17·8	−1·0	17·3	18·5	−1·2	17·9	18·6	−0·7
M	19·0	20·1	20·1	−1·1	18·6	19·8	−0·8	19·7	19·7	0·0	18·6	20·2	−1·6
N	21·9	20·4	20·6	1·3	23·0	22·2	0·8	22·1	20·8	1·3	21·4	20·7	0·7
O	13·3	15·4	16·2	−2·9	11·3	13·6	−2·3	13·9	15·0	−1·1	13·0	15·9	−3·9
Q_1	19·9	20·3	18·8	1·1	21·5	21·2	0·3	20·4	19·7	0·6	19·7	19·8	0·1
Q_2	14·1	14·1	14·7	−0·6	15·9	14·5	1·4	15·7	14·0	1·7	13·6	14·6	−1·0
Q_3	25·8	24·3	23·2	2·6	26·7	24·6	2·1	25·8	24·3	1·5	26·0	23·6	2·4
Q_4	14·7	16·3	16·4	−1·7	12·0	15·0	−3·0	14·5	16·0	−1·4	14·7	16·0	−1·3
No. of cases	90	140	90		43	100		39	271		92	233	

ds significant at the 5 per cent level are underlined.
Those significant at the 1 per cent level are doubly underlined.

141

Table 2

Significant Personality Differences between Leaders and
Nonleaders for Four Criteria of Leadership

	1. Problem-solving leaders	2. Salient leaders	3. Sociometric leaders	4. Elected leaders
A	–	–	–	–
B	4·2	–	–	–
C	–	2·2	–	–
E	–	–	3·1	–
F	2·5	–	–	4·6
G	3·1	–	–	3·6
H	3·1	3·4	–	3·2
I	–	–	–	–
L	–	–	–	–
M	–	–	–	−2·5
N	–	–	1·9	–
O	−2·2	−2·4	–	−2·7
Q_1	–	–	–	–
Q_2	–	–	2·4	–
Q_3	3·4	2·2	2·0	2·1
Q_4	–	−2·2	–	–

1. Differences are reported as critical ratios. Only differences which are significant at or beyond the 5 per cent are shown.

2. The negative sign preceding a *C.R.* indicates that the leader score mean is lower than that of the nonleader mean.

are significant at the 5 per cent (*C.R.* [Critical Ratio] = 1·96) and at the 1 per cent (*C.R.* = 2·58) levels of confidence, and that in most cases there is a *tendency* for the *same* personality factors to show differences for each of the four different criteria of leadership. Personality factors showing differences in the same direction for all four criteria are:

C Emotional maturity or ego strength

E Dominance

G Character integration or super-ego strength

H Adventurous cyclothymia

N Polished fastidiousness

O (—) Absence of worrying anxiousness (free anxiety)

Q_3 Deliberate will control

Q_4 (—) Absence of nervous tension (somatic anxiety)

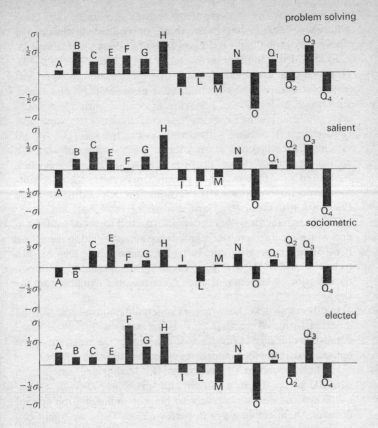

Figure 1 Mean personality scores for leaders and nonleaders. The unit of comparison is the standard deviation of the distribution of nonleaders' scores. Thus, the mean elected leader score on factor F is 0·83 σ units higher than the mean score for group members who were never elected leader

On the other hand, special criteria of leadership selectively emphasize some factors (e.g. B, E, F, and O) much more than other criteria, and in the case of factor A and Q_2 there are even differences in what is the predisposing direction of endowment for leadership according to the concept of leadership used.

From what has been established about the nature of these

143

personality factors in personality research generally, it is comparatively easy to see why these particular dimensions of personality should have such significant relations with leadership.

In regard to the three most consistently differing factors – H, O, Q_3 – which are generally near, or well beyond, the 5 per cent level of certainty, the explanation is clear enough. The timid, withdrawn and hesitant behavior associated with $H-$ would certainly militate against leadership. The anxious, worrying, cautiousness in dealing with people associated with $O+$ would not inspire confidence from others. The absence of the will characters, the stability of purpose, and organizational precision, associated with Q_3 would not permit a person of otherwise suitable temperament to see his decisions through and to organize the group with consistency and a high degree of planning.

The fourth factor which is demanded in all forms of leadership and which reaches levels of significance almost equal to the above is G, or super-ego strength. In so far as conscience may be said to be the 'will of the group' – a regard for supernatural values – the selection of leaders with high G represents a dynamic gain for the group.

In discussing next those factors which differ appreciably for the different forms of leadership, it is necessary to review in some detail the differing conditions of selection. The reader may be reminded that the four categories of leaders (pp. 138–9), are:

1. Those observed to give most 'leadership act' interaction with the group. These we might call 'problem solvers'.

2. Those noted by observers to be most influential on special occasions in affecting a group performance. These we might call 'salient leaders'.

3. Those reported to be leaders by group members in retrospective checking. These we shall call 'sociometric leaders'.

4. Those actually elected by the groups as leaders in the election situations. These are simply 'elected leaders'.

The significant differences between kinds of leaders is presented in Table 3.

For the selection of problem solvers (leader type 1), judged by the 'quantity of observed leadership', a high score is dependent upon the frequent appearance, at least momentarily, of influential behavior in a wide variety of situations, but not necessarily a large amount, or a continuing influence in any one situation. Thus, it makes good sense that here the *level of general ability* (factor *B*) shows more discrimination of problem solvers than of other leaders. Similarly, the spontaneous fluency of ideation and im-

Table 3

Critical Ratios found between the Mean Personality Trait Scores for Leaders Selected by Different Criteria

| Personality trait | Paired differences | *Method of selection* | | | | | |
| | | *1 = Problem solving* | *2 = Salient* | *3 = Sociometric* | *4 = Elected* | | |
		1:2	1:3	1:4	2:3	2:4	3:4
A	–	(1·60)	–	–	(1·5)	2·1	(1·8)
B	–	2·3	3·2	2·7	–	–	–
C	–	–	–	–	–	–	–
E	–	–	–	–	(−1·5)	–	(1·7)
F	–	2·6	2·7	−2·6	–	−5·0	−5·0
G	–	–	–	–	–	–	–
H	–	–	–	–	–	–	–
I	–	–	–	–	–	–	–
L	–	–	–	–	–	–	–
M	–	–	–	–	–	–	–
N	–	–	–	–	–	–	–
O	–	–	–	–	–	–	(1·7)
Q_1	–	–	–	–	–	–	–
Q_2	–	− 2·3	−2·7	–	–	2·8	3·2
Q_3	–	–	–	–	–	–	–
Q_4	–	–	–	–	–	–	–

1. All critical ratios which reach the 15 per cent level of significance (1·46) are shown in this table. It will be recalled that a *C.R.* of 1·96 is significant at the 5 per cent level and 2·58 at the 1 per cent level.

2. A minus sign preceding the *C.R.* indicates that the left-hand (lower numbered) criteria has a lower mean (Table 1).

pulsiveness associated with surgency (factor *F*) could lead to frequent bits of influential behavior, while the driving, persistent, group-concernedness associated with the super-ego-like character integration factor (*G*) would be expected to show a significant association through interest in the problems of the group.

Criterion 2, salient leadership, on the other hand, was meant to select the people who, in at least one specific situation, evidenced reasonably clear and persistent leadership: these people were not merely influential, but the 'most influential' for the whole situation. The predominant influence had moreover to be reasonably clear, in order for the two observers to agree upon it. Since leadership by this criterion must have involved stepping into and holding the center of attention for fairly long periods of time, it is not surprising that it is here that the separation is greatest for the adventurousness-shyness (H) factor and significant for both of the measures of anxiety (O and Q_4). It is perhaps surprising that the dominance (E) difference is not more marked, at least if we give any heed to one popular, over-simplified view which immediately associates dominance and leadership.

The sociometric criterion, consisting of weighted retrospective reports of leadership, is more similar in pattern to criterion 2 than to the others, indicating, we believe, a close correspondence between the salient and the sociometric definition of leadership (see Table 3). It would appear, however, that the group member, in *recalling* his leaders, was *more* influenced by dominance behavior (E), and less by adventurousness (H), and the 'anxious, worrying, apprehensiveness' measured by factor O, than are observers on the lookout for behavior which influences what the group does. Furthermore, it should be noted that there is essentially *no* difference between the *level of ability* for leaders and nonleaders as selected by this criterion. If, as we have supposed, the intelligence measure can be taken as a rough index of effectiveness in problem solving and in the influencing of group behaviour, then we are led to the interesting hypothesis that the sociometrically selected leader is not so much influential as he is attention-getting and dominating. He is the person who is recalled as having captured the group members attention, but he is not necessarily the person who did the things which were decisive with regard to the course of the group's progress.

Turning last to the elected leaders we notice that the chief way in which they differ from leaders by other criteria is on factor F, surgency. It is particularly remarkable that, while a high endowment on this trait is useful in securing election, it bears almost no relation to who is selected when the group member is asked to recall 'Whom do you judge to have been the leaders of this group throughout these meetings?' Indeed, if we could partial out the responses to this question which simply listed the elected leaders, it might be that, by the sociometric criteria, the low F person is in fact recalled as exercising more influence.

While the differences between leaders and nonleaders in factors A and Q_2 (friendly cyclothymia and independent self-sufficiency) are not significant, some of the differences *between leaders* selected by the different criteria are. Thus, it would appear that the warm friendly characteristics associated with $A+$, and the willingness to go with the group and obtain major dynamic gratification from interpersonal stimulation associated with $Q_2(-)$ make for election and for group influential behavior over a wide spectrum of situations. But, to an even greater extent the persistence in inner principles and lack of concern for the wishes of peers, associated with $A-$ and Q_2+, (perhaps well illustrated by Woodrow Wilson) appears to be associated with criteria 2 and 3.

These differences call for further examination in terms of (a) the relative satisfaction which group members received from the $A-$, Q_2+, in comparison with the $A+$, Q_2- leader, and (b) the dimensions of syntality that are altered by the two types of leaders. In the absence of further analysis of data, we would hypothesize that, because he will be more successful, the $A-$, Q_2+ leader will, in the long run, prove more popular in groups where the primary problem is to attain a difficult goal, but less successful and popular in groups and situations where the means of goal attainment are simple but the maintenance of contentment and morale of members is difficult. Similarly, the $A-$, Q_2+ leader will probably have his greatest effect upon the syntality dimensions related to group performance, while the $A+$, Q_2- leader will more likely influence the dynamic and interactional dimensions of structure and behavior.

While no direct measurement of the effects of leadership upon group productivity is as yet available, it seems probable to us that the observer ratings, in particular criterion 2, will more closely reflect changes in productivity. Extrapolating from this assumption, and by reference to Figure 1, we may predict that the leader who had greatest influence upon the syntality of the group, will characteristically be much more adventurous ($H+$), less anxious (Q_4- and $O-$), more emotionally mature ($C+$) and more persistent and wilful (Q_3+) than the typical member of the population from which he is drawn.

Summary

1. Basically there are two ways of designating and measuring leaders: (a) by interaction observations and (b) by syntality change observations.

2. Although (b) is not yet fully practicable we have taken four operational definitions of leadership which range from (a) toward (b) and measured the personalities of individuals picked out by each, contrasting them with one another and with nonleaders.

3. The experimental situation was one in which 34 groups of 10 young men in each performed for 3 sessions of 3 hours each in a wide variety of common small group performances (e.g. committee decisions, construction, tug-of-war, cryptogram solving). The 13 syntality dimensions, factored out of 150 measures of external behavior and internal, structural, interactional observations, were not directly used here.

4. The four leadership categories may be designated:

(i) *Persistent momentary problem solvers*, picked for frequency of brief acts of leaders. The equivalent of these in a role-structured group would probably be the 'technical leaders'. This is an interaction count. This comes near to defining the leader by his persistent influence on syntality.

(ii) *Salient leaders* picked by outside observers as most powerfully influencing the group syntality on at least one total situation and occasion. This, like (i) above, comes near to designating leaders by group performance.

(iii) *Sociometric leaders*, picked by frequency of subjectively reported perception of leadership by group members. This is a subjective, sociometric, rather than a behavioral, interactional, source of evidence on structure, and has nothing demonstrable to do with syntality change.

(iv) *Elected leaders*, picked by voluntary election after experience. A structural measure interactionally based.

5. Comparing leaders with nonleaders, differences significant at the 1 per cent and 5 per cent level were found for factors G, O, H, and Q_3 (for leaders $+$, $-$, $+$, and $+$). These, and lesser differences on factors C, E, N, and Q_4, are in the same direction for all four classes of leaders.

6. In terms of the number of significant critical ratios, the greatest resemblance exists between salient and sociometric leaders and the least between sociometric and elected leaders.

7. The differences between leader types which have a significance at the 5 per cent level or beyond are that problem solvers are higher in general intelligence, and elected leaders are higher in surgency.

8. Four formulae, in the form of optimum factor patterns, may be gathered from the above tables, for selecting leaders according to these four conceptions. Any of these can be put alternatively into specification equation form, in order to utilize the 16 P.F. measures to give a simple prediction of leadership effectiveness. We have chosen to illustrate this by the elected leaders pattern, for this is probably of the widest practical application. From the above differences of means bi-serial correlations were worked out for each personality factor in relation to leadership. (As McNemar, for example, points out, the assumption that the dichotomized variable is continuous generally makes best sense, and it certainly does so in this case, where we are aiming to predict a continuous variable of 'fitness for leadership' which may be cut at any point according to the number of leaders required from the given population.)

The equation works out at:

$$P_L = 0·16A + 0·11B + 0·09C + 0·10E + 0·50F + 0·22G \\ + 0·35H - 0·13I - 10L - 0·21M + 0·09N - 0·27O \\ - 0·16Q_2 + 0·30Q_3 - 0·28Q_4$$

Using this as a specification equation assumes that the factors are uncorrelated (this is true for the ideal personality factors but only approximately true for the present means of measuring them – The 16 P.F. Questionnaire), and that linear relations exist between the criterion and the personality factor endowments. This is a rather potent specification equation, perhaps because it covers so wide an array of personality aspects: for it accounts for

82 per cent of the variance of the criterion and gives a multiple correlation of 0·91. It remains to be seen (1) how well this will stand up to cross validation with other groups; and (2) when more refined measures eliminate the over-determination introduced by the neglect of slight correlations between the factors mentioned above. However, as it stands it appears the highest prediction of leadership that we have encountered in the literature.

References

1. CARTER, L., HAYTHORN, W., SHRIVER, B., and LANZETTA, J. (1951), 'The behavior of leaders and other group members', *Journal of Abnormal and Social Psychology*, vol. 46, pp. 589–95.
2. CATTELL, R. B. (1948), 'Concepts and methods in the measurement of group syntality', *Psychological Review*, vol. 55, pp. 48–63.
3. CATTELL, R. B. (1949), 'r_p and other coefficients of pattern similarity', *Psychometrika*, vol. 14, pp. 279–98.
4. CATTELL, R. B., SAUNDERS, D. R., and STICE, G. F. (1951), *The 16 P.F. Questionnaire*, Institute of Personality and Ability Testing, Illinois.
5. CATTELL, R. B. (1950), *Personality: A Systematic, Theoretical and Factual Study*, McGraw-Hill.
6. CATTELL, R. B. (1951), 'New concepts for measuring leadership in terms of group syntality', *Human Relations*, vol. 4, pp. 161–84.
7. CATTELL, R. B. (1953), 'On the theory of group learning', *Journal of Social Psychology*, vol. 37, pp. 27–52.
8. CATTELL, R. B., SAUNDERS, D. R., and STICE, G. F. (1953), 'The dimensions of syntality in small groups: I. The neonate group, *Human Relations*, vol. 6, pp. 331–56.
9. CATTELL, R. B., and STICE, G. F. (1953), *The Psychodynamics of Small Groups*, mimeographed report, Human Relations Bureau, ONR.
10. CATTELL, R. B. (1952), *The IPAT Humor Test of Personality*, Institute of Personality and Ability Testing, Illinois.
11. CATTELL, R. B., and ANDERSON, J. (1953), 'The measurement of personality and behavior disorders by the I.P.A.T. music preference test', *Journal of Applied Psychology*, vol. 37, pp. 446–54.
12. GIBB, C. A. (1947), 'The principles and traits of leadership', *Journal of Abnormal and Social Psychology*, vol. 42, pp. 267–84.
13. GIBB, C. A. (1949), *The Emergence of Leadership in Small Temporary Groups of Men*, Ph.D. thesis, University of Illinois.
14. GIBB, C. A. (1954), 'Leadership', in G. Lindzey, ed., *Handbook of Social Psychology*, Addison-Wesley.

15. HEMPHILL, J. K. (1949), *Situational Factors in Leadership*, Personnel Research Board, Ohio State University.
16. JENNINGS, H. H. (1950), *Leadership and Isolation*, Longmans Green.
17. STOGDILL, R. M. (1950), 'Leadership, Membership and Organization', *Psychological Bulletin*, vol. 47, pp. 1–14.
18. THURSTONE, L. L. (1947), *Multiple Factor Analysis*, Chicago University Press.

7 R. D. Mann

A Review of the Relationships between Personality and
Leadership and Popularity

Excerpts from R. D. Mann, 'A review of the relationships between personality and performance in small groups', *Psychological Bulletin*, vol. 56
(1959), pp. 241–70.

A wide range of practical and theoretical interests have found expression in the study of small groups. As the major bibliographic
sources (Hare, Borgatta, and Bales, 1955; MacGrath, 1957;
Strodtbeck and Hare, 1954) amply attest, small group research has
proceeded along numerous independent lines. One interest, however, has been dominant for more than 50 years. While phrased in
various ways, the relationship between the personality characteristics of the individual and his performance in the group has
remained a central concern.

There have been at least three conceptual approaches to this
problem. One approach considers the individual as having various
needs and as being motivated to satisfy some of these needs
through interaction with others; the point of interest is the relation between the individual's personality and his goal-directed
behavior in groups. In another view, the individual is conceived
of as a stimulus, or set of stimuli, for the other members of the
group, and the relation between the individual's personality and
the way in which he is perceived and judged by his peers assumes
primary importance. In the third approach, the group is conceptualized as a system confronted with various problems, external and internal, and attention shifts to the processes whereby
particular individuals volunteer or are selected to occupy various
positions and perform various roles necessary for the solution of
the problems. Although these three approaches have generated
many non-overlapping research questions, they have produced
a body of data which may be considered meaningfully as a
whole.

This review attempts to summarize the present state of knowledge about the relationship of an individual's personality to his behavior or status in groups. Although the independent effects of varying the nature of the sample and history or size of the group upon the performance of individuals are not considered, an effort is made to determine the effect of such situational factors on the relationships observed between personality and performance.

While the purpose of this review is to provide an adequate and accurate description of the present state of knowledge in the field, its intent is to stimulate research rather than to make a final summary. It is thought that an organized presentation of the findings to date may help to clarify relationships which have been overlooked or misunderstood. Moreover, it is hoped that this summary may be used as a target and a taking-off point for future research, thus encouraging publication and helping to make knowledge in this field more cumulative.

Selection of the Studies

The studies selected for detailed examination meet the following five criteria: (a) the sample was drawn from a population of high school age or older; (b) the groups studied were face-to-face groups; (c) some assessment was made of the individual's personality; (d) some assessment was made of the individual's behavior or status in the group; and (e) the results were either in correlational form or made use of a control group, i.e. studies testing only leaders or only social isolates are not considered. [. . .]

This review covers the available literature from 1900 through October, 1957. The bibliography was collected by searching the most relevant journals and published abstracts, by following the network of references from article to article, and by obtaining as much unpublished research as possible. In addition, the earlier reviews (Bass, 1954; Borgatta, 1954; Gibb, 1950, 1954; Jenkins, 1947; Roseborough, 1953; Smith and Krueger, 1933; Stogdill, 1948) which emphasize leadership or popularity to the exclusion of other aspects of performance covered here have been useful. No claim is made to completeness, but no sources of known relevance have been deliberately overlooked.

The Personality Variables

The studies which meet the criteria for selection used over 500 different measures of personality. However, less than a quarter of these measures appear in more than one study. As a commentary on the level of integration within the field, this fact needs little amplification. There is a noticeable failure throughout these studies to resolve methodological issues in a consistent fashion.

Clearly, it is not feasible to present each separate personality variable and its correlates. Some organization of the measures was called for. But what organization? The field of personality assessment is test rich and integration poor. The 500 measures all have labels, to be sure, but they are as divergent as oral sadism, the F scale, spatial ability, adventurous cyclothymia, hypochondriasis, and total number of vista responses. Yet all of these measures have been used to predict something about an individual's performance in groups. In addition, there are innumerable adjectives used for ratings and self-descriptions. The situation required a set of personality factors small enough to remain manageable and pure enough to be meaningful, and then empirical grounds on which to classify as many of the variables as possible into the selected set of factors.

To arrive at a useful set of personality dimensions, the empirical work in the field of personality assessment, particularly the work of French (1953), Cattell (1946, 1956, 1957) and Eysenck (1953) was examined. With one exception, the seven dimensions or factors chosen are those frequently isolated in the study of personality by factor analytic techniques, although two emerge only as second-order factors in some reports. A brief description of each personality factor is presented here.

Intelligence

This factor includes all the diverse and specific mental abilities. 69 of the 500 different variables included in the research reviewed are measures of this factor; of these 69 measures 45 are derived from questionnaire and objective tests, 24 from adjective ratings. The 4 most frequently used measures of intelligence are: school or college grades, American Council of Education (A.C.E) Psychological Exam, Cattell's Sixteen Personality Factor Questionnaire (16 P.F.) Factor *B*, and total number of responses on the Rorschach.

Adjustment

The positive end of this dimension has been called adjustment, ego strength, and normality, while the negative end has been called maladjustment, emotionality, neuroticism, psychoticism, and anxiety. 71 objective test and questionnaire variables and 60 adjectives are considered as measures of this factor. The most frequently used measures of this factor are derived from standard personality inventories: Minnesota Multiphasic Personality Inventory (M.M.P.I.), Guilford–Zimmerman, Bernreuter, and 16 P.F.

Extroversion–introversion

Eysenck (1953) presents the fullest discussion of this dimension, although the need to integrate as many variables as possible led to the use of a broader definition. Extroversion–introversion as used in this review, more closely resembles one of Cattell's (Cattell, Saunders, and Stice, 1951) second-order factors from the 16 P.F., which pulls together the dimensions of sociability, surgency, and cyclothymia *v.* schizothymia. Frequently used measures of this factor are: the Bernreuter *F*-2 scale (self-sufficiency), M.M.P.I. hypomania scale, ratings on 'sociable', and the relevant scales from the 16 P.F. (Cattell, 1956) and Guilford–Zimmerman (French, 1953). A total of 38 questionnaire and objective test variables and 61 adjective ratings were used in the studies reviewed.

Dominance

The positive end of the dimension is described by dominance or ascendance, the negative end by submissiveness or helplessness. 17 objective test and questionnaire variables and 12 adjective-ratings which have been found to measure dominance were employed in these studies.

Masculinity–femininity

This factor measures the extent to which an individual's interests or preferences resemble those common to his own or the opposite sex. Of the 14 questionnaire and objective test variables and 6 ratings, the ones most frequently used in these studies are the masculinity–femininity scales from the M.M.P.I., Guilford–Zimmerman, and Goodenough Speed of Association Test.

Conservatism

The positive end of this dimension is defined by conservatism, conventionalism, or authoritarianism, the negative end by radicalism. In the studies reviewed, the measures of this factor include 36 questionnaire and objective test variables and 11 adjective-ratings. By far the most frequently used are the F scale and factor Q_1 from the 16 P.F.

Interpersonal sensitivity

This factor has not been found in factor analytic studies of personality, and some authors have questioned whether it is proper to speak of empathy and insight as characteristics of the individual. However, it is included in this review because it has been related to an individual's status in groups a sufficient number of times to merit separate treatment. For the most part, the measures describe an individual's ability to guess (a) his own status in a group, (b) the status hierarchy of the entire group, as determined by the pooled estimates of the members, or (c) the opinions and attitudes of the other group members.

150 variables out of the total of over 500 could not reasonably be classified into any one of the seven factors. Some of these 150 variables fall into other known factors or clusters, but the number of additional results which could be included by considering them is too small to justify the consequent complexity of the presentation. The majority of the excluded variables, however, come from projective tests; in such cases, both the titles and the known correlations with other personality measures combined to mystify this reviewer as to what meaning they might have outside the language system of the particular technique. Many projective test variables do not fall into stable and identifiable clusters or factors; further, the level of description used in projective tests makes it difficult to bridge the gap between the seven aspects of personality examined in this review and the various projective measures. Except for the measures of inter-

personal sensitivity, the distribution of variables into factors was determined by the empirical evidence for the measure's validity. Where no validity data were found for a measure, a calculated risk was taken in assigning it to a factor if the title and operation closely resembled the set of variables already chosen on empirical grounds as measures of the factor; this process accounted for no more than 50 of the variables classified.

The Status and Behavior Variables

In contrast to personality variables, measures of an individual's status and behavior in groups fall easily into a small number of classes. On the basis of both operations and labels the following six dependent variables were selected: leadership, popularity, total activity rate, task activity, social–emotional activity, and conformity. Leadership and popularity are considered to be status variables; the remaining four are considered to be behavior variables.

Leadership has been measured in four ways: by having an observer rate the individual's attained leadership, by having an individual's peers rate him, by using an individual's formal selection for office as the criterion of leadership, or by having the individual rate himself. The only measures included in the discussion of leadership which do not bear that label are a few measures on the individual's productivity and effectiveness. Popularity has been measured by having an individual's peers rate him on such dimensions as the extent to which they like him, find him acceptable as a friend, would choose him for leisure-time activities, or perceive him to be popular.

The remaining dependent variables are based upon actual observations of the individual's behavior in the group. Activity rate has been measured in terms of either the number of acts initiated or the number of seconds spent talking. The distinction between task activity and social–emotional activity is made by Bales (1950). He distinguishes between task acts, relevant to the external-adaptive problems of the group (suggestions, opinions, orientations, and task questions), and social–emotional acts, relevant to the internal-integrative problems of the group (agreeing and disagreeing, showing tension release and tension, showing solidarity and antagonism). Measures of behavior other than those employing the Bales categories were matched as carefully as possible to the Bales categories and classified on that basis. Conforming behavior includes all measures of an individual's tendency to yield to the opinions or pressures of the group. [. . .]

Method of Presentation

One final issue, the most appropriate unit of research, must be discussed before the presentation of the findings. The problem arises from the fact that a single study may contain, for example, more than one measure of leadership and more than one measure of intelligence. On the one hand, we might consider the study as the unit, examining only the over-all trend of the many results. On the other hand, we might consider each result as the unit, examining the findings from a study in as much detail as possible.

The advantage of using a whole study as the unit is that units are then independent, and, therefore, statistical tests of the significance of the trends are possible. Another approach is to consider as the separate unit each result, that is, each correlation or measure of difference between groups. This can lead to overrepresentation of a particular sample and a particular set of measures in the total summary of research to date. Moreover, it is not possible to use statistical tests to evaluate trends based on more than one result per study, since using the same subjects and then using independent or dependent variables which are highly correlated with each other would violate the assumption of independence which underlies statistical tests.

If each relationship had been investigated in a sufficient number of studies to permit statistical tests in most cases, we would have chosen studies as the units. Because such is not the case, we have chosen the result as the unit of research, but it is recognized that, for the above-mentioned reasons, any trends based on separate results must remain as descriptive indications of the findings to date. Where the number of studies is sufficient to provide an opportunity to use statistical tests, the tests will be made.

There are a number of advantages, however, to using the results as units. Over 1400 results are examined in this review. The far greater number of results may compensate for the disadvantages of this approach by offering greater stability to the trends.

The association between a personality variable and a status or behavior variable is reported in one of eight forms:

(a) positive and significant
(b) positive and not significant
(c) positive but no report of significance
(d) negative and significant
(e) negative and not significant
(f) negative but no report of significance
(g) zero correlation,
(h) not significant but no report of direction.

Throughout this review a positive finding refers to the association between the positive ends of the personality and performance variables as described earlier, not to the confirmation of an hypothesis. The 0·05 level is accepted as the criterion of significance.

Each relationship for which five or more results are available and which has been investigated in more than one study is examined in detail. Three summary statistics are used throughout to describe the findings for each relationship. First, the over-all direction of the results is shown by the percentage of results which are positive; this is calculated by dividing the number of positive results ((a), (b), and (c) above) by the number of results which indicate direction (the total number minus (g) and (h)). Second, the over-all direction of the results is further shown by the percentage of significant results which are positive; this is calculated by dividing the number of results which are significantly positive (a) by the total number of significant results ((a) and (d)). Third, as a way of examining the significance of the results underlying the trends, the percentage of the total number of results which are significantly positive or negative, depending on the direction of the trend, is shown. If the trend is positive, this is calculated by dividing the number of significantly positive results (a) by the total number of results minus the number which are positive but untested (c); if the trend is negative, this is calculated by dividing the number of significantly negative results (*d*) by the total number of results minus the number which are negative but untested (*f*).

There appears to be a general belief that many inconclusive and negative findings are filed away into obscurity, doomed never to enter the professional literature. To the extent that this bias exists in the area reviewed, the trends are misleading. This reviewer has succeeded in obtaining some unpublished data and doctoral dissertations in an effort to counterbalance the alleged distortion in the published materials. However, it may be noted that the unpublished data included here are in almost perfect agreement with the data in the journals and monographs. This seems to suggest that considerations other than the conclusiveness of the results operate to determine which results will be published.

Leadership

Viewed historically, the study of leadership has stimulated more than its share of controversy. The trait approach to leadership, the view that leadership is an attribute of the individual, has received the harshest treatment throughout the years. To have spoken of an individual as possessing a measurable quantity of leadership was perhaps an unfortunate choice of words. The clear implication of such a statement is that since leadership is specific to the individual, it will remain constant for the individual regardless of the situation in which he finds himself. Investigations of the actual consistency with which an individual maintains leadership status in different groups and under varying conditions have yielded results sufficiently equivocal to permit a new bifurcation of the field. On the one hand, the trait approach has been modified to imply that an individual's achieved leadership status is a function of his personality. On the other hand, sufficient evidence has been accumulated to give impetus to the situational approach to leadership, which maintains that leadership is an emergent phenomenon, created through the interaction of individuals (leaders and followers), and that the selection and stability of any leadership pattern is a function of the task, composition, and culture of the group. From all this work has emerged some such summary formulation as that an individual's leadership status in groups is a joint function of his personality and the particular group setting. There is an interesting parallel here to the controversy over the role of heredity and environment in determining behavior; the initial criticisms and intensity gave way to concessions that each factor sets limits for the operation of the other, and researchers turned to studying the relative importance of and the interaction between the two major factors.

Table 1 presents a summary of the relationships between seven aspects of personality and leadership. Shown there are the number of relevant studies, the number of results contained in those studies, the distribution of results into the various forms in which they are reported, and the three summary statistics. The results are reported in eight forms: the positive and negative associations may be significant (Sig.), not significant (N.S.), or untested (Unt.); the remaining two forms, zero correlation (zero) and not significant but no direction reported (?N.S.) are combined in the table. The base numbers for the summary percentages are enclosed in parentheses below the percentages. The base number for the percentage of results which are positive (i) is the total number of results which indicate direction; the base number for the percentage of significant results which are positive (j) is the total number of significant results; the base number for the percentage of results which are both significant and in the direction of the over-all trend (k) is the total number of results minus the positive but untested (c) or negative but untested (f) results, depending on the direction of the trend. A separate section covers each relationship between an aspect of personality and leadership.

Intelligence

28 of the studies reviewed (Arbous and Maree, 1951; Bass, 1951; Bass and Coates, 1952; Bass, McGehee, Hawkins, Young, and Gebel, 1953; Bass and Wurster, 1953a; Bass, Wurster, Doll, and Clair, 1953; Borgatta, 1953; Carter and Nixon, 1949; Cattell and Stice, 1954; Cobb, 1952; Cowley, 1931; Dunkerly, 1940; Flemming, 1935; French, 1951; Gibb, 1949; Gordon, 1952; Gowan, 1955; Green, 1950; Howell, 1942; Hunter and Jordan, 1939; McCuen, 1929; Richardson and Hanawalt, 1943; Riggs, 1953; Slater, 1955a; Stolper, 1953; Sward, 1933; Wurster and Bass, 1953; Zeleny, 1939) have investigated the association

Table 1
The Relationship between Personality Factors and Leadership

Personality factors	No. of studies	No. of results	Positive			Negative			Zero ?N.S. (g, h)	Positive % (i)	% of Sig. (j)	% Sig. and in dir. of trend (k)
			Sig. (a)	N.S. (b)	Unt. (c)	Sig. (d)	N.S. (e)	Unt. (f)				
Intelligence	28	196	91	68	14	1	22	0	0	88 (196)	99 (92)	50 (182)
Adjustment	22	164	50	55	14	2	28	0	15	80 (149)	96 (52)	33 (150)
Extroversion	22	119	37	38	6	6	23	3	6	72 (113)	85 (43)	33 (113)
Dominance	12	39	15	9	3	6	4	0	2	73 (37)	71 (21)	42 (36)
Masculinity	9	70	11	37	0	1	19	0	2	71 (68)	92 (12)	16 (68)
Conservatism	17	62	3	18	0	17	21	3	0	38 (62)	15 (20)	29 (59)
Sensitivity	15	101	15	55	3	1	25	0	2	74 (99)	94 (16)	15 (98)

between an individual's intelligence and his leadership status in one or more groups. These studies contain 196 results, 173 (or 88 per cent) of which indicate a positive relationship between intelligence and leadership. Furthermore, 91 (or 99 per cent) of the 92 significant results are in the positive direction. Omitting those results which are positive but untested for significance, exactly half of the remaining 182 results are both positive and significant at the 0·05 level. Considering independent studies as the units of research, the positive association between intelligence and leadership is found to be highly significant ($p < 0.01$) by the sign test. However, the magnitude of the relationship is less impressive; no correlation reported exceeds 0·50, and the median r is roughly 0·25.

There is some indication that verbal intelligence is a better predictor of leadership than such non-verbal factors as memory and numerical ability. Grades are not strongly related to leadership in college social groups, although this fact may reflect competition between scholastic and social activities for the student's time and energy.

There would seem to be little doubt that higher intelligence is associated with the attainment of leadership in small groups. That the null hypothesis may be emphatically rejected should not obscure the fact that the magnitude of the relationship is not high.

Adjustment

The 22 studies (Bass, McGehee *et al.*, 1953; Bass, Wurster *et al.*, 1953; Borgatta, 1953; Carter and Nixon, 1949; Cattell and Stice, 1954; Cowley, 1931; Dexter and Stein, 1955; Dunkerly, 1940; Flemming, 1935; French, 1951; Gibb, 1949; Gordon, 1952; Gowan, 1955; Holtzman, 1952; Hunter and Jordan, 1939; Richardson and Hanawalt, 1943, 1944, 1952; Slater, 1955a; Stolper, 1953; Williamson and Hoyt, 1952; Zeleny, 1939) relating the personal adjustment of the individual to his leadership status yield 164 results. The trend of the results is clearly positive, as indicated by the fact that 80 per cent of the results are in the positive direction. If only the 52 significant results are considered, the proportion of positive results rises to 96 per cent. One-third of the results are both positive and significant. The over-all trend within every study but one is positive, and the sign test indicates that the null hypothesis of no association may be rejected at the 0·01 level. No single variable measuring adjustment is correlated with leadership over 0·53, and the median correlation appears to lie close to 0·15.

Four studies using the Bernreuter (Gowan, 1955; Richardson and Hanawalt, 1943, 1944, 1952) and one using the 16 P.F. (Cattell and Stice, 1954) present the most striking evidence of this positive association but the various techniques for measuring adjustment (questionnaires, objective tests, and ratings) are about equally productive of positive results. While no single measure of adjustment can be expected to be an efficient predictor of leadership, there is strong evidence to indicate a positive relationship between an individual's adjustment and the leadership status he is likely to attain.

Extroversion–introversion

Twenty-one studies (Bass, McGehee *et al.*, 1953; Bass, Wurster *et al.*, 1953; Borgatta, 1953; Carter and Nixon, 1949; Cattell and Stice, 1954; Cowley, 1931; Dexter and Stein, 1955; Dunkerly, 1940; Flemming, 1935; French, 1951; Gordon, 1952; Gowan, 1955; Hunter and Jordan, 1939; Moore, 1935; Richardson and Hanawalt, 1943, 1952; Slater, 1955a; Stolper, 1953; Sward, 1933; Williamson and Hoyt, 1952; Zeleny, 1939) have investigated the association between extroversion and leadership; 72 per cent of the results are positive, and 85 per cent of the 43 significant results are positive. The non-chance character of this association is suggested by the fact that 33 per cent of the results are both significant and positive. Finally, the sign test on the over-all trends for the independent studies reveals that the positive association is significant at the 0·01 level.

No single measure of extroversion is consistently related to leadership, with the possible exception of the relevant Guilford–Zimmerman scales. The median correlation is roughly 0·15, and the highest correlation reported is 0·42. Those individuals who tend to be selected as leaders are more sociable and outgoing, although the process of inferring such a characterization from the titles of the personality scales is a tenuous matter at best.

Dominance

Twelve studies (Bass, McGehee *et al.*, 1953; Bass, Wurster *et al.*, 1953; Borgatta, 1953; Carter and Nixon, 1949; Cattell and Stice, 1954; Cobb, 1952; Cowley, 1931; Dexter and Stein, 1955; Gordon, 1952; Moore, 1935; Stolper, 1953; Zeleny, 1939) have investigated whether dominance, as measured by personality scales, is associated with an individual's leadership status; 73 per cent of the results are positive, and 71 per cent of the 21 significant results are positive. The significance of the positive association is suggested by the fact that 42 per cent of the results are both positive and significant. No correlation reported exceeds 0·42, and the median correlation is roughly 0·20.

The two measures of dominance which yield the best evidence for a positive relationship between dominance and leadership are the Ascendence and Dominance scales from the Guilford–Zimmerman and 16 P.F., respectively. Particularly unsuccessful, however, have been the attempts to use Allport's Ascendence-Submission Test. Although the trend is not very strong, these data suggest that dominant or ascendent individuals have a greater chance of being designated leader.

Masculinity–femininity

There is a slight positive association between masculinity and leadership status; 71 per cent of the results are positive. Although 92 per cent of the 12 significant results are positive, significant results are found in only two of the nine studies. No single measure of masculinity relates to leadership in a consistently positive direction, and the correlations are uniformly low (Bass, Wurster *et al.*, 1953; Bell, 1952; Carter and Nixon, 1949; Cobb, 1952; Dexter and Stein, 1955; Gordon, 1952; Slater, 1955a; Stolper, 1953; Zeleny, 1939).

Conservatism

Only one measure of this factor displays any consistency in its association with leadership. The California *F* scale, a measure of authoritarian trends within the personality, has been used 10 times in the prediction of leadership. In each case, high-*F*, or authoritarian, individuals were found to be rated lower on leadership than nonauthoritarian individuals. In general, there is a negative association between conservatism and leadership. This is especially evident within the significant results, 17 out of 20 being in the negative direction (Bass and Coates, 1952; Bass, McGehee *et al.*, 1953; Bass, Wurster *et al.*, 1953; Carter and Nixon, 1949; Cattell and Stice, 1954; Cowley, 1931; Flemming, 1935; French, 1951; Hays, 1953; Haythorn *et al.*, 1956; Hollander, 1954; Hunter and Jordan, 1939; Martin, Gross and Darley, 1952; Masling, Greer and Gilmore, 1955; Slater, 1955a, 1955b; Stolper, 1953).

Interpersonal sensitivity

Few areas covered by this review contain so much research which builds upon prior results as this one. Unfortunately, few are so plagued by difficulties and contradictory evidence. The over-all trend of the results is positive; in 74 per cent of the cases leaders are found to be more accurate in estimating various aspects of the opinions of other group members than nonleaders. More impressive is the fact that 15 out of the 16 significant results indicate greater insight among leaders. Although two of the relevant studies report a zero correlation between interpersonal sensitivity and leadership, the trends of the results in the remaining 13 studies are positive. It would appear that while most researchers have been unable to obtain positive results which are statistically significant, they have obtained positive results with impressive consistency (Bell, 1952; Bell and Hall, 1954; Campbell, 1953; Chowdhry, 1948; Chowdhry and Newcomb, 1952; Gage and Exline, 1953; Green, 1948; Greer, Galanter, and Nordlie, 1954; Hites and Campbell, 1950; Nordlie, 1954; Smith, Jaffe, and Livingston, 1955; Sprunger, 1949; Stolper, 1953; Trapp, 1955; Zeleny, 1939).

According to Campbell (1955) one part of these results is open to a serious methodological criticism. When interpersonal sensitivity is measured in terms of an individual's accuracy in guessing how his peers will rate him on leadership, the correlation between interpersonal sensitivity and leadership is spuriously positive. If accuracy is measured by the discrepancy between an individual's actual leadership status and his guessed leadership status, and if, further, there is a tendency for most individuals to guess that they will be rated as having fairly high status, then the higher the actual status, the less the discrepancy and the higher the apparent interpersonal sensitivity. Thus, the positive correlation between actual leadership status and this accuracy score is a statistical artifact. The cogency of Campbell's criticism may be reflected in the fact that 14 of the 17 correlations reported between actual leadership status and accuracy about one's own leadership status are positive. Since the proportion of these questionable results which are positive (82 per cent) is higher than the proportion of results remaining (70 per cent) when these are eliminated, the validity of Campbell's criticism is at least suggested.

There are a number of problems of interpretation in this area of research. Gage and Cronbach (1955) have written a penetrating analysis of the difficulties in measuring interpersonal sensitivity. Among other things, they point out the importance of controlling the contribution of the individual's actual similarity to others in measuring his empathic ability. To conclude that the leader is more aware of group opinion is a different matter than to conclude that his opinion is more similar to the average opinion. More rigorous examination of the components of interpersonal sensitivity and their various associations with leadership remains a task for future research.

A second problem arises when one attempts to specify which of the many items of group opinion leaders may be expected to estimate more accurately than nonleaders. According to Chowdhry and Newcomb (Chowdhry, 1948; Chowdhry and Newcomb, 1952) the item cannot be too irrelevant to the group under study or the leader will not have adequate data on which to base his estimate. On the other hand, according to Newcomb (1954) the item cannot be too relevant or everyone will know the opinion of everyone else, and the difference will disappear. Chowdhry and Newcomb are proposing a range of relevance within which accuracy in estimating group opinion will be positively related to leadership status. In the absence of an objective definition of relevance, this proposition, for all its attractiveness on the common sense level, has remained an *ad hoc* instrument to be wielded against conflicting results. An examination of five studies (Campbell, 1953; Gage and Exline, 1953; Greer *et al.*, 1954; Hites and Campbell, 1950; Trapp, 1955) subsequent to Chowdhry and

Newcomb's reveals a low positive relationship between leadership and accuracy, but fluctuations in the magnitude of the association cannot be related to the relevance of the items because no valid scale of relevance can be applied across studies.

One additional fact emerges from the research in this area. Group members believe that their leaders are more aware of their opinions and feelings than the nonleaders of the group (Campbell, 1953; Sprunger, 1949; Zeleny, 1939). In summary, there appears to be a low but clearly positive relationship between interpersonal sensitivity and leadership. However, methodological and conceptual problems remain which can be resolved only by future research.

Techniques of measurement

Leadership status has been measured in at least four ways: by observer ratings, by peer ratings, by criterion measures, and by self-ratings. The latter technique has been used only once in these studies, but for the three remaining techniques it is possible to ask whether different results are obtained when different techniques are used.

Peer ratings and criterion measures rest upon the estimates of an individual's peers. Peer ratings are essentially descriptions of an individual's present leadership status, whereas criterion measures reflect the group's selection for future leadership. The peer ratings are assessments of the informal leadership structure, whereas criterion measures reflect the formal leadership structure. Numerous studies have noted that there is seldom complete correspondence between the designations which emerge from these two approaches. Observer ratings measure the present informal leadership structure of the group, but the evaluation is made by someone outside the group, in most cases by someone not personally involved in the future of the group, and, therefore, the observer is not implicitly locating himself on the status hierarchy by the act of rating. Finally, the observer is a member of a unique species of judging humanity, a social scientist, with special training and perhaps even special criteria of leadership.

In the cases of intelligence, adjustment, and extroversion vs. leadership, the number of results is large enough to permit detailed analysis of the relationships in terms of the different measuring techniques employed. Table 2 shows the percentage of results which are positive when the three techniques of measuring leadership are related to the personality factors of intelligence, adjustment, and extroversion. The base numbers are shown in parentheses.

Table 2

The Relationship Between Personality Factors and Leadership Using Three Different Techniques of Measuring Leadership

| | Percentage of results positive | | |
	Peer ratings	Criterion measures	Observer ratings
Intelligence	91	85	89
	(66)	(40)	(69)
Adjustment	97	76	76
	(31)	(87)	(41)
Extroversion	50	86	70
	(30)	(58)	(35)

The relationship between intelligence and leadership appears to be quite independent of the techniques of measuring leadership. On the other hand, there is a striking difference between the way adjustment and extroversion are related to leadership as the technique of measurement varies. Adjustment is positively related to peer ratings on leadership in 97 per cent of the cases, while it is positively related to criterion measures in only 76 per cent of the cases. Extroversion is not related to peer ratings at all, but it is consistently related to criterion measures. It appears that an individual's adjustment is more important in determining his informal leadership status (peer ratings) than his formal leadership status (criterion measures). In contrast, extroverted individuals are no more likely than introverted individuals to be rated as informal leaders by their peers, but they are quite likely to be selected as the formal leader for the future. Finally, scanning the third column of the table, it may be noted that intelligence is more consistently related to observer ratings than either adjustment or extroversion.

It does appear that different aspects of an individual's status are being measured by these techniques, and that these different aspects are not uniformly related to his personality. This crude division of the operations into peer ratings, criterion measures, and observer ratings suggests at least two dimensions of possible relevance. It may be important to differentiate between descriptions of present or informal leadership and choices for future or formal leadership; to rate on leadership and to select for leadership may engage quite different standards on the part of the group member. Secondly, it may be critical to know more about who is doing the judging, about the judge's training and his involvement in the group and in the outcome of the rating process itself.

Summary

A number of relationships between an individual's personality and his leadership status in groups appear to be well established. The positive relationships of intelligence, adjustment, and extroversion to leadership are highly significant. In addition, dominance, masculinity, and interpersonal sensitivity are found to be positively related to leadership, while conservatism is found to be negatively related to leadership. Finally, evidence has been presented to indicate that the relationship between personality factors and leadership varies with the technique of measuring leadership.

Popularity

The personality determinants of individual popularity have received less attention than the determinants of leadership. At the same time, however, the importance of personality factors has been more or less assumed, and the situational approach to popularity is not well developed. While less is known about the actual consistency with which an individual maintains his popularity in different groups and across changing conditions, there is reason to believe that popularity, no less than leadership, may be profitably examined in terms of both personality and situational factors.

Table 3 presents a summary of the relationships between seven aspects of personality and an individual's popularity in groups. Since this table is constructed in a manner parallel to Table 1, no detailed explanation of its form will be given.

Table 3
The Relationship Between Personality Factors and Popularity

Personality factors	No. of studies	No. of results	Positive			Negative			Zero ?N.S. (g, h)	Positive % (i)	% of Sig. (j)	% Sig. and in dir. of trend (k)
			Sig. (a)	N.S. (b)	Unt. (c)	Sig. (d)	N.S. (e)	Unt. (f)				
Intelligence	13	38	6	23	0	1	6	0	2	81 (36)	86 (7)	17 (36)
Adjustment	18	78	15	34	5	0	19	0	5	74 (73)	100 (15)	21 (73)
Extroversion	13	46	9	13	9	1	5	0	9	84 (37)	90 (10)	24 (37)
Dominance	6	9	0	5	0	2	1	0	1	63 (8)	0 (2)	0 (9)
Masculinity	4	8	0	5	0	0	3	0	0	63 (8)	— (0)	0 (8)
Conservatism	11	18	3	7	1	2	2	0	3	73 (15)	60 (5)	18 (17)
Sensitivity	11	38	6	16	0	1	13	0	2	61 (36)	86 (7)	16 (38)

Intelligence

Thirteen studies (Bass, Wurster *et al.*, 1953; Bonney, Hoblit, and Dreyer, 1953; Borgatta, 1953; Burks, 1937; Cronbach, 1950; Fiedler *et al.*, 1957; French and Mensh, 1948; Kelly, 1957; Mill, 1953; Reilly, 1947; Riggs, 1953; Shapiro, 1953; Slater, 1955a) have related an individual's intelligence to his popularity. An examination of the 38 results shows that 81 per cent are positive and 86 per cent of the seven significant results are positive; 17 per cent of the results are both positive and significant. The maximum correlation obtained is 0·37, and the median correlation is no higher than 0·10.

College grades are more strongly related to popularity than any other measure of intelligence. In contrast, it may be remembered that grades were less strongly related to leadership than other measures of intelligence. In general, there appears to be a tendency for intelligent individuals to be more popular.

Adjustment

All of the 15 significant results relating an individual's personal adjustment to his popularity are in the positive direction, but when the insignificant and untested results are included, the proportion falls to 74 per cent. Although several of the correlations reported are over 0·50, the median is close to 0·10 (Bass, Wurster *et al.*, 1953; Bonney *et al.*, 1953; Borgatta, 1953; Burks, 1938; Cattell, 1934; Cohen, 1954; Cronbach, 1950; Fiedler *et al.*, 1957; French and Mensh, 1948; Guthrie, 1956; Kelly, 1957; Martin *et al.*, 1952; Mill, 1952, 1953; Shapiro, 1953; Slater, 1955a; Tagiuri, 1952).

No single measure of adjustment is convincingly related to popularity, with one exception (Guthrie, 1956), an opinion survey designed to measure 'satisfactory personal habits'. There is some indication in these data that more popular persons are better adjusted.

Extroversion

When the separate results within each study are pooled and the trend over independent studies is assessed, it is found that 11 of the 12 trends are in the positive direction. Further indication that extroversion is positively associated with popularity comes from the 46 separate results; 84 per cent of the results and 90 per cent of the significant results are positive.

The scales measuring extroversion on the 16 P.F. are better predictors of popularity than the corresponding scales on the Guilford–Zimmerman, and ratings on extroversion are more highly related to popularity than either. The highly chosen, popular individual emerges from these studies as a sociable, surgent, and emotionally labile person (Bass, Wurster *et al.*, 1953; Bonney *et al.*, 1953; Borgatta, 1953; Burks, 1938; Cattell, 1934; Cronbach, 1950; French and Mensh, 1948; Kelly, 1957; Lemann and Solomon, 1952; Mill, 1952, 1953; Shapiro, 1953; Slater, 1955a).

Dominance

On the basis of nine contradictory results little can be said about the relationship between dominance and popularity. The trend is positive, but the two significant results are negative (Bass, Wurster *et al.*, 1953; Bonney *et al.*, 1953; Borgatta, 1953; Kelly, 1957; Lemann and Solomon, 1952; Shapiro, 1953).

Masculinity–femininity

None of the attempts to relate masculinity to popularity have yielded significant results, and the trend, though positive, is weak (Bass and Wurster, 1953a; Mill, 1953; Shapiro, 1953; Slater, 1955a).

Conservatism

Conservatism is positively associated with popularity in 73 per cent of the results. More popular individuals tend to be more conservative, conventional, or authoritarian (Bass, Wurster *et al.*, 1953; Bonney *et al.*, 1953; French and Mensh, 1948; Hays, 1953; Kelly, 1957; Martin *et al.*, 1952; Masling *et al.*, 1955; Rohde, 1951; Shapiro, 1953; Slater, 1955a).

Interpersonal sensitivity

The relationship between empathy or interpersonal sensitivity and popularity has been investigated in 11 studies (Ausubel, 1955; Ausubel and Schiff, 1955; Gage and Exline, 1953; Greer *et al.*, 1954; Lemann and Solomon, 1952; Nordlie, 1954; Norman, 1953; Singer, 1951; Taylor, 1956; Trapp, 1955; Van Zelst, 1953), but the criticisms applied to the studies of empathy and leadership are equally relevant to this body of research. Although 61 per cent of the results are positive, this summary statistic must be examined more carefully.

If Campbell's (1955) criticism is valid, it is improper to relate an individual's popularity to his awareness of that popularity, using the latter as the measure of interpersonal sensitivity. Since the accuracy score is based in part on the person's actual status, this produces spuriously positive correlations. Eliminating the results to which Campbell's criticism would be directed, the proportion of positive results among those remaining is only slightly over 50 per cent. Until the possibility can be discounted that a number of spurious results are embedded in this body of data, the direction of this relationship cannot be estimated with safety.

Summary

Extroversion, intelligence, adjustment, and conservatism are found to be positively related to popularity. The research to date, for various reasons, provides no definite answer to the question of how dominance, masculinity, and interpersonal sensitivity are related to popularity. [. . .]

References

ARBOUS, A. G., and MAREE, J. (1951), 'Contribution of two group discussion techniques to a validated test battery', *Occupational Psychol.*, vol. 25, pp. 73–89.

AUSUBEL, D. P. (1955), 'Sociempathy as a function of sociometric status in an adolescent group', *Human Relations*, vol. 8, pp. 75–84.

AUSUBEL, D. P., and SCHIFF, H. M. (1955), 'Some intrapersonal and interpersonal determinants of individual differences in sociempathic ability among adolescents', *Journal of Social Psychology*, vol. 41, pp. 39–56.

BALES, R. F. (1950), *Interaction Process Analysis: A Method for the Study of Small Groups*, Addison-Wesley.

BASS, B. M. (1951), 'Situational tests: II. Leaderless group discussion variables', *Educational and Psychological Measurement*, vol. 2, pp. 196–207.

BASS, B. M. (1954), 'The leaderless group discussion', *Psychological Bulletin*, vol. 51, pp. 465–92.

BASS, B. M., and COATES, C. H. (1952), *Situational and Personality Factors in Leadership in ROTC*. Unpublished manuscript, Louisiana State University.

BASS, B. M., MCGEHEE, C. R., HAWKINS, W. C., YOUNG, P. C., and GEBEL, A. S. (1953), 'Personality variables related to leaderless group discussion behavior', *Journal of Abnormal and Social Psychology*, vol. 48, pp. 120–8.

BASS, B. M., and WURSTER, C. R. (1953a), 'Effects of company rank on LGD performance of oil refinery supervisors', *Journal of Applied Psychology*, vol. 37, pp. 100–4.

BASS, B. M., and WURSTER, C. R. (1953b), 'Effects of the nature of the problem on LGD performance of oil refinery supervisors', *Journal of Applied Psychology*, vol. 37, pp. 96–9.

BASS, B. M., WURSTER, C. R., DOLL, P. A., and CLAIR, D. J. (1953), 'Situational and personality factors in leadership among sorority women', *Psychological Monograph*, vol. 67, no. 16 (whole no. 366).

BELL, G. B. (1952), *The Relationship between Leadership and Empathy*. Unpublished doctoral dissertation, Northwestern University.

BELL, G. B., and HALL, H. E. (1954), 'The relationship between leadership and empathy', *Journal of Abnormal and Social Psychology*, vol. 49, pp. 156–7.

BONNEY, M. E., HOBLIT, R. E., and DREYER, A. H. (1953), 'A study of some factors related to sociometric status in a men's dormitory', *Sociometry*, vol. 16, pp. 287–301.

BORGATTA, E. F. (1953), *Project 1*. Unpublished manuscript, Harvard University.

BORGATTA, E. F. (1954), 'Analysis of social interaction and sociometric perception', *Sociometry*, vol. 17, pp. 7–31.

BURKS, F. W. (1937), 'The relation of social intelligence test scores to ratings of social traits', *Journal of Social Psychology*, vol. 8, pp. 146–53.

BURKS, F. W. (1938), 'Some factors relating to social success in college', *Journal of Social Psychology*, vol. 9, pp. 125–40.

CAMPBELL, D. T. (1953), *A Study of Leadership among Submarine Officers*. Ohio State University Research Foundation.

CAMPBELL, D. T. (1955), 'An error in some demonstrations of the superior social perceptiveness of leaders', *Journal of Abnormal and Social Psychology*, vol. 51, pp. 694–5.

CARTER, L. F., and NIXON, M. (1949), 'Ability, perceptual, personality, and interest factors associated with different criteria of leadership', *Journal of Psychology*, vol. 27, pp. 377–88.

CATTELL, R. B. (1934), 'Friends and enemies: A psychological study of character and temperament', *Character and Personality*, vol. 3, pp. 55–63.

CATTELL, R. B. (1946), *Description and Measurement of Personality*, World Book.

Personality

CATTELL, R. B. (1956), 'Second-order personality factors in the questionnaire realm', *Journal of Consulting Psychology*, vol. 20, pp. 411–18.

CATTELL, R. B. (1957), *Personality and Motivation Structure and Measurement*, World Book.

CATTELL, R. B., SAUNDERS, D. R., and STICE, G. F. (1951), *The 16 P.F. Questionnaire*, Institute of Personality and Ability Testing, Illinois.

CATTELL, R. B., and STICE, G. F. (1954). 'Four formulae for selecting leaders on the basis of personality', *Human Relations*, vol. 7, pp. 493–507.

CHOWDHRY, K. (1948), *Leaders and their Ability to Evaluate Group Opinions*. Unpublished doctoral dissertation, University of Michigan.

CHOWDHRY, K., and NEWCOMB, T. M. (1952), 'The relative abilities of leaders and nonleaders to estimate opinions of their own groups'. *Journal of Abnormal and Social Psychology*, vol. 47, pp. 51–7.

COBB, K. (1952), 'Measuring leadership in college women by free association', *Journal of Abnormal and Social Psychology*, vol. 47, pp. 126–8.

COHEN, A. R. (1954), *Personality and Sociometric Choice*. Unpublished manuscript, University of Michigan.

COWLEY, W. H. (1931), 'The traits of face-to-face leaders'. *Journal of Abnormal and Social Psychology*, vol. 26, pp. 304–13.

CRONBACH, L. J. (1950), 'Studies of the group Rorschach in relation to success in the college of the University of Chicago', *Journal of Educational Psychology*, vol. 41, pp. 65–82.

DEXTER, E. S., and STEIN, B. (1955), 'The measurement of leadership in white and negro women students', *Journal of Abnormal and Social Psychology*, vol. 51, pp. 219–21.

DUNKERLY, M. D. (1940), 'A statistical study of leadership among college women', *Studies in Psychology and Psychiatry*, vol. 4, pp. 1–65.

EYSENCK, H. J. (1953), *The Structure of Human Personality*, Methuen.

FIEDLER, F. E., DOYLE, J. S., JONES, R. E., and HUTCHINS, E. B. (1957), *The Measurement of Personality Adjustment and Personality Change in Non-clinical Populations*, Group Effectiveness Research Laboratory, University of Illinois.

FLEMMING, E. G. (1935), 'A factor analysis of the personality of high school leaders', *Journal of Applied Psychology*, vol. 19, pp. 596–605.

FRENCH, J. R. P. (1951), 'Group productivity', in H. Guetzkow (ed.), *Groups, Leadership, and Men: Research in Human Relations*, Carnegie Press, pp. 44–54.

FRENCH, J. W. (1953), *The Description of Personality Measurements in Terms of Rotated Factors*, Educational Testing Service, New Jersey.

FRENCH, R. L., and MENSH, I. N. (1948), 'Some relationships between interpersonal judgment and sociometric status in a college group', *Sociometry*, vol. 11, pp. 335–45.

GAGE, N. L., and CRONBACH, L. J. (1955), 'Conceptual and methodological problems in interpersonal perception', *Psychological Review*, vol. 62, pp. 411–22.

GAGE, N. L., and EXLINE, R. V. (1953), 'Social perception and effectiveness in discussion groups', *Human Relations*, vol. 6, pp. 381–96.

GIBB, C. A. (1949), *The Emergence of Leadership in Small Temporary Groups of Men*. Unpublished doctoral dissertation, University of Illinois.

GIBB, C. A. (1950), 'The research background of an interactional theory of leadership', *Australian Journal of Psychology*, vol. 2, pp. 19–42.

GIBB, C. A. (1954), 'Leadership', in G. Lindzey (ed.), *Handbook of Social Psychology*, Addison-Wesley. pp. 877–920.

GORDON, L. V. (1952), 'Personal factors in leadership', *Journal of Social Psychology*, vol. 36, pp. 245–8.

GOWAN, J. C. (1955), 'Relationship between leadership and personality factors', *Journal of Educational Research*, vol. 48, pp. 623–7.

GREEN, G. H. (1948), 'Insight and group adjustment', *Journal of Abnormal and Social Psychology*, vol. 43, pp. 49–61.

GREEN, N. E. (1950), 'Verbal intelligence and effectiveness of participation in group discussion', *Journal of Educational Psychology*, vol. 41, pp. 440–45.

GREER, F. L., GALANTER, E. H., and NORDLIE, P. G. (1954), 'Interpersonal knowledge and individual and group effectiveness', *Journal of Abnormal and Social Psychology*, vol. 49, pp. 411–14.

GUTHRIE, M. R. (1956), 'The measurement of personal factors related to success of office workers', *Journal of Applied Psychology*, vol. 40, pp. 87–90.

HARE, A. P., BORGATTA, E. F., and BALES, R. F. (1955), *Small Groups: Studies in Social Interaction*, Knopf.

HAYS, D. G. (1953), *The F-scale as a Predictor of the Post-meeting Reactions of Small Group Members*. Unpublished manuscript, Harvard University.

HAYTHORN, W., COUCH, A. S., HAEFNER, D., LANGHAM, P., and CARTER, L. F. (1956), 'The behavior of authoritarian and equalitarian personalities in small groups', *Human Relations*, vol. 9, pp. 57–74.

HITES, R. W., and CAMPBELL, D. T. (1950), 'A test of the ability of fraternity leaders to estimate group opinion', *Journal of Social Psychology*, vol. 32, pp. 95–100.

HOLLANDER, E. P. (1954), 'Authoritarianism and leadership choice in a military setting', *Journal of Abnormal and Social Psychology*, vol. 49, pp. 365–70.

HOLTZMAN, W. H. (1952), 'Adjustment and leadership: A study of the Rorschach test'. *Journal of Social Psychology*, vol. 36, pp. 179–89.

HOWELL, C. E. (1942), 'Measurement of leadership', *Sociometry*, vol. 5, pp. 163–8.

HUNTER, E. C., and JORDAN, A. M. (1939), 'An analysis of qualities associated with leadership among college students', *Journal of Educational Psychology*, vol. 30, pp. 497–509.

JENKINS, W. O. (1947), 'A review of leadership studies with particular reference to military problems', *Psychological Bulletin*, vol. 44, pp. 54–79.

KELLY, E. L. (1957), *Medical School Project*. Unpublished manuscript, University of Michigan.

LEMANN, T. B., and SOLOMON, R. L. (1952), 'Group characteristics as revealed in sociometric patterns and personality ratings', *Sociometry*, vol. 15, pp. 7–90.

McCUEN, T. L. (1929), 'Leadership and intelligence', *Education*, vol. 50, pp. 89–95.

McGRATH, J. E. (1957), *A Framework for Integration of Small Group Research Studies*, Psychological Research Associates, Virginia.

MARTIN, W. E., GROSS, N., and DARLEY, J. G. (1952), 'Studies of group behavior: Leaders, followers, and isolates in small organized groups', *Journal of Abnormal and Social Psychology*, vol. 47, pp. 838–42.

MASLING, J., GREER, F. L., and GILMORE, R. (1955), 'Status, authoritarianism, and sociometric choice', *Journal of Social Psychology*, vol. 41, pp. 297–310.

MILL, C. R. (1952), *Personality Patterns of Socially Selected and Socially Rejected Male College Students*. Unpublished doctoral dissertation, Michigan State College.

MILL, C. R. (1953), 'Personality patterns of sociometrically selected and sociometrically rejected male college students', *Sociometry*, vol. 16, pp. 151–67.

MOORE, L. H. (1935), 'Leadership traits of college women', *Sociology and Social Research*, vol. 20, pp. 136–9.

NEWCOMB, T. M. (1954), Personal communication, cited in F. L. Greer, E. H. Galanter, and P. G. Nordlie 'Interpersonal knowledge and individual and group effectiveness', *Journal of Abnormal and Social Psychology*, vol. 49, p. 413.

NORDLIE, P. G. (1954), *The Performance of Small Military Groups as a Function of Intragroup Knowledge*. Unpublished master's thesis, University of Maryland.

NORMAN, R. D. (1953), 'The interrelationships among acceptance-rejection, self-other identity, insight into self, and realistic perception of others', *Journal of Social Psychology*, vol. 37, pp. 205–35.

REILLY, J. W., and ROBINSON, F. P. (1947), 'Studies of popularity in college: I. Can popularity of freshmen be predicted?' *Educational and Psychological Measurement*, vol. 7, pp. 67–72.

RICHARDSON, H. M., and HANAWALT, N. G. (1943), 'Leadership as related to Bernreuter personality measures: I. College leadership in extra-curricular activities', *Journal of Social Psychology*, vol. 17, pp. 237–49.

RICHARDSON, H. M. and HANAWALT, N. G. (1944), 'Leadership as related to the Bernreuter personality measures: III. Leadership among adult men in vocational and social activities', *Journal of Applied Psychology*, vol. 28, pp. 308–17.

RICHARDSON, H. M., and HANAWALT, N. G. (1952), 'Leadership as related to the Bernreuter personality measures: V. Leadership among adult women in social activities', *Journal of Social Psychology*, vol. 36, pp. 141–54.

RIGGS, M. M. (1953), 'An investigation of the nature and generality of three new personality variables: Part II. Related behavior', *Journal of Personality*, vol. 21, pp. 411–40.

ROHDE, K. (1951), 'The relation of authoritarianism of the aircrew member to his acceptance by the airplane commander', *American Psychologist*, vol. 6, p. 323.

ROSEBOROUGH, M. E. (1953), 'Experimental studies of small groups', *Psychological Bulletin*, vol. 50, pp. 275–303.

SHAPIRO, D. (1953), *Psychological Factors in Friendship Choice and Rejection*. Unpublished doctoral dissertation, University of Michigan.

SINGER, E. (1951), 'An investigation of some aspects of emphatic behavior', *American Psychologist*, vol. 6, pp. 309–10.

SLATER, P. E. (1955a), *Psychological Factors in Role Specialization*, Unpublished doctoral dissertation, Harvard University.

SLATER, P. E. (1955b), 'Role differentiation in small groups', *American Sociological Review*, vol. 20, pp. 300–310.

SMITH, A. J., JAFFE, J., and LIVINGSTON, D. G. (1955), 'Consonance of interpersonal perception and individual effectiveness', *Human Relations*, vol. 8, pp. 385–97.

SMITH, M., and KRUEGER, L. M. (1933), 'A brief summary of literature on leadership', *Bull. Sch. Educ. Indiana U.*, vol. 9, no. 4.

SPRUNGER, J. A. (1949), *The Relationship of Group Morale Estimates to other Measures of Group and Leader Effectiveness*, Unpublished master's thesis, Ohio State University.

STOGDILL, R. M. (1948), 'Personal factors associated with leadership: A survey of the literature', *Journal of Psychology*, vol. 25, pp. 35–71.

STOLPER, R. (1953), *An Investigation of some Hypotheses concerning Empathy*, Unpublished master's thesis, Louisiana State University.

STRODTBECK, F. L., and HARE, A. P. (1954), 'Bibliography of small group research: (From 1900 through 1953)', *Sociometry*, vol. 17, pp. 107–178.

SWARD, K. (1933), 'Temperament and direction of achievement', *Journal of Social Psychology*, vol. 4, pp. 406–29.

TAGIURI, R. (1952), 'Relational analysis: An extension of sociometric method with emphasis upon sociometric perception', *Sociometry*, vol. 15, pp. 91–104.

TAYLOR, F. K. (1956), 'Awareness of one's social appeal', *Human Relations*, vol. 9, pp. 47–56.

TRAPP, E. P. (1955), 'Leadership and popularity as a function of behavioral predictions', *Journal of Abnormal and Social Psychology*, vol. 51, pp. 452–7.

U.S. OFFICE OF STRATEGIC SERVICES (1948), *Assessment of Men*, Rinehart.

Personality

VAN ZELST, R. H. (1953), 'Validation evidence on the empathy test', *Educational and Psychological Measurement*, vol. 13, pp. 474–7.

WILLIAMSON, E. G., and HOYT, D. (1952), 'Measured personality characteristics of student leaders', *Educational and Psychological Measurement*, vol. 12, pp. 65–78.

WURSTER, C. R. and BASS, B. M. (1953), 'Situational tests: IV. Validity of leaderless group discussions among strangers', *Educational and Psychological Measurement*, vol. 13, pp. 122–32.

ZELENY, L. D. (1939), 'Characteristics of group leaders', *Sociology and Social Research*, vol. 24, pp. 140–9.

8   C. Clifford and T. S. Cohn

The Relationship between Leadership and Personality attributes perceived by Followers

C. Clifford and T. S. Cohn, 'The relationship between leadership and personality attributes perceived by followers', *Journal of Social Psychology*, vol. 64 (1964), pp. 57–64.

Introduction

Social scientists investigating leadership have shown an increasing consideration of group-members' perception [4, 7, 9, 10, 11, 12]. This is evident both in research oriented around leader behavior, *per se*, and in trait-oriented studies.

In some of the latter studies that utilize a perceptual approach, a trend can be detected toward repeating the earlier futile attempts to establish universal traits for leaders. For example, in spite of reference to 'specific social milieu', Jennings [4] hypothesizes that certain qualities, such as freedom from self-concern, may generalize to other sociogroups.

Van Dusen [10] attributes possible wide applicability to his results after analysing description of the 'good' leaders. He states that his study 'represents a technique for the eventual isolation of factors which may be common to leadership in "all" groups'. After reviewing the leadership literature, Gibb [2] makes the statement: 'There are indications certain traits . . . are frequently found to characterize leaders of various types, in a variety of situations.'

Despite these intuitive feelings that some sort of universal traits will be found, following their thinking through to a logical conclusion would indicate the contrary. If the leadership role is determined by the group-members' perceptions, then as the leader role varies there should be a corresponding change in group-members' perceptions. There is some reason to believe that a limited range of leader roles has been investigated, which could account for the discoveries of apparently common traits among different groups.

The present study was an attempt to vary the leader roles to a greater extent than done before and to relate them to concomitant variations in group-members' perceptions of the individual elected to fill these roles.

The hypotheses were formulated as follows:

1. Leadership is a function of the personal attributes of the leader as perceived by the followers.

2. As the situation changes, the perceived personal attributes of the individual selected for the leader role will change.

Subjects

Seventy-nine boys and girls, in a summer camp, ranging in age from 8 to 13, composed the sample. They were organized into twelve groups determined by the camp procedure of assigning campers of the same age and sex to a cabin. They spent four weeks together. The majority of the children were from the upper-middle socioeconomic group.

Procedure

To measure perceived personality attributes of leaders, a questionnaire asking 'Who is best?' on twelve items (see Table 1) was

Table 1

The Questionnaire

Name.......................... *Observer*........................ *Date* ....

1. Which kid gives orders best?
2. Which kid has the best ideas?
3. Who is the smartest kid in the cabin?
4. Who is the friendliest kid?
5. Which kid is liked the most in the cabin?
6. Who is the best baseball player? (*boys only*)
   Who is the best housekeeper in the cabin? (*girls only*)
7. Which kid is best at knowing how the other kids feel?
8. Who is the best looking kid in the cabin?
9. Who is best at sports?
10. Who is the best swimmer?
11. Who can get the others to do good things?
12. Who can get the others to do bad things?

---

administered in private to each camper seventeen days after camp started. Nine elections by secret ballot in various camp situations were later obtained during the four-week period. For each election, enough time had elapsed so that the election could be based on actual performance. Kendall's tau [5], calculated on the IBM 650, was used to determine the relationship between each perceived personality attribute and each leadership index.

Results and Discussion

Eleven of the twelve attributes and seven of the nine elections (one item and two elections pertained to the sex variable alone) were intercorrelated, and 26 per cent ($n = 20$) of the taus ($n = 77$) computed were significant beyond the 0·05 level (see Table 2). These results support the hypothesis that leadership is correlated with the personal attributes of the leader as perceived by the followers.

For the total group, there was only one duplication in the 'patterns' of perceived attributes required in various roles. This finding supports the second hypothesis that, as the situation changes, the perceived personal attributes of an individual selected for the leader role will change. For example, the social-chairman role was similar to the rest-monitor role in that there were no perceived attributes in relation to either role for the total group, in spite of the statistically significant relationship of the perceived attribute of 'best ideas' to the social-chairman role and the perceived attributes of 'smartest' and 'best looking' to the rest-monitor role for the girls. However, as reported in the research cited earlier, there was some overlapping of role requirements with similar situations. 'Best ideas' was related to four of the seven roles for the total group, and the perceived attributes of 'best at giving orders' and 'best at getting others to do good things' were related to three each.

In contrast to this slight generalization of attributes, the perceived attribute of 'best at knowing how the others feel', which has been described as a prerequisite for the leadership role by Chowdry and Newcomb [1], was related to only one role – that of the planner.

This variability in the role requirements suggests support for

Table 2

Taus for Total Group

Attribute	Planner	Banquet chairman	Rest monitor	Wish-loader	Swimming captain	Arts and crafts	Reporter
Orders	0·28**	0·21*	-0·12	0·11	0·09	0·35**	0·11
Ideas	0·38**	0·26**	0·07	0·13	0·14	0·18*	0·23*
Smart	0·24*	0·05	0·16	0·13	0·07	0·14	0·39**
Friendly	0·23*	0·19*	-0·02	0·04	0·06	0·16	-0·10
Liked	0·23*	0·26	-0·07	-0·11	0·12	0·13	-0·12
Empathy[1]	0·44**	-0·03	-0·07	0·15	0·01	0·09	0·14
Looks	0·13	0·14	0·18	-0·02	0·04	0·12	0·31**
Sports	0·14	0·19*	0·10	-0·12	0·03	0·45	-0·01
Swimming	-0·10	0·07	0·05	-0·05	0·37**	0·09	0·25*
Good influence	0·31**	0·03	0·08	0·18	0·19*	0·27**	0·10
Bad influence	-0·07	-0·04	-0·11	0·01	-0·01	-0·16	-0·13

* Significant beyond 0·05 level.

** Significant beyond 0·01 level.

1. From the question: 'Which kid is best at knowing how the other kids feel?'

Sanford's [8] assertions that the followers may choose a functionally competent leader when the group goal involves a task requiring competence, but a warm, approving leader when competence is not essential.

In this study, situations in which there were frequent planning and directions of group action required perceived functional competence. For example, the planner and the arts-and-crafts roles, in which both daily planning and daily responsibility for group action were required, are related to 'best at giving orders', 'best ideas', and 'best at getting others to do good things'. Emphasis on functional competence was notable, also, in the swimming-captain's role, in which the pattern of required perceived attributes consisted of 'best swimmer' and 'best at getting others to do things'.

With decreasing 'group task orientation' as exemplified by the reporter role, and increasing 'social orientation' as exemplified by the banquet-chairman role, the perceived role requirements changed from 'giving orders' or 'getting others to do good things' to a pattern including attributes specific to the role alone or indicating such pre-eminence as 'best looking', 'smartest', or generally 'good at sports'.

Finally, in situations which were purely social in nature (or 'flunky', as the rest monitor might be dubbed), we find either no perceived attributes statistically significant or idiosyncratic factors operating.

The results, also, suggest an answer to the question asked by Lippitt et al. [6]: 'Why do certain members with high attributed power demonstrate low manifest power?' The findings in our study indicate that the definition of Lippitt et al. that attributed power in terms of group-members' perceptions of 'who can get others to do things' is too limited. As an example, in the planner role, 'knowing best how the others feel' may be a better indicator of who may gain the leader role than the perceived attribute of 'best at getting others to do things', which was not related alone – or at all, in some roles – to manifest power as indicated by elections.

Although the boys and girls agree on parts of the requirements for four roles – the planner, arts-and-crafts, swimming, and reporter roles – there are more sex differences than similarities (see

185

Table 3
Taus for the Boys

Attribute	Planner	Banquet chairman	Rest monitor	Wish-loader	Swimming captain	Arts and crafts	Reporter	Baseball
Orders	0·23	0·10	−0·16	−0·05	0·21	0·30*	0·15	0·47*
Ideas	0·20	0·16	−0·04	−0·02	0·21	0·05	0·19	0·01
Smart	0·04	−0·05	0·06	0·02	0·22	0·08	0·48**	0·01
Friendly	0·34*	0·04	0·10	−0·03	0·20	0·05	−0·40*	0·25
Liked	0·35*	0·21	−0·01	−0·24*	0·21	0·22	−0·25	0·51**
Empathy	0·32*	0·02	−0·16	0·10	0·13	0·16	−0·04	0·03
Looks	0·18	0·26*	0·07	0·03	0·17	0·05	0·54**	0·17
Sports	0·09	0·09	0·20	−0·28*	0·01	0·05	−0·15	0·29
Swimming	−0·31*	0·06	−0·23	0·06	0·31*	0·03	0·20	0·09
Good influence	0·27	−0·09	0·00	0·16	0·36*	0·29*	0·10	0·12
Bad influence	−0·05	−0·12	−0·03	0·01	−0·18	−0·21	−0·03	−0·14
Baseball	0·02	0·19	0·20	−0·22	0·05	0·05	0·02	0·34*

* Significant beyond 0·05 level.
** Significant beyond 0·01 level.

Table 4
Taus for the Girls

	Planner	Banquet chairman	Rest monitor	Swimming captain	Wish-loader	Reporter	Arts and crafts	House-keeping
Orders	0·34*	0·26	−0·08	−0·06	0·16	0·20	0·40*	0·35
Ideas	0·54**	0·29*	0·19	0·02	0·32*	0·26	0·48**	0·19
Smart	0·43**	0·20	0·32*	−0·13	0·09	0·31*	0·22	0·14
Friendly	0·17	0·33*	−0·13	−0·12	0·28	0·06	0·26	0·32
Liked	0·11	0·30*	−0·15	0·03	0·13	−0·03	0·00	0·14
Empathy	0·55**	−0·07	0·04	−0·12	0·24	0·19	0·03	0·33
Looks	0·08	−0·00	0·31*	−0·11	−0·08	0·28*	0·22	0·44
Sports	0·18	0·40**	−0·04	0·06	0·15	0·08	0·45**	0·37
Swimming	0·08	0·11	0·12	0·37*	−0·22	0·27*	0·03	0·17
Good influence	0·33*	0·16	0·17	−0·08	0·18	0·18	0·24	0·31
Bad influence	−0·11	0·04	−0·21	0·28*	0·04	−0·23	−0·11	−0·18
Housekeeping	−0·10	−0·06	0·15	−0·02	−0·04	0·12	0·26	0·37

* Significant beyond 0·05 level.
** Significant beyond 0·01 level.

Tables 3 and 4). The girls narrow their choices in contrast to the boys. The girls place more emphasis on functional competence in the planner's role, whereas – for the boys – 'liking' has something to do with election to this role. In addition, it is of interest to consider negative relationships for leadership among the boys. The boys elected to the social-activity role are poor at sports and are disliked; and the newspaper reporter might be smart and good looking, but is perceived as being unfriendly. This suggests again, that certain leader roles were 'unloaded' on some children and supports the notion that focal positions are not always desired positions. Perhaps some of the contradictions in research in this area may be a function of including in the same category individuals in desirable leader roles and individuals in undesirable leader roles.

Another additional finding is that, in accord with Hollander's and Webb's study [3], friendliness has little to do with elective leadership.

Summary

The hypothesis was advanced that there is a relationship between the leader role and perceived attributes and, as the situation changes, the perceived attributes required for the leader role will change. In a camp setting with seventy-nine children, perceptions of peer-group members on twelve attributes were ascertained. Sociometric questions indicating leadership and results of elections for nine different leader roles were obtained. Kendall's tau was used to determine the relationship between each perceived attribute and each elective position. The results supported the conclusion that leadership is – in part, at least – a function of personal attributes perceived by the followers. This means that personality variables may still play a part in understanding leadership. However, the problem should be rephrased in terms of personality variables required of a leader role in a specific situation which is in turn a function of the followers' perceptions.

References

1. CHOWDRY, K., and NEWCOMB, T. M. (1952), The relative abilities in leaders and nonleaders to estimate opinions of their own groups', *Journal of Abnormal and Social Psychology*, vol. 47, pp. 51–7.
2. GIBB, C. A. (1954), 'Leadership', in G. Lindzey, ed., *Handbook of Social Psychology: Vol. 2. Special Fields and Applications*, Addison-Wesley, pp. 877–920.
3. HOLLANDER, E. P., and WEBB, W. B. (1955), 'Leadership, followship and friendship: An analysis of peer nominations', *Journal of Abnormal and Social Psychology*, vol. 50, pp. 163–7.
4. JENNINGS, H. H. (1950), *Leadership and Isolation*, Longmans, Green.
5. KENDALL, M. G. (1948), *Rank Correlation Methods*, Griffin.
6. LIPPITT, R., POLANSKY, N., and ROSEN, S. (1952), 'The dynamics of power', *Human Relations*, vol. 5, pp. 37–64.
7. SANFORD, F. H. (1951), 'Leadership identification and acceptance', in H. Guetzkow, ed., *Groups, Leadership and Men*, Carnegie Press, pp. 158–76.
8. SANFORD, F. H. (1952), 'The follower's role in leadership phenomena', in G. E. Swanson, T. M. Newcomb, and E. L. Hartley, eds., *Readings in Social Psychology*, Holt, pp. 325–40.
9. SCOTT, E. L. (1956), 'Leadership and perceptions of organization', *Bureau of Education Research Monograph*, no. 82. Ohio State University.
10. VAN DUSEN, A. C. (1948), 'Measuring leadership ability', *Personnel Psychology*, vol. 1, pp. 67–79.
11. WILK, R. E. (1957), 'The self perceptions and the perceptions of others of adolescent leaders elected by their peers', *Dissertation Abstracts*, vol. 17, no. 9.
12. WILLIAMS, S. D., and LEAVITT, H. J. (1947), 'Group opinion as a predictor of military leadership', *Journal of Consulting Psychology*, vol. 11, pp. 283–92.

9 A. M. Rose

Alienation and Participation: A Comparison of Group Leaders and the 'Mass'

A. M. Rose, 'Alienation and participation: a comparison of group leaders and the "Mass"', *American Sociological Review*, vol. 27 (1962), pp. 834–8.

There have been many studies of leaders, but the great majority of them deal with these persons as individuals who have certain distinctive psychological characteristics that have caused them to be 'selected' as leaders. Leaders may also be seen as group functionaries who develop certain social characteristics as a result of the influence of the group which they lead and of their position in the group. This paper will seek to test a number of hypotheses about the characteristics of leaders that can be expected to occur because of their role as active participants in groups (Rose, 1954).

The effort was made to study as leaders the presidents of all of the statewide organizations in Minnesota in 1959 that carried on some kind of a program in relationship to the public. The list had been developed through several years of operation of the State Organization Service of the University of Minnesota, and included 151 organizations, so that the initial sample consisted of 151 presidents. These were sent questionnaires through the mails and, with one follow-up letter, 71 (or 47 per cent) responded. This proportion of return is not bad for busy people solicited through the mails, but it does not allow for generalization to the total sample or to the universe of American voluntary association presidents. Thus, this study of 71 organization presidents must be regarded as exploratory in character. While we cannot claim that non-respondents do not differ in some ways from respondents, it should be understood that all respondents are leaders of statewide organizations.

The leaders will be compared with a cross-section of the married population of the Twin Cities, selected by a random procedure from the city directories. Men and women were alternated in the cross-section sample. Those who failed to respond to mail solicitation were interviewed in their own homes, so that total response was 90 per cent (195 respondents out of 220 in the original sample). Differences are reported between the leaders and the cross-section only if they are large enough to be statistically significant at the 5 per cent level, except when noted as non-significant differences.

The Leaders and the General Population

Relatively speaking, the group leaders are of the élite. Seventy-five per cent of the group leaders, as compared to 25 per cent of the general population, have at least some college education. Among the group leaders, 52 per cent have professional or managerial occupations whereas in the general population the proportion is 12 per cent. When asked to rank themselves along a six-category continuum of class, 90 per cent of the group leaders, as compared to 55 per cent of the cross-section, ranked themselves as upper-uppers, lower-uppers or upper-middles. All of these differences are highly significant statistically. But they are not categorical differences: the numerical majority of the group leaders is closer to the averages for the general population than they are to the averages for the élite among the group leaders (except possibly in education). Still, groups are likely to select as leaders those who have the educational background, the vocational skills, and the status to make them effective leaders.

Participation itself tends to be a 'trait'. We hypothesize that the group leaders are also more participant than the general population in organizations other than those in which they are leaders. This is true for church membership, although the difference is not statistically significant: 91 per cent of the group leaders, as compared to 85 per cent of the general population, are members of churches. Group leaders are more likely to be members of a union or business group than are the individuals in our cross-section, and here the difference is statistically significant (54 compared to 36 per cent). Group leaders are also more likely to attend meetings of these groups: 28 per cent of the group leaders reported themselves as attending 13 or more meetings a

191

year of their occupational group, as compared to only 8 per cent of the general population.

Group leaders are also more participant in voluntary associations other than those in which they are leaders. Whereas 51 per cent of the group leaders were members of a social club or recreational organization, this was true of only 18 per cent of the cross-section. The difference is somewhat less, but still significant, for membership in social welfare or social reform organizations (24 compared to 14 per cent). Reflecting this participation were answers to a question asking 'How many evenings during the past month (30 days) have you spent with people who are *not* members of your immediate family?' Mentioning more than 10 evenings were 32 per cent of the group leaders and 20 per cent of the cross-section. Group leaders also claim to have more close friends than do persons in the general population. While indicating these various forms of group participation to a greater extent, group leaders are no different from the cross-section in the extent to which they feel they are non-conformists: 25 per cent of both samples say they 'enjoy being different from other people in (their) behavior'.

Another subjective or psychological reflection of social participation is 'need inviolateness', or the expression of need to avoid social contact or exposure. This was measured by a six-item scale. Only 13 per cent of the group leaders agreed with any one or more of these items, as compared to 28 per cent of the general population sample.

Social Integration

It is because of the facts listed in the three preceding paragraphs that we can consider group leaders as more socially integrated than the average persons in the general population sample. We hypothesize, further, that they are less alienated from their society in various subjective or psychological ways because of this social integration. In stating this hypothesis, we again emphasize that we are dealing with statistically significant differences in proportion, not with categorical or qualitative differences. We do not expect, nor do we find, that the general population is alienated or anomic. It is merely true, but nevertheless important to note, that the general population contains a statistically significantly larger proportion of alienated or anomic individuals.

A first approach in support of this hypothesis would be to ascertain if group leadership tends to give a person some sense of satisfaction with his power in the community. When asked, 'Do you think people like yourself should have more to say about the running of things in this country?' 5 per cent fewer of the group leaders than of the cross-section (45 compared to 40 per cent) answered in the affirmative. This is not a statistically significant difference. At the same time, group leaders are somewhat less likely than the general population to indicate that they are manipulated by a power élite: In response to the question 'To what extent do the people who run this country make you do things that you don't really want to do?' 9 per cent of the leaders, as compared to 22 per cent of the cross-section, said they felt this way more than 'once in a while'. While the difference is statistically significant, the proportions are not large. The same pattern emerges in response to the question 'How often do you feel that you are not given the chance to show what you can do?' 3 per cent of the group leaders answered 'most of the time', as compared to 8 per cent of the cross-section. The difference is not significant, and the proportions are small. Thus, in terms of sense of power in the community and feeling of freedom to take independent action, which form one axis of absence of alienation, not many of the two groups of citizens we are comparing exhibit such alienation. Group leaders feel somewhat more integrated into the social structure, but their difference from the cross-section of citizens is not great.

In another sense, however, the group leaders are much less alienated than is the general population. This is in regard to knowledge of how the social system works. Group leaders are constantly acquiring social knowledge, and using it to lead or control a segment of society, no matter how small or specialized. To prove this, we did not present respondents with a test of factual social knowledge, because an adequate test would have to be quite extensive, and because to a considerable degree *relevant* social knowledge differs from one person to another according to where he is placed in the social system. Rather, we utilized a seven-item scale designed to measure feelings of bewilderment and confusion. Differences in scores can be measured in a number of ways, but if we take all those who gave at least one answer indicating bewilderment or confusion, we get the largest number who may be said to feel this way. The proportion on this basis for group leaders was 24 per cent, while for the general population it was 48 per cent. The difference is highly significant statistically, and the proportions are large (although it should be recalled that our measure encourages large proportions by being based on agreement with any one of seven items). The same point can be made by comparing responses on a single, direct question. When asked 'How well do you feel you understand what is going on in the world today?' 88 per cent of the group leaders, as compared to 65 per cent of the general population, answered either 'very well' or 'fairly well'. Again, the difference is highly significant, and the proportion indicating lack of understanding ('not very well' or 'not well at all') is moderately high (35 per cent) in the general population.

One of the more familiar indices of alienation, which leadership in voluntary associations might be expected to counteract, is Leo Srole's five-item scale of anomie (Srole, 1956). As anticipated the group leaders are significantly less likely to give any indication of anomie than does the cross-section: Only 3 per cent of the group leaders agreed with any of the anomie items, as compared to 20 per cent of the cross-section. Even so, the percentage among the cross-section who indicate this slight degree of anomie is not large.

One of the long-noted manifestations of alienation is intergroup prejudice. Stouffer has shown that group leaders are more inclined to support civil liberties than is the general population (Stouffer, 1955), and we shall now see that they are also more inclined to support civil rights. On a three-item scale of social distance toward Negroes, 70 per cent of the group leaders showed willingness to associate with Negroes in at least two of the three respects, as compared to only 44 per cent of the general population. On a separate social distance item, 'Negroes should be put on separate jobs from whites'. 97 per cent of the group leaders disagreed, as did 77 per cent of the general population. On a series of items regarding Jews, group leaders showed themselves much less anti-Semitic than did the general population. On four items the percentage differences ranged from 16 to 25·6 per cent. Similarly, on one item regarding Catholics, leaders showed themselves somewhat less prejudiced, although the difference is less here, probably because the general population included a larger percentage of Catholics than did the leaders' sample. In response to the item, 'In general, Catholics should not be allowed to hold high political office', 89·6 per cent of the leaders disagreed, as compared to 72·8 per cent of the cross-section.

Satisfaction with Democracy

Another hypothesis concerning the effects of high group participation on the individual is that participation in voluntary associations provides a sense of satisfaction with democratic processes. This sense of satisfaction was measured along two dimensions: responsible action expected of a citizen in a democracy and belief in the responsiveness of government to the wishes of the people. To get at the action dimension, respondents were asked if they were registered to vote, how often they voted, and how systematically they read the front pages of the newspapers. In all three respects, group leaders were significantly more active than the general population. For example, when asked 'How often do you read the front page of a newspaper carefully?' only 1 per cent of the group leaders, as compared to 10 per cent of the cross-section, admitted they did this only 'once in a while'.

In two of the three questions used to tap attitudes as to whether American government is responsive to the wishes of the people, the differences between leaders and the general population were large and statistically significant; for the third question the difference was in the expected direction but not large enough to be significant.

1. When asked, 'To what extent do the people who run this country care about what ordinary people think or want?', those answering at least 'most of the time' were 90 per cent of the leaders and 57 per cent of the cross-section.
2. When asked, 'To what extent do the people who run this country have at heart the best interest of the United States', the proportions answering at least 'most of the time' were 88 per cent among the group leaders and 75 per cent of the cross-section.

3. When asked, 'How good a job does the government do in representing the interests of the American people?', those answering 'a fairly good job' or 'a very good job' were 87 per cent of the group leaders and 84 per cent of the general population. While this difference is not significant, it is to be noted that the general population here comes up to the high belief in responsiveness of government held by the group leaders, rather than the leaders falling to the relatively low level of the general population on the preceding two items. The lack of discrepancy here is especially interesting in view of the fact that the 'government' at the time of the survey was headed by President Eisenhower, and there was a significantly larger proportion of Republicans among the leaders than among the population cross-section.

Life Views

Thus far we have examined the 'traits' and attitudes of group leaders in so far as they relate to the social environment. Our general theory also anticipates that there are differential patterns between group leaders and the general population in how they view their own lives. To a significantly greater extent the group leaders are satisfied with their career or occupational choice: 69 per cent, compared to 52 per cent for the cross-section, would follow the same occupations if they 'could go back to age 18 and start over again'. On the other hand, leaders are significantly less likely to be satisfied with what they have achieved in life: In response to the question 'Do you think you have done the best you could have done with your life, considering the circumstances?' 83 per cent of the leaders, as compared to 97 per cent of the cross-section, answered either 'yes, entirely so' or 'yes, fairly much so'. Apparently, some group leaders are negative toward their achievements, but not toward their occupations. This mixed attitude toward personal achievement is reflected in answers to a general question concerning life satisfaction, 'In general, how satisfied are you with your life?' The proportion responding 'very satisfied' or 'fairly satisfied' is slightly greater among the group leaders, but not significantly so (82 per cent among the group leaders compared to 76 per cent among the general population).

The dissatisfaction with their achievements among some group leaders is apparently not due to a belief that they have suffered handicaps. In response to the question 'How difficult has your life been?' the proportion answering either 'not difficult at all' or 'not very difficult' is practically identical for the two samples (72 and 71 per cent, respectively). A free-response type of question did best in getting at the source of achievement-dissatisfaction among the group leaders: 'If you could change yourself over into any kind of person, what kind of person would you want to be?' The answers given more frequently by the leaders were that they wanted to be more aggressive, more active, better educated, and, specifically, better leaders. In other words, the achievement dissatisfactions of the leaders were precisely in the area of their group leadership, not their occupations.

Characteristic of their greater realism and lesser alienation, the group leaders have a clearer and more definite idea about these personal aspirations. In response to the question 'How clear an idea do you have as to what would be best for you?' the proportion responding 'very clear idea' or 'fairly clear idea' was 94 per cent among the group leaders as compared to 72 per cent among the general population. Similarly, in response to the question 'How sure are you that you know what the best way of living is?' 87 per cent of the leaders, compared to 77 per cent of the general population, said 'very sure' or 'fairly sure'. Another indication that group leaders are positively oriented to their leadership role is that they are significantly likely to say they would likely carry on their present activity when asked 'In general, what would you like to do when you are past 65 years old?' Group leaders are more likely to be decided as to what they plan to do when they are past 65 than is the general population; 79 per cent of the group leaders, as compared to 64 per cent of the cross-section, claim to be decided.

Interpretations

The findings of this study support certain interpretations of social phenomena which, while not original with this author, run contrary to the dominant interpretations of those phenomena. First, we have shown that group leaders are more likely to be socially integrated and less likely to be alienated from the society than the general population. We interpret this in terms of the very participation and activity of the group leaders in the groups of which they are leaders, rather than in terms of their individual personalities. Since this is a correlational rather than an experimental study, we cannot prove this interpretation, although all our findings are compatible with the interpretation.

Second, our findings do not indicate that the general population differs in kind from the group leaders in such manner as would permit us to call it an anomic 'mass'. There are differences between the two groups sufficiently large as to be statistically significant, and no doubt there is a significant minority of the general population which is alienated. But such persons are still a minority, and do not justify speaking of the population, in general, as anomic, alienated, or a 'mass'.[1] As all societies must be, in order to function and deserve the name of society, ours is sufficiently integrated so that most of the time its members are able accurately to predict what others will do under given conditions, in terms of their understanding of the cultural meanings and values. One is justified in characterizing American society, either now or in the latter half of the nineteenth century, as a mass society only in so far as it differs in degree, not in kind, from the more thoroughly integrated societies of preliterate peoples or of those of our own ancestors in the pre-industrial era.

Third, in accord with the preceding point, leaders or the 'élite' of our society are not completely distinguishable from 'the mass' in their monopoly of power or their absolute class differentiation, in contrast with the viewpoint expressed by Floyd Hunter (1952, 1959) and C. Wright Mills (1956). It is true that more of the leaders have more social power than is to be found among the average member of the general population and they have a higher average class position. But our findings are much more compatible with the interpretation that power is dispersed somewhat in the general population and that there is a wide range of class differentiation in the non-leadership general population. Also contrary to Hunter and Mills, there is no evidence in our data that the local leaders studied believe they are manipulated by a higher power élite (only 9 per cent of them said that 'people

1. These findings are in accord with a number of recent researchers on group participation and extended family contacts.

who run this country make you do things you don't really want to do'). And just as many of the local leaders as of the general population (25 per cent) said they 'enjoy being different from other people in (their) behavior'.

In sum, our interpretation of the data of this study is that group leaders differ only in degree and proportion, not in kind or absolutely, from the general population, and that what differences there are are due to the more active social participation of the leaders. Our findings cannot be regarded as definitive because of the limitations of our method, but they provide suggestive evidence against certain prevalent ideas about differences between leaders and 'the mass'.

References

HUNTER, F. (1952), *Community Power Structure*, University of North Carolina Press.

ROSE, A. M. (1954), 'A theory of the function of voluntary associations in contemporary social structure', *Theory and Method in the Social Sciences*, University of Minnesota Press, pp. 50–71.

SROLE, L. (1956), 'Social integration and certain corollaries', *American Sociological Review*, vol. 21, pp. 709–16.

STOUFFER, S. A. (1955), *Communism, Conformity and Civil Liberties*, Doubleday.

WRIGHT MILLS, C. (1956), *The Power Elite*, Oxford University Press.

Part Four Interaction Theory

Research findings lack much of their value until they have been incorporated in a theory which at the same time fits them and runs beyond them. Theory it is which casts up hypotheses for further research and propositions for trial application in situations of greater complexity and wider scope. The basic aim of science is theory, that is to say to find general explanations of natural events.

There is, at this time, no strong theory of leadership in the sense that explanations and predictions may be made from it to apply widely to many people in many groups in many places. On the other hand it is possible to meet Wolman's criteria for the acceptability of a scientific theory that it be a set of propositions free from internal contradiction and free from contradiction with data obtained by observation or experimentation. (See Wolman, 1965, p. 14.)

Gibb's 1947 statement of theory (Reading 10) which had a considerable history (see Reading 5 and Gibb, 1950) was little more than an empirical generalization derived from the many researches which preceded it and from generalizations already present in the literature but which had largely fallen out of sight in the immediate pre-war years. As so often happens in the history of science this statement achieved very considerable notice and influence principally because of its timeliness. It simply gave form to ideas which, though not new, had come to be understood by the many social scientists and others who had been concerned with leadership under conditions of war. Gibb's 1958 paper (Reading 11) has rather greater claims to state a theory of leadership in that the propositions are here more orderly and thinking is carried beyond empirical generalization. A system is devised which permits projection beyond known facts and suggests propositions which are capable of empirical test and verification – in essence that theory avers that:

1. People interact in groups to achieve personal satisfaction.

2. Leadership is part only of a broader system of role differentiation, directed to the satisfaction of personal needs.

3. The leader relation has both cognitive and affective components which together define a variety of forms of leadership and predict changes in these forms as time goes by and formal structures are consolidated.

Hemphill, whose work was contemporaneous with Gibb's and completely independent of it, and originally independent of Stogdill's too, came to a very similar position through very different procedures. A brief account of his research and its findings (Reading 12) is included here for its value in indicating the group dimensions Hemphill set up, and for its independent confirmation that leader behaviour and judgements of leadership quality vary with varying characteristics of the groups in which the leadership is reported.

Hollander may be said to have contributed to the development of interaction theory in a paper (Hollander, 1958) to which reference is made in Reading 18. It is a merit of Hollander's approach that it emphasizes the importance of expectancies in the determination of behaviour. Leader behaviour is no exception in that the leader retains his status to the extent that he meets the expectations of other active group members. Through the concept of idiosyncrasy credit Hollander

looks upon the leader's status as an accumulation of positive impressions from past interactions with other group members. In operational terms, they provide the basis for the leader's taking actions which would be seen to be nonconforming for other members of the group. The important point is that innovation in the face of situational demands is expected of the leader as a feature of his role. (Hollander, 1967, p. 439.)

However, the greatest advance in interaction theory in the sense of adapting it to give it wider application particularly in more complex situations has been made by Fiedler in what he has called a *Contingency Model of Leadership Effectiveness* (see Fiedler, 1964, 1967 and Reading 13). Basically this theory postulates that the effectiveness of a group is contingent upon the interaction between leadership style and the degree to which the group situation is favourable to the leader by providing him with influence over his group members. This theory suggests that group performance can be improved *either* by modifying leader behaviour *or* by modifying the group-task situation.

While Fiedler has operated in terms of two highly specialized measures of leadership style it is apparent to him and to others that the styles he identifies have much in common with consideration and structuring behaviour as these have been defined in the Ohio Leadership Studies (see Fleishman and Harris, Reading 22) and as they have found their way into much of the leadership literature. Considerate, relationship-oriented leaders are found to perform best in situations in which they have only moderate influence either because the task is relatively unstructured or because when the task is structured they are not well-liked. On the other hand task-oriented structuring leader behaviour is effective in situations which are highly favourable because the task is structured and leader-member relations are good, or in situations which are highly unfavourable because the task is unstructured and leader-member relations are poor. Fiedler (1967) himself has shown that the contingency model does fit a number of complex situations though it may require some modification when it is carried into the study of organizational management.

Finally in this section is included a comment, almost an aside, by two psychologists with practical experience but no history of professional participation in the development of a psychology of leadership. Reading 14, by Cooper and McGaugh, is interesting for the freshness of its approach as well as for what it accepts and what it rejects of the work in this field. The present excerpt is a fitting comment upon the selections included in this part in that it emphasizes the motivational quality of the leadership relation and in so doing recognizes a need to differentiate leadership and domination as Pigors had done in 1935. It bears a good deal of thinking about too that Cooper and McGaugh wish to incorporate both of these in a concept of leadership and propose to do so by recognizing both 'push' and 'pull'.

References

FIEDLER, F. E. (1964), 'A contingency model of leadership effectiveness', in L. Berkowitz, ed., *Advances in Experimental Social Psychology*, vol. 1, Academic Press, pp. 150–90.

FIEDLER, F. E. (1967), *A Theory of Leadership Effectiveness*, McGraw-Hill.

GIBB, C. A. (1950), 'The research background of an interactional theory of leadership', *Australian Journal of Psychology*, vol. 1, pp. 19–41.

HOLLANDER, E. P. (1958), 'Conformity, status and idiosyncrasy credit', *Psychological Review*, vol. 65, pp. 117–27.

HOLLANDER, E. P. (1967), *Principles and Methods of Social Psychology*, Oxford University Press.

WOLMAN, B. B. (1965), *Scientific Psychology*, Basic Books.

10   C. A. Gibb

The Principles and Traits of Leadership

Excerpts from C. A. Gibb, 'The principles and traits of leadership', *Journal of Abnormal and Social Psychology*, vol. 42 (1947), pp. 267–84.

[. . .] Leadership has usually been thought of as a specific attribute of personality, a personality trait, that some persons possess and others do not, or at least that some achieve in high degree and others scarcely at all. The search for leaders has often been directed toward finding those persons who have this trait well developed. The truth would seem, however, to be quite different. In fact, viewed in relation to the individual, leadership is not an attribute of the personality but a quality of his role within a particular and specified social system. Viewed in relation to the group, leadership is a quality of its structure. And, depending upon the definition of 'group', this particular quality may become a '*sine qua non*'. Without leadership, there is no focus about which a number of individuals may cluster to form a group. A group is here defined as two or more people in a state of social interaction. Group activity means that individuals are acting together in some fashion; that there is some order of the different lines of individual action. There is a division of labor within a group that is accepted by all members of the group. In a discussion group, for example, the speaker performs a task different from that of other members. Both he and the members act in expected ways, and yet their behavior may be collective. The coherence occurs because of the common understandings or cultural traditions as to how they should behave. Similarly, the concept of leadership as a cultural norm plays a considerable part in the emergence of a leader. And this would seem to be the significance of Warren's parenthetic statement [11] that 'leadership depends on attitudes and habits of dominance in certain individuals and submissive behavior in others.' It is not implied that these are instincts variously strong in some individuals and weak in others, but that these are accepted ways of behaving within the cultural framework and that therefore they tend to determine the field forces acting in a group situation.

Leadership Theory

This dynamic conception of groups composed of dynamic entities or personalities interacting will accord well with Lewin's notion [6] that the individual's characteristics and actions change under the varying influence of 'the social field'. It does not seem unreasonable to claim that groups have a capacity to propel to leadership one or more of their number; and, what is more, the choice of a specific individual for the leadership role will be more dependent upon the nature of the group and of its purpose than upon the personality of the individual; but it will be most dependent upon the relation between the personality and the group at any particular moment. That is to say, in Linton's terms, that the group choice of a leader will be determined by the status of individual members. This claim does not lose sight of the nature of the individuals who constitute the group, and it does not assert that any member may be propelled to leadership nor does it suggest that the social situation alone makes the leader. Leadership is both a function of the social situation and a function of personality, but it is a function of these two in interaction; no additive concept is adequate to explain the phenomenon. There is no justification for saying that personality qualities which make for leadership exist in a latent form when not being exercised in a social situation. Any qualities of personality common to leaders in varying situations may also exist in persons who never achieve leadership status. What might be called the attributes of leaders are abstracts from a total interactional situation and are qualities of a particular social role. In the absence of this kind of social situation the latent existence of the same pattern of qualities cannot be inferred. Again, this does not mean that there can be no potential leaders, but it does mean that the potentiality cannot be directly known any more than capacity can be known except as a back-inference from expressed ability.

Leadership is not usually an enduring role unless an organization is built up which enables an individual to retain the role after he ceases to be qualified for it. In this case leadership becomes domination or mere headship. In the absence of such an artificial restriction, the interaction within the group is very fluid and the momentary group leader is that person who is able to contribute most to progress toward the common goal. Ten men previously unknown to each other are set a common problem, such as transporting heavy radio equipment to the top of a steep cliff. In the initial stages they are ten individuals thinking of possible solutions. One may find a solution which he communicates to the others. Usually this establishes interaction. The ten now become one group and the group focus is the man (A) who offered the solution. He is the leader at the moment. He is in the position of influencing their behavior more than they influence his. He is in the role of initiator of group action, which at this point consists of discussion. If now his plan is accepted, the group goal changes. It has been the choice of a plan and for that phase A occupied the leadership role. The goal now, however, is the execution of the plan. Two things may happen. A, by virtue of a prestige he has acquired, may continue in the role of leader or he may find another individual (B) naturally taking over. The group problem is now more practical, and B may, by virtue of his different innate capacities or previous experiences, be better able to contribute to the group project. Leadership then passes naturally to B, and, if difficulties are met and a third man (C) offers a solution, the role may pass to him. On the other hand, it is possible that all of these individuals, A, B, and C, may find their retention of the leadership role very short lived and even momentary only because another member of the group, D, rises to a more permanent occupancy of the role by virtue of his ability to translate suggestions into working orders, and by virtue of his greater social effectiveness.

Observation of group behavior in this way strongly supports the contention that leadership is not an attribute of personality or of character. It is a social role, the successful adoption of which depends upon a complex of abilities and traits. But even more, the adoption of a leadership role is dependent upon the specific situation. The same individual in the same group may alternate between the role of leader and follower as the group goal changes. Most frequently the individual is propelled into a position of leadership by virtue of his capacity for interpersonal contribution in the specific situation. There is, however, a generic aspect to leadership as Du Vall [2] has pointed out. This is indicated by the fact that the person of all-round superiority is more frequently in situations in which he is able to make a contribution.

The first main point to be made, then, in leadership theory is that leadership is relative always to the situation. Men may come together and yet not constitute a group. Until the individuals of the aggregation are given a common object or goal, there will be no social interaction and consequently no group formation. Each may face an individual problem and achieve an individual solution. But when many face a common problem and one or more of the individual solutions is communicated to others then there is interaction, and, if that interaction is focused upon one or two individuals in the group, then he or they are leaders for the time being. Clearly, in order that such a situation may develop, it is necessary that there should be a problem, and that it should be such a problem as to afford an opportunity for the play of individual differences in its solution. The circumstances must be such as to require a choice. As Schneider [9] has pointed out, it is the social circumstances which make particular attributes of personality attributes of leadership. While the social circumstances are such as to demand the original formulation of a plan, inventing ability will be an attribute of personality determining the adoption of a leadership role. But, the plan having been formulated, the social circumstances then demand not invention but social effectiveness as an attribute of personality essential for the leadership role. And, unless the same individual possesses both attributes, the leadership passes from one to another. The situation determines which of many attributes of personality will be attributes of leadership at any given moment. That is why Pigors [8] observes that, 'whenever an obstacle physical or mental prevents the flow of action, the group welcomes any manifestation of individual difference that tends to resolve this uncertainty or to facilitate group action'.

Leadership, then, is always relative to the situation (a) to the extent that a certain kind of situation is required before the leadership relation will appear at all, and (b) in the sense that the particular set of social circumstances existing at the moment determines which attributes of personality will confer leadership status and consequently determines which members of a group will assume the leadership role, and which qualities of personality function to maintain the individual in that role. This was one of the things indicated by Thrasher's study of juvenile gangs in Chicago. Leadership seemed to be a quality that came out as the group moved about together – it was the result of the social situation. This is, in fact, the second principle of leadership theory. It is that individual accession to the leadership role is dependent upon the group goal and upon the capacity of the individual to contribute to the achievement of the goal. Pigors says, 'It is nonsense to talk of leadership in the abstract since no one can just lead without having a goal. Leadership is always *in* some sphere of interest, and *toward* some objective goal seen by leader and follower' [8].

Only in so far as the individual can contribute to group progress in the required direction has he any claim to a hearing, and, unless he can establish himself with his fellow members, he will not receive recognition as their leader. This is, of course, to raise the question whether the leader can exercise a creative influence upon the group's goals and activities or whether he can do no more than express and exemplify already accepted ideals and contribute to progress in the direction of an accepted goal perhaps by pin-pointing and clarifying a previously vague conception. Klineberg [4] suggests that a compromise is indicated in that 'the leader has great influence but only on certain groups under certain conditions. Change these or change him', he says, 'and the resulting behavior is markedly altered.' Schneider [9], on the other hand, claims that the 'new' history as written by Marx, Turner, Beard, and others, 'sees leaders as a product of the times and leadership as a function of the circumstances of the moment'. The problem seems to be indeterminate because there is no denying that the 'great men' of history have been responsible for changes in the social situation of which they were a part, but there is no way of telling to what extent these changes would have occurred anyway or under the leadership of another group-chosen personality.

The third characteristic of the leadership process to which attention may be drawn is that its basic psychology is that of social interaction. There can be no leadership in isolation, it is distinctly a quality of a group situation. There can be no leader without followers. An individual's intellectual quality may be very superior and his individual solution of a group problem may be excellent, but he is not a leader until his solution is communicated, and then not until other people are associated with him in giving expression to his ideas. Leader and follower must be united by common goals and aspirations and by a will to lead, on one side, and a will to follow, on the other, i.e. by a common acceptance of one another. From this it follows that the individual must have membership character in the group which makes him its leader, because leaders and followers are interdependent. This is the first of Brown's [1] 'field dynamical laws of leadership', and the first of Du Vall's [2] criteria of the leadership process. The leader must be a member of the group; he must share the group objectives and aspirations. Stated in other words, this principle of mutual interaction between the leaders and the group implies that the individual chosen leader must have certain qualities of personality which, derived as they are from his group-membership-character, confer upon him a certain social effectiveness and determine his acceptability.

Having group-membership-character, it is upon individual differences that one depends for election to leadership status. It is because there are individual differences of capacity and skill that one, and usually only one, of a group emerges having a pattern of qualifications superior to others for meeting present group needs. But these 'superior' persons must not be too different. Followers subordinate themselves not to an individual who is utterly different but to a member of their group who has superiority at this time and who is fundamentally the same as they are, and who at other times is prepared to be a follower just as they are. [. . .]

The determination of the role to be played by the individual is the group reaction to his interpersonal contribution. The close relation between leader and followers is therefore apparent.

The leader inevitably embodies many of the qualities of the followers. Any individual's personality at a given point in time reflects the field forces with which it is interacting. The personality which most adequately reflects those forces is the one most likely to be propelled to leadership. Thus it is that La Piere and Farnsworth [5] are led to make the point that because there is such close interaction between the leader and the led it is often difficult to determine just who affects whom and to what extent. For this reason it is possible for leadership to be nominal only. This possibility is emphasized by a carry-over of prestige from one point in time to another. The fact that individual A in our earlier example was intellectually quickest with a suggested solution of the group problem established him as a focus of attention in the minds of the others. Momentarily, at any rate, he became their leader and they became followers. A definite interactional pattern was established. A social–cultural evaluation was made of him by the others. That is precisely what is meant by prestige. Prestige is a distinction attaching to a person in the minds of others. It depends, as we have now seen, on the qualities ascribed to the individual by other members of the group. As Young points out, prestige is a special case of the point, 'that a man's personality reflects others' image and recognition of him. A leader's prestige rests upon the apperceptive background of the followers. The leader takes on the qualities which his adherents project on him' [12].

This, too, is Brown's [1] second 'field dynamical law of leadership', that the 'leader must represent a region of high potential in the social field', i.e. that he must have prestige and this he acquires by symbolizing the ideals of all members of the group. In some instances it may be said that prestige within a group is acquired by virtue of an external appointment or by virtue of a certain status in an institution which embraces that group, as in the case of a parish priest. In such a case the assumption of a leadership role is made easier, but it is still true that it will be retained only while the individual so appointed is able to symbolize the ideals of the group members. In other words, the personality thus 'made' leader must so reflect the field forces within the group with which it is interacting as to have had potential leadership status if membership without leadership could have been granted by the appointment.

Reviewing leadership theory one may say, then, that its three most important principles are, first, that leadership is always relative to the situation – relative, that is, in two senses; (a) that leadership flourishes only in a problem situation and (b) that the nature of the leadership role is determined by the goal of the group; and this is, in fact, the second principle of leadership, that it is always toward some objective goal. The third principle is that leadership is a process of mutual stimulation – a social interactional phenomenon in which the attitudes, ideals, and aspirations of the followers play as important a determining role as do the individuality and personality of the leader.

These principles lead us to accept Pigors' [8] definition of leadership as a 'process of mutual stimulation which, by the successful interplay of relevant individual differences controls human energy in the pursuit of a common cause'. And any person may be called a leader 'during the time when and in so far as, his will, feeling, and insight direct and control others in the pursuit of a cause which he presents.'

As Jennings says, 'the "why" of leadership appears not to reside in any personality trait considered singly, nor even in a constellation of related traits, but in the interpersonal contribution of which the individual becomes capable in a specific setting eliciting such contribution from him' [3], provided that the individual superiority is not so great as to preclude solidarity of purpose.

Such a theory of the leadership process excludes such group situations as those organized for professional tuition, expert advice, management, and the like, and excludes the concept of headship. When once the group activity has become dominated by an established and accepted organization, leadership tends to disappear. Even if this organization originally served the leadership role, any continuance of the organization as such, after the causal set of circumstances has ceased to exist, represents a transition to a process of domination or headship, where headship is regarded, as Warren [11] defined it, as 'a form of authority determined by caste, class or other factors than popular selection and acceptance', and where domination is defined by Pigors [8] as:

a process of social control in which accepted superiors assume a position of command and demand obedience from those who acknowledge themselves as inferiors in the social scale; and in which by the forcible assumption of authority and the accumulation of prestige a person (through a hierarchy of functionaries) regulates the activities of others for purposes of his own choosing.

The characteristics of this process of domination as distinct from that of leadership are that: (*a*) the position of headship is maintained through an organized system and not by the spontaneous recognition of the individual contribution to the group goal; (*b*) the group goal is arbitrarily chosen by the autocratic head in his own self-interest and is not internally determined; (*c*) there is not really *a group* at all, since there is no sense of shared feeling or joint action; and (*d*) there is in this process a wide social gap between the group members and the head, who strives to maintain this social distance as an aid to his coercion of the group through fear.

This concept of domination and headship is important because it is so different from that of leadership and because so much so-called leadership in industry, education, and in other social spheres is not leadership at all, but is simply domination. It is not, however, necessary that headship should preclude leadership. [. . .]

References

1. Brown, J. F. (1936), *Psychology and the Social Order*, McGraw-Hill.
2. Du Vall, E. W. (1943), *Personality and Social Group Work*, Associated Press.
3. Jennings, H. H. (1943), *Leadership and Isolation*, Longmans, Green.
4. Klineberg, O. (1940), *Social Psychology*, Holt.
5. La Piere and Farnsworth (1942), *Social Psychology*, McGraw-Hill, 2nd edn.
6. Lewin, K. (1935), *A Dynamic Theory of Personality*, McGraw-Hill.
7. Linton, R. (1945), *The Cultural Background of Personality*, Appleton-Century.
8. Pigors, P. (1935), *Leadership or Domination*, Harrap.
9. Schneider, J. (1937), 'Social class, historical circumstances and fame', *American Journal of Sociology*, vol. 43, pp. 37–56.
10. Schneider, J. (1937), 'The cultural situation as a condition of the achievement of fame', *American Sociological Review*, vol. 2, pp. 480–91.
11. Warren, H. C. (1934), *Dictionary of Psychology*, Houghton Mifflin.
12. Young, K. (1945), *Social Psychology*, Crofts, 2nd edn.

11   C. A. Gibb

An Interactional View of the Emergence of
Leadership

Excerpt from C. A. Gibb, 'An interactional view of the emergence of
leadership', *Australian Journal of Psychology*, vol. 10 (1958), pp. 101–10.

[. . .] Leadership may be best conceptualized as a group function.
Leadership emerges in a group as part of a more diffuse differentiation of roles by which group members more expeditiously achieve
group goals and satisfy their individual group-invested needs.
Leadership is a part of the problem-solving machinery of groups.
Modifying slightly Pigors' [10] definition, it may be said that
leadership is a concept applied to the structure of a group to
describe the situation when some personalities are so placed in the
group that their will, feeling, and insight are perceived to direct
and control others in the pursuit of common ends. Leaders in the
group are those persons who are perceived most frequently to perform those roles or functions which initiate and control behaviour
of others towards the achievement of group goals or sub-goals.
The implication of such a definition is that in any group there may
be, at any time, a *number* of leaders. This, of course, is so. There is
still a tendency among psychologists and sociologists to think of
every group as having *a* leader, though many will go so far as to
recognize that, as group goals change through time, a succession
of persons may occupy this office. Anybody who has worked with
traditionless laboratory groups, however, is well aware that un-
equivocal unipersonal leadership rarely, if ever, occurs. Many
members perform leader functions and the question as to who are
the leaders can be answered only by drawing an arbitrary line on
a frequency continuum. It may well be, of course, that not all
leader functions are equally important in terms of group movement towards group goal. In this case, the simple count is inappropriate, and weighting techniques are called for. There is no
doubt but that individual observers indulge in such weighting
subjectively, but no practicable objective system is yet available

to us. It is such a subjective weighting of the many leader functions which has given us the variety of definitions to be found in the literature. It has sometimes been suggested that the leader be regarded simply as the individual occupying a given office, but leadership is frequently apparent *before* group development has proceeded to the point of designated offices. Furthermore, it is a common occurrence, both in the laboratory and in real-life groups, that persons other than the office-holders are observed to initiate and control group action most frequently. In the case of minimal effectiveness of the office-holder, it may be said that this is definition of the leader in terms of the single function of meeting the culture-carried expectation that there will be one such officer in every group. Another suggestion has been that the leader is that individual upon whom the behaviour of group members is focused. But a disturbing influence in a group may be the focus of attention and we would not wish to designate him 'leader'. This may be regarded as definition in terms of a unifying function, though the degree of unity is minimal, and is no different from that which could be achieved by a purely fortuitous event in the environment. Yet another procedure – now generally called sociometric – regards the leader as that group member who is so chosen by his colleagues. In this case, the varying subjective emphases of the many functions become apparent. As the sociometric questions asked alter, even slightly, the role-emphasis, there is a significant shift of persons being most frequently designated. And there is a significant correlation between each of these perceptions of function and the recognition of leadership, if the latter be left undefined, or defined in terms of the exercise of influence over others.

The purpose of the foregoing remarks has been to reassert the proposition that leadership is a concept applied to the *interaction* of two or more persons. Any group is a system of interactions. The emergence of group structure is strictly a structure-in-interaction. By it each member is assigned a position within the system, and this position, or status, is an expression of his interactional relations with all other members. Thus, the particular role an individual member achieves within the group is determined both by the functional or role needs of the group-in-situation, and by the particular attributes of personality, ability, and skill, which differentiate him perceptually from other members of the group. Leadership is a function of personality. It is also a function of the social system. But more basically it is a function of these two in interaction.

Much of the confusion with which recent explanations of leadership have been endowed stems from this fact. Where persons constitute an interactive system and we concern ourselves with the perception – or better still, the cognition – of one by another as we do in discussing leadership, we must find, as Parsons [9] claims, that the other is both a person and a relation in the structure of the interactive system. Thus, to borrow his example, if I say that John is my friend, I am characterizing him as a participant in a system of social interaction in which I also am involved. The psychology of leadership is probably the first place in which we, as psychologists, are attempting to pin down and to study the dynamics of this relational meaning of persons to one another. It may, of course, be studied in other places. A valuable extension of this work will be into such relationships existing in the family system as are designated by our terms brotherhood, fatherhood, and motherhood, etc.

A major advantage of conceptualizing leadership as a property of interaction is placed in clear perspective by this quotation from Parsons [9, p. 16]:

It may first be pointed out that two interacting persons must be conceived to be objects to each other in *two primary* respects, and in a third respect which is, in a sense, derived from the first two. These are (1) cognitive perception and conceptualization, the answer to the question, *what the object is*, and (2) cathexis – attachment or aversion – the answer to the question of *what the object means* in an emotional sense. The third mode by which a person orients himself to an object is by evaluation – the integration of cognitive and cathectic meanings of the object to form a system, including the stability of such a system over time.

Much of the complexity of the concept 'leadership' has been due to the unavailability of this insight. The relation connoted by the idea 'leader' is evaluational, and, therefore, has both cognitive and cathectic components. In so far as structure-in-interaction is concerned, the essential feature of the cognitive component is perception of another individual's instrumentality in need satisfaction. It is this perception which confers power and status. From any individual participant's point of view those persons who, in this interactive system, can contribute most to the satisfaction of those needs which are system-related, are ascribed power and high status. Status hierarchy as described by the external observer represents a sum of such ascribed statuses inferred by the observer from the quality of the interactions which take place in his presence. In addition, as Sherif [12] has recently demonstrated, group-valued performance may also reflect status, though there would seem to be very definite limits to the phenomena he observes.

There has been much concern with types of leadership, usually differentiated in terms of the nature of the relation between leader and led. But, aside from one very interesting paper by Redl [11], the cathectic component has been very much neglected. A very rewarding job waiting to be done in this area is to catalogue in some way the variety of emotional relations possible in the interactive system, and then to attempt identification of those which may, by various criteria, be regarded as characteristic of the leadership relation. It seems that as a first attempt at this, and by way of illustration, it may be said that within common concepts of leadership at least two basic emotional qualities have been apparent. One of these is fear and the other is love, in the broad sense of this term. If each of these is thought of as varying in degree from little to much, four common forms of authority and influence are immediately identifiable. Where the cognitive component of the interaction involves the recognition of status-higher, and where the cathectic component of the interaction is characterized by a high degree of fear *and* a high degree of love, the emotional quality of the relation may now be said to be that of *awe* and the literary term for the quality of the entire interaction would be patriarchy. If the cognitive component remains unchanged, but the cathectic component entails a high degree of fear and little or no love, the quality of tyranny exists. Where both love and fear are minimal, and the status-higher person does not engender any emotional relationships with himself, the relationship may be characterized as organizational, meaning that the cognitive meaning this person has is a function only of his perceived relation to need–satisfaction. Where, finally, the relation entails love or attachment and little or no fear, the phrase 'ideal-leader' is frequently applied. Ordinarily, when we talk about leadership as a set of functions through which the group co-ordinates the activities of individuals, the entire question of cathexis, or meaning of the object in an emotional sense, may be irrelevant. But, if the time dimension is admitted to our thinking, then the cathection of the parties to the interaction to one another seems inevitable. It is a part of this theory then, that even if we consider only those autonomous groups in which the sources of all influence and control are intra-group (that is to say, if we ignore the most common of the real-life situations to which the term headship applies), even then, the concept of leadership embraces a wide variety of interactional relationships, all of which must be expected to have quite different effects in terms of group behaviour.

Further, it may be hypothesized that there is an inherent tendency for the leadership function to move from organization towards tyranny and from ideal leadership towards patriarchy. This hypothesis is offered without any deep conviction, but it does seem to be the result of the cultured-carried expectation of persisting organization. In the early stages of group development persons emerge in the organizational role by virtue of their control over problem-related resources. Or, they emerge as positively cathected leaders by virtue of their control over problem-related resources, and by virtue of the readiness we show to relate ourselves emotionally to others on the basis of first impressions. It was one of the interesting and surprising findings of the Illinois researches [Gibb, 6] on the emergence of leadership in small temporary groups of men that preferences expressed within a few minutes after strangers had met one another, and after very little interaction had occurred, were significantly correlated with leadership evaluations at the end of ten hours of interaction in the laboratory. In other words, it is contended that in auto-nomous groups where the sources of control and authority are all within the group itself, the first emergent structure-in-action to which the concept of leadership applies is that in which one, or a few, persons are perceived to control the resources for problem solution. Theoretically, one would expect this primary relation to have little or no cathectic component. However, because each person has a history of prior interaction, there is 'love-at-first-sight', or cathection-with-first-impression. As a result, the first observable emergent structure-in-interaction may have both cognitive and cathectic components and thus be a truly evaluative leadership relation. As interaction persists, organization or structure-in-interaction solidifies. This would seem to be largely a result of a cultural concept of stable organization shared by all group members. But, whatever its origin, structure-in-interaction undergoes definite differentiation. Now, the early congruence of the cognitive relation to the person controlling resources and the positive cathexis of that same person is reduced. Bales' [1] data lend themselves to this kind of interpretation and are consistent with this theory. Where he has sought to identify, in small groups of five, those persons most frequently contributing best ideas and guidance, and those persons best liked, he finds that there is a striking incompatibility of these two roles and that this incompatibility increases from one group meeting to the next. Carter's [2] findings, and our own [Gibb, 7], that independent observations of leadership are correlated with sociometric identifications of 'liked' persons only to the extent of about 0·4, also fit this hypothesis well. When, then, the culture-borne concept of stable organization is carried to the extent of formalization so that roles are assigned for a stated period of time, without reference to actual cognitive status evaluation, i.e. without reference to control over resources or to contributory strength in group problem solving, leadership becomes less functional and the office-holder is supported by organization rigidity rather than by the functional evaluations of his fellows-in-interaction. His leadership has now become headship, and the dynamics of the group will almost certainly have become complicated by the emergence of new organizers and new leaders thrown up by the complex of forces, which now includes, of course, the behaviour of the formal office-holders. These latter, who will have attached status symbolism to their offices, now move in the direction of coercion. Frequently this is done through the establishment of power cliques or bureaucracies; and fear relationships – or aversions at any rate – enter the interactive system, tending to give to the exercise of authority a tyrannical or patriarchal twist, depending upon the degree of positive emotional relationship.

This identification of two components of evaluation-in-interaction is not unrelated to Cattell's [4] differentiation between effective and maintenance functions in the group. Elaborating this differentiation, Cartwright and Zander [3, p. 541] offer, as examples of effective or goal achievement behaviours, such things as: 'initiates action', 'keeps members attention on the goal', 'clarifies the issue', 'develops a procedural plan' and 'makes expert information available'. Examples offered of behaviours that serve functions of group maintenance include 'keeps interpersonal relations pleasant', 'provides encouragement', 'gives the minority a chance to be heard', and 'increases the interdependence among members'. These lists suggest the hypothesis that the cognitive component, or perception of instrumentality in need satisfaction, tends to be weighted more heavily in evaluation when the ratio of effective synergy to maintenance synergy is greater. This hypothesis is congruent with observations we have made of experimental groups, that leadership activity (as we have thought of it) occurs most frequently when these groups are faced with a problem. This hypothesis is another way of stating Cartwright and Zander's expectation [3, p. 542] that goal achievement functions become more valuable to the group when it accepts an important goal, or when goal achievement is threatened. A corollary, which elicits less confidence, is that the cathectic component, or the emotional meaning of the other, tends to be weighted more heavily in evaluation when the ratio of effective synergy to maintenance synergy is smaller. Some supporting evidence for the corollary may be found. In therapy groups where there is not, as a rule, any clear-cut group goal, the emotional relationships of members to one another, and of the members to the therapist, become highly important to all members. The familiar phenomenon of transference in the clinical relation of therapist and patient is perhaps another instance. One may suggest that Jennings' [8] pioneering sociometric studies of leadership emphasized cathexis to the detriment of cognitive evaluation because she was dealing with situations in which maintenance synergy was a relatively high proportion of total synergy.

Another fact of leadership, with which an interactional theory is best equipped to deal, concerns the effect a leader can have on the dynamics of a group. At times, when an organized group is moving at a relatively slow pace, i.e. when effective synergy is low absolutely rather than relatively, a leader can have considerable effect provided that he remains within the framework of the general group goals. On the other hand, when a group is highly polarized and effective synergy is high, a leader may be powerless to divert its attention from its immediate object. Leadership means that leaders are perceived to contribute positively to the satisfaction of individual's group-invested needs. To the extent that one does this in a variety of situations, and over a span of time, he may remain a leader; when he fails to be thus evaluated he has been superseded; and he does so fail as soon as the followers perceive his needs and his goal to be divergent from their own.

The important aspects of this interactional theory are the following. First, groups are mechanisms for achieving individual satisfactions and, conversely, persons interact with other persons for the achievement of satisfactions. Secondly, role differentiation, including that complex called leadership, is part and parcel of a group's locomotion towards its goals and thus towards the satisfaction of needs of individual members. Thirdly, leadership is a concept applied to the *inter*action of two or more persons, when the evaluation of one, or of some of the parties to the interaction is such that he, or they, come to control and direct the actions of the others in the pursuit of common ends. Fourth, evaluation of one party to interaction by another is itself an integration of cognitive perception of the other and of cathexis. In other words, evaluation is a product of (a) perception of instrumentality in need satisfaction, and (b) emotional attachment. Fifth, this form of conceptualization leads to a recognition of a complex of emotional relationships which, in turn, define a variety of leadership relations. Finally, this view of social interaction gives rise to a number of hypotheses concerning leadership for which there is already some evidence in sociological observations and in the findings of psychological experimentation.

References

1. BALES, R. F. (1953), 'The equilibrium problem in small groups', in T. Parsons, R. F. Bales and E. Shils, eds., *Working Papers in the Theory of Action*. Free Press, pp. 111–61.
2. CARTER, L. F. (1953), 'Leadership and small-group behaviour', in M. Sherif and M. O. Wilson, eds., *Group Relations at the Crossroads*. Harper, pp. 257–84.
3. CARTWRIGHT, D., and ZANDER, A. (1953), *Group Dynamics*. Row, Peterson.
4. CATTELL, R. B. (1948), 'Concepts and methods in the measurement of group syntality', *Psychological Review*, vol. 55, pp. 48–63.
5. CATTELL, R. B. (1951), 'New concepts for measuring leadership in terms of group syntality', *Human Relations*, vol. 4, pp. 161–84.
6. GIBB, C. A. (1949), *The Emergence of Leadership in Small Temporary Groups of Men*, University Microfilms, no. 1392, University of Michigan.
7. GIBB, C. A. (1950), 'The sociometry of leadership in temporary groups', *Sociometry*, vol. 13, pp. 226–43.
8. JENNINGS, H. H. (1950), *Leadership and Isolation*, Longmans, Green, 2nd edn.
9. PARSONS, T. (1953), 'The super-ego and the theory of social systems', in T. Parsons, R. F. Bales and E. Shils, eds., *Working Papers in the Theory of Action*, Free Press, pp. 13–29.
10. PIGORS, P. (1935), *Leadership Domination*, Houghton-Mifflin.
11. REDL, F. (1942), 'Group emotion and leadership', *Psychiatry*, vol. 5, pp. 573–96.
12. SHERIF, M., WHITE, B. J., and HARVEY, O. J. (1955), 'Study of status relations in experimentally produced groups through judgmental indices', *American Journal of Sociology*, vol. 60, pp. 370–9.

12 J. K. Hemphill

The Leader and His Group

J. K. Hemphill, 'The leader and his group', *Educational Research Bulletin*, vol. 28 (1949), pp. 225–9.

One of the most urgent necessities for the social scientist today is an understanding of man's activities as a leader. Questions of who shall lead and how individuals may be prepared for effective leadership pose problems of primary concern for education in a democracy.

The popular idea that leaders are born, not made, stresses the importance of individual traits which make for successful leadership but ignores another factor of equal importance: the characteristics of the social group which is to be led. It is the interaction of the leader who possesses a given set of personal attributes and the group whose efficient functioning demands that particular combination of attributes which results in successful leadership. In other words, there are no absolute leaders, since successful leadership must always take into account the specific requirements imposed by the nature of the group which is to be led, requirements as diverse in nature and degree as are the organizations in which persons band together.

This paper reports some tentative conclusions about characteristics of groups which are important in determining what types of behavior will be considered by group members to be conducive to successful leadership. In order to determine the relationships between the characteristics of groups and the behavior of the successful leader, information is needed in the following areas: what a given leader does, the characteristics of the group he leads, and the degree of success he achieves as a leader.

In planning the investigation, a part of which this paper reports, it was decided to utilize the member of a group as a source of information about the characteristics of the group, the leader's behavior, and the quality of his leadership. The member of a group has at least a modicum of information about each of these three areas. Under ordinary circumstances he has an opportunity to observe the leader's behavior, either directly or indirectly. He has information about the nature of the group of which he is a member. Certain members, by virtue of seniority or an important position in the group, have a greater amount of information than others, but each one can describe his group as it appears to him. It would also seem safe to assume that each member of a group is able to make a judgment about the quality of leadership shown by the person who leads the group.

After extensive pre-testing, a satisfactory questionnaire was constructed. It was so arranged that when properly completed, several types of information could be obtained from it. It asked, first, for a description of the group to which the respondent belonged and his relation to it; second, a report of the frequency with which the leader engaged in 70 specific types of behavior; and finally, his comprehensive judgment of the quality of leadership possessed by the leader of the group. Adequate replies were received from the members of 500 separate groups.

Two procedures were used in analysing the data. First, the responses to 50 items on the questionnaire which described the group and the respondent's relation to it were coded into 15 dimensions. The second part of the analysis consisted of examining the relations between group dimensions, items of leader behavior, and judgments of leadership quality. These two steps in the analysis of the data will be discussed briefly.

Ten categories were set up to describe the group, and five categories to show the respondent's relation to his group. These categories were called *group dimensions*, because they were constructed to express degrees of characteristics ranging continuously from a low to a high degree. The 15 dimensions, briefly defined, are as follows:

Group characteristics

1. Size – the number of members in the group.
2. Viscidity – the degree to which the group functions as a unit.
3. Homogeneity – the degree to which group members are similar with respect to age, sex, background, and so on.

4. Flexibility – the degree to which the group has established rules, regulations, and procedures.

5. Stability – the frequency with which the group undergoes major changes or reorganizations.

6. Permeability – the degree to which the group resists admission of new members.

7. Polarization – the degree to which the group works toward a single definite goal.

8. Autonomy – the degree to which the group operates independently of direction by other or larger groups.

9. Intimacy – the degree to which group members are acquainted with one another.

10. Control – the degree to which the group restricts the freedom of members' behavior.

Characteristics expressing the respondent's relation to his group

11. Participation – the degree to which a member takes part in the group's activities.

12. Potency – the degree to which the group meets important needs of a group member.

13. Hedonic tone – the degree to which group membership is pleasant and agreeable to a group member.

14. Position – the location of a member within the group's status hierarchies.

15. Dependence – the degree to which a member relies upon his group.

In coding the information gained from the responses to the items on the questionnaire, a 9-point score was obtained for each of the 15 dimensions listed. Each group was described in terms of 15 numerical scores, one for each dimension. Reliability of the coding procedure was checked by comparing the coding done by two independent workers. These reliabilities ranged from 0·53 to 0·95, and were considered sufficiently high for the purpose of the study. The intercorrelations between the dimension scores were, on the average, low (0·18).[1]

1. The correlations were averaged without regard to signs, following Fisher's technique.

The analysis of the relationship between the three areas of information was carried out by the computation of contingency coefficients. For example, one of the relationships examined was that between the size of the group and the item of behavior 'He was lax with the group.' Of the 500 leaders described by the respondents, 19 were 'always' lax; 46 were 'frequently' lax; 103 were 'occasionally' lax; 154 were 'seldom' lax; 121 were 'never' lax; and 57 respondents reported that the item did not apply or that they were not able to judge the degree of laxness of their leader. The 500 groups were divided into two categories according to size, 250 large groups having 31 or more members and 250 small groups having fewer than 31 members. The contingency coefficient expressing the relationship between size of the group and this item of behavior was found to be -0.16. This indicates a slight tendency for leaders in small groups to be described by group members as more frequently 'lax with the group'.

The relationships between each item of leader behavior and general leadership quality, and between leader behavior and four combinations of leadership quality, with dimension scores, were also determined.[2]

Altogether, approximately 5000 contingency coefficients were computed. By examining interrelationships between group dimensions, items of leader behavior, and judgments of leadership quality, it was possible to make tentative statements about what types of leader behavior were most frequently associated with successful leadership in groups having varying characteristics. In interpreting the results of the study, one must bear in mind that the same respondent furnished the information from which the

2. Groups having an approximate median score on a group dimension, and in which leadership quality was judged 'good' or 'excellent', composed one combination; groups having 'good' or 'excellent' leadership and less than a median dimension score formed a second combination; a third was made up of groups having an above-median dimension score and leadership judged to be 'fair', 'poor', or 'bad'; while the fourth combination contained groups having less than a median dimension score and less than 'good' leadership. Because of limitations of space, detailed statistical data will be omitted in this paper. For a complete presentation of the data upon which this report is based, *see* Hemphill, *Educational Research Bulletin*, vol. 28 (1949), pp. 84–95.

nature of his group was inferred and served as the judge of whether or not the leader he described was successful. Findings which illustrate some of the problems involved in leadership are presented and discussed as tentative statements about the nature of groups and successful leader behavior.

Speed in making decisions has often come under consideration in connection with successful leadership. On the one hand, we hear that a leader must make his decisions quickly in order to avoid giving the impression of hesitation or insecurity. On the other hand, we are told, the leader needs time to consider many factors in order to reach sound decisions. The findings of this study would suggest that speed in arriving at decisions is a critical attribute of successful leadership in certain types of groups. Pressure on the leader for quick decisions is likely to be exerted by groups which have a large membership, groups which lack well-defined organization, in cases where the group is part of a larger body or is subject to frequent change and reorganization, as well as by members who participate to a high degree in the activities of their groups. There is also evidence bearing on the subject of decision-making that leaders who give the impression of having confidence in their decisions are found in groups in which membership is relatively pleasant.

Another recurrent problem in connection with leader behavior is the degree to which a leader should assume a role of authority. The findings of this study suggest that authoritative behavior on the part of the leader is most successful in groups which closely restrict membership, in groups described by members who have high status in their groups, and in groups described by members who do not feel dependent on their groups. Bearing on this same problem is the finding that in groups which have little stability, that is, are subject to frequent change, leaders who lose prestige by allowing members to 'get the better of them' are less successful. In the more stable organizations, leaders appear to be under less pressure to maintain their prestige. Other findings in this same area have to do with the tendency of leaders to subordinate personal gain to group welfare, as indicated by one of the 70 items of leadership behavior, 'He stuck his neck out for the group.' In groups with a single definite purpose and in those which exert a high degree of control over the behavior of members, successful leaders risk their personal welfare for the good of the group more frequently than they do in the less polarized or less highly controlled groups.

A third area of conflict in leader behavior associated with the nature of the group is the problem of whether a leader who exhibits belief in his superiority to his group is more or less successful than one who does not. Our findings indicate that the successful leader tends to avoid giving the impression that he is superior to his group, particularly in large groups, in formal groups, and in groups with a low degree of autonomy. In these types of groups, leaders have greater opportunity to display an attitude of superiority, and are more likely to have their behavior misinterpreted by group members as expressing superiority. The successful leader maintains the belief among group members that he is not superior to them, even though the group is structured in such a way that his behavior might be interpreted as showing the opposite. The indications are that members of groups whose leaders exhibit an attitude of superiority find membership relatively unpleasant and describe their groups as lacking unity of action.

Inconsistency and display of emotion present a fourth area in which there seems to be variation in the acceptance of a leader's behavior according to the nature of his group. Lack of emotional control is less acceptable as a part of successful leadership in the highly structured group than in the informal. Moreover, groups in which leaders 'fly off the handle' find membership relatively unpleasant. Inconsistency in behavior, as revealed, for instance, by reversing decisions, is found more frequently among successful leaders of less flexible, more permeable, less polarized, less pleasant, less united groups than in those with opposite degrees of these characteristics. Inconsistent behavior is better tolerated, if a leader is to be considered successful by group members, when the group lacks established rules and procedures, a simple definite goal or purpose, or a tendency to work together as a unit.

The statements made here about leader behavior and the nature of the group must at present be considered hypotheses. They are all seriously in need of further investigation. However, the conclusion is inevitable that an understanding of leadership involves far more than the isolation of traits of personality. Once we know the conditions, situations, and group characteristics which are associated with successful leadership, we shall be able to add specific content to leader-training courses which should greatly increase their effectiveness.

13 F. E. Fiedler

Leadership – a New Model

Excerpt from F. E. Fiedler, 'Leadership – a new model', *Discovery*, April 1965.

Should a leader concentrate mainly on giving clear and concise directions or should he concern himself first with the feelings and the attitudes of his men, so that he can establish a true partnership with them? Should he be decisive and plan for his group, or should he encourage its members to think and work with him so that they will be self-motivated to perform their best? These questions represent in somewhat simplified terms today's major controversy in leadership training and management theory. The orthodox training doctrine, which has enjoyed unquestioned preeminence until relatively recent times, has held that the leader must be the brain of the group. He must plan, direct, co-ordinate, supervise, and evaluate work done by members of his group. The newer approach evolved in the 1940s and known variously as human relations oriented, non-directive, or group centred, has proposed that the leader's main function lies in enabling his men to become self-directing, and in developing an atmosphere which will permit group members to contribute most creatively and constructively to the task. This approach has led most recently to developments such as brain storming and sensitivity training.

The issues which this controversy involves are by no means trivial. These two types of philosophies have determined in large measure the training programme of industry, the military services and government, and executive selection and development.

The seemingly simple question, asking which of two approaches is the more effective, has been surprisingly resistant to yielding a satisfactory answer. There have been studies supporting each of these two points of view, and many management theorists have come to the conclusion that different types of group require different types of leadership. But this knowledge is not very helpful unless we can also specify the exact conditions under which each of these two leadership styles will work best.

Leadership Abilities and Styles

Intellectual abilities and technical competence play an important part in leadership, but within any given situation, or supervisory level, differences in intelligence and ability tend to be small. The majority of top executives tend to fall into the superior intelligence group, and most shop foremen tend to have a high degree of technical knowledge of the work. Moreover, the relationship between intelligence and ability of a leader and the performance of his group tends to be small. Most research on leadership and supervision has concerned itself with personality and behaviours which are related to the two major types of leadership styles.

The classical studies by K. Lewin and his associates comparing autocratic and democratic boys' groups, set in motion a number of research programmes in this area. Most of these studies have moved towards the use of personality and behaviour for comparing task centred and person centred styles of leadership – autocratic versus democratic, structuring versus considerate, directive versus non-directive leadership.

The emphasis on these particular styles of leadership and attitudes is not too surprising. Leadership is essentially a relationship in which one person uses his power and influence in getting a number of people to work together and accomplish a common task. There are, after all, only a limited number of ways in which one person can get others to do his bidding. He can drive, order, or direct them, or he can guide, cajole, or get them involved in the task. The leader can devote himself to directing the task, or he can devote himself to seeing to it that his members become self-motivating and self-directing.

The research programme on leadership effectiveness which we conducted under a contract from the United States Office of Naval Research was concerned with predicting group performance, and it used a measure related to two types of leadership. In a simple test an individual thinks of all the people with whom he has ever worked and then he is asked to describe the one person with whom he had most difficulty in working – his least preferred

231

co-worker (L.P.C.). The description is made on 20 items such as friendly or unfriendly, cooperative or uncooperative. The so-called L.P.C. score is obtained by giving each of the 20 scale items a weight of one to eight points, with eight points indicating the favourable pole of the item, and totalling the points for the various items. Thus, a person with a high L.P.C. score is one who describes his least preferred co-worker in relatively favourable, accepting terms; someone with a low score describes his least preferred co-worker in relatively unfavourable, rejecting terms. As previous studies have shown, leaders with high L.P.C. scores tend to be permissive, non-directive, considerate in their reactions to group members, while leaders with low scores tend to be directive, managing, task controlling in their leadership behaviour.

Our research programme has involved a wide variety of groups, from basketball teams and surveying parties to military combat crews, open hearth steel shops, small business concerns, and various laboratory and field experimental groups engaged in creative tasks. These studies have yielded high correlations between the L.P.C. score of the leader and measures of actual group performance. However, in some studies the permissive, considerate leaders had the best performing groups while the managing, controlling, directive leaders had groups which yielded the best results in other cases.

Major Factors Affecting Leader Influence

A review of these studies indicated the need for a system of classification which would identify the type of leader required for a particular group and task. Such a classification would have to consider the nature of interaction between the leader and the members of his group, and in particular, the ease with which the leader can exert his influence over his group. Our previous studies suggested a classification based on three major factors: the leader–member relationship, the nature of the task, and the power of the leader's position.

Leader–member relations

These involve the degree to which the leader is personally accepted and liked, that is, the members' esteem for, and loyalty to, their leader. This is, undoubtedly, the most important single factor determining interaction between the leader and his group. If the leader has the loyalty and confidence of his group he needs little else to influence the group. The personal power of the leader can be measured by techniques such as asking members to name the individual in their organization or group whom they would most prefer as leader, who has the best ideas, or who contributes most to the results of the group. It can also be assessed by asking the leader to describe the group climate by completing a short questionnaire, such as the L.P.C. score, but describing the group rather than his least preferred co-worker. This score measures indirectly the leader's acceptance by the group. Obviously it will be fairly easy to lead a group in which one is liked or accepted. It will be difficult to be a leader of a group in which one is disliked or rejected.

Task structure

A board of directors will require different leadership from an infantry squad or a group of dockers. However, what characteristics of the task determine the best type of leadership? The primary dimension which suggested itself in this connexion is the task structure – the degree to which the task is defined. Group tasks are almost invariably assigned by the organization to which the group belongs and the tasks are obviously designed to promote its goals even in the case of *ad hoc* laboratory groups. When the task is highly structured, the organization through its group leader can control how well the task will be done. Consider, for example, a group which counts down a space probe. The leader and the organization prescribe exactly each step of the operation and the sequence in which it is to be performed. And if the group follows instructions it will complete the task. Any man who fails to perform his job, or who performs it in the wrong sequence, can immediately be spotted and corrected. If he fails to obey, he is liable to disciplinary action or court martial.

This is, however, not possible when the task is vague and unstructured. Developing a new product or a new policy, presents quite a different problem. Here the leader neither knows nor can he control the steps which are necessary to achieve a successful result. In fact, the leader frequently cannot even spell out exactly what a successful product should look like. In such a situation, the organization also cannot be of much help to the leader. One cannot, for example, punish a man for failing to be maximally creative, or for misjudging a difficult problem. The unstructured task obviously presents a much more difficult situation for the leader than does a task which can be neatly programmed and controlled.

Task structure can be measured by rating the task on four aspects, namely, decision verifiability – the degree to which the correctness of the solution can be demonstrated; goal clarity – the degree to which the desired outcome is clearly stated; goal path multiplicity – the number of possible methods for performing the task; and solution specificity – the degree to which there is more than one correct solution.

Power of position

Finally, we must consider the power inherent in the position of the leader apart from his personal attraction or ability to command respect and loyalty. The leader who can hire and fire, promote or demote, can obtain compliance under conditions which might be impossible for the leader in a relatively powerless position, such as the chairman of a volunteer group whose members are at liberty to walk out at any time.

While such power is often signified by rank insignia as well as various perquisites, it is frequently less important than the structure of the task. To cite one example, the army frequently details a non-commissioned officer or a low ranking officer to lead or instruct groups of higher ranking officers on certain tasks such as the handling of new weapons or equipment. Incoming medical officers are frequently trained in army procedures by non-commissioned officers. These tasks are, however, highly structured, and the low ranking leader is always able to count on the backing of the organizational hierarchy.

In our studies we have assessed the power of position by means of a simple check list which includes such items as the ability of the leader to promote or demote, and his special rank or title.

Classifying Groups

Having measured or judged each of the group-task situations on the three dimensions of leader–member relations, task structure, and position power, we can locate the group-task situation in a three-dimensional space represented by a cube. We may further classify the groups so that they fall on the upper or on the lower half of each of the three dimensions, which leads to an eight-celled cube. Thus groups falling into cell 1 have good leader–member relations, high task structure, and the leader has a powerful position. Groups in cell 2 have good leader–member relations, high task structure, but the leader's position carries little power, and groups in cell 8 have relatively poor leader-

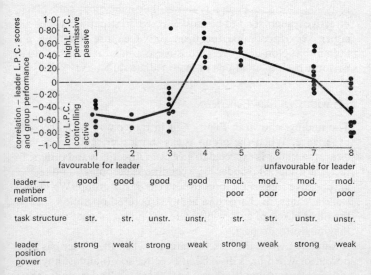

Figure 1 Leaders fit for the situation. Situations which require different attitudes on the part of the leader emerge from this graph showing the relation between group-task structure, group performance, and the leader's L.P.C. score – a measure of the style of the leader. Managing, directive leaders are usually most effective in situations which are very favourable for them (*left*) or relatively unfavourable (*right*). Permissive, considerate leaders are best suited to intermediate situations (*centre*). Each point represents a set of groups – the results from over 800 groups are presented on this graph

member relations, low task structure, and the leader is weak or has little power.

We assume that it is easier to be a leader when one is liked, has a powerful position, and a clearly defined task, than to be a disliked and powerless leader with a vague task. It is then possible to arrange the eight situations according to their favourableness for the leader. This can be done by first arranging groups on leader-member relations, the dimension we considered most important, then on task structure, and lastly on power of position which seems somewhat less important than the other two factors.

We can now ask whether different situations require different types of attitudes on the part of the leader. This is done by plotting the correlations between the leader's L.P.C. score and performance of the group for each type of group-task situation. The resulting plot (see Figure 1) shows that managing, controlling, directive leaders tend to be most effective in situations which are either very favourable for them or which are relatively unfavourable. Non-directive, permissive, considerate leaders tend to perform best in situations of intermediate difficulty.

Fit with Everyday Experience

The findings shown in Figure 1 fit in rather well with everyday experience. When the group backs the leader, and the task is clear, the leader is expected to give clear directions and orders. In fact, the leader who under these conditions becomes non-directive and passive frequently loses the esteem of his group. We do not want a leader, in charge of a highly structured operation such as the flight check of an aeroplane, to ask his crew what they think they ought to do next.

Similarly, when the task is confused, when the leader has little power, or when he is disliked, it is better to do almost anything rather than to stand helplessly by. Where the leader, under these conditions, does not take charge, his group is likely to fall apart.

The permissive, non-directive, human relations oriented approach is most appropriate in two types of situations. In one the leader deals with a group which is engaged in a highly unstructured task, such as one requiring problem solving, decision making, or creativity. Here, the liked leader must be non-threatening, accepting, permissive, and group-centred, since he must depend upon the contributions of his members. The threatening person, or one who is critical and directive, will find it difficult to encourage members of his group to express their ideas freely for fear that they might be judged unfavourably or criticized by the leader. The second type of situation is one in which the not-too-well accepted leader has a structured job. Even though his position may hold power, the leader may have to step softly, and to be diplomatic to avoid being completely rejected by members of his group. He may have to pander to their wishes, and he may have to seek their agreement and advice. The leader with a high L.P.C. score who is permissive and group-oriented is likely to perform better under these conditions.

Changes in Leadership Over Time

The interaction between appropriate leadership and the group-task situation can also be seen whenever a major change makes the situation less structured. This happens, for example, in business organizations during a crisis. By definition a crisis implies a situation which provides no guide lines for behaviour. The typical pattern under these circumstances is for the manager to call his assistants together for consultation. After the crisis has passed, the organization generally returns to routine and fairly well-structured tasks which require directive, managing, controlling leadership.

The opposite situation exists in such organizations as research groups. Here the task begins in a very unstructured manner. The research director and his assistants plan, discuss, consult, and weigh various approaches and research designs. Unless the director decides to do all the planning by himself, this phase of the work requires a high degree of permissiveness. The director soft-pedals, for the time being, the high position-power he may have. He treats his subordinates as equals and gives few, if any, orders. This situation changes dramatically once the research plan has been completed and the design has been frozen. Now the task becomes quite structured and the director, or one of his subordinates, assumes a very directive managing role. Assistants are required to perform their functions exactly as called for by the plan, and any 'creativity' in giving instructions or devising new methods *ad lib*, as the study progresses, is strictly forbidden.

Testing the Hypothesis

The original model classified group-task situations on the basis of three major dimensions, namely, the leader–member relations, the leader's position power, and the task structure. The more general hypothesis which this model suggests is, however, that the type of leadership attitude and behaviour which will be most effective is dependent, or contingent, upon the favourableness of the group-task situation. We can therefore speak of a 'contingency model'.

It is obvious that the three dimensions in the original model are not the only factors determining the favourableness of the group-task situation for the leader. Other aspects of the situation undoubtedly could also play an important part. One of these is the degree to which the group members share similar or dissimilar technical training – as is the case in interdisciplinary research, or the degree to which members have the same cultural and linguistic background. It is especially easy in the latter case to 'misunderstand' instructions, or to become involved in attitudes towards fellow group members which are detrimental to the group task. As a consequence, the leader's job becomes more difficult since he has to watch not only over the task but also over the potentially explosive social situation.

We recently tested the contingency model in multi-lingual military groups of the Belgian Navy. The study involved Flemish- and French-speaking petty officers and men who were assigned to three-man teams half of which had petty officers and half had recruits as leaders, thus varying the leader's power of position. Each team performed two types of tasks. One of these was an unstructured task which required the composition of a recruiting letter urging 16- to 17-year-old boys to join the Belgian Navy. Two short structured tasks were given which required computing the shortest route for ships, one through ten ports, the other through twelve ports, given certain conditions as a result of fuel capacity and obligatory sections of route.

Group atmosphere scores, to determine the leader–member relations were obtained from the leader after each task. In addition, however, the study also involved groups with homogeneous membership – three Flemish-speaking men or three French-speaking men – and groups with heterogeneous membership – Flemish-speaking leader and two French-speaking members, or a French-speaking leader and two Flemish-speaking members.

A further factor affecting the difficulty of the group-task situation arose because the leader of the newly assembled group had a more difficult job than the leader of a group which had had some practice in working together. Thus, the first task would present a

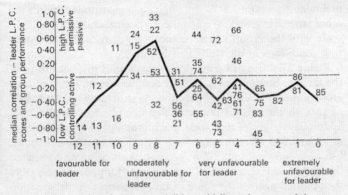

Figure 2 Testing 'contingency model' in multi-lingual groups of the Belgian Navy. This graph showing the effect of the leader's L.P.C. score and group performance on the favourableness of the situation for the leader fits very closely to the theoretical curve predicted by the contingency model. Table 1 indicates the significance of the two digit numbers plotted above – the first refers to left and the second to right

Table 1

Composition	Power of position	High group atmos.	Low group atmos.	Type of task	1st task	2nd task
Homogeneous	high	1	5	Structured I	1	2
Homogeneous	low	2	6	Structured II	3	4
Heterogeneous	high	3	7	Unstructured	5	6
Heterogeneous	low	4	8			

more difficult problem than the same task after the group had worked together for two hours. Secondly, the study involved two structured tasks. Here again, the leader would find it easier to handle his group on the second structured task than on the first.

The study used a total of 96 three-man groups, all of which were tested on the same day to prevent the groups from communicating with each other about the tasks or procedures. There were 48 homogeneous and 48 heterogeneous groups, half with petty officers as leaders and half with recruit leaders, half beginning the study with the structured tasks and half with the unstructured task. The groups were matched on the basis of preliminary tests on L.P.C., intelligence, and attitude towards the other language group. We again correlated each leader's L.P.C. score with the group's performance with each of the 48 group-task conditions in the study (see Figure 2).

Figure 2 includes all group-task situations by giving to three of the factors, homogeneity, high leader position power, and high group atmosphere, a weight of three, to structured tasks a weight of two, to the second task and the second structured task an additional weight of one point. Each group participated in three tasks, and was therefore classified in three group-task situations. For all groups within the same group-task situation we correlated the leader's L.P.C. score and the group performance. These were then plotted against the score of favourableness of the situation for the leader (see Figure 2). As can be seen, the results of this study give a very close fit to the hypothesized curve, thus supporting the contingency model. Other tests likewise have supported this hypothesis. A more detailed treatment of the theory and a review of the research conducted between 1951 and 1967 is presented in a recently published book by the author, entitled *A Theory of Leadership Effectiveness*, McGraw-Hill, 1967.

Implications

This model suggests that up to now we may have paid too much attention to selecting and training leaders and too little attention to the situation. It is obviously easier to change someone's rank and power, or to modify the job he is supposed to do, than it is to change his personality or leadership style. We can improve the effectiveness of leadership by accurate diagnosis of the group-task situation and by altering the leader's work environment. It is then possible for the organization to provide greater control over the performance of its subordinate groups than has been hitherto possible.

It is even possible, as we have seen in the Belgian Navy study, to change the leader–member relationship to some extent. This can be done by changing the composition of the group, by including or excluding individuals whose background and language differ from that of the leader.

The model which has been presented is, of course, only a model – a theory with some supporting data. It has several limitations which must be carefully considered. It is, above all, applicable only to interacting groups in which the task requires close cooperation among group members. It is not applicable to groups, such as sales teams, or bowling teams, in which the performances of each member are added together to yield a group score. The primary virtue of this model, as of any similar theory, lies in presenting the problem of leadership from a new point of view, and in suggesting a new method for dealing with this highly complex aspect of modern life.

14   J. B. Cooper and J. L. McGaugh

Leadership

Excerpts from J. B. Cooper and J. L. McGaugh, 'Leadership', *Integrating Principles of Social Psychology*, Schenkman Publishing Company, 1963, ch. 9.

The interest of social psychology in leadership is closely allied to its interest in social organization. As we have seen, many social organizations incorporate distributions of influence and power. Influence and power positions within a social organization are conveniently referred to as positions of leadership, and individuals who occupy these positions we call leaders.

The term leadership is an abstraction that refers to a particular kind of social expectation. It is a phenomenon which humans observe. As a consequence of social experience, we come to expect certain regions within social organization to be power-laden and the individuals who occupy such regions to wield power. For example, one expects a college to have an office known as the presidency, and the person who occupies that office to be president. Beyond this, it is expected that the president will exercise the power of that office. Thus, the office is a perceived region of the social organization, and from that region certain performances are expected. That such performances are not always forthcoming, and may be far out of line with that which is expected, supports the view that *leadership* and *leader* are not synonymous.

Types of Leadership

Distribution of power within human organization has both adaptive and survival value and is analogous to the distribution and specialization of function so clearly found among many of the infrahumans. Many instances of such distribution and specialization are, of course, individually destructive, and conducive to social disorganization. Leadership and leaders, however, are indispensable to human adaptation and survival.

'Push' leadership

Although the genesis of human leadership phenomena is not to be found in lower species, in the broadest perspective, the same basic, necessary social phenomenon is evident among all the social animals. Within a colony of animals there may be marked differences in status. With many species of birds there are 'pecking orders' which are scrupulously observed by members of the flock. Dominant males have greater access to both food and females. Very subordinate males may constantly refrain from approaching females even though the dominant male has been removed. And dominant hens permit mating less often than subordinate hens. In reviewing the literature on the establishment and maintenance of dominance, Collias has concluded that a dominance–submission relationship between two species members is usually established during the initial encounter or during a series of early encounters. Fighting, bluffing, or passive submission appear to be the most important variables in determining the outcome of such early encounters, and

success in initial encounters depends upon a variable complex of factors and is generally favored by maturity, maleness, familiarity with the locale, help from other individuals, high social status in the home group, isolation from dominating individuals, experience in winning, signs of fear or unaggressiveness in the opponent, body weight, endurance, skill, endocrine balance, good health, and various unknown factors (Collias, 1951, p. 392).

Douglis (1948) has shown, for instance, that a hen that was rotated systematically from one flock to another established and maintained a different status in as many as five different flocks simultaneously. Obviously, for many infrahuman species dominance–submission relationships are important social organizational features, and the behavior of individuals may be better understood if we know something about the establishment and use of these relationships. Leadership within such dominance–submission relationships may be characterized as the 'push' type.

'Pull' leadership

In addition to the 'push' type there is also the 'pull' type among some of the infrahumans. By the 'pull' type is meant one of several animals out in front followed by another or many others. Again, among many migratory species of birds, one bird is first in formation with others following. With sheep, typically '. . . the old female with the largest number of descendants consistently leads the flock' (Scott, 1958, p. 170). As with 'push' type leadership, this, too, is adaptively important behavior since those species that demonstrate leader–follower ('pull') type interrelationships seem to have 'imprinting' propensities. The young have a native capacity for learning to follow particular moving stimulus objects. This aids survival since those objects are likely to help provide conditions (e.g. nourishment and shelter) necessary for survival. For instance, the young lamb nurses and the gosling is brought into areas of food supply.

Of course, with both types – 'push' and 'pull' – there are many subtleties which are not understood. For example, why do members of a 'push' type organization stay together? While it is not our purpose to pursue questions of this sort here, we believe it is important to emphasize that many, if not most, social organizations incorporate power differentials. The members of a social organization are, of course, not all necessarily alike in terms of the reasons for their responses to social influences. Some group members may respond in particular ways because they are afraid of others, and pattern their social behavior largely in terms of avoidance of those (a) they have learned to fear, and (b) those who are afraid of them. In other instances, animals follow other animals, we might suppose, because of previous affective satisfaction. At the lower animal level, these two principal conditions of leadership seem reasonably evident. But at the human level leadership phenomena are comparatively complex because of the emergences to which we have so frequently alluded.

At the human level we also find 'push' and 'pull' leadership phenomena. It is by no means as clear, however, as at the infrahuman level. In broadest perspective, human goals are ego-related. In his constant ego-protection striving, man, in common with many of the lower species, learns to use others as 'tools'. In some instances he bows to the behavior of others, and in some he is bowed to. However, man's social behavior is typically a confused mixture of the two. He may simultaneously bow and be bowed to, and he usually has some complex planning which lies behind the complex, multiple role he is playing.

In previous chapters [not included here] we have suggested several human capacities that characterize man as psychologically unique among the many species. It was further suggested that the unique nature of social organization at the human level is partly a function of these unique human capacities. The same may be said of human leadership. Man's capacities for religious experience, esthetic appreciation, political thought and action, systematic inquiry, and language, to mention some of his more important unique capacities, add new dimensions to human leadership. But it is by comparing human leadership with examples from the infrahuman levels that these new dimensions may most clearly be seen in relief.

While there are both 'push' and 'pull' leadership processes at the human level, just as there are at infrahuman levels, there are additional features. For the 'pull', something more than simple imprinting or reward training operates. A human may generate enthusiasm for, or an affectively toned desire to follow, another. In addition he may develop a highly structured cognitive organization to support his desire to follow. At the human level 'push' type leadership also evidences certain unique features. Its uniqueness lies principally in two human features. First is man's tremendous capacity to anticipate, to plan. Humans are capable of behavioral logistics that find them often even 'willingly' being dictated to, directed, and pushed into behavior they very much dislike. Second, man is capable of showing signs of interpreting a situation as pull, when in reality he interprets it as push. The human may act as though he admires the person in command and professes a desire to follow, though in reality he may be working out a compromise. Being pushed around now in order to gain a favorably anticipated position later is common practice among humans. While some few descriptions of infrahuman behavior somewhat similar to this have been recorded, principally among chimpanzees (Hebb and Thompson, 1954), man's capacity to use it is so great by comparison that it may be considered unique at the human level.

Classical Leadership Theories

Psychologists are by no means alone in their interest in leadership. Philosophers, historians, political theorists, theologians, and others have given much attention to this social phenomenon. Long before psychology was established as a science scholars had developed theories of leadership and some students of social–political processes had explained in detail rules for successful leadership. For instance, as early as the sixteenth century Machiavelli, the Florentine statesman and political writer, had described in great detail the ways by which the head of state could rule effectively and the machinations he must employ in order to maintain his position of power. Philosopher–statesmen such as Francis Bacon and Thomas Hobbes showed an active interest in the problem of leadership and wrote extensively on the subject. Down to the present time men of learning have been fascinated by leadership phenomena. On the one hand, there have been attempts to explain leadership by the development of theories. On the other hand, practical guide lines have been sought by which leadership positions may be obtained and consolidated.

As a background it is helpful to look to the main lines of classical theory which have served as basic orientations for contemporary psychological approaches. In broadest outline, two basic leadership theories grew out of the thinking of the early political philosophers. They are usually referred to as the 'great man' (sometimes, 'hero') and the 'times' (sometimes, 'history') theories. In their extreme forms, these theories are in direct opposition to each other. As J. F. Brown (1936) pointed out some years ago, each represents either–or thinking and they are analogous to the traditional nature–nurture dichotomy. In general, the 'great man' theory has received the greater amount of attention and support in western society. This is quite understandable when we stop to think that the intellectual élite in western society has, for the most part, come from privileged societal groups. Since this élite has in the past written most about leadership, we should expect that most writers would have sought to show natively determined characteristics as responsible for the occupancy of leadership regions. We have but to examine the chronicles of history to realize that most history has been written around particular leaders. To say the least, the 'times' theory has been given much less attention, and since the variables which support it are relatively difficult to identify, it is much less appealing and personally related than the 'great man' theory.

Great man theory

In general, the 'great man' theory holds that particular individuals are natively endowed with characteristics that cause them to stand out from the many and permit them to guide, direct, and lead the majority. This is a view that fits well the doctrine of the divine right of kings. It is not uncommon to any élite, whether economic or intellectual. In its extreme, this theory views social organization and social change as functions of unusual foresight and action on the part of a select few. The select few are natively endowed with qualities that make their leadership possible; and their responsibility is to guide society and direct the behavior of the many. This position is the general thesis which underlies the thesis of Plato's *Republic*.

Times theory

The 'times' theory views leadership as a function of the given social situation. At a particular time, a group of people has certain needs and requires the services of an individual to assist it in meeting its needs. Which individual comes to play the role of leader in meeting these needs is essentially determined by chance, that is, a given person happens to be at the critical place at the critical time. The particular needs of the group may, of course, be met best at a given time by an individual who possesses particular qualities. This does not mean that this particular individual's peculiar qualities would thrust him into a position of leadership in any other situation. It means only that the unique needs of the group are met by the unique qualities of the individual. It has often been said that had Hitler espoused his doctrine in the United States rather than in Germany, he would have been committed to a mental institution. It may very well be that the need to 'escape from freedom' was so great in post-World War One Germany that a majority seemed to believe that their needs could be met only by a person who held the megalomaniac views and action plans Hitler espoused. The 'times' theory is somewhat less rigid than the 'great man' theory, since it does assume a part of the great man theory. It agrees that humans are not all alike – that there are individual differences, and that the unique characteristics of a given person may at a given time meet the needs of a given group most adequately. [. . .]

The Leader as Differentiated from the Head

Gibb (1947) [see also Reading 10] has for some time maintained that leadership, headship, and domination should be distinguished. He believes that one meets the true definition of a leader only when the influence he exerts is accepted voluntarily by others, or when it is in 'a shared direction'. Again, this is an arbitrary definition of leadership which says, in effect, only the 'pull type' influence process is leadership. However, according to Gibb, we should think of influence exerted by one person over another or others as lying somewhere along the leadership–headship–domination continuum.

Such a theoretical scheme permits several combinations or overlappings. The real leader may also be the legally appointed head. A good example of this is the military officer who occupies a leadership-expectancy region by virtue of his legally bestowed rank. To the men over whom he has this jurisdiction, he may also be respected, and his men might wish to follow him with no regard to his leadership status at all. This condition, Gibb points out, '. . . is the assumption which underlies the selection of military officers'. The fact that such appointments do not always turn out so happily brings us to a second combination. The military officer may, instead of being voluntarily accepted as a 'real leader', be a dominator. He may influence his subordinates only by punitive acts and threats. Third, an individual may be a 'real leader', though he has no rank, no headship status. Workers may take their leads from another rank and file worker and pay only lip-service to the foreman. Fourth, the head may be completely ineffectual, neither 'real leader' nor dominator. Yet, he is head by virtue of an external power that maintains him in office. History is replete with accounts of monarchs who have fallen into this category. Finally, there is the dominator who influences the behavior of others by virtue of his own power. The 'self-made' tycoon who controls powerful financial networks and politics by virtue of the fact that he is feared is a type well known to all through fiction and film.

The value of Gibb's scheme is great from the standpoint of functional analysis. It represents a framework for describing interpersonal influence combinations. At the same time, there are two apparent limitations. First, there is a semantic problem. What Gibb chooses to call leadership could more profitably be referred to as a type of leadership. Domination behavior also influences the behavior of others, even though our preference for democratic behavior leads us to dislike and try to prevent domination. Second, group processes are fluid, dynamic. A given individual may play a variety of roles and occupy different positions of status within a given group over a period of time. One is reminded of J. M. Barrie's play, *The Admirable Crichton*, about the butler who, during a crisis, became the truly respected, high status leader of the household. Once the crisis had ended he returned to his butlership, and influence again emanated from the employer. The parent generally is leader to his child. He has status – is 'head of the household'. At times he is loved and respected by his child, and at such times the child wants to follow. At other times the father may dominate his child, and his dominant behavior may be motivated from a punitive basis or from the standpoint that the child must be forced to do a certain thing for his own good.

Our preference is to think of influence effectively exerted on others as leadership. From this we may then go along with Gibb and agree that at any given time interpersonal influence may be voluntarily accepted in a shared direction (common motivation), or it may be domineering in nature and result in resentful acquiescence. In either circumstance the person doing the influencing may or may not command a headship status. Finally, in some situations influence may be exerted only symbolically; that is, a leadership expectancy region is merely occupied by an individual who actually exerts no influence, either as a person others want to follow or as a dominator. These are conditions of leadership that must be studied in the light of their unique psychological characteristics and constant fluidity. [. . .]

References

BROWN, J. F. (1936), *Psychology and the Social Order*, McGraw-Hill.

COLLIAS, N. E. (1951), 'Problems and principles of animal sociology', in C. P. Stone (ed.), *Comparative Psychology*, Prentice-Hall.

DOUGLIS, M. B. (1948), 'Social factors influencing the hierarchies of small flocks of the domestic hen: Interactions between resident and part-time members of organized flocks', *Physiological Zoology*, vol. 21, pp. 147–82.

GIBB, C. A. (1947), 'The principles and traits of leadership', *J. Abnorm. Soc. Psychol.*, vol. 42, pp. 267–84.

HEBB, D. O., and THOMPSON, W. R. (1954), 'The social significance of animal studies', in G. Lindzey (ed.), *Handbook of Social Psychology*, Addison-Wesley.

SCOTT, J. P. (1958), *Animal Behavior*, University of Chicago Press.

Part Five Emergence of Leaders

The emergence of leaders is not easily studied in real groups and certainly not in large complex hierarchical organizations. In small temporary and neonate groups, however, some quite striking observations have been made which undoubtedly have meaning for those more complex groups in which men and women experience direction and leadership. One of the earliest attempts to study factors determining leadership by studying its emergence in newly formed collections of strangers was made by Gibb (1950, 1951). Among the interesting observations of this investigation was that just a few minutes after being introduced to each other strangers were able to express sociometric 'likes', apparently based upon first impressions and this impression was positively and significantly related to leadership choices after many hours of active interaction. Whatever may be the complex personality dynamics of 'love at first sight' the phenomenon appeared to be present in making sociometric choices in like-sex small groups.

If the emergence of leadership seemed to be set off by what might have been thought to be a small and insignificant variable, other work has shown that this is not an isolated instance. Festinger, Schachter and Back (1950) found that architectural features of a housing development which determined the frequency of inter-person contact determined in turn the formation of friendships and the flow of interpersonal influence. Steinzor (1950), reported that in general, members facing each other in a small discussion group tended to interact more frequently than did those seated next to each other. Howells and Becker in a simple but elegant little experiment which is included in this part (Reading 17) have shown that seating not only influences the flow of communication, but that presumably because of this, as other work would have led one to expect, it is a determiner of leadership emergence.

Another of the seemingly irrational determinants of the emergence of leadership which is clearly related to findings mentioned above, is the observation that there is a relationship between leadership and rate of participation especially in traditionless discussion groups. Bernard Bass (1954, p. 471) has indicated that a number of studies report such a relationship, and he comments:

> This high correlation is disturbing at first, since it suggests that L.G.D. (leaderless group discussion) ratings primarily discriminate the verbose from the terse. However the relationship can be shown by a series of deductions to logically follow if we assume that almost all participation in the L.G.D. is *attempted* leadership behavior, that L.G.D. ratings are assessments of *successful* leadership behavior, and that attempted leadership must occur in order for some of it to be judged successful.

Whether this argument will be seen as logic or rationalization probably depends a good deal upon one's attitude towards and respect for chosen or elected leaders. In any event Kirscht, Lodahl and Haire designed a study (Reading 16) to investigate the extent to which meaning could be given to this relationship by hypothesizing that leadership is attributed not simply for participation frequency but for participation of an organizational-integrative kind. While they are forced to conclude that sheer amount of participation is an important variable, some encouragement may be taken from the fact that their leaders were also task and problem oriented and their participation was organizational and integrative.

The most important observations to emerge, however, from the detailed investigation of neonate laboratory groups are those of Bales and his associates in the Harvard Department of Social Relations. These have been described in a number of papers to which reference is made in Reading 15 by Bales and Slater. While these studies are notable for a number of contributions including Bales (1950) it is intended to place emphasis here upon the recognition that in such groups two distinct role patterns are associated with the attribution of leadership, those which serve to solve the task and the social-emotional problems of the group. Furthermore, Bales notes, the most effective groups are those in which a mutual respect exists, and a useful working relationship is worked out, between these two role 'specialists'. This has proved to be an insight derived from the study of emergence which has been found to have meaning also in more real and complex organizations as Etzioni attests (see Reading 24). It is probably not too much to claim that Bales' recognition of dual leadership has contributed more to an understanding of leadership and group process than has any other single experimental finding.

References

BALES, R. F. (1950), *Interaction Process Analysis*, Addison-Wesley.

BASS, B. (1954), 'The leaderless group discussion', *Psychological Bulletin*, vol. 51, pp. 465–92.

FESTINGER, L., SCHACHTER, S., and BACK, K. (1950), *Social Processes in Informal Groups*, Harper.

GIBB, C. A. (1950), 'The sociometry of leadership in temporary groups', *Sociometry*, vol. 13, pp. 226–43.

GIBB, C. A. (1951), 'An experimental approach to the study of leadership', *Occupational Psychology*, vol. 25, pp. 233–48.

STEINZOR, B. (1950), 'The spatial factor in face-to-face discussion groups', *Journal of Abnormal and Social Psychology*, vol. 45, pp. 552–5.

15   R. F. Bales and P. E. Slater

Role Differentiation in Small Decision-Making Groups

Excerpts from R. F. Bales and P. E. Slater, 'Role differentiation in small decision-making groups', in T. Parsons and R. F. Bales (eds.) *Family, Socialization and Interaction Process*, Free Press, 1955, ch. 5.

Introduction

One important aspect of the social organization of groups which endure over any considerable time is the fact that usually roles within the organization are differentiated from each other. The members of the organization possess a common culture, part of which consists of the expectations they have developed as to how each person will behave. When roles are differentiated, overt acts of certain qualities are expected of certain persons at certain times, while overt acts of other qualities are expected of other persons at other times. Furthermore, there is some permanence in the expectations which apply over extended time periods.

In a more general sense, however, one can think of 'differentiation' as a process of development by which such a constellation of roles comes to be recognizable. Presumably, high degrees of differentiation generally trace back to more simple beginnings. There may even be a kind of 'evolutionary tree' – a branching process of development in which certain divisions or differentiations are not only primary in time for a given group, but also functionally more fundamental, and so likely to be similar from one type of group to another.

In the present chapter we report certain data on differentiation between members in small decision-making groups. The degree to which differentiated roles in the fully developed structural sense appear in these small decision-making groups is perhaps a moot point. Certainly some of the characteristics are present in some of the groups. On the other hand, data on certain aspects, particularly direct measures of expectations are not available for this study. Expectations in the present analysis are inferred from consistencies in overt behavior, consensus in ratings, and congruence between behavior and received ratings. Furthermore, the time periods involved are short, so that the degree of permanence is relatively slight.

But in any case, degrees of complexity, clarity, and permanence are surely relative matters. The aim of the present analysis is to catch role-differentiation 'in the making' from some minimal level, in the hope that the character of the minimal phenomena may give clues as to very general forms and reasons for development of role differentiation. We hope that a study of the most general aspects of differentiation in small groups through microscopic time spans can provide a useful conceptual model for understanding role differentiation on a more complex structural level.

The Experimental Setting and the Sample

A number of other reports have preceded this one (Bales, 1950a, 1950b, 1951, 1953; Bales and Strodtbeck, 1951; Bales *et al.*, 1951; Heinicke and Bales, 1953). The sample used for the present study overlaps in part with that used in previous studies, but not completely. The cases used for the present study are part of a larger series that will include groups of sizes two to seven inclusive, four groups of each size, each group meeting four times. The present sample consists of four 3-man groups, two 4-man groups, four 5-man groups, and four 6-man groups, or fourteen separate groups. Each group was observed through four sessions, making a total of fifty-six sessions.

All of the groups in this sample were composed of paid male undergraduates at Harvard, recruited through the student employment office. Every effort was made to ensure that none of the subjects knew one another, but there were a few pairs where this condition was not met. The subjects were not introduced to each other by name, and no leader was appointed by the experimenter. The aim was to start the members on as equal a footing as possible, and leave them to solve all of their problems of social organization by themselves. We wanted to observe the development of role differentiation from some minimum starting point.

The task given to each group was the same. They were told we were interested in group discussion and decision making, and that the physical facilities had been designed to make our observations as easy as possible. Microphones were pointed out, the subjects were told a sound recording would be made, and that they would be observed from an observation room divided from the discussion room by a one-way mirror, in order to avoid distracting them with observers. Each subject was given a five-page written summary of facts about an administrative problem of the sort familiar in college case discussion courses. They were asked not to show these summaries to each other. The summaries were collected after they had been read by the subjects individually.

The subjects were asked to consider themselves as members of the administrative staff of the central authority in the case. They had been asked by their superior to consider the facts and return a report to him which would give their opinion as to why the persons involved in the case were behaving as they did, and their recommendation as to what he should do about it. They were to take forty minutes for the discussion, and in the final one or two minutes to dictate their decisions for the sound record. They were asked for a 'group decision' without further specification as to what this meant or how they were to arrive at it.

The host experimenter left the room at this point, taking the written case with him. The discussion was recorded and the interaction observed by Bales' set of categories.[1] At the end of the session the host experimenter returned and the subjects filled out a questionnaire which included the following questions:

(a) Who contributed the best ideas for solving the problem? Please rank the members in order. *Include yourself*.

(b) Who did the most to guide the discussion and keep it moving effectively? Please rank the members in order. *Include yourself*.

(c) How well did you personally like each of the other members? Rate each member on a scale from 0 to 7, where zero means 'I feel perfectly neutral toward him', and seven means 'I like him very much'.[2]

1. Described in detail in Bales (1950b).
2. A different form of question was used for the earlier part of the sample, but both forms were reduced to rank order of liking for the present study.

Each group met four times at intervals of one week, in order to get a sample of developmental trends. Four similar cases were used, given in a rotated order from group to group in a latin square design in order to compensate for differences in the case material. The questions above were answered at the end of each of the four sessions. At the end of the fourth session an additional question was asked:

(d) Considering all the sessions, which member of the group would you say stood out most definitely as a leader in the discussion? How would you rank the others? *Include yourself*. [. . .]

Differentiation in Overt Interaction

The method used to observe and classify interaction starts with the assumption, that probably the simplest possible set of categories we can imagine involves: (a) a discrimination in *quality* or type of activity (at least the distinction of 'overt action' and 'no overt action'): (b) a discrimination in *who performs* the activity; and (c) a discrimination in *time* of occurrence.

If these discriminations are taken as the starting point, perhaps the next step in refinement consists in the development of a finer qualitative classification. We wish to make further distinctions which will reduce the degree of abstraction and include more information.[3] Table 1 shows a set of categories for the classification of acts of communication which have been developed with criteria of this sort in mind. It is still a highly schematic classification system, but is believed to be logically exhaustive at its own level of abstraction. There are four major sections of qualitative types: Questions (categories 7, 8, 9), Problem Solving Attempts (categories 4, 5, 6), Positive Reactions (categories 1, 2, 3), and Negative Reactions (categories 10, 11, 12). Each section in turn is subdivided into three types. Each of these types in turn subsumes a great multiplicity of sub-types.

The distinction of who performs the act is made by identification numbers assigned arbitrarily to the subjects. An apparatus

3. The further distinctions involved are best described in Bales (1953, pp. 194–202), where it is shown that they are essentially the distinctions made by Parsons' 'pattern variables'.

has been constructed which provides a paper tape moving horizontally, over which the vertical list of categories is placed. An action is recorded by writing down on the moving paper tape an identification number designating the person speaking, followed

Table 1

Categories for the Classification of Acts of Communication

Qualitative Type	Communicative Act
A: Positive reactions	1. Shows solidarity, raises others' status, jokes, gives help, reward 2. Shows tension release, shows satisfaction, laughs 3. Agrees, shows passive acceptance, understands, concurs, complies
B: Problem-solving attempts	4. Gives suggestion, direction, implying autonomy for other 5. Gives opinion, evaluation, analysis, expresses feeling, wish 6. Gives orientation, information, repeats, clarifies, confirms
C: Questions	7. Asks for orientation, information, repetition, confirmation 8. Asks for opinion, evaluation, analysis, expression of feeling 9. Asks for suggestion, direction, possible ways of action
D: Negative reactions	10. Disagrees, shows passive rejection, formality, withhold help 11. Shows tension increase, asks for help, withdraws 'Out of Field' 12. Shows antagonism, deflates others' status, defends or asserts self

by a number designating the person spoken to. The score is placed on the tape in a vertical position which indicates the category of the act. The time order is provided automatically by the horizontal order of scores. The behavior unit scored is a single simple sentence of verbal communication or its non-verbal equivalent as understood by the observer. The scoring is continuous. Every act which occurs is thus classified as to its quality, who performed it, toward whom, and when. [. . .]

Differentiation in Subject Ratings

Measures of how much a man talks and receives are obtained from the interaction records. Measures of how the members judge each other's ideas, guidance ability, and how much they like each other are obtained by questions after each meeting. A simple measure of the degree to which these measures may tap different aspects of differentiation can be obtained by asking the question: how many times do we find a rank one man on a given one of these characteristics who is not rank one on any other of the four remaining characteristics? A 'specialist' might be considered to be a man who achieves isolated prominence in only one of these areas. Similarly, if there is any characteristic in which this kind of specialization occurs more often than in the others, this characteristic might be considered to identify an 'axis' of differentiation. . .

The principal type of differentiation is a *separation of the rankings on likes from the rankings on other measured characteristics.* Apparently there are more cases in which the best liked

Table 2

Percentage of Cases in which the Same Man holds Top
Position on Liked Ranking and either Idea or Guidance
Rankings at the Same time, by Sessions

| | *Sessions* | | | |
Coincidence between	1	2	3	4
Ideas and likes	52·1	8·6	16·4	8·6
Guidance and likes	34·3	25·0	12·1	23·6

man holds top ranking in only that one characteristic than cases of any other sort of isolated prominence. For all groups, the difference between this characteristic and the others is significant at the 0·001 level, using a chi-square test. . .

The probability that the person holding top position on one of the 'task characteristics' (Idea and Guidance rankings) will be the same person who holds top position on the Like rank order appears to be higher in the first meetings than in any meeting following. One can calculate the percentage of cases in which the same man holds top position in both rank orders by sessions and find out whether there is a decrease. Data are shown in Table 2. The trend toward separation of top position on idea rank order and being best liked is significant at the 0·05 level, but the trend toward separation of guidance and likes is not.

Profiles of Idea Specialists and Best Liked Men

This tendency for the best liked man not to be the man chosen as having the best ideas – a tendency which seems to increase over time – raises the question as to whether men of these two types, high on one characteristic but not on the other, will show congruent differences in overt behavior. The following procedure was followed for obtaining cases: (1) All sessions were eliminated in which ties for top rank occurred in either the idea or the like ranking. (2) All sessions were eliminated in which the best liked man was also top man on the guidance or idea ranking. (3) The remaining 23 sessions constituted the sample. About two-thirds of the sessions in the sample are drawn from low status consensus groups, and about two-thirds are drawn (in equal numbers) from 5- and 6-man groups. In most of the sessions the top man on the idea ranking also holds top position on the guidance ranking.

Table 3 shows the composite profiles in percentages of own initiated and received interaction for the twenty-three top men on the idea ranking and for the twenty-three top men on the like ranking obtained from the same sessions. Note that the man in the top idea position is higher in giving suggestions and opinions whereas the man in the top liked position is higher in giving and receiving solidarity and tension release. The idea man seems to receive more agreement. The liked man, perhaps somewhat paradoxically, shows more negative reactions although he does not receive significantly more. The liked man also may be slightly higher than the idea man in asking for opinion and suggestion. These differences may perhaps be best summarized by saying that

261

Table 3

Composite Profiles of 23 Top Men on Idea Ranking and
23 Top Men on Like Ranking for the Same Sessions*

Interaction Category	Initiated		Received	
	Idea men	Liked men	Idea men	Liked men
1. Shows solidarity	4·19	4·79	2·90	3·68
2. Shows tension release	5·97	7·71	8·40	10·38
3. Shows agreement	14·60	14·97	22·92	17·88
4. Gives suggestion	8·66	5·68	6·14	6·36
5. Gives opinion	31·30	27·20	26·28	28·86
6. Gives orientation	17·90	17·91	15·24	13·73
7. Asks orientation	3·66	3·43	2·78	3·01
8. Asks opinion	2·39	2·73	2·00	1·98
9. Asks suggestion	0·98	1·58	0·72	0·33
10. Shows disagreement	7·31	8·43	9·50	10·21
11. Shows tension increase	1·97	3·67	1·30	1·37
12. Shows antagonism	1·07	1·90	1·74	2·21

* Differences between the two men were tested on the following sets of categories. Levels of significance are shown in parentheses:

Initiated: 1 + 2 (0·05 level)
4 + 5 (0·01 level)
10 + 11 + 12 (0·05 level)

Received: 1 + 2 (0·05 level)
4 + 5 (not significant)
10 + 11 + 12 (not significant)

the idea man shows a concentration of activity in the task area, whereas the liked man shows a concentration in the socio-emotional types of activity, both positive and negative.[4]

4. A recent study by Richard Mann, based on two much larger samples of groups of the same kind as reported here shows that this general type of differentiation is not confined to those with the highest positions. A comparison of the position of a man on the two criteria of task ability and being liked yielded two types. Subjects who are evaluated by their peers as having a *higher* position on task ability than on being liked are found to have 'giving suggestions' as significantly more characteristic of their behavior than the other type, whereas those subjects whose position on being liked is higher are found to have 'showing tension release' as significantly more characteristic of their behavior. Unpublished honors thesis, Harvard College: *The Relation of Informal Status to Role Behavior in Small Discussion Groups*.

The problem of testing the significance of these differences is a vexed one, largely because of the problem of interdependence among the categories. The use of raw scores, which would minimize this effect, would be misleading, since the idea man tends to both initiate and receive more interaction in absolute terms than the best-liked man. We have therefore resorted to performing correlated t-tests on individual percentage profiles. We assume that, since the tests were performed on only three groups of categories, comprising about half of the total, the dependence effect will not be too great. Although these tests do not directly test the differences in Table 3, which are based upon composite profiles of raw scores rather than means of individual percentage profiles, we assume that the differences are of the same order and the tests therefore relevant. The results of the tests are shown in Table 3.

A different test of significance may be made by constructing an index for each man, based on his own raw profile, including all categories of action given and received, arranged to fit the actual differences between the different profiles. The numerator will include all categories in which the idea man scored higher in the composite profiles than the liked man, while the denominator will include all categories in which the liked man scored higher than the idea man. The higher the index for a given man, the closer he approaches the hypothetical idea type. Using this method, the mean index for the twenty-three idea men is 0·766, and for the twenty-three liked men it is 0·597. The difference between these means is significant at the 0·01 level.

A simpler and less *ad hoc* index may be constructed for each man by placing in the numerator the raw number of positive reactions (categories 1, 2, 3) he initiates, and in the denominator the raw number of task oriented attempts (categories 4, 5, 6) he initiates. This index is the reverse of the other – the higher the index for a given man, the closer he approaches the hypothetical liked type. Using this method the mean index for the idea men is 0·458, and for the liked men it is 0·582. The differences between these means is significant at the 0·01 level. That there are real differences in the quality of overt behavior between the men in these two status positions seems fairly clear from these findings.

In the present section we have found that of the several rankings examined the two which diverge from each other most markedly are the ranking on 'who has the best ideas?' and the ranking on 'how well do you like each of the other members?' On this basis two status types can be recognized. It has been shown that men occupying one of these status positions but not the other show significant and complementary differences between the types of overt behavior they tend to initiate and receive.

We are now in a position to note a fact which suggests that this type of differentiation is of more general significance. The quality of behavior shifts markedly from the last act of the contribution of a given member (his Proaction) to the first act of the member who responds to his contribution (the Reaction of another). This is perhaps the most striking phenomenon of differentiation on the miscroscopic behavioral level.

The remarkable fact is that the behavior differences between the two status types occur along the same axis of differentiation as that which distinguishes the Proactive Profile from the Reactive Profile. In other words, the differentiation of activity that appears in the behavior of the *same* person, as he passes from the reactive to the proactive phase of his own participation in a microscopic time span, is essentially the prototype of a more macroscopic differentiation in the activity of *two different* types of persons, as measured by the ratings of members of *each other* in post meeting reactions. This congruence between microscopic and macroscopic levels of differentiation suggests that the cause for this type of division may be common to behavior systems at several degrees of molarity, and is in this sense fundamental.

Interaction Between Specialists

The complementarity of the two patterns of behavior characteristic of the idea man and the best liked man strongly suggests that a good deal of interaction may take place directly between the members of this pair. They may, in some groups, constitute a dominant or central pair, supporting each other, and dividing between them the performance of the major activities necessary for the task accomplishment and social–emotional recovery of the group.

Table 4

Characteristics of Interaction between Top Ranking Men on
Ideas (I) and Top Ranking Men on being Liked (L)

Characteristic of interaction observed	Percentage of cases in which characteristic occurred		Significance level for high and low groups combined
	High groups	Low groups	
I *interacted* with L more than he did with any other member	57·1	52·9	**
I *interacted* with L more than any other member interacted with L	64·3 *	50·0	**
I *agreed* with L more than he did with any other member	57·1	44·1	*
I *agreed* with L more than any other member agreed with L	75·0 **	44·1	**
L *interacted* with I more than he did with any other member	92·9 ***	47·1	***
L *interacted* with I more than any other member interacted with I	71·4 **	32·4	*
L *agreed* with I more than he did with any other member	85·7 ***	44·1	***
L *agreed* with I more than any other member agreed with I	46·4	29·4	—
Percentage expected by chance	32·1	28·8	

Level of significance:
No asterisk: non-significant
  * 0·05
  ** 0·01
  *** 0·001

The study of pair relations within the group can become exceedingly complicated, and analysis of this kind is only beginning. However, in the present context it would be particularly interesting to know: (*a*) whether the idea man and the best liked man interact more with each other than with other members; (*b*) whether they agree more with each other than with other members; and (*c*) whether they are the top two interactors. These questions apply, of course, only to sessions where these two statuses are held by different members. Any differences between high and low status consensus groups will be of particular interest.

Table 4 shows the results of such a study. All of the characteristics examined are in the expected direction, and all except one are significant when the data for high and low groups are combined. When the low groups are examined alone, however, not one of the characteristics reaches the 0·05 level of significance. The high groups are markedly different. In these groups it is very characteristic that the best liked man talks more and agrees more with the top ranking idea man than he does with any other member. No other member is likely to talk as much to the idea man as the best liked does, but sometimes some other member may agree more with the idea man than he does. Apparently, simply saying 'yes' to the idea man is not enough to make one best liked. The idea man on the other hand, talks more and agrees more with the best liked man than any other member does typically, but does not confine his attention to the best liked man, and sometimes talks and agrees with other members about as frequently as with the best liked man.

The general picture is clear. In the groups with high status consensus particularly, a heavy traffic of interaction passes between these two specialists, and it is of a generally supportive nature. In the low status consensus groups there is some tendency in this direction, but the pattern in every respect is less clearcut and frequent. Inter-specialist support in overt interaction is a phenomenon associated most frequently with high status consensus.

One is led to expect, by the nature of the findings, that both specialists must generally be high interactors, perhaps the first and second high interactors in the group. The average talking rank for idea men in this sample is 1·6 (1·1 in the high groups), and for best liked men 2·9 (2·6 in the high groups). The expectation thus holds better for the high groups than for the low. However, there is also an indication that the best liked man is third or lower in a fair number of cases, and thus may be interacting with the idea man more frequently than his own interaction rank would warrant [. . .]

The Attribution of Leadership

How do the subjects in these groups conceive 'Leadership'? It will be recalled that at the end of the last session the members were asked: 'Considering all the sessions, which member of the group would you say stood out most definitely as a leader in the discussion? How would you rank the others? Include yourself.' To investigate the relationship between 'Leadership' and the five other measures we found the top man for all four sessions taken together, on each measure, and then found the percentage coincidence of top position on Leadership with top position on each of the five rank orders.

By this method it turns out that top position on Leadership coincides in 50 per cent of the cases with top position on talking, in 60·7 per cent with receiving, 59·3 per cent with ideas, 78·6 per cent with guidance, and only 14·3 per cent with liking. The highest association is with guidance.

Leadership might best be described as a generalized role. It is perhaps the most unspecialized and diffuse designation of high status that can be found in a small group situation. When members of a group designate a particular individual as 'leader' in answer to a question such as the one above, that individual is perhaps felt to possess those qualities which best serve to solve both the task and social–emotional problems of the group. Since different groups emphasize task and social emotional problems in varying proportions, the attribution of leadership will depend not only upon the choice of one person over another but also upon the differential stress placed upon these group problems by the group. The group problems might thus be conceived as factors, with weights assigned to them by the group according to some elementary kind of value consensus.[5] One group, e.g. might

5. There may well be other factors in addition to the two mentioned – the findings for the Low groups suggest amount of participation as a third.

A factor analysis by Couch and Carter of some nineteen different sorts of ratings of individuals made by observers of groups somewhat similar to those in this sample indicated three orthogonal factors: (1) a 'group goal facilitation' factor which is probably similar to our variable of task ability; (2) an 'individual prominence' factor which is probably similar to gross participation rate, and (3) a 'group sociability' factor which seems very similar to our likeability measure. See Carter (1953).

attribute leadership on the basis of, say, 0·7 task ability, 0·3 likeability; another might reverse the weights. Consensus on leadership attribution according to this notion would depend upon (*a*) the amount of group agreement upon the weights to be assigned (value consensus), and (*b*) the amount of group agreement upon ratings given each member on each factor (rating consensus). Leadership would thus be thought of as tending to 'bridge the gap' among the more specialized roles, and perhaps also to 'shift in time' being attributed now to one sort of specialist, now to another, according to the most pressing problems or the major values of the group.

The fact that liking coincides so seldom with leadership suggests that in our present sample likeability is given a rather low weight, possibly because of the heavy task demands placed upon the group by the experimental situation. Among the task characteristics those that seem to coincide most often with leadership show some signs of being the least specialized. [. . .] Unfortunately there are too few cases to show any clear trend as yet, but we propose the tentative hypothesis that attribution of leadership will tend to be associated with prominent performance of highly generalized rather than with highly specialized functions.

Personality Factors and Relations Between Specialists

The low groups tend to be distinguished by a lack of fusion or congruence between amount of overt interaction of the given member and his rank on either idea or liking criteria. Furthermore, in the low groups the fusion of status on ideas and likes is minimal. The low groups tend to show a high degree of differentiation in these particular respects. On the other hand there is little evidence of 'reintegration' as compared to the high groups. As we have seen in the examination of the interaction between specialists, the evidence of cooperation between members of the top pair is minimal in the low groups. The differentiation in the low groups appears not to rest on consensus, but on personality differences among members which impel them in different directions. We are thus led to propose a distinction between *consensual* differentiation and *de facto* differentiation.

If the low groups are characterized by *de facto* rather than *consensual* differentiation one might hypothesize that they may be composed of members whose tendencies to specialize in particular kinds of behavior may be somewhat chronic, compulsive responses to personality needs rather than flexible responses to the needs of the particular group situation. They may be somewhat 'rigid' in their perceptions, and 'absolutistic' in their values, as well as compulsive in their behavior.

The relation of personality to role and status in the group constitutes a very large problem area in which there are probably few simple answers. The hypothesis just suggested is obviously highly over-simplified. However, we do have one additional item of information about each individual in the sample which bears upon the hypothesis. All subjects were given the thirty item California *F*-Scale. High scores on this scale are thought to indicate one kind of rigidity and absolutism, associated with the authoritarian personality (Adorno, 1950). (Probably extremely low scores do also, but this is a complication that will be ignored for the present.) Table 5 shows the mean *F*-scores of the various top men and the chosen leader, in both high and low groups. In

Table 5

Mean Scores on 30-item *F*-Scale for Top Men on Five Characteristics and Leader, in High and Low Groups

	High groups	*Low groups*	*All groups*
Leader	76·2	85·2	80·7
#1 Guidance	88·7	79·2	83·9
#1 Receiving	83·3	94·2	88·7
#1 Talking	74·9	103·8	89·3
#1 Ideas	82·3	101·2	91·7
#1 Liking	91·1	99·9	95·5

general, top men in high groups have lower *F*-scores than top men in low groups. The difference between high and low groups is particularly clear for the idea specialist and the top man on talking.[6] If we compare the idea men and the best liked men with each other, we find no difference in the low groups, but in the high groups the idea men have a significantly lower mean *F*-score

6. These differences are significant at the 0·01 level.

than the best liked men.[7] The best liked men show up as high in F-score.

Analysis of the data on attribution of leadership suggested that certain measures tend toward minimum association with each other (ideas *v.* liking) while others, like leadership, guidance, receiving, tend to 'bridge the gap', and to be associated to some extent with both of these. Those that show the greatest tendency toward separation may be said to be specialized; those that bridge the gap may be called generalized. Table 5 is arranged vertically with the most generalized attributes at the top and the most specialized at the bottom. As we move in the direction of greater specialization, the mean F-scores for high and low groups combined appear to become progressively higher. Top men on the three most generalized characteristics taken together have in fact significantly lower F-scores than the top men on the three more specialized characteristics (at the 0·05 level, using a standard t-test).

In general, then, if a relatively high F-score is associated with rigidity, and the relatively lower score with greater flexibility, we can say that the top men tend to be more flexible in high groups than in low groups,[8] that in high groups the social–emotional specialist is less flexible than the task specialist, and that there is some suggestion that individuals with more specialized characteristics are less flexible than individuals with more generalized characteristics.

Another possible index of 'rigidity' may be found in the like ratings that each individual makes. Some subjects do not make any differentiation in their professed likes toward other members. They say that they like all members equally, and in most cases strongly. Examination of the data indicates that these subjects who do not differentiate their sociometric choices show a significantly (0·01 level) higher F-score than those who do differentiate. If we compare the incidence of undifferentiated choices among top men on the five roles, we find that 42 per cent of best liked men fail to differentiate, as compared with 23 per cent of top men on talking, 33 per cent of top men on receiving, 20 per cent

7. Significant at the 0·05 level.
8. With the exception of top men on guidance – an exception for which the hypothesis provides no explanation.

of top men on ideas, and 27 per cent of top men on guidance. The difference between the best liked men and the other four types is significant at the 0·06 level, using a Chi-square test.

These best liked men, then, say in effect, 'I like everyone.' In connection with their high F-score, this suggests the possibility of a certain rigidity in the attitudes of many best liked men toward interpersonal relationships. They may 'have to be liked' and may achieve prominence in this respect because of the ingratiating skills they have acquired during their lives in bringing this desired situation about. Their avoidance of differentiation in ratings may be an expression of the compulsive and indiscriminate nature of this striving.

If this interpretation is correct, it provides another possible explanation as to why the best liked man is so seldom chosen as the leader of the group. If leadership, as we have suggested, is implicitly or unconsciously attributed on the basis of several weighted factors, the tendency of the best liked man toward 'rigidity' or overspecialization would tend to lower his rating on the task ability and other factors, and so lower his chances of being chosen leader.

This discussion of 'rigidity' in relation to status consensus would lead us to expect that more best liked men will fail to differentiate in the low groups than in the high groups. About 62 per cent of the non-differentiating best liked men are found in low groups, but the difference is not significant.

In any case, there is a sizeable group of best liked men who may achieve this position through behavior designed to avoid negative reactions from others. It is interesting to note, in this connection, that the task specialist (operationally defined as the best idea man) refuses to differentiate less often than any of the other top men. It would seem to be important for the task specialist to be able to face a certain amount of negative feeling toward him without abandoning his role, and his apparent willingness to make differentiated liking choices may be indicative of at least a minimal ability of this kind. Not to have to like everyone implies an awareness and acceptance of the fact that everyone may not have to like him.

It is interesting now to ask whether the high groups differ from the low groups in the liking choices the best liked man gives the top idea man. The interaction data reported above on the relation between these two specialists might lead us to expect that in the high groups the best liked man may more often express liking for the top idea man than in the low groups. Examination of the data, however, reveals no differences between high and low groups. However, pooling high and low groups, in the 23 relevant cases the average liking given by the best liked man to the top idea man was significantly higher (at the 0·01 level) than the average rating that others gave the top idea man in the same session. This is not simply a result of the fact that the best liked man tends to rate everybody high. The rating he gives to the best idea man is also significantly higher (at the 0·01 level) than the rating he gives to others in the group. The fact that this occurs in both high and low groups, though interaction support is more marked in the high groups, again seems to indicate something over-determined in the like ratings made by the best liked man. It appears that regardless of what his interactive relationship with the top idea man has been, the best liked man will tend to express positive feeling toward him once the meeting is over.

Other members may exhibit other types of rigidity. One other type, for example, is suggested by the lack of congruence in the low groups between amount of participation and status on either ideas or likes. A reasonable assumption is that the flexible person adjusts his amount of participation according to the esteem and acceptance he receives. The low groups more often contain persons who persist in very high rates of activity in spite of low acceptance and esteem. Evidence from another study[9] indicates that this type is often 'deluded' as to his popularity – he guesses that other persons like him, whereas in fact they do not.

In the low groups, there is not only a relative lack of consensus as to who stands where in various status orders, but also the lack of consensus appears in conjunction with certain rigidities in perception, value judgments, and overt behavior stemming presumably from personality characteristics of members. It is suggested that the differentiation in the low groups is more heavily influenced by *de facto* personality differences of members than by consensus on an appropriate division of labor.

9. Edgar F. Borgatta and Robert F. Bales, *Sociometric Status Patterns and Characteristics of Interaction*. Unpublished manuscript.

Interpretive Summary

Against the background of findings we may now attempt an interpretive summary. The evidence suggests that the degree of consensus on who stands where on various status orders is a critical factor in the structure and development of the group. Consensus in this respect is probably itself a complicated end result of the social process, but one would suppose that it is affected by the values members hold when they first come together. Measures of values of members were not available for the present sample, but are being attempted for groups at present under observation, and eventually data will be brought to bear on this area of problems.

For the present, we suspect that the groups high on status consensus are those in which it happens, through original composition, that a fairly high degree of latent consensus in critical values exists. Given this common base, a common interpretation of the nature and importance of the task might reasonably follow, and the result is a high degree of consensus on who is producing the best ideas for task solution. Those so perceived are allowed or encouraged to specialize in the task area, and so build up their total amount of participation.

At the same time, we suppose, even in the high groups, a certain amount of ambivalence tends to center on the task specialist. He tends to be liked because he is satisfying needs in relation to the task area. But he also tends to arouse a certain amount of hostility because his prestige is rising relative to the other members, because he talks a large proportion of the time, and because his suggestions constitute proposed new elements to be added to the common culture, to which all members will be committed if they agree. Whatever readjustments the members have to make in order to feel themselves committed will tend to produce minor frustrations, anxieties, and hostilities. These are centered to some degree on the object most active in provoking the disturbance – the task specialist.

The more the task specialist talks, the more ambivalent the attitudes of other members toward him presumably become, and as a solution, they tend to withdraw some liking from him, and center it on some other person who is less active and may in some way reciprocate their positive affect, or express their negative affect. If some person in the group acts in such a way as to attract positive affect on either or both of these bases, he may become the best liked man – and in his activity may become a kind of social–emotional specialist.

If the differentiation goes this far, and the evidence indicates that it is fairly typical, even in the high groups, the task specialist can be thought of as 'representing' the task values of the members. The social–emotional specialist 'represents' other values and attitudes which tend to a certain degree to be disturbed, de-emphasized, threatened, or repressed by the requirements of the emerging task solution. The two specialists interact with high frequency in the high groups, and in a generally supportive manner, though probably also with occasional altercations. They constitute a prominent pair within the group, and their complementarity in interaction represents a high degree of closure which might well be referred to as the 'inner circle' within the total circle of interaction.

Specialization in the high groups arises in response to a complex of situational demands, the demands of personalities, and the demands of the social system, but it takes place in the context of a fundamental consensus as to how the roles should be performed and how they should complement each other. Inter-specialist interaction and support ensures the maintenance of this consensus and prevents the specialization from taking a rigid or disruptive form.

Leadership and perhaps guidance are attributed to that member, one of the pair or occasionally a third person, who best symbolizes the weighted combination and integration of the two more specialized functions. The two directions of specialization, though complementary and supporting in the long run, in the short run tend in some degree to conflict with each other in a way that makes it difficult for the same man to be top specialist on both. In the present sample, the stronger probability is that leadership will be attributed to the task specialist, although the concept of weighted factors implies that if the task specialist is *too* low on likeability, or if the social–emotional specialist is very high on task ability leadership may be attributed to the social-emotional specialist. The data suggest that guidance and leadership tend to be attributed to the person who accomplishes or symbolizes a higher order integration of the two more specialized task and social–emotional functions.

In the low groups, we suppose, the low order of consensus as to who stands where is in part a result of an original low degree of similarity in basic values of members. The members differently evaluate the nature and importance of the task, and so lack a common base for arriving at a consensus as to who has the best ideas. Talking and receiving time are not determined by tacit agreement that participation time should be allocated to any particular persons rather than others. Individual participation is not regulated by a sensitive adjustment to the response received from others. Individual members may perceive themselves as liked, whereas in fact they are not. Others may believe they like everybody, whereas unconsciously they feel fear and hostility.

Neither the task specialist nor the most active participant in the low groups is often best liked, although the latter achieves this position more often than the former. There is a high turnover of personnel in the top ranks of the various status orders. It is difficult for a person who attains top rank in some respect in a given meeting to hold it in the next. Specialization occurs in response to individual needs which are only tangentially related to the demands of the group problem-solving situation. Because the specialized behavior serves the individual who performs it more than it does others, inter-specialist support does not occur systematically. No one individual is able to combine a high activity rate with a high status on both task ability and likeability, and hence adequately to symbolize the balance of functions which leads to the stable attribution of leadership. [. . .]

References

ADORNO, T. W. (1950), *The Authoritarian Personality*, Harper.

BALES, R. F. (1950a), 'A set of categories for the analysis of small group interaction', *American Sociological Review*, vol. 15, pp. 257–63.

BALES, R. F. (1950b), *Interaction Process Analysis, A Method for the Study of Small Groups*, Addison-Wesley.

BALES, R. F. (1951), 'Some statistical problems of small group research', *Journal of the American Statistical Association*, vol. 46, pp. 311–22.

BALES, R. F. (1953), 'The equilibrium problem in small groups', in T. Parsons, R. F. Bales, and E. A. Shils, eds., *Working Papers in the Theory of Action*, Free Press, ch. 4.

BALES, R. F., and STRODTBECK, F. L. (1951), 'Phases in group problem solving', *Journal of Abnormal and Social Psychology*, vol. 46, pp. 485–95.

BALES, R. F., STRODTBECK, F. L., MILLS, T. M., and ROSEBOROUGH, M. (1951), 'Channels of communication in small groups', *American Sociological Review*, vol. 16, pp. 461–8.

CARTER, L. F. (1953), 'Leadership and small group behavior', in M. Sherif and M. O. Wilson, eds., *Group Relations at the Cross Roads*, Harper, ch. 11.

HEINICKE, C. M., and BALES, R. F. (1953), 'Developmental trends in the structure of small groups', *Sociometry*, vol. 16, pp. 7–38.

16   J. P. Kirscht, T. M. Lodahl and M. Haire

Some Factors in the Selection of Leaders by Members of Small Groups

J. P. Kirscht, T. M. Lodahl and M. Haire, 'Some factors in the selection of leaders by members of small groups', *Journal of Abnormal and Social Psychology*, vol. 58 (1959), pp. 406–8.

Several studies have reported the relationship between leadership and the rate of participation. Bass (1949) found a correlation of 0·93 between ratings on leadership and the amount of participation time in ten-person groups. However, the size of this correlation may be partially the effect of using the subjects as raters and of the prior acquaintance of the subjects in a class. A study by Borgatta and Bales (1956) reports that high ratings on leadership by group members tends to be associated with high rates of interaction initiation. Moderate but consistently positive correlations between amount of participation and sociometric scores were found by Peterman (1950).

Although such findings are not unexpected because of the generally task-oriented behavior of laboratory discussion groups, participation, by itself, may not be very predictive of leadership. Slater (1955) reports that leadership as rated by other group members coincided with highest participation in only 11 of 20 discussion groups.

Other researchers have attempted to specify the particular kinds of interaction that differentiate the leaders of small groups. Carter, Haythorn, Shriver, and Lanzetta (1951), using four-person groups, examined the interaction in 53 scoring categories. Two of these categories consistently differentiated leaders in three kinds of tasks: 'diagnoses situation – makes interpretation' and 'gives information on carrying out action'. Other categories that showed differences but not as reliably were: 'proposes course of action for others', 'initiates action toward problem solving which is continued', and 'integrates group behavior'. It was also found that in the reasoning task, leaders ask for information or facts significantly more often than nonleaders. Furthermore, Shaw and Gilchrist (1956) found that leader rank and the number of written communications sent were positively related and that the major source of the difference for leaders was communications about organizing the group and giving factual information.

Thus it seems that leaders are persons who organize the group, solicit and integrate contributions, and propose courses of action. A high rate of participation would not necessarily be associated with these behaviors.

The present study was designed to investigate the relationship between amount of participation, frequency of task- and group-oriented interaction, and the selection of leaders by other group members. The general hypothesis was that amount of participation and organizational-integrative interaction are both associated with leader selection but that each may reflect different aspects of the criterion.

Method

Two three-person groups met simultaneously in separate rooms and were given identical instructions by the experimenters. Each group discussed a human relations problem for about 20 minutes, reaching a group consensus in that time. The groups were then told that a second meeting would take place immediately in which one person from each group would act as a representative; the two representatives would discuss a concrete problem related to the previously discussed topic. Each group then selected one of the members to act as representative.

Tape recordings of the meeting were scored for the amount of time each participant talked. Also, each meeting was scored with a system of eight categories based on Bales' (1950) system. In general, the unit of analysis was one simple statement. The three relevant categories and their definitions follow:

D. Gives suggestion (any statement which proposes a course of procedure but is *not* simply an expression of opinion, e.g. 'Let's have each person give his solution' not 'I think teachers should unionize').

E. Asks for suggestion, opinion, fact (any request which is not for repetition or rhetorical purposes, e.g., 'What do you think?' or 'Would you agree that. . .').

F. Sums up, integrates (any statement attempting to organize the points covered in the discussion, or to bring together diverging opinions, or to re-word or make explicit opinions of others, e.g. 'We seem to agree that strikes are bad'; 'These restrictions would qualify what we said earlier').

These three categories will be referred to as 'DEF'. They define group-oriented, organizational kinds of interaction and are similar to the categories that differentiated leaders in the Carter *et al.* (1951) study. It was hypothesized that the interaction scored in these categories would distinguish those members who would be chosen by the group as representatives from those not chosen.

Data were obtained on 26 three-person groups. Two of the groups were discarded because of incomplete interaction records and two were also discarded because they used random devices (flipping coins, etc.) to select the representative.

Results

For the total sample of 66 Ss, data on time-talked were put into percentage form for each meeting. Those members who were chosen as representatives talked an average of 44·8 per cent of the meeting time; nonrepresentatives talked an average of 27·6 per cent of the time. This difference yields a t of 5·2, significant beyond the 0·001 level. The average number of DEF interactions per meeting was 12·6 for representatives and 6·1 for nonrepresentatives. However, the variances are heterogeneous in this case, so a median test was used, yielding a chi square of 8·79, significant beyond the 0·01 level. Thus, both on measures of amount of participation and DEF interaction, those members chosen as representatives were higher.

The time-talked measure correlated with DEF scores +0·39, p less than 0·01. Although a moderate, positive relationship exists between participation and DEF, the two variables do not measure the same thing. When the DEF scores were put into percentage of total DEF per group, the correlation between DEF and time-talked is +0·44, not significantly higher than the former correlation.

Since the measure of leadership was a discrete variable, point-biserial correlations were computed to determine the amount of relationship between leader choice and the two interaction measures. It was found that the time-talked measure correlated with leadership $+0.543$; for DEF scores, the point-biserial correlation coefficient was $+0.527$. Both of these correlations are significant beyond the 0.01 level.

A weighted combination of the two interaction variables was made up using the discriminant function (McNemar, 1955, pp. 210–11). The relative weights were 0.26 for time-talked and 0.16 for DEF. This combination yields the best discrimination between the distributions of scores for representatives versus non-representatives. When composite scores were made up using these weights, they correlated with leadership $+0.632$.

If the selection of leader is examined group by group, the predictive power of the interaction measures can be determined and compared. That person who talked the most was chosen as representative in 14 of the 22 groups. Since the chance level of selection is one out of three, this represents a highly significant ($\chi^2 = 9.15$, $p < 0.01$) prediction, if not too reliable in a practical sense. In those groups where one person dominated the discussion, i.e. talked over 50 per cent of the time ($N = 8$), time-talked accounts for the representative in seven of the eight cases.

In 14 of the 22 cases, the person with the highest DEF score was chosen as representative. In two of the negative cases, two members were tied in DEF score, and one of the two was chosen. There are 10 cases in which the highest DEF score does not coincide with the highest time-talked. Thus, it is apparent that the two variables do not account for the same thing.

If the dominant person is predicted in those cases in which one person talks over 50 per cent of the time, and where this is not applicable, DEF scores are used, 16 of the 22 cases are accounted for. This method of combining the two variables yields the best practical prediction that can be made from the data.

Although one of the DEF categories may be more crucial than the others, none of the three was found to predict as well by itself as the combined score. It may be that there are particular kinds of groups or situations in which different types of integrative behaviors are particularly appropriate, but these refinements are not possible with the present data.

The other categories used in scoring the interaction yielded no significant differences between representatives and nonrepresentatives. These categories included agreement, positive social interaction, tension release, disagreement, and hostility.

Discussion

The major problem in this experiment is the isolation of variables that can be used to account for the perception of leadership by group members. The data show that amount of participation and DEF interaction are significantly related to leadership choice.

Participation and DEF interaction are neither independent nor highly correlated. They show a moderate, positive relationship. Conceptually, we might think of the group discussion situation in functional terms. The task set by the experimenter defines the goal of the group. Analytically, the process of reaching this goal can be broken down into several components, as is done by Bales (1950). One set of problems involves the production of relevant ideas by the group members; a second set is concerned with the organization and integration of these ideas into a solution that is acceptable to the group. If it can be assumed that the perceptions of the group members of each other with respect to leadership center around the group's functioning, then it appears that the relationship between these two aspects of problem-solving is not a simple one. Within the area of perceived leadership are two subregions: amount of participation and organizational behavior. In general, these two overlap partially, but it appears from our data that the relative importance and the amount of overlap varies from group to group. In some groups, it appears that any person who takes over the task and produces something will be chosen as leader. In other groups, ideas may be plentiful and the problem is to work out a mutually acceptable result. While this scheme makes difficult a simple prediction of leader choice, it appears to do more justice to the data than a monolithic concept of leadership in small groups.

Another way to state this interpretation is in terms of the differentiation of roles in small groups. Where one member talks a great deal, he is perceived as an appropriate representative, but in a more equal participation situation, group-centered, integrative behavior is relatively more important. In the latter case, persons are differentiated with respect to functioning in synthesizing the group. Even in this case, however, there is undoubtedly a minimum amount of participation necessary before the group-oriented behavior is noticed.

It must be remembered that these groups met only once and that the members were unacquainted with each other prior to the meeting. The representatives are leaders only in the narrow sense that they are empowered to act for the group. While these results may not pertain to a wide range of leadership situations, many short term, problem-solving groups are found that are similar to the experimental situation. Furthermore, the results with respect to DEF interaction seem to corroborate the findings of Carter *et al* (1951) regarding the types of interaction which are important in leader behavior. This confirmation includes Carter's negative findings also: the expression of agreement, 'personal feelings', and disagreement did not reliably differentiate emergent leaders from nonleaders. In addition, the results on amount of participation tend to confirm the importance of this variable, as has been found by other experimenters.

In summary, the general picture of a small group leader which appears to be common to various researches shows a group member who tends to have a high rate of participation in the discussion; he is task-oriented, attempts to specify the problem, to suggest courses of action, to seek out the members' contributions, to integrate these and to propose solutions in the attempt to secure consensus in the group.

References

BALES, R. F. (1950), *Interaction Process Analysis*, Addison-Wesley.

BASS, B. M. (1949), 'An analysis of the leaderless group discussion', *Journal of Applied Psychology*, vol. 33, pp. 527–33.

BORGATTA, E. F., and BALES, R. F. (1956), 'Sociometric status patterns and characteristics of interaction', *Journal of Social Psychology*, vol. 43, pp. 289–97.

CARTER, L., HAYTHORN, W., SHRIVER, B., and LANZETTA, J. (1951), 'The behavior of leaders and other group members', *Journal of Abnormal and Social Psychology*, vol. 46, pp. 589–95.

MCNEMAR, Q. (1955), *Psychological Statistics*, Wiley.

PETERMAN, J. N. (1950), *Verbal Participation, its Relation to Decision Satisfaction and the Leader Function in Decision Making Groups*, Univer. of Michigan Conference Research Project.

SHAW, M. E., and GILCHRIST, J. C. (1956), 'Intra-group communication and leader choice', *Journal of Social Psychology*, vol. 43, pp. 133–8.

SLATER, P. E. (1955), 'Role differentiation in small groups', *American Sociological Review*, vol. 20, pp. 300–10.

17 L. T. Howells and S. W. Becker

Seating Arrangement and Leadership Emergence

L. T. Howells and S. W. Becker, 'Seating arrangement and leadership emergence', *Journal of Abnormal and Social Psychology*, vol. 64 (1962), pp. 148–50.

In task oriented discussion groups a leader will tend to emerge as a result of interaction among the group members. Bavelas (1950) and Goldberg (1955) have concluded that the size of the group and the type of communication pattern used are determiners of leadership emergence. Heise and Miller (1951) presented evidence to support the hypothesis that the most centrally located member of a group is likely to emerge as leader. Bales (1953) also found after analyzing communication patterns and leadership that 'the communication pattern tends to "centralize" . . . around a leader through whom most of the communication flows'. Excluding Bales' analysis the experimental conditions in these studies were characterized by controlled communication patterns where the number of channels and the direction of communication were fixed.

With free communication possible, i.e. where all channels are available to all members of the group, Festinger, Schachter, and Back (1950) found that communication among individuals tends to be maximized between individuals positioned opposite to one another and conversely, that there is less communication between people placed side by side. A similar conclusion was drawn by Steinzor (1950) who stated that 'the greater . . . the expressive stimulus value a member of a group has for others the more nearly opposite he sits from one in a circle' (p. 554). Because his subjects were seated in a circle, it was also possible for Steinzor to conclude that a participant who had a greater mean seating distance from all the other participants would be likely to attain higher leadership status.

Bass and Klubeck (1952) partially tested Steinzor's (1950) conclusions by arranging subjects on each side of a V-shaped arrangement. With this arrangement the mean seating distances varied and following Steinzor it was expected that the subjects on the open end of the V would more frequently emerge as leaders. The data did not conform to this expectation and Bass concluded that the 'particular seat a person occupied was of negligible importance in determining a participant's tendencies to attain leadership status . . .' (p. 727).

From the Festinger *et al.* (1950) and Steinzor (1950) results one could deduce that the communications of a small group sitting at a table will tend to flow 'across' rather than 'around' the table. Further, from the Bevelas' (1950) and Bales' (1953) results it can be stated that the individual who controls communication, i.e. the individual who sends and receives more messages, will emerge as leader.

If these two conjectures are correct then, despite Bass' (1953) failure to find the effect, seating arrangements can affect communication flow which, in turn, will influence leadership emergence. Accordingly, the general hypothesis to be tested in the present study is that *seating position, by influencing the flow of communication, is a determiner of leadership emergence.*

Method

One hundred undergraduate men enrolled at the University of Chicago volunteered in order to earn $1.00 as experimental subjects. Twenty groups of five were constituted by random selection from the pool of 100 subjects with the restriction that all members of a group be unable to recognize the names of the remaining group members.

For purposes of identification as each group member appeared for his evening session he was given a colored wrist band (Blue, Red, Green, White, or Yellow) to which he had been randomly assigned and instructed to sit in the chair with the matching color. The colors on the chairs were rotated so that over the 20 sessions each color was assigned to each chair position an equal number of times. The chairs were arranged so that two were evenly spaced along one of the long sides of a 6 ft × 3 ft table and three were evenly spaced on the opposite, long side of the table. The subjects were informed that the purpose of the experiment was to investigate the effects of various communication patterns on creativity after which the instructions pertinent to the task were given.

The instructions included an explanation of the task, anagrams, and the rules for evaluating the group's production. The subjects were told that each word was worth a number of points and that some words were worth more than others, and furthermore that as they generated words it would be possible to establish a hypothesis about the kinds of words which have greater value. They were also told that a clock was set at random so that the alarm signaling the end of the session would ring sometime between 15 and 45 minutes after they started working. In reality all groups worked for 25 minutes. At the alarm the group was required to submit the product of their effort on one sheet of paper.

The task selected, and the conditions imposed on its completion, were designed to stimulate group interaction and to enhance the chances for development of group structure. That is, it was possible for one member to designate another as recorder so the requirement of submitting 'one sheet representing the group's effort' would be satisfied. Decisions had to be made on the division of time and labor with regard to generating words and looking for the clue.

When the alarm rang ending the work session, questionnaires were distributed and completed by the group members. The questionnaires required each subject to rank the other four subjects, but *not* himself, on 15 personality characteristics and also to compare each subject with all the other subjects, again excluding himself, for leadership qualities demonstrated during the session. Since it has been shown that nominations by group members are more reliable leadership measures than are observer ratings or other leadership criteria (Carter, Haythorn, and Howell, 1950), the subjects' leadership ratings were taken as the criteria of leadership. Where there was a 4–1, or 3–2 vote favoring a single person, he was considered the leader of the group. Any other vote was deemed inconclusive and the leader was assumed to be on the side of the table mitigating against the hypothesis.

The procedures provided for two subjects to face three subjects across a table and engage in a problem-solving task. Based on the theoretical considerations described above it was expected that communication would flow across rather than around the table. Thus, it was expected that each of two subjects would exert influence on three subjects and each of three subjects would exert influence on two subjects. Leadership ratings made by the members of the group provided data for a test of the following hypothesis:

A greater number of leaders than would be expected by chance will emerge from the two-seat side of the table.

Results and Discussion

The analysis of the data was based on the assumption that each person in the group had an equal chance of being voted leader. As such, it would be expected that 8 leaders would emerge from the two-seat side of the table and 12 from the three-seat side. Since the observed results are in the predicted direction and differ significantly from those expected by chance it is concluded that seating position influences communication and so is a determinant of leadership emergence in a task oriented group.

Table 1

Number of Leaders Emerging from Two- and Three-Seat Sides of Table

Two-seat side	Three-seat side
14	6

Note.—$\chi^2 = 7\cdot5, p < 0\cdot01$.

Given these data it seems possible to reconcile the differences between Steinzor's (1950), Bass and Klubeck's (1952), and the present study. Steinzor found that a person sitting opposite another around a circle provided more stimulus for that other and also that the largest mean seating distance was a determiner of leadership. That the second conclusion may be viewed as an artifact of the circular arrangement of subjects seems possible, especially since Bass and Klubeck failed to support the conclusion with subjects arranged around a V-shaped arrangement. If 'oppositeness' rather than seating distance is important then Bass and

Klubeck could have expected no differences in their situation, since no subject had an advantage in the number of other subjects he faced. Differences could be expected in the situation reported here, i.e. two subjects opposite three subjects, for each of two could possibly influence each of three.

Summary

Based on the proposition that seating position effects the flow of communication which, in turn, effects leadership emergence 20 groups of five subjects performed a problem-solving task and then rated the group members on exhibited leadership. The seats were arranged so that two subjects were opposite three subjects. A greater number of leaders than would be expected by chance emerged from the two-seat side of the table, thus, lending support to the hypothesis.

References

BALES, R. F. (1953), 'The equilibrium problem in small groups', in T. Parsons, R. F. Bales, and E. A. Shils, eds., *Working Papers in the Theory of Action*, Free Press, pp. 111–61.

BASS, B. M., and KLUBECK, S. (1952), 'Effects of seating on leaderless groups', *Journal of Abnormal and Social Psychology*, vol. 47, pp. 724–7.

BAVELAS, A. (1950), 'Communication processes in task-orientated groups', *Journal of the Acoustical Society of America*, vol. 22, pp. 725–30.

CARTER, L. F., HAYTHORN, W., and HOWELL, M. A. (1950), 'A further investigation of criteria of leadership', *Journal of Abnormal and Social Psychology*, vol. 45, pp. 350–60.

FESTINGER, L., SCHACHTER, S., and BACK, K. (1950), *Social Processes in Informal Groups: A Study of a Housing Project*, Harper.

GOLDBERG, S. C. (1955), 'Influence and leadership as a function of groups structure', *Journal of Abnormal and Social Psychology*, vol. 51, pp. 119–22.

HEISE, G., and MILLER, G. (1951), 'Problem solving by small groups using various communication nets', *Journal of Abnormal and Social Psychology*, vol. 46, pp. 327–35.

STEINZOR, B. (1950), 'The spatial factor in face-to-face discussion groups', *Journal of Abnormal and Social Psychology*, vol. 45, pp. 552–5.

Part Six Followers

Followers are, of course, essential to leadership and these have always been clearly understood as reciprocal roles just as truly as are the roles of husband and wife. In recent years, however, with more detailed and systematic empirical study of small groups there has come a change in the understanding of following. Whereas a great many of the studies reviewed by Stogdill (Reading 5) differentiated only between leaders and non-leaders or leaders and other group members in their attempts to discover the distinctive differences between leaders and others, it has been shown by the study of both real and laboratory groups that the 'rest' or the non-leaders in any group also require differentiation. In any given task and set of circumstances some may be identified as leading, others as following and still others as being indifferent, apathetic, or acquiescent. Such a differentiation has led to recognition that followers are more active group members and that group executive functions depend heavily on them. It may even be suggested that leadership requires a leader–follower coalition for effectiveness and research has indicated that followers are more like leaders than they are like the 'rest'. It is a question of some importance whether these followers should not, in fact, be seen as members of a leadership team, even though their own personal influence over others may be undetectable. Certainly they enter into a circular interaction process with the leaders and by their very responses to leadership they influence that leadership in very significant ways. Probably the first psychologist to focus attention upon the follower as an alert, that is a differentiated, participant was Sanford (1950), whose telling observation is quoted by Hollander in Reading 18, page 296. Hollander more than any other has taken up this suggestion and his paper with Webb (Hollander and Webb, 1955) is a notable contribution to the understanding of leadership. While it is summarized in Reading 18 it is worthwhile to quote some of its conclusions, among them that

followership status is not necessarily implied by non-leader status on peer nominations. It appears evident that the popular dichotomy between leadership and followership is in need of reappraisal. . . . It may be realistic, therefore, to consider characteristics of followership as one functional component of good leadership (Hollander and Webb, 1955, p. 167).

Reading 19 by Paul Nelson follows up some aspects of Hollander and Webb's conclusions. Nelson's work is of special interest because it relates to a real, rather than a laboratory, group which was nevertheless sufficiently subject to continuous and prolonged observation to give its measures an unusual degree of reliability. Unfortunately Nelson has equated followers with non-leaders and his 'leadership' scale with its anchor descriptions 'marked ability to lead his fellows' and 'always follows, never leads' is in all probability non-linear. Indeed it would represent a somewhat special set of circumstances if 'always follows' and 'never leads' were synonymous. However, the point that Nelson does pursue is of interest for the comment it makes upon the conclusions of Hollander. Hollander's use of a sociometric choice technique gave him chosen or liked leaders and followers who were often ($r = 0.92$) the same persons. Nelson suggests that the relationship may be due at least as much to the 'liking' as to the similarity of functional roles. However, he does believe that 'the underlying orientation in common to *liked* leaders (and non-leaders) was an attitude of teamwork and respect for various forms and sources of authority'. In other words it may be claimed that non-leaders are chosen or liked as followers because with the leaders they share an active commitment to the group's task and mission.

References

HOLLANDER, E. P., and WEBB, W. B. (1955), 'Leadership, followership and friendship', *Journal of Abnormal and Social Psychology*, vol. 50, pp. 163–7.

SANFORD, F. H. (1950), *Authoritarianism and Leadership*, Institute for Research in Human Relations, Philadelphia.

18 E. P. Hollander

Emergent Leadership and Social Influence

E. P. Hollander, 'Emergent leadership and social influence', *Leaders,
Groups and Influence*, Oxford University Press, N.Y., 1964, ch. 2.
(Adapted from Chapter Three, 'Emergent leadership and social influence',
by E. P. Hollander, from *Leadership and Interpersonal Behavior*, edited by
L. Petrullo and B. M. Bass; Holt, Rinehart and Winston, 1961.)

The term *leader* is used so broadly that it is best to define our use
of it at the outset. In general, leader denotes an individual with
a status that permits him to exercise influence over certain other
individuals. Specifically, our concern is directed toward leaders
deriving status from followers who may accord or withdraw it, in
an essentially free interchange within a group context. Group consent is therefore a central feature in the leader–follower relationships touched on here, although this limitation does not mean
that we will totally neglect the possible implications for all kinds
of groups, from the simple dyad to the institutionally based
formal group or society.

Primarily, our intention is to offer some observations and empirical findings which strike at the persisting notion of a dichotomy between leadership and followership. We first present some
results of sociometric research, followed by a theoretical model
that treats the emergence of status and assertion of influence as
outputs from interaction centered in interpersonal perception.
Finally, we introduce some findings from a laboratory experiment
with groups to underscore particularly conceptions from this
model which concern the different effects of perceived competence
and conformity on the emergence of status and the assertion of
influence.

Status in General

There are different bases for status and different expectations regarding its operational features. These defy ready cataloguing,
but in our usage here, status refers to the placement of an

individual along a dimension, or in a hierarchy, by virtue of some criterion of value. To say that an individual has 'status' does not describe an intrinsic attribute or a stable pattern of his behavior; rather it describes the relationship of that individual to certain others and their attendant behavior toward him. Interpersonal perception is a necessary part of this process.

Who perceives what about whom is of central importance not just in terms of the literal case, but also in terms of expectancies. The behavior of the object person is not seen just by itself; it is also effectively *matched* against a standard of expectation held by the perceiver. Before a status distinction can arise, therefore, two things must hold: an arousal of a socially conditioned expectancy, and a flow of information regarding the object person. The perceiver will have had some exposure to the perceived through direct experience or through secondary sources; this leads to a perceptual differentiation which underlies a shift in 'behavior toward'.

Granting, as an example, that a millionaire possesses a fairly uniform degree of higher status in our society, he operates without it if unshaven, unkempt, and unknown, he moves about among strangers. Even though an economic criterion and an expectancy already exist for a status distinction, the relevant information is absent. In this instance, the emergence of status is linked to one kind of standard, though a wide variety of others could apply (Hyman, 1942). What the relative impact of these will be resides in complex issues of value. In any case, status is not a sole and stable function of some given feature of social interaction between two particular individuals. Cross-pressures of time and place affect the balance.

If leaders occupy a given status relative to followers, this is one function of the way the former are at some moment perceived and reacted to by the latter. Gibb (1954, p. 915) has made the point this way: 'Followers subordinate themselves, not to an individual whom they perceive as utterly different, but to a member of their group who has superiority at this time and whom they perceive to be fundamentally the same as they are, and who may, at other times, be prepared to follow.' Being a follower is not inconsistent with being a leader, in time. This begs the question of the persisting dichotomy, so some history may be useful here.

The Changing Approach to Leadership

The tradition of concern and controversy about leadership extends far back into the history of social philosophy. This was to stamp related empirical work with a decided bent toward enumerating qualities of the leader. While recent research has seen the leader displaced from this traditional position at center-stage, not very long ago it was typical to indulge in a quest for broad traits of leadership.

Though essentially a matter of emphasis, as in the work of Cowley (1931), traits were selected without regard for situational variants. Gradually a useful distinction between appointed leaders and those who emerged through the willing response of followers was recognized. This was partly a reaction to the burgeoning interest in informal groups with their self-generating status hierarchies, and partly a result of the accessibility of sociometric devices which provided means for studying the consensual choice patterns of various groups.

During this phase, popularity as a feature of group-emergent leadership was given disproportionate importance. Much of the earlier sociometric work equated choice as a room-mate or study companion with choice as a leader, and several well-known and substantial studies gave credence to this presumed parity, though only within a limited context (for example, Jennings, 1943).

Eventually, both the trait and popularity emphases were subordinated to an approach which focused on the varying demands for leadership imposed by an immediate situation (Hemphill, 1949; Carter *et al.*, 1951). The literature survey by Stogdill (1948) on personal factors associated with leadership was quite decisive in pointing up the disordered state of the earlier viewpoint, which disregarded situations. It was not as though the situational view prevailed entirely, however; influential as it was, the literature reflected some dissent (Gibb, 1950; Bell and French, 1950). We have this appropriate comment by Gouldner (1950, p. 13):

The group contexts of leadership must be specified if a formalism sterile of action utility is to be avoided. Leadership must be examined in specific kinds of situations, facing distinctive problems. The opposite shortcoming must also be detoured; in other words, the similarities among *some* leadership situations or problems must be emphasized.

Failure to do so would enmesh our investigation in an infinite analysis of unique situations as devoid of practical potentiality as the formalist approach.

Still another refinement within the situational framework was an awareness that followers define a situation in responding to leadership; they are not passive creatures of a frozen social matrix. Of his research on the follower as an alert participant, F. H. Sanford (1940, p. 4) has said:

There is some justification for regarding the follower as the most crucial factor in any leadership event and for arguing that research directed at the follower will eventually yield a handsome payoff. Not only is it the follower who accepts or rejects leadership, but it is the follower who *perceives* both the leader and the situation and who reacts in terms of what he perceives. And what he perceives may be, to an important degree, a function of his own motivations, frames of reference, and 'readinesses'.

Thus it is seen, several viewpoints have been held concerning leadership and followership: first, a search for characteristics of the leader on the supposition that there is some universality among these; second, a concern with group-emergent leadership where popularity among followers may be of significance; third, a focus upon situational factors that determine, or program, the demands made upon leadership and for leadership; and finally, an interest in the more subtle interplay of motives and perceptions between followers and their leaders.

If any current leaning is discernible, it seems to be toward a focus upon the interaction between individuals and its relation to influence assertion and acceptance. In this way, we are becoming more acute in noting how interpersonal perception affects and is affected by status differentiation, as shown, for example, in the work of Jones and deCharms (1957), Dittes and Kelley (1957), and the research reported in Chapter 18 [not included here].

While it is true that two individuals may bear a stable relationship to one another in a given situation, the demands made upon them in a changing situation could reasonably alter their interpersonal behavior, assuming the necessary volitional conditions; being a leader or follower through the course of time or within a given group setting is not then a fixed state. The context for study consequently becomes more than the immediate situation in which interactions occur, since it includes the past interactions of the parties involved and their impressions of each other as well. The development of newer sociometric approaches has abetted this focus.

Sociometric Techniques in the Study of Leadership

Leadership and interpersonal attraction have been studied more by sociometric techniques than in any other way. It is useful, therefore, to note in perspective the changing complexion of the service these techniques have provided. In early work with the sociogram the essential thing was the interpersonal choice pattern, especially in indicating group members to be isolates or stars. In time, scores were generated through the adaptation of peer nomination as one kind of peer-rating procedure for evaluation (Hollander, 1954a and 1954b). This approach, which makes it possible to derive useful indexes of a person's qualities as seen by his fellow group members, is discussed more fully in Chapter 8 [not included here].

A significant parallel development centers about the attempt to determine the basis for group members' perceptions of one another. This extension answers questions regarding the locus of evaluation – whether in the perceiver, the perceived, the situation in which they are immersed, or various possible combinations and weightings of these. Use of sociometric techniques in this more analytic fashion exposes bases for interpersonal attraction and reciprocal choice (Tagiuri, 1952). For the simple case of two persons interacting, attraction is often attributed to a similarity of perception (cf. Homans, 1950; Newcomb, 1956 and 1961). The literature on complementary roles bears out the contention that a common frame of reference, some commerce of understanding, disposes toward interpersonal attraction (Mead, 1934). Thus, in the simplest case of friendship formation, mutually reinforcing patterns of behavior derive from a shared perception or attitude.

For several reasons, though, it is mistaken to take this as a direct paradigm of leadership choice. Jennings (1947) has made a useful distinction in this vein, that between 'psyche-tele' attraction directed by personal feelings, and 'socio-tele' attraction governed at least in part by a group standard. The chooser is of course the interpreter of this standard. Nevertheless, a greater degree of restraint is introduced into the process of choice by imposing this group set. The situational demands of the group or encompassing institution have a discernible impact on the chooser, as is evident from sociometric analysis. Thus, depending upon the context, members of a group do indeed distinguish between those they like as friends and those they would wish to have as a leader, and this has been amply demonstrated in a number of studies. In one such study, reported in Chapter 12 [not included here], the friendship choices of officer candidates at the Newport O.C.S. were found to be related variously to choices for other positively loaded continua, that is 'leadership qualities', 'probability of success in O.C.S.', and 'interest in and enthusiasm for training'. Simply liking an individual did not mean a positive evaluation of him so far as these other characteristics were concerned. A counterpart of this finding occurs in the laboratory work of Bales and Slater (1955), among others.

The traditions of sociometry set limits, however, on our understanding of leadership and followership. We continue to find, for instance, the supposition of an identity between leadership and such criteria as 'want to study with' or 'want to play with'. Their utility for pinpointing leadership in the influence sense is questionable. In this regard, Criswell (1949) has noted that these 'sets' involve choice in the face of some expectation of reciprocation, thus making mutuality important; leadership choice makes it less important. Generally speaking, whether the leader chooses those who choose him is quite irrelevant to the more central consideration of the *frequency* with which he is chosen by others.

A collateral issue has to do with the criteria set for leadership and the extent to which these are rigorously specified within an operational setting. If we conceive of the leader's influence in terms of a continuum of power, then we may have a *low* power loading, as in the case of 'lead this group in a discussion', or a *high* power loading, as in 'command this squad in combat'. Though an obvious distinction, it has too often been plainly absent from research; one suspects that a push is made for 'some measure of leadership' or a 'sociometric', and anything at hand or easily concocted gets used. No wonder then that the potential follower, asked to make an evaluation, seeks in vain for a meaningful frame of reference, and then either haphazardly makes a choice or bases his decision on some abstract orientation toward the class called 'leaders'.

These particulars are directed only incidentally at clarifying the use of sociometric techniques, a matter taken up in greater detail in Chapter 8 [not included here]. More to the point here are the related and troublesome rubrics that still pervade the study of leadership. One of the more basic of these holds that some members of the group are perceived to have qualities appropriate to leadership and thus are frequent choices for that status. This may be referred to as the 'pyramid model', with its peak comprised of leaders and its base of followers; it also may be reduced to a simple continuum from those of high choice, presumed to be leaders, to those of less choice, presumed to be followers. In either case, the assumption is implicit that there exists a universe of peers among which individuals, placed in the vantage point of followers, differentiate others perceived to be leaders. Followership thus becomes defined by sheer exclusion.

But supposing followership to be more active than passive, this would hardly prove an adequate basis for its appraisal. Is the follower, after all, just someone who is *not* a leader? To really pursue this one should invert the usual question of 'whom to follow?' so as to render it 'whom to have follow?' Group members thus placed in the position of leader would be called upon accordingly to differentiate individuals regarding characteristics appropriate to followers.

If the pyramid or continuum models are sound, one would expect that such an inversion of procedure would yield a diffusion of choice reflecting the operation of a friendship variable, or at least it should be so if followers are mainly friends. This might mean that some of the individuals otherwise selected as leaders would also be selected as followers, though on the whole one would expect that leaders should have a relatively lower standing on followership than the average standing for group members.

Research Findings on the Pyramid Model

A study taking account of the aforementioned points was reported by the author with Webb in 1955 and is presented in

Chapter 6 [not included here]. Prominent among the considerations prompting that research was the view that the traditional sociometric model of leadership and followership might be open to challenge. Since our procedure followed closely the approach discussed, our data serve to address the issue squarely.

Eight sections of aviation cadets (total $N = 187$) were asked to complete three peer nominations upon graduation from a sixteen-week preflight course at Pensacola. The first two of these were on leadership and followership, the third on friendship. On both the leadership and followership form each cadet was asked to assume that he was assigned to 'a special military unit with an undisclosed mission'. Then, for leadership, he was directed to nominate in order three cadets from his section whom he considered best qualified to lead this special unit and three cadets from his section whom he considered least qualified. A similar set was presented for followership with the instruction that the cadet assume that *he himself had been assigned to the leadership* of this special unit; from among the members of his section, he was instructed to nominate three cadets whom he would want as part of his unit and three whom he would not want.

Correlational analysis revealed leadership and followership nominations to be related to a high degree, $r = 0.92$. Friendship had a significantly higher relationship with followership, $r = 0.55$, than with leadership, $r = 0.47$. But apart from this, friendship nominations were not found to bear appreciably on the basic leadership–followership relationship. Of the three friendship nominees designated by each subject, an average of more than two were not mentioned at all in the leadership nominations made by these same subjects.

One further finding deserves attention in light of the previous remarks. If, as has been contended here, followership may be studied in terms of the desires of potential leaders, then a reasonable question is whether actual status on the leadership continuum renders a difference in followership choice. An analysis then correlated the followership scores derived from nominations made by individuals in the top half and by those in the bottom half of the leadership score distribution. Its value for followership scores independently summed from these two nominator segments was 0.82. It would seem therefore that chooser status did not make an appreciable difference in the choice of followers within these groups.

On this the results were clear: the more desired followers tended to be chosen from the upper extremes of the leadership distribution; indeed, the correspondence was marked. Furthermore, the influence of friendship, so often taken for leadership under the heading of 'popularity', had little effect on this relationship.

In a later study by Kubany (1957) quite comparable results were found with medical school *graduating seniors* ($N = 87$). A high correlation obtained between peer-nomination scores for choices on 'family physician' and 'turn over practice to' ($r = 0.85$). Neither of these were as highly correlated with 'friend and social associate', and each was differentially correlated with peer-nomination scores for professional knowledge, skill, and favourable interpersonal behaviors, with professional knowledge and skill typifying more closely the 'family physician' choice. We may consider that where one physician is prepared to give himself over to another for his own personal care and that of his family, the latter may be viewed as a leader. Though operating within a professional relationship, his influence in interpersonal relations may be quite real; therefore, choices for 'family physician' betray a view of the individual more in keeping with leadership. On the other hand, when one physician sees another as someone to whom he would 'turn over his practice', this signifies a disposition more in line with followership since the chooser says in effect that this is someone whom he believes would take his directions and conscientiously fulfill them as a self-surrogate (Hollander, 1958)

These data bolster the previous findings, but mainly in highlighting competence as a valued feature in a multiplicity of joint work situations. That individuals should choose potential leaders as those whom they would also wish to have as followers is not in itself surprising. For one thing, institutional hierarchies plainly create such demands, so that responding well as a follower is apt to be demanded at all levels. Common areas of competence are to be expected, but more important is the way in which competence may contribute to the development of leadership status, particularly when combined with still other interpersonal characteristics.

Beyond one's ability at the task, followership holds an incipient state of leadership. Consequently, any model of leadership is deficient if it fails to account for transitions in status, especially as these are occasioned through the time-linked features of interaction.

Some Implications of Emergent Status

The findings amassed suggest that two things in particular are important in an individual's attainment of leadership. First, that he be seen as competent in the group's central task; and second, that broadly speaking he be perceived as a member of the group – what Brown (1936) has called 'membership character'.

Any group member is bound by certain expectancies – whether norms or roles – which prevail at a given time. To directly challenge these would very likely limit his upward mobility, unless a person were extremely competent and, what is more important, widely perceived as such. In most instances, adherence to the prevailing expectancies of the group is essential for the group member's acceptance. We are in effect speaking then of conformity, but not in the usual sense of fixed behavioral norms to which all group members are expected to display manifest allegiance. We conceive of conformity in terms of *group expectancies* which may be person-specific and fluid or more generally applicable and static. Thus, what may be perceived to be nonconforming behavior for one group member may not be so perceived for another. Moreover, this is a function of status accumulated from past interactions, and is taken up more fully in Chapter 15 [not included here] where we present the construct *idiosyncrasy credit* to refer to status as a summative consequence of being perceived by others as contributing to the group's task and living up to expectancies applicable at any given time. These 'credits' are in essence positively disposed impressions of a person held by others; operationally, they provide the basis for influence assertion and its acceptance. The apparent paradox that leaders are said to be at once innovators and also to be conformers to group norms may be seen therefore as a matter of sequence.

So long as the person does not lose credits by sharp breaks with a past record of competence and conformity to expectancies, he rises to a level of credit which permits deviation from, and even open challenge of, prevailing social patterns of the group. In attaining this level, however, the particular expectancies applicable to him will have undergone change, so that it may be less appropriate to behave in the same way.

Guided by this credit model, an experiment with problem-solving groups was conceived to test the effects upon influence acceptance produced by the nonconformity to procedural norms of a confederate of the experimenter who was very competent in the task. It is reported in Chapter 17 [not included here].

The key manipulation in that experiment was nonconformity by the confederate, through various zones of five trials each, to procedures previously agreed upon by the group in a pre-trial discussion. The fifteen trials were considered as three zones – early, middle, and late – with the discussion taken to be part of the first zone. A group choice, whether by majority rule or otherwise (this determined by the group) was required for each trial, following the three minutes permitted for considering alternatives. At the conclusion of each trial, the experimenter announced the outcome, that is, a negative or positive sum of varying magnitudes representing funds won or lost.

Six treatments were used: nonconformity throughout; nonconformity for the first two zones; for just the first zone alone; for the last two zones; for just the last zone alone; and not at all, as a control condition. Each subject was heard to report his recommended choice at least once during every one of the trials. Had it been *accepted* by the group as its own, the choice recommended by the confederate would have yielded the higher payoffs on all but four trials.

In the zones calling for nonconformity, the confederate violated procedures by speaking out of prescribed turn, by questioning the utility of majority rule, and by unsupported – but not harsh – challenges to the recommendations made by others. He manifested such behaviors on an approximate frequency of at least one per trial with a mean of two per trial considered optimum. Thus, he would break in with his choice immediately after an earlier respondent had spoken and before the next in sequence could do so; when there were periods of silence during a trial, he would observe aloud that maybe majority rule didn't work so well; and he would show a lack of enthusiasm for the choice offered by various others on the matter of basis.

The findings revealed the ongoing effect of task competence in increasing influence acceptance over time, seen in the rising means across zones. While current nonconformity does not yield a significant effect, past nonconformity does. In those groups where the confederate began nonconforming after the first zone, both his suggestions and nonconformity were accepted with minimal challenge; by the third zone, his suggestion that majority rule was faulty typically netted a rubber-stamping of his choice. Again, if he had already accrued credit, the pattern of interrupting people out of turn was simply imitated by others. However, where he exhibited nonconformity from the outset, quite opposite effects were elicited from the others, notably with comments of censure.

Summary

In this chapter we have considered variables yielding emergent status in terms of potential influence. It has been shown that social interaction gives rise to a kind of interpersonal assessment, and that this is made up of task-related elements and behaviors matched by the perceiver against some social standard, referred to here as an 'expectancy'.

Where an individual fulfills these conditions of competence and an adherence to group expectancies over time, he is said to have accumulated 'idiosyncrasy credits' and, at some threshold, these credits permit innovation in the group as one evidence of social influence. Thus the task-competent follower who conforms to the common expectancies of the group at one stage may emerge as the leader at the next stage. Correspondingly, the leader who fails to fulfill the expectancies associated with his position of influence may lose credits among his followers and be replaced by one of them. Which person achieves and retains leadership will therefore depend upon the perceptions of others from ongoing social interaction.

References

BALES, R. F., and SLATER, P. E. (1955), 'Role differentiation in small decision-making groups', in T. Parsons *et. al.* (eds.), *Family, Socialization and Interaction Process*, Free Press.

BELL, G. B., and FRENCH, R. L. (1950), 'Consistency of individual leadership position in small groups of varying membership', *Journal of abnormal and social Psychology*, vol. 45, pp. 764–7.

BROWN, J. F. (1936), *Psychology and the Social Order*, McGraw-Hill.

CARTER, L. F., HAYTHORN, W., SHRIVER, B., and LANZETTA, J. (1951), 'The behavior of leaders and other group members', *Journal of abnormal and social Psychology*, vol. 46, pp. 589–95.

COWLEY, W. H. (1931), 'The traits of face-to-face leaders', *Journal of abnormal and social Psychology*, vol. 26, pp. 304–13.

CRISWELL, J. H. (1949), 'Sociometric concepts in personnel administration', *Sociometry*, vol. 12, pp. 287–300.

DITTES, J. E., and KELLEY, H. H. (1957), 'Effects of different conditions of acceptance upon conformity to group norms', *Journal of abnormal and social Psychology*, vol. 53, pp. 100–7.

GIBB, C. A. (1950), 'The sociometry of leadership in temporary groups', *Sociometry*, vol. 13, pp. 226–43.

GIBB, C. A. (1954), 'Leadership', in G. Lindzey (ed.), *Handbook of Social Psychology*, vol. II, Addison-Wesley.

GOULDNER, A. W. (ed.) (1950), *Studies in Leadership*, Harper.

HEMPHILL, J. K. (1949), *Situational Factors in Leadership*, Ohio State Univ.

HOLLANDER, E. P. (1954a), 'Authoritarianism and leadership choice in a military setting', *Journal of abnormal and social Psychology*, vol. 49, pp. 365–70.

HOLLANDER, E. P. (1954b), 'Buddy ratings. Military research and industrial implications', *Personnel Psychology*, vol. 7, pp. 385–93.

HOLLANDER, E. P. (1958), 'Some further findings on leadership, followership and friendship', *O.N.R. Technical Report IV.*, Carnegie Institute of Technology.

HOMANS, G. C. (1950), *The Human Group*, Harcourt-Brace.

HYMAN, H. H. (1942), 'The psychology of status', *Archives of Psychology*, no. 269.

JENNINGS, H. H. (1943), *Leadership and Isolation*, Longmans.

JENNINGS, H. H. (1947), 'Sociometry of leadership', *Sociometry Monographs*, vol. 14, pp. 12–24.

JONES, E. E., and DECHARMS, R. (1957), 'Changes in social perception as a function of the personal relevance of behavior', *Sociometry*, vol. 20, pp. 75–85.

KUBANY, A. J. (1957), *Evaluation of Medical Student Clinical Performance: A Criterion Study*. Unpublished doctoral dissertation, Univ. of Pittsburgh.

MEAD, G. H. (1934), *Mind, Self, and Society*, Univ. of Chicago.

NEWCOMB, T. M. (1950), *Social Psychology*, Holt, Rinehart, and Winston.

NEWCOMB, T. M. (1956), 'The prediction of interpersonal attraction', *American Psychologist*, vol. 11, pp. 575–86.

SANFORD, F. H. (1950), *Authoritarianism and Leadership*, Institute for Research in Human Relations, Philadelphia.

Followers

STOGDILL, R. M. (1948), 'Personal factors associated with leadership: a survey of the literature', *Journal of Psychology*, vol. 25, pp. 35–71.

TAGIURI, R. (1952), 'Relational analysis: an extension of sociometric method with emphasis upon social perception', *Sociometry*, vol. 15, pp. 91–104.

19 P. D. Nelson

Similarities and Differences among Leaders and Followers

P. D. Nelson, 'Similarities and differences among leaders and followers', *Journal of Social Psychology*, vol. 63 (1964), pp. 161–7.

Background

In support of their contention that followership should not be considered the antithesis of leadership, Hollander and Webb [8] observed a high correlation between peer nominations of desired leaders and desired followers for an hypothetical small-group situation. In keeping with such a finding, it is theoretically sound to consider a good leader to be a good follower in any of several contexts, whether in regard to the leader's responsiveness to the needs of group members or his responsiveness to the demands of higher levels of authority within an organizational structure. By and large, however, even though the form of leadership may vary [10], there is evidence to support the hypothesis that individuals tend to persist in either predominantly leader or follower types of behavior across groups and situations [2, 3, 4, 5].

In view of the apparent consistency of individual behavior, the implications of the Hollander and Webb study seem not to be that leaders and followers are necessarily the same person, but rather that leaders and followers have something in common, particularly when they are valued as individuals by group members. In this regard another finding in the Hollander and Webb study was a moderate positive correlation between friendship (popularity) and both leadership and followership nominations. The moderate correlation suggests, of course, that there can be leaders and followers who are either popular or not so popular. Given this assumption, there may be as many personal characteristics common to leaders and followers of equated popularity as there are in common to either leaders or followers *per se*.

The purpose of the present study was to evaluate similarities and differences in personal characteristics among four types of individuals – namely, liked leaders, less-liked leaders, liked followers, and less-liked followers. Based upon the assumption that individuals tend to pursue either a predominantly leader or follower role within groups, one expectation of the present study was that liked and less-liked leaders should have some personal characteristics in common which differentiate them from followers. In contrast, on the basis of the Hollander and Webb study, it was also expected that liked leaders and followers should have certain characteristics in common which differentiate them from less-liked leaders and followers.

Method

1. Subjects

The Ss in the present study were 72 men who had wintered-over at Antarctic scientific stations. The men represented four different stations, group size of which ranged from 17 to 19 men. Approximately half the Ss were military enlisted personnel (median age of 28 years) and the remaining Ss were civilian scientists and technicians (median age of 26 years). The men at each station worked and lived together in relative isolation from the outside world for 12 continuous months.

2. Procedure

Periodically through the year and at the end of the Antarctic year, a designated military and a civilian supervisor at each station independently evaluated each station member on his overall performance and on each of 21 personal characteristics. The evaluations were made on nine-point rating scales. Of the total number of personal characteristics on which ratings were given, the following were subject to consideration in the present study: leadership, likability, adaptability, emotional control, acceptance of authority, self-confidence, job motivation, alertness, industriousness, problem sharing, aggressiveness, frustration tolerance, motivation to be an efficient group member, and satisfaction with the job assignment.[1]

1. Several characteristics, most of which were emotional symptoms, were omitted from the present study since they were highly correlated with more general inclusive characteristics, such as emotional control.

Experimental groups were derived from the leadership and likability ratings. Anchor descriptions on the leadership scale were 'marked ability to lead his fellows' and 'always follows, never leads', with intermediate descriptions referring to the relative frequency with which the individual led or followed. Both the leader and the follower groups were therefore obtained from the leadership scale. The likability scale was anchored with the descriptions of 'extremely well-liked by others' and 'tendency to be avoided by others'. For each group member an average rating was obtained from each supervisor on leadership–followership and on likability. With use of Fisher's z transformation to obtain an average of the correlations between station supervisors' ratings, average Pearson coefficients of 0·53 and 0·66 were obtained as estimates of supervisor agreement on leadership and likability ratings respectively ($SE_{z \text{ avg}} = 0·13$). By the same method, an average correlation of 0·43 was obtained across stations between peer nominations of friendship and a combined supervisor rating of likability. Across supervisors, the average correlation between leadership and likability ratings was 0·06 ($SE_{z \text{ avg}} = 0·09$).

With use of the combined average of both station supervisors' ratings, the members of each station group were dichotomized as close to the median as possible on both leadership-followership and likability scales. Pooling Ss across stations, four experimental groups were therefore derived, these being liked leaders (L+), less-liked leaders (L−), liked followers (F+), and less-liked followers (F−). As suggested by the zero-order correlation between leadership and likability, an approximately equal number of Ss fell within the four experimental groups.

On each of the remaining 13 personal characteristics of interest in the present study, a combined average of both station supervisors' ratings was obtained for each station member. Employing Student's t-test of mean differences, the four experimental groups were then compared on each of the different characteristics. Major comparisons made were between liked and less-liked leaders, liked and less-liked followers, liked leaders and liked followers, and less-liked leaders and less-liked followers.

Results

Results of the comparison of four experimental groups on personal characteristics are shown in Table 1. In terms of average ratings on likability and leadership, the four groups were significantly different from one another in the expected manner, i.e. leaders from followers and liked individuals from less-liked individuals.

Both groups of leaders, liked and less-liked, were more self-confident, alert, job motivated, and aggressive than the follower groups of comparable likability. On none of these characteristics were the two leader groups significantly different from each other.

Liked leaders and liked followers were both more satisfied with the job assignment, emotionally controlled, and accepting of authority than the less-liked leaders and followers, but not significantly different from one another on these characteristics. The liked leaders and followers were also more motivated to be efficient group members, although liked leaders displayed more of this characteristic than liked followers. On none of these characteristics were the less-liked leaders significantly different from the less-liked followers.

Each of the four experimental groups was in some way different from the others, leaders being somewhat different from followers, and liked individuals being somewhat different from less-liked individuals. In an effort to assess the overall similarity of each group with the others, the four experimental groups were compared two at a time on their attitudinal and behavioral profiles derived for each group by ranking the 13 personal-characteristic average ratings from most to least characteristic. Using the Spearman rank-order correlation, the only groups found to be significantly similar were the liked leaders and the liked followers (rho = 0·87, $df = 12$); all other values of rho ranged from 0·00 to 0·41. Significance was tested by the t approximation suggested by McNemar [9].

Discussion

Consistent with the summary presented by Gibb [6] on behavioral correlates of leadership, leaders in the present study were more

Table 1

Comparison of Leader and Follower Groups on Supervisor Trait Ratings[1]

Traits	Group (L+) N = 15 Mean	SD	(L−) N = 20 Mean	SD	(F+) N = 20 Mean	SD	(F−) N = 17 Mean	SD	Student t-test values[2] (L+/L−)	(F+/F−)	(L+/F+)	(L−/F−)
Leadership (crit.)	6·44	1·17	5·98	0·76	3·94	0·82	3·87	0·90	1·278	0·220	6·882**	7·421**
Likability (crit.)	7·31	0·51	4·67	1·67	6·94	0·96	4·78	1·26	6·463**	5·620**	1·417	0·225
Self-confidence	6·19	1·40	5·80	0·88	5·07	0·85	4·73	1·28	0·950	0·995	2·732**	2·893**
Alertness	6·70	0·97	6·31	0·84	5·56	1·18	5·28	0·91	1·246	0·819	3·109**	3·555**
Job motivation	6·71	0·97	5·90	2·34	5·70	1·41	4·66	1·19	1·407	2·428*	2·510*	2·063*
Adaptability	6·83	1·11	5·72	1·70	5·65	1·30	4·91	1·15	2·334*	1·834	2·886**	1·705
Industrious	7·57	1·00	5·76	1·42	5·79	1·60	4·78	1·32	4·435**	2·108*	4·044**	2·177*
Aggressiveness	5·17	1·04	5·92	1·44	4·14	1·09	4·95	1·18	1·638	2·152*	2·827**	2·245*
Problem sharing	4·16	1·16	4·26	1·30	4·25	1·12	4·57	1·46	0·251	0·739	0·230	0·667
Frustration tolerance	5·29	1·11	5·50	1·92	4·70	1·46	5·64	1·46	0·422	1·945	1·350	0·234
Maturity	5·86	1·31	4·42	1·57	4·74	1·23	3·86	1·39	2·940**	2·013	2·571*	1·150
Job satisfaction	5·66	1·35	4·50	1·90	5·20	1·57	3·74	1·61	2·103*	2·755**	0·920	1·333
Group motivation	6·69	1·12	5·11	1·26	5·83	1·14	4·89	1·41	3·926**	2·196*	2·243*	0·487
Emotional control	7·46	1·08	5·48	1·87	6·79	1·15	5·50	1·41	3·931**	2·918**	1·762	0·047
Accept authority	6·73	1·06	4·89	1·82	6·74	1·12	5·02	2·21	3·760**	2·900**	0·018	0·198

1. For all traits except frustration tolerance, higher ratings imply more of the particular trait.
2. Student t-test values derived prior to rounding off for tabular presentation; direction of differences is ignored.
 * Significant at the 0·05 level.
 ** Significant at the 0·01 level.

self-confident, alert, and aggressive than nonleaders (followers). But in terms of overall similarity on attitudinal and behavioral profiles, liked leaders and liked followers were more similar than any other groups. These two groups were particularly similar to one another, and different from the less-liked leaders and followers, on satisfaction with assignment, emotional control, acceptance of authority, and motivation to be a part of the group. The fact that liked leaders were even more motivated toward the group than liked followers may be accounted for in part by the hypothesis that a critical expectation held of the leader, if he is to maintain esteem, is that he display strong motivation to belong to the group [7].

Individuals judged by their supervisors as leaders in the present study appear to have demonstrated what Bass [1] would refer to as attempted leadership behavior. That is, they were the individuals most likely to initiate task-oriented behavior within the group. But the individuals who attempted leadership and were more effective in so doing, as judged in this study by their popularity, appear to be characterized by an attitude or orientation of teamwork and respect for other sources of authority whether it be a station supervisor, a set of group norms or rules, or perhaps even the opinion of a follower who is particularly knowledgeable in regard to the task at hand. It is in this sense of teamwork and respect that the liked follower is similar to the liked leader in a small group, the major difference between the two types of individuals being that the follower tends to be less assertive.

The results of this study and of that by Hollander and Webb seem particularly relevant for future studies of leadership characteristics. If one operationally defines leadership in the form of attempted leadership, such as by assertiveness, it is likely that both the potentially effective and less-effective leader would be pooled together under the common label of 'leader'; it would then seem likely that the only characteristics on which leaders would be found different from nonleaders would be those characteristics related to assertiveness. On the other hand, if leaders are operationally defined as those group members nominated by peers as 'good leaders' or 'persons you would like to follow', the nonleader group against which the leader group would be compared would be composed of individuals defined in the present study as less-liked leaders, liked followers, and less-liked followers. Again, since liked leaders have characteristics in common with both less-liked leaders and liked followers, the presence of the latter two groups in the nonleader category would make it unlikely that many attitudinal or behavioral characteristics would emerge as differentiating leaders from nonleaders.

Thus, the problem of leadership–followership is probably best approached with an experimental design which accounts for the possibility of there being liked and less-liked leaders as well as liked and less-liked followers. If we are interested primarily in the effective leader and the effective follower, such individuals must in some way be experimentally differentiated from their less-effective counterparts.

Summary

On the basis of the Hollander and Webb study [8] which clearly demonstrated a positive relationship between desirability as a leader and desirability as a follower, the present study was conducted to assess similarities and differences in personal characteristics among four types of individuals – namely, liked leaders, less-liked leaders, liked followers, and less-liked followers. It was expected that while both types of leaders would in some way be different from the followers, leaders and followers of equated popularity would also have certain characteristics in common.

A total of 72 men who had wintered-over at four Antarctic scientific stations served as *S*s. Based upon a year's experience with the men at their stations, two supervisors at each station independently evaluated all station members on several attitudinal and behavioral characteristics, one of which was a leadership-followership scale and another of which was a likability scale. By dichotomizing the members of each station on both the leadership and the likability scales, four experimental groups of liked and less-liked leaders and followers were obtained for comparison on other personal characteristics.

Both liked and less-liked leaders were more self-confident, alert, job motivated, and aggressive than the follower groups of comparable likability. On the other hand, liked leaders and liked followers, in contrast to the less-liked leaders and followers, were more satisfied with the assignment, emotionally controlled, accepting of authority, and motivated to be efficient group members. In terms of their overall profile of attitudes and behavior, the liked leaders and the liked followers were found to be most similar – more so than liked leaders with less-liked leaders, liked followers with less-liked followers, or less-liked leaders with less-liked followers. It was suggested that the underlying orientation in common to liked leaders and followers was an attitude of teamwork and respect for various forms and sources of authority.

References

1. BASS, B. M. (1960), *Leadership, Psychology, and Organizational Behavior*, Harper.
2. BELL, G. B. and FRENCH, R. L. (1955), 'Consistency of individual leadership position in small groups of varying membership', in A. P. Hare, E. F. Borgatta and R. F. Bales (eds.), *Small Groups: Studies in Social Interaction*, Knopf, pp. 275–9.
3. BORG, W. R. (1957), 'The behavior of emergent and designated leaders in situational tests', *Sociometry*, vol. 20, pp. 95–104.
4. BORGATTA, E. F., BALES, R. F., and COUCH, A. S. (1954), 'Some findings relevant to the great man theory of leadership', *American Sociological Review*, vol. 19, pp. 755–9.
5. GALLO, P. S., and McCLINTOCK, C. G. (1962), 'Behavioral, attitudinal, and perceptual differences between leaders and nonleaders in situations of group support and nonsupport', *Journal of Social Psychology*, vol. 56, pp. 121–33.
6. GIBB, C. A. (1954), 'Leadership', in G. Lindzey (ed.), *Handbook of Social Psychology*, Addison-Wesley, pp. 877–920.
7. HOLLANDER, E. P. (1958), 'Conformity, status, and idiosyncratic credit', *Psychological Review*, vol. 65, pp. 117–27.
8. HOLLANDER, E. P., and WEBB, W. B. (1955), 'Leadership, followership, and friendship: an analysis of peer nominations', *Journal of Abnormal and Social Psychology*, vol. 50, pp. 163–7.
9. McNEMAR, Q. (1949), *Psychological Statistics*, Wiley.
10. SLATER, P. E. (1955), 'Role differentiation in small groups', in A. P. Hare, E. F. Borgatta and R. F. Bales (eds.), *Small Groups: Studies in Social Interaction*, Knopf, pp. 498–515.

Part Seven A Contemporary View

While Parts One to Six of this collection have revealed a common core of thinking about leadership they have also revealed a good deal of difference at least in detail. There is a need to draw the threads together and to consider how the contemporary psychologist and sociologist see the leadership process before an attempt is made in Part Eight to think about the adequacy of our understanding for application to real-life situations.

Any one of a number of selections might have been chosen to represent a contemporary overview. The chapter on 'Leadership' (Secord and Backman, 1964) is a very good one which represents the position well:

The current approach to leadership emphasizes leadership behavior: those actions that are functionally related either to goal achievement or to the maintenance and strengthening of the group. Such behavior is engaged in to a varying degree by all members (p. 370).

Leadership in the organizational setting is subjected to a valuable analysis by Katz and Kahn (1966) and in the course of this analysis much that is known about leadership is drawn together. Discussion ranges over problems of definition, the need for leadership, cognitive and affective requirements of leadership, two-way orientation of leaders, and the distribution of the leadership function.

Other summary statements may be found in the new *International Encyclopedia of the Social Sciences* (Sills, 1968) and in Lindzey and Aronson (1968).

The selection chosen (Reading 20) has the advantages that

its authors are well versed in both the psychological and the sociological literature; it shares the dynamic-interaction-process approach of the volume; and it illustrates well incorporation of empirical research into an integrative summary statement. While these authors do not emphasize all that may be said to be established in the study of leadership, they do record well and succinctly the major understandings. The most essential understanding of leadership is that it is one, rather special, manifestation of a broader system of role relationships. It is consistent with this that the personality characteristics of leaders reveal little of the nature of leadership because leadership is an interactive phenomenon, and that it is more harmful than helpful to think that a group necessarily has or requires a single leader. Leadership is accepted as being a matter of degree rather than an all-or-none affair, and leaders are continuous participants in a circular interaction process in which they exercise influence, but not without being influenced both by followers and by other leaders in other functional groupings. Finally, attention is drawn to the place occupied by position power and visibility in conferring or continuing leadership status.

While as is indicated in Part Eight, there is not enough specificity in the knowledge of leadership to enable yet a 'how-to-do-it' manual, the work of the post-war years has given a good understanding of the basics of the process and the general agreement about a number of propositions is at least sufficient to guide both groups and leaders in the better execution of their tasks.

References

KATZ, D., and KAHN, R. L. (1966), *The Social Psychology of Organizations*, Wiley.

LINDZEY, G., and ARONSON, E. (1968), *Handbook of Social Psychology*, Addison-Wesley.

SECORD, P. S., and BACKMAN, C. (1964), *Social Psychology*, McGraw-Hill.

SILLS, D. L. (ed.) (1968), *International Encyclopedia of the Social Sciences*, Crowell Collier and Macmillan.

20 T. M. Newcomb, R. H. Turner and P. E. Converse

Leadership Roles in Goal Achievement

Excerpt from T. M. Newcomb, R. H. Turner and P. E. Converse, 'Leadership roles in goal achievement', *Social Psychology: The Study of Human Interaction*, Holt, Rinehart, and Winston, 1965, pp. 473–85.

As groups proceed with their various kinds of activities, it is easy to observe that different members make different contributions to whatever their group's objectives are. Their contributions differ both in degree and in nature; that is, some members make contributions that are more important or more indispensable than those of other members; and some of them facilitate goal achievement in one way and some in other ways. Insofar as any member's contributions are particularly indispensable, they may be regarded as leaderlike; and insofar as any member is recognized by others as a dependable source of such contributions, he is leaderlike. To be so recognized is equivalent to having a role relationship to other members, since it is not necessarily any specific behaviors on the part of a leaderlike person that make his contributions of special importance, but rather his relationship to other members. His end of such a role relationship is well described as that of a facilitator toward group goals.

This way of looking at leadership is quite different from several more conventional points of view, and sometimes in outright opposition to them. For example, a person who holds a high-status position of power or authority may or may not be a particularly valuable or indispensable facilitator, and even if he is he may not be generally recognized as such by those who work with and under him. Merely to hold a leaderlike position does not necessarily mean that one's role relationships with other group members are leaderlike. For similar reasons, leadership, if viewed as a facilitative role relationship, cannot very well be defined in terms of specific kinds of behavior. For example, the mere giving of orders is not necessarily facilitative, nor is a commanding air or a domineering manner. As noted in Research Illustration 2, there appear to be at least two very broad categories of behavior, one or both of which often characterize persons recognized as special facilitators, but the specific forms of their contributions may vary widely.

It is often assumed that individuals recognized as leaders must have certain kinds of personal characteristics in common. With comparatively few exceptions, however, the facts are solidly against this assumption. In a review of twenty different investigations of the traits of individuals regarded as leaders in various kinds of groups (Bird, 1940), altogether seventy-nine different traits were mentioned. Less than half of these seventy-nine traits appeared on more than one of the twenty lists, even allowing for near synonyms. Only one trait, intelligence, was included in as many as ten of the twenty lists. Not only was there little agreement among these lists; there was actually a good deal of contradiction: some included aggressiveness, ascendance, and decisiveness, whereas adaptability, tactfulness, mildness, and suggestibility appeared in others. It is not hard to see what lies behind such diversity. Different kinds of groups, existing for different purposes, are likely to find that different kinds of persons best serve as facilitators, even the same group, as a matter of fact, may find that quite different sorts of persons are equally good facilitators. Thus we cannot learn much about the nature of leadership by studying the personal characteristics of persons who are regarded as leaders.

Viewing leadership as a facilitative role relationship forces us to question another common assumption: that for each single group there is a single leader. We would not need to question this assumption if it were true that in most groups there is just one person who is recognized as *the* special facilitator in *all* ways that are important to goal achievement. Very often, however, this is simply not the case. Bales and others have shown, as in Research Illustration 2, that many groups distinguish between persons who are particularly good facilitators with respect to task achievement, and others whose distinctive contribution is toward the personal satisfaction of group members, both in relation to the task and to each other. It may commonly be observed, moreover, that during the course of one or more group sessions the role of principal facilitator shifts back and forth between two or more persons. It is often impossible, even with respect to one particular kind of contribution, to assert that any single person is *the* special facilitator. Such considerations suggest that it may be more harmful than helpful to think of leadership as necessarily concentrated in a single person.

Finally, the definition of leadership as a facilitative role relationship is not consistent with the rather common view that 'the leader is the man who exerts the most influence'. It is often the case that actual influence, in the sense of affecting the course of events, may be exercised in ways that are hardly recognized at all by other group members. Tremendous influence may stem from a person who works behind the scenes, examples from recent American history are Edward M. 'Colonel' House in President Woodrow Wilson's administration, or Harry Hopkins, to whom President Franklin D. Roosevelt delegated so many crucial responsibilities. It can also happen that a titular leader who, because he works inconspicuously, is considered weak and ineffective by his associates, is in fact the controlling source of crucial decisions. Group members whose facilitative effects are not recognized by others do not thereby cease to be facilitators, but it is more accurate to say that their contributions are leaderlike than that they themselves are leaderlike. Other members cannot take their parts in a role relationship to a leader whose facilitative contributions they do not recognize. The interactional aspects of leadership (which we shall discuss further at the end of this section) depend, as do other role relationships, on the sharing of attitudes and expectations by role participants.

Hence we shall think of leadership as a matter of degree and kind of facilitation, rather than as an all-or-none affair; and as a role relationship in which the distinctive contributions of the various participants are commonly recognized, and expectations concerning one another's contributions are shared.

Modes of Facilitation

It is to be expected that the ways in which different forms of leader facilitation can most readily be distinguished will correspond to the kinds of facilitation that groups typically need. Most of this section is devoted to an examination of three kinds of group requisites, and of the ways in which interaction between leaders and other group members contributes to providing these requisites. Although they are all very common ones, it is not necessarily true that they apply to every group, nor to any group at any particular moment.

Research Illustration 1 presents one way of showing that group members tend to be valued by each other for different kinds of contributions. The persons who (on the average, for forty-eight sessions held by four groups) were best liked were not the most active members, but the second and third most active members. The most active members typically received the most 'dislike' ratings, and also the third most 'like' ratings, together with the highest rating for their ideas. These and other similar findings have led Bales to propose 'the hypothesis of two complementary leaders', labeled 'task specialist' and 'social-emotional specialist'. These specialized kinds of facilitation correspond to group requisites that have to do with efficiency and with member satisfaction, respectively. We shall now examine each of these kinds of role relationships.

Research Illustration 1

Using the Interaction Process Recorder, Bales observed the frequencies of each of the twelve categories of behavior on the part of each member of four 5-man groups that met for twelve sessions (1958). The task assigned to each group was 'to decide what should be recommended as action' in order to solve a 'human-relations case'. Each member, individually, was first given a five-page presentation of a problem facing an organization administrator; although all read the same material, in order to stimulate discussion they were left uncertain as to whether all had been given exactly the same information. Members were allowed to take notes, but not to consult the printed material after reading it through. Each group was allowed forty minutes, the last one or two of which were used to dictate the group's solution of the problem. There follows a brief excerpt describing a sequence of interaction on the part of one of the groups, together with the category assigned to each response in parentheses.

Member 1: I wonder if we have the same facts about the problem? (*Asks for opinion.*) Perhaps we could take some time in the beginning to find out. (*Gives suggestion.*)

Member 2: Yes, we may be able to fill in some gaps in our information. (*Gives opinion.*) Let's go around the table and each tell what the report said in his case. (*Gives suggestion.*)

Member 3: Oh, let's get going. (*Shows antagonism.*) We've all got the same facts. (*Gives opinion.*)

Member 2: (*Blushing and showing tension*): . . .

At the end of each session every member was asked to rank each of the other members as to liking for him, disliking for him, and as to the value of his ideas. These rankings were later averaged for all forty-eight group sessions in order to relate them to indices of total activity on the part of each man – that is, 'the total interaction initiated' by each man. In the accompanying figure, which summarizes the findings concerning this relationship, the 'activity rank' refers not to any particular person in each group, but to whatever man was most active in each of the forty-eight sessions. Thus the values at the left of the figure, above Rank 1, are averages of the ratings received for whatever men happened to be most active in each session, whether or not the same individual. The figure shows that, typically, the most active man was thought to have the best ideas, but not to be the best liked.

Bales's data also show that this inverse relationship between having good ideas and being liked is characteristic of all sessions except the first one. In the first session (according to later data based on a larger

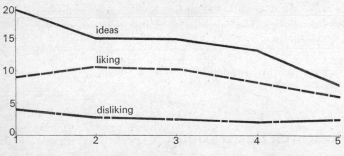

activity rank

Figure 1 Average ratings received on ideas, liking and disliking by men of each activity rank

number of groups), the top man in idea rank was also the top man in liking rank in more than half of the groups, but this occurred far less often during second sessions, and less than 10 per cent of the time by the fourth session. Bales's own interpretation of such findings is stated, in part, as follows: 'Could it be that there was something about arriving in a top-status position, owing to technical contributions to the task problems of the group, that tended to "lose friends and alienate people"? If so, was another man likely to arise who paid more attention to the social-emotional problems of the group and so tended to collect more liking? The idea that this happens with sufficient frequency that it can be viewed as typical may be called "the hypothesis of two complementary leaders"'. (Bales, 1958, p. 441.)

Facilitating task achievement

In so far as a group is task-oriented, its achievement depends not only on working out solutions and plans but also, very often, on carrying them to completion. In groups that have had a history of experience in working together toward their goals, one or more members are likely to become recognized as dependable facilitators because they are perceived as having some or possibly all of such resources as these:

1. They are knowledgeable about matters related to the task.
2. They are imaginative, innovative.
3. They are hard-headed, realistic.
4. They are persuasive, convincing in obtaining group consensus.
5. They are good at formulating problems or summarizing discussions.
6. They are skilled in planning, organizing, coordinating.
7. They can be depended on to carry through.

Research Illustration 2

For a period of many years the Survey Research Center of The University of Michigan has studied relationships between working groups and their supervisors in varied settings. The results here reported are from section gangs on a railroad, work groups in a tractor factory, and clerical workers in an insurance company; about 2500 workers in some 400 different groups, together with supervisors in all groups, responded to interviews or questionnaires. Kahn and Katz (1960), the authors of the report, have this to say about their data-gathering procedures: '. . . methodological emphasis was placed upon checks and controls in the field studies undertaken. Unquantified anthropological observation was replaced by standardized interviews with carefully defined samples of respondents. Impressionistic accounts of attitude and morale . . . were replaced with measures of workers' psychological responses. Effects of supervisory practices were not judged on the basis of what management assumed the results to be. Independently derived measures were employed in testing relationships. For example, supervisory behavior was measured independently of its effects upon productivity and morale of workers' (p. 555).

Kahn and Katz report four ways in which high-producing groups differ from low-producing ones. The first of these is *role differentiation*: supervisors in high-producing groups typically do not perform the same tasks as do rank-and-file workers; in particular, they spend more time in planning, as reported both by themselves and by their supervisees. For example, 72 foremen in high- and in low-producing railroad groups replied as follows to the question, 'How much of your time do you usually spend in supervising, and how much in straight production work?'

Production level	50% or more time spent in supervising	Less than 50% of time spent in supervising	Response not obtained	Total
Higher	20	11	5	36
Lower	9	22	5	36

(The differences between higher and lower production levels, in this table and in the two that follow, are highly significant: the probabilities that they are due to chance are less than 0·01.) Kahn and Katz regard the effects of supervising as being of two kinds: coordination and organization of tasks make for efficiency, and at the same time increases workers' motivation to produce.

A second difference between supervisors of high- and low-producing groups was that the former exercised *less close supervision* and delegated more authority. According to coders' assessments of lengthy interviews about their own jobs as supervisors of clerical workers in an insurance company, the two groups of supervisors differed as follows:

Production level	Close supervision	General supervision	Not ascertained	Total
Higher	6	5	1	12
Lower	11	1	0	12

Workers' own responses showed very similar differences. Close supervision (frequent checkups, detailed and frequent instructions, limitations upon employees' freedom to work in their own way) is generally intended either to keep men on the job or to make sure that their work is done in a specified manner. But it may also reduce a worker's sense of independence, and thus his motivation. According to Kahn and Katz's data, the latter effect tended to be predominant.

High-production supervisors tended, in the third place, to be more '*employee-oriented*' than other supervisors. In contrast to 'production-oriented' supervisors, they give serious attention to matters of employee motivation, as reported by employees as well as by themselves. Examples of supervisors' employee-orientation include 'understanding' rather than punitiveness when mistakes are made: helping employees to qualify for promotion; taking a personal interest in employees – even including their off-the-job problems. High-production supervisors were generally felt to be supportive.

As a fourth factor, though one that is less directly related to leadership, the high-production group members showed greater *cohesiveness* and pride in their jobs than the members of other groups. In the railroad study, both foremen and men in high-producing groups believed that their groups' production was 'better than most', even when they had no means of knowing that this was in fact true. Clerical workers in an insurance company showed the following differences, with respect to pride in their own groups:

Production level	High pride	Medium pride	Low pride	Total
Higher	47	53	43	143
Lower	14	58	70	142

Typical comments by men in high-production groups include these: 'I really feel a part of this group'; and 'I'd rather have my job in this group than an identical one in another group'. Such comments are particularly impressive in view of the fact that the men who made them did not believe that their own groups were superior in respect to skill, know-how, or education.

Finally, Kahn and Katz remind their readers that productivity is by no means perfectly correlated with supervisors' role differentiation, their not-too-close supervision, or their employee-orientation, nor with group cohesiveness; high productivity can occur in the absence of some or perhaps all of these conditions. They note that this is to be explained, in part at least, by the fact that a supervisor can increase productivity in *either* of two ways: through his technical skill or through his ability to motivate his men.

Some of these resources enable persons who possess them to make particularly useful contributions themselves, directly. Others refer to less direct forms of facilitation: insofar as any member can stimulate others to use *their* resources more fully, he has, so to speak, a multiplying effect, and this may be more significant than his own direct contributions. Some of the skills, habits, and practices on the part of supervisors of work groups that have such multiplying effects are described in Research Illustration 2. The more productive groups, according to these and other findings, were facilitated in either or both of these ways: (1) They were *enabled* to be effective because their supervisors provided technical know-how, planning, and coordination; (2) their members were *motivated* to be effective because their supervisors were generally supportive, and because they were proud of belonging to a successful work group. It is probable that comparatively few of the supervisors studied by Kahn and Katz combined both unusual enabling and unusual motivating skills, just as Bales found that 'idea men' in his problem-solving groups were usually not 'social-emotional' leaders also. Work groups are fortunate, apparently, if their appointed supervisors are particularly skillful either as enabling or as motivating facilitators. In either case, the achievement of high productivity as a group goal is dependent on those interactional processes by which group members respond to facilitating behaviors on the part of their supervisors.

The findings reported by Kahn and Katz do not necessarily mean that supervisors were influencers without themselves being influenced by interaction processes. For example, the supervisor of a group that is already a productive one sees little need of doing 'straight production work', or of providing close supervision. Circular rather than one-way effects are probably the rule: an effective supervisor contributes to productivity, and is thereby encouraged to continue his effective procedures. We shall later note other instances of such circularity in interaction.

Maintaining satisfying interpersonal relationships

Some groups exist, ostensibly at least, solely for the purpose of accomplishing certain tasks, but the achievement of such goals is likely to be aided or hindered by members' interpersonal satisfactions or dissatisfactions, as the studies by Bales and by Kahn and Katz have shown. Other groups have few or no objectives other than the satisfactions that members find in interacting with one another. Most if not all groups whose members continue to interact share, briefly and episodically at least, both kinds of concerns. Regardless of the nature of a group's dominant goals, therefore, their achievement can be facilitated by any member insofar as he contributes to making intermember relationships satisfying. Leaderlike behaviors that are directly facilitative in such ways include the following:

1. Providing warmth, friendliness.
2. Conciliating, resolving conflict, relieving tension.
3. Providing personal help, counsel, encouragement.
4. Showing understanding, tolerance of different points of view.
5. Showing fairness, impartiality.

The would-be facilitator of satisfying interpersonal relationships faces a special dilemma, however: How can he, especially if he occupies a formal position of leadership, show warmth and supportiveness in an impartial manner and at the same time let both effective participators and ineffective or disturbing ones know how he assesses their work? Fiedler's studies, as summarized in Research Illustration 3, point to what appear to be common practices on the part of accepted leaders of effective groups, as they confront this dilemma. They tend to depersonalize their relationships to group members; that is, they are task-oriented rather than person-oriented even in their personal relationships. But Fiedler's findings, as he carefully notes, apply only to groups in which 'the leader is sociometrically endorsed by the men on whom his authority depends. . . . Where his subordinates will not "listen" to him, his attitudes cannot affect the group's behavior.' All this suggests that in at least some task-oriented groups of men, a leader who discriminates between effective and ineffective workers is not regarded as unfair. When task goals are shared, personal warmth can be made subsidiary to task accomplishment, and under such conditions discrimination is facilitative; a discriminating leader is not only accepted but also, apparently, respected.

Fiedler's findings, like those of Kahn and Katz, point to ways in which through facilitative behavior a person can multiply his own effectiveness by making the group as a whole an effective one.

These findings and those of Katz and Kahn do not, however, suggest exactly the same conclusions. The importance of psychological distance in Fiedler's studies has a good deal to do with two facts: most if not all of his groups were rather small; and his 'leaders' were sociometrically chosen individuals, and not necessarily official ones. Under these conditions group members can accept discrimination on the part of a leader whom they know and trust, and can profit by his somewhat cold-blooded supervision. But in larger groups, whose leaders are considered to be official supervisors who are not necessarily sociometrically preferred or even particularly trusted, the characteristics of employee-orientation and supportiveness on the part of supervisors may be fully as important as the maintaining of psychological distance.

Research Illustration 3

Fiedler (1960) has made a number of studies of one aspect of relations between leaders and other members of a wide variety of natural groups. His work began with discoveries that are consistent with principles of balanced interpersonal systems: most members of a college fraternity, for example, were found to see more similarity between themselves and their most preferred associates than between themselves and their least preferred ones. Such tendencies were not universal, however, and so he began to study group leaders in terms of the degree to which they did or did not perceive most and least preferred co-workers as being different; this variable he labeled *assumed similarity of opposites* (ASo). His rationale for applying this variable to group leaders was as follows: Those who discriminate sharply between the characteristics of their most and their least preferred co-workers are, in effect, rejecting the latter, whereas those who do not so discriminate are persons who prefer to keep close relationships with as many people as possible, whether or not they are desirable co-workers. Assumed *dis*similarity of opposites is thus, hypothetically, an index of interpersonal distance, in the sense of revealing more concern with work relationships than with personal involvement; assumed similarity of opposites reveals the opposite tendency.

One of the first kinds of groups that Fiedler studied was a league of fourteen high school basketball teams; the measure of a team's effectiveness was simply the proportion of games won during a season. The informal leader of each team (not necessarily the same as its captain) was designated as whatever man was most preferred by his teammates as a player, according to sociometric responses. Contrary to what you might expect, the more successful teams had chosen as their informal leader not the persons who made few discriminations among team members but those characterized by dissimilarity of opposites. In Fiedler's words, '. . . we expected that members of good teams would have relatively close interpersonal relations with each other . . . that members of teams [whose members] accepted one another and felt close to others on the team would also feel more secure, and that this security would allow them to devote proportionally greater efforts to the task than to activities designed to consolidate their own status within the team. While this was a beautiful hypothesis, it failed to be supported. Much to our surprise, we found that the good teams had . . . chosen as their informal leaders the low ASo persons [perceiving much dissimilarity], while the poorer teams had selected the warmer, more accepting, high ASo persons as informal leaders. The correlation between the informal leader's ASo score and the proportion of games the team had won . . . was −0·69, a very high relationship for studies of this nature.' A comparable study of a second set of basketball teams yielded similar results. Later studies of student surveying teams, bomber crews, Army tank crews, shift workers in open-hearth steel mills, and staffs of consumer cooperatives provided general support for the original investigations of basketball teams, and in some cases even stronger support. Fiedler's interpretations of these findings are offered, in part, in response to the question, Why is psychological distance relevant to team performance? '. . . we cannot adequately control and discipline people to whom we have strong emotional ties. If a man is emotionally dependent on another, he cannot afford to antagonize him since this might deprive him of the other man's support. Similarly, we can evaluate only those people, objectively, and we can control only those on whose good will we do not want to depend.' (Fiedler, 1960.)

Whatever the leaderlike behaviors that contribute to satisfying interpersonal relationships, they will be most facilitative if (as in the case of task achievement) they enable a group member to multiply his own effectiveness through others. In so far as one of Fiedler's informal leaders facilitates the arousal of a group norm of impersonality, according to which task achievement is rewarded and laxity is not, then he has multiplied his own effectiveness because group members themselves enforce the norm. In so far as one of Kahn and Katz's supervisors contributes to the creation of cohesiveness and consensual pride in their group, he too is multiplying his effectiveness. Satisfying interpersonal relations, like task achievement, are outcomes of interaction within the group as a whole; it is the facilitative effects on members' interaction that are the essence of leadership.

Sources of Individuals' Potential for Facilitation

It is obvious that no one can be an effective facilitator in ways that are beyond his capacities or that are personally repugnant to him. But attempts to identify leaders merely in terms of their personal characteristics have not, as we indicated at the outset of this chapter, been very fruitful. Our concern is with the social sources, not the intrapersonal ones, of individuals' potential for facilitating the achievement of group goals. More specifically, our present questions are of this kind: What are the social conditions that tend to elicit whatever abilities group members have to become facilitators?

Since we have already considered some motivational aspects of this question in Chapter 9 [not included here], we shall concentrate on group-structural considerations. Certain kinds of positions make it possible for their occupants to be particularly facilitative – and equally possible, of course, for them to provide obstacles to goal achievement. We shall consider two general ways in which recognized positions – especially formal ones, like those of a president, a manager, or a foreman – carry with them a potential for facilitation.

Facilitation through power

An individual's social power refers to the resources that he can muster by way of bringing influence to bear on one or more others. It is his potential to exert influence, with or without the willing consent of anyone who is the object of influence. Such power may or may not be resisted, it refers to influence potential, not to effectiveness in any particular instance.

Many formal positions confer power, in this sense, on their occupants, and this may also be true of informal positions, as in the case of some of Fiedler's more effective leaders. Two somewhat different bases of position-associated power may be distinguished: authority, and control of resources. *Authority* refers to consensually supported power; that is, the power behind a position of authority lies in the probability that others will support attempts by the position holder to exert influence, and if necessary help make his attempts successful. Consensual support for authority may be internal (on the part of group members themselves) or external (on the part of outsiders, as in the case of a group of managers who support a foreman's attempts to influence his workers). Group members may accept the authority of a position holder (that is, submit to his influence) either out of respect for his personal characteristics or out of deference to the position, regardless of who occupies it, or for some combination of these. The essence of authority is that its strength lies in group norms; members share acceptance of rules according to which authority is granted to someone.

There are many forms of *resource control*. A foreman, for example, has it in his power to make equipment or materials available to his men, and a corporation president can allocate financial resources in various ways. Control over information is a particularly effective form of exerting influence that is often available to officials. Persons who occupy key positions in communication networks tend to be thought of as leaders. Top officials of groups or organizations often owe a great deal of their power to the fact that they have both internal and external communicative access – that is, both to their subordinates and to outsiders. Members at lower-status levels usually have less access to internal sources of information, and little or none externally.

Facilitation through visibility

In so far as special facilitators, whether or not they hold formal positions, are consensually recognized as such, they are generally visible to other group members. This fact in itself adds to their facilitative potential, in either or both of two ways. Their visibility, in the first place, makes them *symbols* of the group, both internally and externally. As personified symbols, both group members and outsiders tend to bring problems to them, rely on their advice, or seek their influence. Recognition as a facilitator results in acceptance as a symbol, which in turn results in increased opportunities for facilitation. Their visibility may also result in their being accepted as *models* for others to follow. In so far as this occurs, their effectiveness may be multiplied in many ways; ineffectiveness, too, may have multiplying effects.

Leadership as a Role Relationship

It is possible for an interaction group to continue to exist, and even attain its goals quite successfully, in the absence of any particularly facilitative contributions on the part of any members;

there would be no leaders in such a group. But the reverse is not true: there could be no leader apart from a group. In this sense a group is more essential to a leader than a leader to a group, and this fact alone makes clear the interactional nature of leadership, which depends quite as much on what group members do to, for, and with a leader as on anything that he does. Facilitation, after all, requires persons to be facilitated, and shared recognition of a facilitator is a matter of response by members not only to him but also to one another.

It is for such reasons that we have described leadership as a role relationship. Once a group member has become recognized by others as particularly facilitative in certain ways, those ways are likely to become habitual on his part as others develop habits of responding to his facilitative ways; thus role relationships develop that are, quite literally, two halves of the same habit. [. . .]

References

BALES, R. F. (1958), 'Task roles and social roles in problem solving groups', in E. Maccoby, T. M. Newcomb, and E. L. Hartley (eds.), *Readings in Social Psychology*, Holt, Rinehart and Winston, 3rd edn.

BIRD, C. (1940), *Social Psychology*, Appleton-Century-Crofts.

FIEDLER, F. (1960), 'The leader's psychological distance and group effectiveness', in D. Cartwright and A. Zander (eds.), *Group Dynamics: Research and Theory*, Harper and Row, 2nd edn.

KAHN, R. L., and KATZ, D. (1960), 'Leadership practices in relation to productivity and morale', in D. Cartwright and A. Zander (eds.), *Group Dynamics: Research and Theory*, Harper and Row, 2nd edn.

Part Eight Leadership in Complex Situations

Relatively few of the empirical studies of leadership have been conducted in complex organizations. In large measure this has been due to a recognition that leadership phenomena in the factory, the warship, the government department, the university, indeed in any hierarchical organization are extremely complex. Even developers of theories have been content, for the most part, to rely upon observations of small groups whether in the laboratory or an aircraft. Their reasoning appears to have been that the essence of the leadership relation must first be captured before the many complexities can begin to be woven in.

Fiedler (1967) notes that 'much of the literature on groups tends to gloss over the fact that task groups in real life are practically always subunits of a larger organization' (p. 17). It has long been recognized that the organizational context plays an essential part in the determination of leadership. One of the studies to have made this point most clearly was that of Pelz (Reading 21) which showed that leadership within an hierarchical organization may be somewhat different from that in isolated small groups, and was able to reconcile what had been hitherto somewhat conflicting results.

Reading 13, included in Part Four as an extension or refinement of interaction theory, is also an attempt to fit the theory to some of the complexities of hierarchical organizations. It demonstrates well that one cannot in complex situations find simple and direct relationships among leadership phenomena – the relationships like the phenomena are complex or as Fiedler has said elsewhere (1967) 'A pretzel-shaped universe requires pretzel-shaped hypotheses'. What in simpler circumstances may be direct linear relationships become, in complex organizations, contingent upon other conditions holding or not holding.

Fleishman and Harris show just this very clearly indeed in Reading 22. Working with the Ohio Leadership Studies and within the International Harvester Company they find significant *non-linear* relationships between foreman behaviour and such indices of industrial well-being as grievance rates and turnover. Desirable patterns of leadership behaviour can be chosen only when a complex web of interrelationships is understood.

More complex models of the relationship between leader behaviour and organizational effectiveness are put to at least a preliminary test by Bowers and Seashore in Reading 23. The multidimensional conception of both leader behaviour and organization effectiveness leads again to a finding of significant contingent relationships. As the authors themselves emphasize, 'The model is not a simple one of managerial leadership leading to peer leadership, which in turn leads to outcomes separately; instead, different aspects of performance are associated with different leadership characteristics, and, in some cases, satisfaction outcomes seem related to performance outcomes' (p. 384). Some relationships here turn out to be strong and direct, others indirect and still others which might have been expected can not be found at all. It is clear that present conceptualizations of leadership are far from explaining all aspects of effectiveness in complex organizations.

Amitai Etzioni is a sociologist well known for his 1964 study of modern organizations (Etzioni, 1964). His paper chosen for inclusion here (Reading 24) deals in a very interesting and thought-provoking way with the application to complex organizations of the important Bales–Parsons model of dual leadership in small groups. In no small way Etzioni establishes the usefulness in a variety of real-life situations of the Bales laboratory analysis, and once again the contingent nature of relationships is emphasized by his thoughtful and suggestive differentiation among complex organizations.

To the reader of these selections and even more to those who read more extended treatments such as Bass (1960), Katz and Kahn (1966), or Fiedler (1967), it will be clear that our knowledge of the constituents of effective leadership in a complex organization is still very limited indeed, but it will be equally apparent that psychology and sociology have made progress in understanding this most subtle relationship. Already replications and extensions of relatively simple and direct findings from small group studies in larger and more directly involved task groups give confidence that some applications may profitably be made.

References

BASS, B. M. (1960), *Leadership, Psychology and Organizational Behavior*, Harper.

ETZIONI, A. (1964), *Modern Organizations*, Prentice-Hall.

FIEDLER, F. (1967), *Theory of Leadership Effectiveness*, McGraw-Hill.

KATZ, D. and KAHN, R. L. (1966), *The Social Psychology of Organizations*, Wiley.

21 D. C. Pelz

Leadership Within a Hierarchical Organization

D. C. Pelz, 'Leadership within a hierarchical organization', *Journal of Social Issues*, vol. 7 (1951), pp. 49–55.

Introduction

Concern with leadership has been central to the Human Relations Program from its beginning. But there have been important shifts in emphasis. Our early concepts and hypotheses drew freely from previous studies on small groups. To discover how the first-line supervisor affected employee attitudes and productivity, the direction of search seemed obvious. One studied the face-to-face interactions between supervisor and work group.

The hard facts of analysis have shown that this approach is incomplete. Leadership in isolated groups is one thing; leadership within large organizations may be something else again. At least, it must be looked at with a fresh view.

The impact of organizational factors on interactions within the work group was suggested by some of our first results. In training courses the supervisor is given this general rule: he should always recognize good work done by employees. He should, for example, recommend deserving employees for promotion. But in the Prudential study supervisors of high producing work groups were found to play one of two roles in the promotion process. Either they made recommendations which generally went through, or they made no recommendations at all. In contrast, the supervisors of low producing work groups often recommended promotions, but these generally did not go through (Katz, Maccoby and Morse, 1950). To recommend promotions was not, as such, related to high employee productivity. A more basic factor seemed to be operating, outside of the sphere of the work group. This factor was the supervisor's power within the larger department. The high producing supervisors were more realistic about their power; they entered the promotion process only when they could influence the outcome. The concept of the supervisor's power or influence within his department is central in a recent study, some details of which are given below (Pelz, 1951).

Superficially the results of such studies might suggest that we need one set of theories to account for leadership in isolated groups, and another set of theories to account for leadership within hierarchical organizations. It is our belief, however, that both situations can be incorporated within a single theoretical framework. In fact, it might be possible to use artificial groups and laboratory methods to reproduce some of the variables of an organizational context. Variables such as power and status have been manipulated in several studies done at the Research Center for Group Dynamics (Kelley, 1951; Pepitone, 1950). Some elements in a theoretical framework designed to include both leadership situations are discussed at this point.

Basic Postulate: Successful Leadership Depends in Part on Helping Group Members Achieve Their Goals

Empirical studies, as shown in reviews of the literature by (Gibb, 1947; Jenkins, 1947; Stogdill, 1948) have failed to find traits that are universal in successful leaders. In different studies, different or contradictory traits in leaders are found related to whatever criterion of success is used. Differences in the situations or in the groups, from study to study, seem to be partly responsible. Gibb concludes that 'leadership is relative always to the situation'.

But it is not enough simply to say that leadership is relative to the situation. Relative to what aspects of the situation? We must identify those factors which make a given leader behavior 'successful' or 'unsuccessful'.

Recent theories have stressed the *needs of group members* as key aspects of the all-important 'situation'. The successful or valued or obeyed leader is one who can help group members achieve their goals. This emphasis on group members' needs and goals appears sound, at least as one beginning of a theory of leadership. In any kind of situation, a basic postulate is that *the more the leader (or any member) helps other members achieve their goals, the greater will be the members' acceptance of him.* By 'acceptance' is meant that members are willing to follow the leader's suggestions, express satisfaction with the leader's conduct, etc.

This basic postulate is not, by itself, a theory. It does not permit us to make specific predictions, and this a genuine theory must be able to do. To make predictions, we must be able to state conditions such as: (*a*) Toward what goals are the group members motivated? (*b*) What acts or characteristics of a leader help the members achieve each of these goals? And finally, (*c*) How do specific leaders measure up on these factors? If the first two conditions are known, and if we have measured each leader on the relevant factors, we can begin to predict the acceptance of particular leaders by their particular groups.

Very probably, the basic postulate will apply to leaders within a hierarchical organization, as well as to leaders in simpler groups. But the conditions which we need to know for prediction may be markedly affected by the organizational context. With regard to (*a*), for example, we shall have to give more weight to what we may loosely call 'organizational goals' and 'group goals'. These must, of course, actually function as goals or as sub-goals for the individual members, if the basic postulate is to apply. With regard to (*b*), the organizational context will have much to do with whether certain acts of the leader can or cannot help his group members achieve their goals. The recent study cited above underscores this point. Major features of this research will now be described.

The Point of Departure: Some Puzzling Results in Previous Analyses of the Data

The data for the study were collected early in 1948 from the personnel of a large electric utility, employing well over 10,000 people, and serving a major midwestern manufacturing city and surrounding urban and rural areas. The work of the company covers many different occupations and skill levels. Attitudes of all non-supervisory employees were ascertained through paper-and-pencil questionnaires. Attitudes and practices of all first-line supervisors – each of the people in charge of a work group, the basic unit – were obtained in personal interviews utilizing open-ended questions. The verbatim replies were later coded with the content analysis procedures of the Survey Research Center.

The author's objective was to determine how measures obtained on the supervisors related to attitudes of employees they supervised. What supervisory practices led to employee acceptance of the supervisor? Three separate analyses had to be done, before answers to this question could be formulated. In the process, the importance of organizational factors became increasingly clear.

The first analysis was of a design frequently found in leadership studies. Forty 'high employee satisfaction' work groups and thirty 'low employee satisfaction' work groups were selected, and the data from their respective supervisors examined on fifty items. While half the differences were in the expected direction, only six differences were statistically significant (at the 5 per cent level of confidence). By chance alone, 2·5 'significant' differences would be expected; the obtained number was little more than twice the chance number.

The inconclusiveness of these results compelled a second analysis. The previous analysis had focused exclusively on the interaction between supervisor and employees in the work group; it had assumed, in all work groups, universal relationships between supervisory practices and employee attitudes. But the evidence on situational effects warns against this assumption. High satisfaction in one group of employees may result from supervisory practices quite different from those used in another well satisfied group. In the second analysis, therefore, different types of employees and situations were handled separately. Separate analyses were performed for men and women, for white collar and blue collar workers, for small work groups and large, for differing educational backgrounds, and for various combinations of these factors.

The results of this analysis were more promising. A direct comparison with the first is not possible – different measures of the supervisory and employee variables were used. It is interesting that statistically significant results numbered seven times chance. But some of these significant results were disturbing; some went *opposite* to predictions based on previous research. One of the supervisory measures, for example, was a scale of 'taking sides with employees in cases of employee–management conflicts', based on three intercorrelated items from the interview. In case of disagreement between the employees under him and his own superiors, whose side did the supervisor take? Did he see his job primarily as selling his employees' viewpoint to management, as selling management's viewpoint to employees, or as remaining independent? Previous evidence suggests that group members will think more highly of the leader who 'goes to bat' for them, who sides with them in cases of conflict with higher authorities. The results supported this hypothesis in small work groups (10 employees or fewer). But in large white collar work groups, employees were significantly *less* satisfied with such a supervisor; they preferred the supervisor who sided with management. Other supervisory variables showed similar contradictory results.

Why? What was there about the large work group situation that produced relationships apparently opposite to those found in small work groups? Still one more analysis was essential, if we were to resolve this predictive tangle and others like it.

The previous section mentions two general areas within which the third analysis design sought some of the responsible factors. Perhaps employees in the larger work groups had different needs and goals from those in the smaller groups. One step, therefore, was to develop, from existing employee data, crude indices of certain needs.

Or perhaps the same supervisory behavior, in small and in large work groups, might have different results with respect to employees achieving their goals. At this point, the factor of the supervisor's *power or influence* within the larger department became crucial.

Two Predictions on Influence and Leadership

The type of theory adopted for the third analysis has already been described. The basic postulate is that the supervisor will be 'accepted' by his work group if his behavior helps them to achieve their goals. The new concept introduced in the third analysis is that of the supervisor's influence within his department. If the supervisor has considerable influence over events within his department, then his attempts to help employees reach

341

their goals are very likely to succeed. If, on the other hand, he lacks influence, then his attempts toward employee goal achievement are likely to fail.

Two related predictions follow. Given supervisors who are influential, the more they behave so as to aid goal achievement, the more satisfied their employees will be toward them. A positive correlation is predicted between the supervisory behavior and employee attitudes. But given non-influential supervisors, there can be no such relationship. Stronger attempts toward helping employees can produce no rise in employee satisfaction. There might be a drop, in fact. The second prediction, then, is that the correlation between the supervisor's helpful behavior and employee attitudes will be significantly less positive (or more negative) under non-influential supervisors.

If variation in influence does produce these changes in the relationships of supervisory behavior to employee attitudes, then influence may be called a 'conditioner' of the relationships, following a useful suggestion by Morris and Seeman (1950). The amount of change – the difference in correlations found under high and low influence supervisors respectively – may be called the 'conditioner effect' of influence.

Because of the initial emphasis on the supervisor's interpersonal relations, a variable of his power or influence was not anticipated when the data were collected. But it appeared possible to construct one. A supervisor was considered to have relatively high 'influence over the social environment in which his employees were functioning' if he reported having a voice in departmental decisions made by his own superior; if he had relatively little contact with his superior – an indication of more autonomy in running his own work group; and if he had a high salary – indicating higher general status.

Two scales of supervisory behavior appeared to measure 'attempts at helping employees to reach their goals'. One was the scale previously described, of 'taking sides with employees in cases of employee–management conflict'. Another was a scale of 'social closeness toward employees', or lack of social distance, based on several items from the supervisor's interview.

Several employee attitudes were used. The most important one was an index of employees' 'general satisfaction with the performance of their immediate supervisor'. Product-moment correlations between the two supervisory behaviors and the various employee attitudes were computed. These correlations were obtained separately under influential and under non-influential supervisors, in each of seven employee sub-populations, defined according to white collar versus blue collar occupations, sex, size of work group, and union coverage.

Major Results

The results, in general, confirm the predictions. For the group of high influence supervisors, we obtained twenty-eight correlations between the two supervisory behaviors and the various employee attitudes, in the several employee sub-populations. For the low influence supervisors, we obtained a parallel set of twenty-eight correlations. Nineteen of the correlations under influential supervisors are at least mildly positive, and seven are significantly positive (at the 5 per cent level of confidence). This is eleven times the chance number (taking direction into account). The first prediction is thus generally confirmed. By contrast, under low influence supervisors, nineteen of the parallel correlations are either zero or slightly negative.

The second prediction concerns the various 'conditioner effects' of the supervisor's influence: the difference in each product-moment correlation between a supervisory behavior and an employee attitude, under high and low influence supervisors respectively. Positive differences are found in the majority of the twenty-eight comparisons, and six of them are significantly positive.[1] This number is ten times what chance alone would produce. Thus the second prediction is generally confirmed. It should be noted that none of these conditioner effects could have been foreseen on the basis of previous findings. They are not the product of empirical hindsight.

The results demonstrate, in short, that a supervisor's influence or power within the department does condition the way his supervisory behavior relates to employee attitudes. When an

1. The significance of differences between correlations was tested by the use of Fisher's z-transformation for r, as described in Q. McNemar, *Psychological Statistics*, John Wiley and Sons, 1950.

influential supervisor uses these helpful practices, positive correlations are found between his behavior and employee attitudes. But in the case of non-influential supervisors, no correlations (or slightly negative ones) are found between the same supervisory behaviors and employee attitudes.

Implications

In the three successive analyses of our supervisory leadership data, the importance of the organizational context has become increasingly clear. The major variable in the third analysis – the supervisor's power or influence within the department – depends on the supervisor's role within the larger organization. It cannot be measured by observing interactions within the work group. (The power of the supervisor over his group members is not the same variable.)

The findings imply that if an influential supervisor attempts to help employees achieve their goals, his efforts will usually succeed. Concrete results will be achieved. Employee satisfactions will rise. But – the data imply – if a non-influential supervisor tries to do the same, his efforts will often fail. Employee expectations will be frustrated. Their satisfactions will not rise, or may even fall.

From a broader view, the data illustrate the futility of studying supervisor–employee relations without regard for the organizational setting. We cannot give all supervisors a set of universal rules on how to behave toward subordinates.

This statement does not imply a pluralism in the laws of leadership. On the contrary, we believe that a variety of leadership phenomena might be accounted for in a single theoretical framework. A basic postulate in such a framework – one expressed by several theorists – is that a leader will be accepted by group members to the extent that he helps them to achieve their goals.

This postulate should apply both to isolated groups and to groups in an organizational setting. Specific goals will differ somewhat in the two cases. In the latter, members will emphasize organizational and group goals more than in the former. Moreover, within large organizations the leader's ability to help the group will depend to a much greater degree upon factors outside of the face-to-face group. As the leader's role in the organization varies, our theory leads us to predict sharp changes in the effect of his behavior upon members' goal achievements, and hence upon their attitudes.

References

GIBB, C. A. (1947), 'The principles and traits of leadership', *Journal of Abnormal and Social Psychology*, vol. 42, pp. 267–84.

JENKINS, W. O. (1947), 'A review of leadership studies with particular reference to military problems', *Psychological Bulletin*, vol. 44, pp.54–79.

KATZ, D., MACCOBY, N., and MORSE, N. C. (1950), *Productivity, Supervision and Employee Morale, Part 1*, Survey Research Center, University of Michigan.

KELLEY, H. H. (1951), 'Communication in experimentally created hierarchies', *Human Relations*, vol. 4, pp. 39–56.

MORRIS, R. T., and SEEMAN, M. (1950), 'The problem of leadership: an interdisciplinary approach', *American Journal of Sociology*, vol. 56, pp. 145–55.

PELZ, D. C. (1951), *Power and Leadership in the First-Line Supervisor*, Survey Research Center, University of Michigan.

PEPITONE, A. (1950), 'Motivational effects in social perception', *Human Relations*, vol. 3, pp. 57–76.

STOGDILL, R. M. (1948), 'Personal factors associated with leadership: a survey of the literature', *Journal of Psychology*, vol. 25, pp. 35–71.

22 E. A. Fleishman and E. F. Harris

Patterns of Leadership Behavior Related to Employee
Grievances and Turnover

E. A. Fleishman and E. F. Harris, 'Patterns of leadership behavior related
to employee grievances and turnover', *Personnel Psychology*, vol. 15 (1962),
pp. 43–56.

This study investigates some relationships between the leader
behavior of industrial supervisors and the behavior of their
group members. It represents an extension of earlier studies
carried out at the International Harvester Company, while the
authors were with the Ohio State University Leadership Studies.

Briefly, these previous studies involved three primary phases
which have been described elsewhere (Fleishman, 1951, 1953a,
1953b, 1953c; Fleishman, Harris and Burtt, 1955; Harris and
Fleishman, 1955). In the initial phase, independent leadership
patterns were defined and a variety of behavioral and attitude
instruments were developed to measure them. This phase confirmed the usefulness of the constructs 'consideration' and 'structure' for describing leader behavior in industry.

Since the present study, as well as the previous work, focused
on these two leadership patterns, it may be well to redefine them
here:

Consideration includes behavior indicating mutual trust, respect,
and a certain warmth and rapport between the supervisor and his
group. This does not mean that this dimension reflects a superficial 'pat-on-the-back', 'first name calling' kind of human
relations behavior. This dimension appears to emphasize a
deeper concern for group members' needs and includes such behavior as allowing subordinates more participation in decision
making and encouraging more two-way communication.

Structure includes behavior in which the supervisor organizes and
defines group activities and his relation to the group. Thus, he
defines the role he expects each member to assume, assigns tasks,

346

plans ahead, establishes ways of getting things done, and pushes for production. This dimension seems to emphasize overt attempts to achieve organizational goals.

Since the dimensions are independent, a supervisor may score high on both dimensions, low on both, or high on one and low on the other.

The second phase of the original Harvester research utilized measures of these patterns to evaluate changes in foreman leadership attitudes and behavior resulting from a management training program. The amount of change was evaluated at three different times – once while the foremen were still in the training setting, again after they had returned to the plant environment, and still later in a 'refresher' training course. The results showed that while still in the training situation there was a distinct increase in consideration and an unexpected decrease in structure attitudes. It was also found that leadership attitudes became more *dissimilar* rather than similar, despite the fact that all foremen had received the same training. Furthermore, when behavior and attitudes were evaluated back in the plant, the effects of the training largely disappeared. This pointed to the main finding, i.e. the overriding importance of the interaction of the training effects with certain aspects of the social setting in which the foremen had to operate in the plant. Most critical was the 'leadership climate' supplied by the behavior and attitudes of the foreman's own boss. This was more related to the foreman's own consideration and structure behavior than was the fact that he had or had not received the leadership training.

The third phase may be termed the 'criterion phase', in which the relationships between consideration and structure and indices of foremen proficiency were examined. One finding was that production supervisors rated high in 'proficiency' by plant management turned out to have leadership patterns high in structure and low in consideration. (This relationship was accentuated in departments scoring high on a third variable, 'perceived pressure of deadlines'.) On the other hand, this same pattern of high structure and low consideration was found to be related to high labor turnover, union grievances, worker absences and accidents, and low worker satisfaction. There was some indication that these relationships might differ in 'non-production' departments. An interesting sidelight was that foremen with low consideration *and* low structure were more often bypassed by subordinates in the informal organizational structure. In any case, it was evident that 'what is an effective supervisor' is a complex question, depending on the proficiency criterion emphasized, management values, type of work, and other situational variables.

The present study examines some of the questions left unanswered by this previous work.

Purpose

The present study focused on two main questions. First, what is the *form* of the relationship between leader behavior and indices of group behavior? Is it linear or curvilinear? As far as we know, no one has really examined this question. Rephrased, this question asked if there are critical levels of consideration and/or structure beyond which it does or does not make a difference in group behavior? Is an 'average' amount of structure better than a great deal or no structure at all? Similarly, is there an optimum level of consideration above and below which worker grievances and/or turnover rise sharply?

The second question concerns the interaction effects of different combinations of consideration and structure. Significant correlations have been found between each of these patterns and such indices as rated proficiency, grievances, turnover, departmental reputation, subordinate satisfactions, etc. (e.g. Fleishman, Harris and Burtt, 1955; Halpin, 1954; Hemphill, 1955; Stogdill and Coons, 1957). These studies present some evidence that scoring low on both dimensions is not desirable. They also indicate that some balance of consideration and structure may be optimal for satisfying both proficiency and morale criteria. The present study is a more intensive examination of possible optimum combinations of consideration and structure.

The present study investigates the relationships between foreman behavior and two primary indices of group behavior: labor grievances and employee turnover. Both of these may be considered as partial criteria of group effectiveness.

Procedure

Leader behavior measures

The study was conducted in a motor truck manufacturing plant. Fifty-seven production foremen and their work groups took part in the study. They represented such work operations as stamping, assembly, body assembly, body paint, machinery, and export. At least three workers, drawn randomly from each foreman's department, described the leader behavior of their foreman by means of the Supervisory Behavior Description Questionnaire (described elsewhere, Fleishman, 1953b, 1957). Each questionnaire was scored on consideration and structure, and a mean consideration score and a mean structure score was computed for each foreman. The correlation between consideration and structure among foremen in this plant was found to be -0.33. The correlation between these scales is usually around zero (Fleishman, 1957), but in this plant foremen who are high in structure are somewhat more likely to be seen as lower in consideration and vice versa. However, the relationship is not high.

Grievance measures

Grievances were defined in terms of the number presented in writing and placed in company files. No data on grievances which were settled at lower levels (hence, without their becoming matters of company record) were considered. The frequency of grievances was equated for each foreman's work group by dividing the record for that group by the number of workers in that group. The reliability of these records, computed by correlating the records for odd and even weeks over an 11-month period and correcting by the Spearman–Brown formula, was 0.73. The entire 11-month record (for each foreman's work group) was used in the present analysis.

Turnover measures

Turnover was figured as the number of workers who voluntarily left the employ of the company within the 11-month period. Again, the records for each foreman's group were equated by dividing the number who resigned by the number of workers in his work group. The nature of the records did not permit an

349

analysis of the reasons which each worker gave for leaving, and so all such terminations are included. The corrected odd–even weeks reliability for this period was 0·59.

The reliabilities for the grievance and turnover measures are for the foremen's work groups and not for the individual worker. In the case of turnover, this reliability is quite high when one considers that different workers are involved in each time period. (Once a worker leaves, of course, he cannot contribute to turnover again.) The findings of stable grievance and turnover rates among groups under the same foremen is an important finding in its own right. The correlation between grievances and turnover is 0·37. This indicates that, while high grievance work groups tend to have higher turnover, the relationship is not very high. Each index is worth considering as an independent aspect of group behavior.

Results

Leader behavior and grievances

Figure 1 plots the average employee grievance rates for departments under foremen scoring at different levels of consideration.

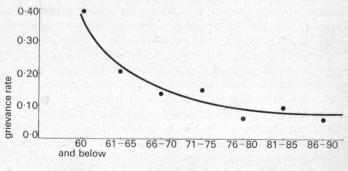

Figure 1 Relation between consideration and grievance rates

From the curve fitted to these points it can be seen clearly that the relationship between the foremen's behavior and grievances from their work groups is negative and curvilinear. For most of the range increased consideration goes with reduced grievance

350

rates. However, increased consideration above a certain critical level (approximately 76 out of a possible 112) is not related to further decreases in grievances. Furthermore, the curve appears to be negatively accelerated. A given decrease in consideration just below the critical point (76) is related to a small increase in grievances, but, as consideration continues to drop, grievance rates rise sharply. Thus, a five-point drop on the consideration scale, just below a score of 76, is related to a small grievance increase, but a five-point drop below 61 is related to a large rise in grievances. The correlation ratio (eta) represented by this curve is -0.51.

Figure 2 plots grievances against the foremen's structure scores. Here a similar curvilinear relationship is observed. In this case the correlation is positive (eta $= 0.71$). Below a certain level

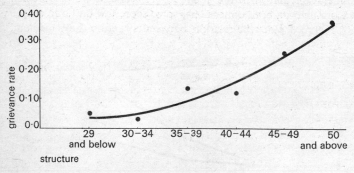

Figure 2 Relation between structure and grievance rates

(approximately 36 out of a possible 80 on our scale) structure is unrelated to grievances, but above this point increased structure goes with increased grievances. Again we see that a given increase in structure just above this critical level is accompanied by a small increase in grievances, but continued increases in structure are associated with increasingly disproportionately large increases in grievance rates.

Both curves are hyperbolic rather than parabolic in form. Thus, it appears that for neither consideration nor structure is there an 'optimum' point in the middle of the range below and above which grievances rise. Rather there seems to be a range within which increased consideration or decreased structure makes no difference. Of course, when one reaches these levels, grievances are already at a very low level and not much improvement can be expected. However, the important point is that this low grievance level is reached before one gets to the extremely high end of the consideration scale or to the extremely low end of the structure scale. It is also clear that extremely high structure and extremely low consideration are most related to high grievances.

Different combinations of consideration and structure related to grievances

The curves described establish that a general relationship exists between each of these leadership patterns and the frequency of employee grievances. But how do *different combinations* of consideration and structure relate to grievances? Some foremen score high on both dimensions, some score low on both, etc.

Figure 3 plots the relation between structure (low, medium,

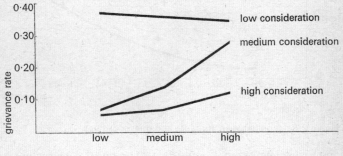

Figure 3 Combinations of consideration and structure related to grievances

and high) and grievances for groups of foremen who were either low, medium, or high on consideration. The curves show that grievances occur most frequently among groups whose foremen are low in consideration, regardless of the amount of emphasis on structure. The most interesting finding relates to the curve for the high consideration foremen. This curve suggests that, for the high consideration foreman, structure could be increased without any appreciable increase in grievances. However, the reverse is not true; that is, foremen who were low in consideration could not reduce grievances by easing up on structure. For foremen average on consideration, grievances were lowest where structure was lowest and increased in an almost linear fashion as structure increased. These data show a definite interaction between consideration and structure. Apparently, high consideration can compensate for high structure. But low structure will not offset low consideration.

Before we speculate further about these relationships, let us examine the results with employee turnover.

Leader behavior and turnover

Figures 4 and 5 plot the curves for the Supervisory Behavior Description scores of these foremen against the turnover criteria. Again, we see the curvilinear relationships. The correlation (eta) of consideration and turnover is -0.69; structure and turnover

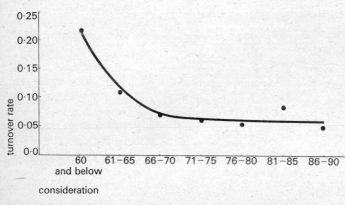

Figure 4 Relation between consideration and turnover rates

correlate 0.63. As in the case with grievances, below a certain critical level of consideration and above a certain level of structure, turnover goes up. There is, however, an interesting difference in that the critical levels differ from those related to grievances. The flat portions of each of these curves are more extended and the rise in turnover beyond the point of inflection is steeper. The

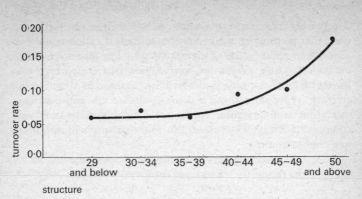

structure

Figure 5 Relation between structure and turnover rates

implication of this is quite sensible and indicates that 'they gripe before they leave'. In other words, a given increase in structure (to approximately 39) or decrease in consideration (to 66) may result in increased grievances, but not turnover. It takes higher structure and lower consideration before turnover occurs.

Different combinations of consideration and structure related to turnover

Figure 6 plots the relation between structure (low, medium, and high) and turnover for groups of foremen who were also either low, medium, or high on consideration. As with grievances, the curves show that turnover is highest for the work groups whose foremen combine low consideration with high structure; however, the amount of consideration is the dominant factor. The curves show that turnover is highest among those work groups whose foremen are low in consideration, regardless of the amount of emphasis these same foremen show on structure. There is little distinction between the work groups of foremen who show medium and high consideration since both of these groups have low turnover among their workers. Furthermore, increased structure does not seem related to increased turnover in these two groups.[1]

1. This, of course, is consistent with our earlier finding that for increased turnover it takes a bigger drop in consideration and a bigger increase in structure to make a difference. Thus, our high and medium consideration groups separate for grievances, but overlap for turnover.

354

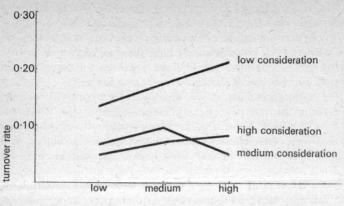

Figure 6 Combinations of consideration and structure related to turnover

Conclusions

1. This study indicates that there are significant r elationship between the leader behavior of foremen and the labor grievances and employee turnover in their work groups. In general, low consideration and high structure go with high grievances and turnover.

2. There appear to be certain critical levels beyond which increased consideration or decreased structure have no effect on grievance or turnover rates. Similarly grievances and turnover are shown to increase most markedly at the extreme ends of the consideration (low end) and structure (high end) scales. Thus, the relationship is curvilinear, not linear, and hyperbolic, not parabolic.

3. The critical points at which increased structure and decreased consideration begin to relate to group behavior is not the same for grievances and turnover. Increases in turnover do not occur until lower on the consideration scale and higher on the structure scale, as compared with increases in grievances. For example, if consideration is steadily reduced, higher grievances appear before increased turnover occurs. It appears that there may be different 'threshold levels' of consideration and structure related to grievances and turnover.

4. Other principal findings concern the interaction effects found between different combinations of consideration and structure. Taken in combination, consideration is the dominant factor. For example, both grievances and turnover were highest in groups having low consideration foremen, regardless of the degree of structuring behavior shown by these same foremen.

5. Grievances and turnover were lowest for groups with foremen showing medium to high consideration together with low structure. However, one of the most important results is the finding that high consideration foremen could increase structure with very little increase in grievances and no increase in turnover. High consideration foremen had relatively low grievances and turnover, regardless of the amount of structuring engaged in.

Thus, with regard to grievances and turnover, leader behavior characterized by low consideration is more critical than behavior characterized by high structure. Apparently, foremen can compensate for high structure by increased consideration, but low consideration foremen cannot compensate by decreasing their structuring behavior.

One interpretation is that workers under foremen who establish a climate of mutual trust, rapport, and tolerance for two-way communication with their work groups are more likely to accept higher levels of structure. This might be because they perceive this structure differently from employees in 'low consideration' climates. Thus, under 'low consideration' climates, high structure is seen as threatening and restrictive, but under 'high consideration' climates this same structure is seen as supportive and helpful. A related interpretation is that foremen who establish such an atmosphere can more easily solve the problems resulting from high structure. Thus, *grievances* may be solved at this level before they get into the official records. Similarly, *turnover* may reflect escape from a problem situation which cannot be resolved in the absence of mutual trust and two-way communication. In support of this interpretation, we do have evidence that leaders high in consideration are also better at predicting subordinates' responses to problems (Fleishman and Salter, 1961).

One has to be careful in making cause and effect inferences here. A possible limitation is that our descriptions of foreman behavior came from the workers themselves. Those workers with many grievances may view their foremen as low in consideration simply because they have a lot of grievances. However, the descriptions of foreman behavior were obtained from workers drawn randomly from each foreman's group; the odds are against our receiving descriptions from very many workers contributing a disproportionate share of grievances. In the case of turnover, of course, our descriptions could not have been obtained from people who had left during the previous 11 months. Yet substantial correlations were obtained between foremen descriptions, supplied by currently employed workers, with the turnover rates of their work groups. Furthermore, we do have evidence that leader behavior over a year period tends to be quite stable. Test-retest correlations for consideration, as well as for structure, tend to be high even when different workers do the describing on the retest (Harris and Fleishman, 1955). Our present preference is to favor the interpretation that high turnover and grievances result, at least in part, from the leader behavior patterns described.

The nonlinear relations between leader behavior and our criteria of effectiveness have more general implications for leadership research. For one thing, it points up the need for a more careful examination of the *form* of such relationships before computing correlation coefficients. Some previously obtained correlations with leadership variables may be underestimates because of linearity assumptions. Similarly, some previous negative or contradictory results may be 'explained' by the fact that (a) inappropriate coefficients were used or (b) these studies were dealing with only the flat portions of these curves. If, for example, all the foremen in our study had scored over 76 on consideration and under 36 on structure, we would have concluded that there was no relation between these leadership patterns and grievances and turnover. Perhaps in comparing one study with another, we need to specify the range of leader behavior involved in each study.

There is, of course, a need to explore similar relationships with other criteria. There is no assurance that similar curvilinear patterns and interaction effects will hold for other indices (e.g. group productivity). Even the direction of these relationships may vary with the criterion used. We have evidence (Fleishman,

Harris, and Burtt, 1955), for example, that consideration and structure may relate quite differently to another effectiveness criterion: management's perceptions of foremen proficiency. However, research along these lines may make it possible to specify the particular leadership patterns which most nearly 'optimize' these various effectiveness criteria in industrial organizations.

References

FLEISHMAN, E. A. (1951), *'Leadership Climate' and Supervisory Behavior*, Personnel Research Board, Ohio State University.

FLEISHMAN, E. A. (1953a), 'Leadership climate, human relations training, and supervisory behavior', *Personnel Psychology*, vol. 6, pp. 205–22.

FLEISHMAN, E. A. (1953b), 'The description of supervisory behavior', *Journal of Applied Psychology*, vol. 37, pp. 1–6.

FLEISHMAN, E. A. (1953c), 'The measurement of leadership attitudes in industry', *Journal of Applied Psychology*, vol. 37, pp. 153–8.

FLIESHMAN, E. A. (1957), 'A leader behavior description for industry', in R. M. Stogdill and A. E. Coons (eds.) *Leader Behavior: Its Description and Measurement*, Bureau of Business Research, Ohio State University.

FLEISHMAN, E. A., HARRIS, E. F., and BURTT, H. E. (1955), *Leadership and Supervision in Industry*, Bureau of Educational Research, Ohio State University.

FLEISHMAN, E. A., and SALTER, J. A. (1961), 'The relation between the leader's behavior and his empathy toward subordinates', *Advanced Management*, March, pp. 18–20.

HARRIS, E. F., and FLEISHMAN, E. A. (1955), 'Human relations training and the stability of leadership patterns', *Journal of Applied Psychology*, vol. 39, pp. 20–5.

HALPIN, A. W. (1954), 'The leadership behavior and combat performance of airplane commanders', *Journal of Abnormal and Social Psychology*, vol. 49, pp. 19–22.

HEMPHILL, J. K. (1955), 'Leadership behavior associated with the administrative reputation of college departments', *Journal of Educational Psychology*, vol. 46, pp. 385–401.

STOGDILL, R. M. and COONS, A. E. (eds.) (1957), *Leader Behavior: Its Description and Measurement*, Bureau of Business Research, Ohio State University.

23 D. G. Bowers and S. E. Seashore

Predicting Organizational Effectiveness with a Four-
Factor Theory of Leadership

D. G. Bowers and S. E. Seashore, 'Predicting organizational effectiveness
with a four-factor theory of leadership', *Administrative Science Quarterly*,
vol. 11 (1966), pp. 238–63.

Recent research in the area of leadership seems to point to the existence
of four basic dimensions of leadership: support, interaction facilitation,
goal emphasis, and work facilitation. Data from a recent study of 40
agencies of one of the leading life insurance companies are used to
evaluate the impact of both supervisory and peer leadership upon
outcomes of satisfaction and factorial performance measures.

Results from the study suggest that this conceptual model is useful
and that leadership's relation to organizational outcomes may best be
studied when both leadership and effectiveness are multi-dimensional.
Both peer and supervisory leadership measures relate to outcomes. In
most instances, the ability to predict is enhanced by taking simultaneous
account of certain non-leadership variables.

For centuries writers have been intrigued with the idea of
specifying predictable relationships between what an organization's leader does and how the organization fares. In our own
time, behavioral science has looked extensively at this question,
yet incongruities and contradictory or unrelated findings seem to
crowd the literature. It is the intent in this paper to locate and
integrate the consistencies, to explore some neglected issues, and,
finally, to generate and use a network of variables for predicting
outcomes of organizational effectiveness.

Leadership has been studied informally by observing the lives
of great men and formally by attempting to identify the personality traits of acknowledged leaders through assessment techniques. Review of the research literature from these studies,
however, reveals few consistent findings (Gibb, 1954; Stogdill,
1948). Since World War Two, research emphasis has shifted from
a search for personality traits to a search for behavior that makes
a difference in the performance or satisfaction of the followers.

The conceptual scheme to be outlined here is an example of this approach.

In this paper, the primary concern is with leadership in businesses or industrial enterprises, usually termed 'supervision' or 'management', although most of the constructs of leadership to be used here apply equally well to social groups, clubs, and voluntary associations.

Work situations in business organizations in a technologically advanced society typically involve a comparatively small number of persons who receive direction from one person. This is the basic unit of industrial society and has been called the 'organizational family' (Mann, 1965). In this modern organizational family, there is usually task interdependence and there is frequently social interdependence as well. The ideal is that of a group of people working effectively together toward the accomplishment of some common aim.

This paper presents a review of the conceptual structure resulting from several programs of research in leadership practices, followed by a reconceptualization that attempts to take into consideration all of these earlier findings. In an attempt to assess the usefulness of the reconceptualization, it is then applied to leadership and effectiveness data from a recent study.

Dimensions of Leadership

It seems useful at the outset to isolate on a common-sense basis certain attributes of 'leadership'. First, the concept of leadership is meaningful only in the context of two or more people. Second, leadership consists of behavior; more specifically, it is behavior by one member of a group toward another member or members of the group, which advances some joint aim. Not all organizationally useful behavior in a work group is leadership; leadership behavior must be distinguished from the performance of non-interpersonal tasks that advance the goals of the organization. On a common-sense basis, then, leadership is organizationally useful behavior by one member of an organizational family toward another member or members of that same organizational family.

Defined in this manner, leadership amounts to a large aggregation of separate behaviors, which may be grouped or classified in a great variety of ways. Several classification systems from previous research have achieved considerable prominence, and are briefly described here.

Ohio State leadership studies

In 1945, the Bureau of Business Research at Ohio State University undertook the construction of an instrument for describing leadership. From extended conversations and discussions among staff members who represented various disciplines, a list of nine dimensions or categories of leadership behavior were postulated. Descriptive statements were then written and assigned to one or another of the nine dimensions, and after further refinement, 150 of these were selected as representing these nine dimensions and were incorporated into the Leader Behavior Description Questionnaire.

Two factor analyses attempted to simplify its conceptual framework further. Hemphill and Coons (1957) intercorrelated and factor-analysed group mean scores for 11 dimensions for a sample composed largely of educational groups,[1] and obtained three orthogonal factors.

1. *Maintenance of membership character*. Behavior of a leader which allows him to be considered a 'good fellow' by his subordinates; behavior which is socially agreeable to group members.

2. *Objective attainment behavior*. Behavior related to the output of the group; for example, taking positive action in establishing goals or objectives, structuring group activities in a way that members may work toward an objective, or serving as a representative of group accomplishment in relation to outside groups, agencies, forces, and so on.

3. *Group interaction facilitation behavior*. Behavior that structures communication among group members, encouraging pleasant group atmosphere, and reducing conflicts among members.

Halpin and Winer (1957) made an analysis using data collected from air-force crews, revising the original measuring instrument to adapt it to the respondent group. Only 130 items were used,

1. The 11 dimensions were made up of the original 9, one of which (communication) had been subdivided, plus an overall leadership evaluation.

with appropriate rewording, and the number of dimensions was reduced to eight. Treatment of the data indicated that five of the eight were sufficient for describing the entire roster, and the correlation of the 130 items with these five dimensions was regarded as a matrix of oblique factor loadings. These item loadings were then factor analysed and the results rotated, producing four orthogonal factors.

1. Consideration. Behavior indicative of friendship, mutual trust respect, and warmth.

2. Initiating structure. Behavior that organizes and defines relationships or roles, and establishes well-defined patterns of organization, channels of communication, and ways of getting jobs done.

3. Production emphasis. Behavior which makes up a manner of motivating the group to greater activity by emphasizing the mission or job to be done.

4. Sensitivity (social awareness). Sensitivity of the leader to, and his awareness of, social interrelationships and pressures inside or outside the group.

The Halpin and Winer analysis has been the more widely known and used. Because the investigators dropped the third and fourth factors as accounting for too little common variance, 'consideration' and 'initiating structure' have become to some extent identified as 'the Ohio State' dimensions of leadership.

Early Survey Research Center studies

Concurrent with the Ohio State studies was a similar program of research in human relations at the University of Michigan Survey Research Center. Approaching the problem of leadership or supervisory style by locating clusters of characteristics which (*a*) correlated positively among themselves and (*b*) correlated with criteria of effectiveness, this program developed two concepts called 'employee orientation' and 'production orientation' (Katz, Maccoby, and Morse, 1950; Katz, Maccoby, Gurin, and Floor, 1951).

Employee orientation is described as behavior by a supervisor, which indicates that he feels that the 'human relations' aspect of the job is quite important; and that he considers the employees as human beings of intrinsic importance, takes an interest in them, and accepts their individuality and personal needs. Production-orientation stresses production and the technical aspects of the job, with employees as means for getting work done; it seems to combine the Ohio State dimension of initiating structure and production emphasis. Originally conceived to be opposite poles of the same continuum, employee-orientation and production-orientation were later reconceptualized (Kahn, 1956), on the basis of further data, as representing independent dimensions.

Katz and Kahn (1951), writing from a greater accumulation of findings, presented another conceptual scheme, with four dimensions of leadership.

1. Differentiation of supervisory role. Behavior by a leader that reflects greater emphasis upon activities of planning and performing specialized skilled tasks; spending a greater proportion of time in actual supervision, rather than performing the men's own tasks himself or absorption in impersonal paperwork.

2. Closeness of supervision. Behavior that delegates authority, checks upon subordinates less frequently, provides more general, less frequent instructions about the work, makes greater allowance for individuals to perform in their own ways and at their own paces.

3. Employee orientation. Behavior that gives major emphasis to a supportive personal relationship, and that reflects a personal interest in subordinates; being more understanding, less punitive, easy to talk to, and willing to help groom employees for advancement.

4. Group relationships. Behavior by the leader that results in group cohesiveness, pride by subordinates in their work group, a feeling of membership in the group, and mutual help on the part of those subordinates.

Differentiation of supervisory role corresponds in part to what the Ohio State studies refer to as initiating structure or objective

363

attainment behavior, and clearly derives from the earlier concept of production orientation. Closeness of supervision, on the other hand, has something in common with maintenance of membership character, consideration, and employee-orientation, but also with objective attainment behavior, initiating structure, and production orientation. Employee orientation clearly corresponds to the earlier concept by the same name, while group relationships is to some extent similar to the interaction facilitation behavior and social sensitivity of the Ohio State studies.

In still another conceptualization, combining theory with review of empirical data, Kahn (1958) postulated four supervisory functions.

1. Providing direct need satisfaction. Behavior by a leader, not conditional upon behavior of the employee, which provides direct satisfaction of the employee's ego and affiliative needs.

2. Structuring the path to goal attainment. Behavior that cues subordinates toward filling personal needs through attaining organizational goals.

3. Enabling goal achievement. Behavior that removes barriers to goal achievement, such as eliminating bottlenecks, or planning.

4. Modifying employee goals. Behavior that influences the actual personal goals of subordinates in organizationally useful directions.

Direct need satisfaction clearly resembles consideration and employee-orientation; enabling goal achievement seems similar to initiating structure or objective attainment behavior; structuring the path to goal attainment and modifying employee goals are probably closer to the Ohio State production emphasis factor.

Studies at the Research Center for Group Dynamics

Cartwright and Zander (1960), at the Research Center for Group Dynamics, on the basis of accumulated findings, described leadership in terms of two sets of group functions.

1. Group maintenance functions. Behavior that keeps interpersonal relations pleasant, resolves disputes, provides encouragement, gives the minority a chance to be heard, stimulates self-direction, and increases interdependence among members.

2. Goal achievement functions. Behavior that initiates action, keeps members' attention on the goal, develops a procedural plan, evaluates the quality of work done, and makes expert information available.

These descriptive terms clearly refer to broader constructs than consideration or initiating structure. Group maintenance functions, for example, include what has been termed consideration, maintenance of membership character, or employee-orientation, but they also include functions concerned with relationships among group members not in formal authority positions. This concept is in some ways similar to group interaction facilitation behavior in the Ohio State factor analysis of Hemphill and Coons (1957). Goal achievement functions seem to encompass what the Ohio State studies referred to as initiating structure and production emphasis or objective attainment behavior, and what early Survey Research Center studies called production orientation.

Mann's three skills

In subsequent work at the Survey Research Center built upon earlier findings, a recent classification, proposed by several writers and developed and operationalized by Floyd Mann (1965), treats leadership in terms of a trilogy of skills required of supervisors or managers. Although behaviors requiring particular skills and those skills themselves are not necessarily perfectly parallel, it seems reasonable to assume at least an approximate correspondence between the two. The three skills are:

1. Human relations skill. Ability and judgment in working with and through people, including knowledge of principles of human behavior, interpersonal relations, and human motivation.

2. Technical skill. Ability to use knowledge, methods, techniques, and equipment necessary for the performance of specific tasks.

3. Administrative skill. Ability to understand and act according to the objectives of the total organization, rather than only on the basis of the goals and needs of one's own immediate group. It includes planning, organizing the work, assigning the right tasks to the right people, inspecting, following up, and coordinating the work.

Likert's new patterns of management

Rensis Likert of the University of Michigan Institute for Social Research, building upon many of the findings of the Survey Research Center and the Research Center for Group Dynamics as well as upon his own early work in the same area for the Life Insurance Agency Management Association, describes five conditions for effective supervisory behavior.

1. Principle of supportive relations. The leadership and other processes of the organization must be such as to ensure a maximum probability that in his interactions and his relationships with the organization, each member will, in the light of his background, values, and expectations, view the experience as supportive, and as one that builds and maintains his sense of personal worth and importance (Likert, 1961, p. 103).

2. Group methods of supervision. Management will make full use of the potential capacities of its human resources only when each person in an organization is a member of one or more effectively functioning work groups that have a high degree of group loyalty, effective skills of interaction, and high performance goals (Likert, 1961, p. 104).

3. High performance goals. If a high level of performance is to be achieved, it appears to be necessary for a supervisor to be employee-centered, and at the same time to have high performance goals and a contagious enthusiasm as to the importance of achieving these goals (Likert, 1961, p. 8).

4. Technical knowledge. The (effective) leader has adequate competence to handle the technical problems faced by his group, or he sees that access to this technical knowledge is fully provided (Likert, 1961, p. 171).

5. Coordinating, scheduling, planning. The leader fully reflects and effectively represents the views, goals, values, and decisions of his group in those other groups where he is performing the function of linking his group to the rest of the organization. He brings to the group of which he is the leader the views, goals, and decisions of those other groups. In this way, he provides a linkage whereby communication and the exercise of influence can be performed in both directions (Likert, 1961, p. 171).

Comparison and integration

These various research programs and writings make it clear that a great deal of conceptual content is held in common. In fact, four dimensions emerge from these studies, which seem to comprise the basic structure of what one may term 'leadership':

1. Support. Behavior that enhances someone else's feeling of personal worth and importance.

2. Interaction facilitation. Behavior that encourages members of the group to develop close, mutually satisfying relationships.

3. Goal emphasis. Behavior that stimulates an enthusiasm for meeting the group's goal or achieving excellent performance.

4. Work facilitation. Behavior that helps achieve goal attainment by such activities as scheduling, coordinating, planning, and by providing resources such as tools, materials, and technical knowledge.

This formulation is obviously very close, except in terminology, to that expressed by Rensis Likert and was, in fact, stimulated by it. Table 1 indicates how concepts from the various research programs relate to these four basic concepts of leadership. More important, however, is the fact that each of these four concepts appears, sometimes separately, sometimes in combination, in all but two (Katz, *et al.*, 1950; Kahn, 1958) of the previous formulations listed. These four dimensions are not considered indivisible, but capable of further subdivision according to some regularity of occurrence in social situations or according to the conceptual preferences of investigators.

Independence of Leadership and Position

Traditional leadership research has focused upon the behavior of formally designated or recognized leaders. This is probably due, at least in part, to the historical influence of the hierarchical models of the church and the army. As a result, it has until recently been customary to study leadership either as an attribute of the person of someone who is authority-vested, or as an attribute of his behavior. More recently, attention has been paid to leadership in groups less formally structured, as illustrated by the work of Bass with leaderless group discussion, the work of Sherif, as well as some of the work of other researchers in the area of group dynamics (Bass, 1960; Cartwright and Zander, 1960; Sherif and Sherif, 1956).

In the previous section, leadership was conceptualized in terms of four social-process functions, four kinds of behavior that must be present in work groups if they are to be effective. The performance of these functions was deliberately not limited to formally designated leaders. Instead, it was proposed that leadership, as described in terms of support, goal emphasis, work facilitation, and interaction facilitation, may be provided by anyone in a work group for anyone else in that work group. In this sense, leadership may be either 'supervisory' or 'mutual'; that is, a group's needs for support may be provided by a formally designated leader, by members for each other, or both; goals may be emphasized by the formal leader, by members to each other, or by both; and similarly for work facilitation and interaction facilitation.

This does not imply that formally designated leaders are unnecessary or superfluous, for there are both common-sense and theoretical reasons for believing that a formally acknowledged leader through his supervisory leadership behavior sets the pattern of the mutual leadership which subordinates supply each other.

Leadership and Organizational Effectiveness

Leadership in a work situation has been judged to be important because of its connection, to some extent assumed and to some

Table 1

Correspondence of Leadership Concepts of Different Investigators

Bowers and Seashore (1966)	Hemphill and Coons (1957)	Halpin and Winer (1957)	Katz et al. (1950)	Katz and Kahn (1951)	Kahn (1958)	Mann (1965)	Likert (1961)	Cartwright and Zander (1961)
Support	Maintenance of membership character	Consideration	Employee orientation	Employee orientation	Providing direct need satisfaction	Human relations skills	Principle of supportive relationships	Group maintenance functions
Interaction facilitation	Group interaction facilitation behavior	Sensitivity		Closeness of supervision / Group relationships			Group methods of supervision	
Goal emphasis	Objective attainment behavior	Production emphasis	Production orientation		Structuring path to goal attainment / Modifying employee goals	Administrative skills	High-performance goals	Goal-achievement functions
Work facilitation		Initiating structure	Differentiation of supervisory role	Differentiation of supervisory role / Closeness of supervision	Enabling goal achievement	Technical skills	Technical knowledge, planning, scheduling	

extent demonstrated, to organizational effectiveness. Effectiveness, moreover, although it has been operationalized in a variety of ways, has often been assumed to be a unitary characteristic. These assumptions define a commonly accepted theorem that leadership (if not a unitary characteristic, then a limited roster of closely related ones) is always salutary in its effect and that it always enhances effectiveness.

The pattern of the typical leadership study has been first, to select a criterion of effectiveness: sometimes a rating of overall effectiveness by superiors, at other times a questionnaire measure of 'morale', on still other occasions a few measures such as output, absence, or accident rates. Next, an attempt is made to relate leadership to the criterion selected. When, in fact, a relationship is obtained, this is accepted. When no relationship or one opposite to that expected is obtained, the investigator often makes some statement referring to 'error' or 'further research'.

It seems that a better strategy would be to obtain: (a) measures reflecting a theoretically meaningful conceptual structure of leadership; (b) an integrated set of systematically derived criteria; and (c) a treatment of these data, which takes account of the multiplicity of relationships and investigates the adequacy of leadership characteristics in predicting effectiveness variables.

In the present study an attempt is made to satisfy these conditions. A conceptual structure of leadership is developed, using empirical evidence. The four concepts of this structure are operationalized in terms of questionnaire items describing behavioral acts largely 'loaded' on one or another of these constructs, and a systematically derived set of criteria of organizational effectiveness is obtained.

Research Methods

Research site

This study was conducted in 40 agencies of a leading life insurance company. These agencies are independently owned businesses, performing identical functions in their separate parts of the country. Only one or two hierarchical levels intervene between the regional manager, at the top of the hierarchy, and the sales agent at the bottom. The typical agency consists of an exclusive territory comprising a number of counties of a state or states. The regional manager ordinarily has headquarters in some principal city of his territory, and contracts with individuals to service the area as sales agents. He receives an 'override' upon the commissions of policies sold by these agents, in addition to the full commissions from whatever policies he sells personally.

If geographical distance or volume of business is great enough, he may contract with individuals to serve as district managers. The district manager is given territorial rights for some sub-portion of the regional manager's territory, is permitted to contract agents to service the area, subject to the approval of the regional manager, and receives a portion of what would otherwise be the regional manager's override upon sales within his territory.

Although this is the usual arrangement, variations occur. Occasionally, for example, a territory will be so constituted as to prevent subdivision into districts. In these cases, the regional manager contracts directly with sales agents throughout his territory. In other cases, the territory is almost entirely urban, in which case the regional manager may substitute salaried or partially salaried supervisory personnel for district managers. In all cases, however, there are at least a regional manager and sales agents, and frequently, in addition, a district manager between these two parties.

In all, the company's field force comprises nearly 100 agencies. Of these, 40 were selected as being roughly representative of them all. Selection was made by company personnel, with an effort to select half of the 40 from the topmost part of the list of agencies ordered by performance, and the other half from among poorer performing agencies, omitting any having recent organizational disruption or change. Questionnaires were mailed out in April, 1961, to all contracted regional managers, district managers, sales agents, and supervisory personnel on full or part salary in these agencies; 83 per cent were returned by June 1961, for a total of 873 respondents.

Measurement

This report is concerned with 20 index measurements obtained through paper-and-pencil questionnaires, and 7 factorial measures of agency performance obtained from company records. A

371

short description of each questionnaire variable appears in Table 2. These measures reflect perceptions of behavior rather than behavior itself, and are therefore no different from any other method of quantifying behavior: all involve the measurement of

Table 2
Content of Variables Used

Area	Description of questionnaire variable
Leadership* Support	Importance of morale
	Willingness to make changes
	Friendliness
	Conversational ease
	Opinion acceptance
Goal emphasis	Importance of competitive position
	Extra work effort
Work facilitation	Stressing standard procedures
	Offering new approaches
	Checking works vs capacity
	Emphasis upon meeting deadlines
Satisfaction†	With company
	With fellow agents
	With income prospects
	With regional manager
	With office costs
	With job
Need for affiliation	Importance of being liked
	Importance of being accepted
Regional manager's expert power	Respect for regional manager's competence and good judgment
Classical business ideology‡	Extent of agreement with statements of value and belief about nature of 'best' economic society
Rivalry among agents	Extent to which some agents are trying to advance at others' expense

* Items in the leadership area were adapted from two sources: items used in the Ohio State studies and those used in previous Survey Research Center studies.

† 11 items, 6 satisfaction areas.

‡ Items based upon conceptualization by Sutton *et al.*, (1956).

behavior, by some person and some mechanism. Close familiarity by the recipients of the behavior – and whatever systematic bias this introduces – is here considered as more desirable than the lack of information and large random error that an outside observer would very probably introduce.

In addition to these questionnaire measurements, the company provided some 70 measures of agency performance, which were then factor analysed,[2] resulting in 7 orthogonal factors.

Factor I. Staff-clientele maturity. This factor reflects a difference in the kind of business produced by the agency attributable to the age and experience of the agent staff and the clientele that they reach. A high score reflects a high average premium per thousand, collected relatively infrequently, with very little term insurance or graduated premium life insurance, a small proportion of the business from new or young agents, and greater profitability from business already on the books.

Factor II. Business growth. This seems to indicate in fairly uncomplicated fashion the growth of business volume over the years immediately preceding the year of measurement.

Factor III. Business costs. Although the principal loadings are on variables measuring the costs per unit of new business, some minor loadings occur on variables relating to costs of renewal business. This factor, therefore, seems to be a business-cost dimension.

Factor IV. Advanced underwriting. This seems to be a factor measuring the extent to which there is emphasis by the agent staff upon advanced underwriting. A high score on this factor reflects a large average face value per life and per policy, comparatively large premiums per collection, a fairly high ratio of cases rejected, very little prepayment, fairly high costs, and high profitability of new business. A low score, of course, reflects a reverse pattern.

Factor V. Business volume. A fairly straightforward dimension measuring the dollar volume of new business done by the agency.

2. The factor analysis method used was that of a principal axes solution with varimax rotation.

Factor VI. Manpower turnover. A measure of the extent to which there was a change in personnel within the agency during 1959. This factor loads most heavily on the ratio of terminations plus appointments to manpower, and on the ratio of terminations alone to manpower.

Factor VII. Regional manager's personal performance. This factor differs from those above by representing the performance of the regional manager, not of the agency as a whole. It seems to reflect the extent to which he is putting energy into agency maintenance and development, as against taking short-run gain. It is, perhaps, an age factor, related in some measure to the regional manager's distance from retirement.

Four of these factors are measures of performance in the usual sense; that is, a positive and a negative value can be placed at opposite ends of these continua: business growth, business costs, business volume, and manpower turnover. Factor I (staff-clientele maturity) and Factor IV (advanced underwriting) are descriptive, rather than evaluative,[3] and Factor VII is peculiar to only one person in the agency.

There are, therefore, within this study multiple-criteria measures, both of satisfaction, described earlier, and of performance. Although the use of multiple-criteria measures has become more common in recent years, it is still infrequent enough to make the study somewhat unique.

From the data that resulted, the following questions suggest themselves:

1. Are both mutual and supervisory leadership measures useful; that is, are there differential effects from the various leadership dimensions such that some criteria are associated with certain measures or combinations of measures and some with others?

2. In what way are mutual leadership measures related to supervisory measures?

3. How adequately may criteria of effectiveness be predicted

3. It should be noted that these factors are interpreted by the authors on the basis of a single set of data. Data from other periods or other firms, as well as interpretations by life insurance experts, might differ from those presented here.

from leadership measures as compared to other kinds of measures?

The reader should from the outset be reminded of several problems of the analysis. First, the analytic model used in this study assumes a particular causal directionality. Since the data are from a single period of time, this directionality cannot be proved. As an operating assumption, it must be either accepted or rejected by the reader, and the relationships otherwise interpreted by him. The assumption of managerial behavior as an organizational prime mover is, however, a common one. Second, since the model starts from assumptions about the nature of leadership, the analysis considers first the relationships of leadership characteristics to criteria of effectiveness. Third, since this is an attempt to locate possible precursors of effectiveness, the analysis then considers the relationship of nonleadership variables to effectiveness, paying serious attention only to those nonleadership variables that can reasonably be interpreted as causes of effectiveness. Fourth, not all of either leadership or nonleadership variables with statistically significant relationships are used to predict effectiveness measures; only the one or two of each category that is most highly correlated.

Results

Relation of leadership to effectiveness

Table 3 presents the correlation coefficients of leadership measures with measures of satisfaction. Table 4 presents similar correlations of leadership measures to performance factors. These data indicate first, that the incidence of significant relationships of leadership to effectiveness is well above the chance level. Of 40 satisfaction-leadership coefficients, 30 are significant beyond the 5 per cent level of confidence. Of 56 performance-leadership coefficients, 13 are significant beyond the 5 per cent level of confidence. Second, the significant coefficients are not uniformly distributed throughout the matrix; instead, certain effectiveness criteria (e.g. satisfaction with income) and certain leadership measures (e.g. peer work facilitation) have many significant relationships, whereas others have few or none (e.g. Performance Factor VI). Third, significant coefficients are as

375

often found in relation to peer as to managerial leadership characteristics.

For parsimony, the leadership characteristic with the largest coefficient in relation to each criterion measure is chosen as the

Table 3

Correlation of Leadership with Satisfactions

Leadership measure	Satisfaction with				
	Company	Fellow agents	Job	Income	Manager
Peer					
Support	0·03 *	0·68	0·39	0·29 *	0·47
Goal emphasis	0·37	0·77	0·26 *	0·42	0·62
Work facilitation	0·29 *	0·68	0·34	0·51	0·45
Interaction facilitation	0·31	0·72	0·30 *	0·42	0·55
Manager					
Support	0·31	0·65	0·35	0·45	0·86
Goal emphasis	0·11 *	0·71	0·09 *	0·43	0·31
Work facilitation	0·31	0·61	0·24 *	0·36	0·41
Interaction facilitation	0·30 *	0·67	0·10 *	0·53	0·78

* All others significant beyond 0·05 level of confidence, 2-tail.

Table 4

Correlation of Leadership with Performance Factors

Leadership measure	Performance factor						
	I	II	III	IV	V	VI	VII
Peer							
Support	0·26	−0·02	−0·27	−0·21	0·23	−0·12	0·27
Goal emphasis	0·49*	−0·05	−0·45*	−0·27	0·15	0·04	0·04
Work facilitation	0·33*	0·14	−0·41*	−0·41*	0·18	0·00	0·04
Interaction facilitation	0·44*	−0·13	−0·44*	−0·24	0·11	0·14	0·05
Manager							
Support	0·28	−0·24	−0·26	−0·12	0·25	0·16	0·10
Goal emphasis	0·31*	0·11	−0·27	−0·18	0·41*	0·03	−0·19
Work facilitation	0·43*	0·13	−0·37*	−0·33*	0·21	0·16	−0·12
Interaction facilitation	0·42*	−0·29	−0·30	−0·21	0·13	0·20	0·01

* Significant beyond 0·05 level of confidence, 2-tail.

analytic starting point in these matrices. To this is then added in turn each of the two significant leadership relationships by means of a two-predictor multiple-correlation technique. Because no r-to-z transformation of multiple correlation coefficients is possible, these cannot be compared with the original r value; therefore, seven correlation points are arbitrarily set as the criterion of significant improvement in prediction.[4]

It is apparent from Table 5, that, with two exceptions, adding other leadership characteristics that display somewhat smaller, but significant, correlations does not improve prediction. It is

Table 5

Improvement of Prediction of Criteria of Effectiveness by Addition of Other Significantly Related Leadership Characteristics

Effectiveness measure	Best predictor	Other measures improving prediction
Satisfaction with		
Company	Peer goal emphasis	None
Fellow agents	Peer goal emphasis	None
Job	Peer support	None
Income	Manager interaction facilitation	Peer goal emphasis
Manager	Manager support	None
Factors *		
I Staff-clientele maturity	Peer goal emphasis	Peer work facilitation
III Business costs	Peer goal emphasis	None
IV Advanced underwriting	Peer work facilitation	None
V Business volume	Manager goal emphasis	None

* Performance Factors II, VI, and VII showed no significant relationships to leadership characteristics.

4. The actual multiple correlation values require much space and are therefore omitted here. Copies of these tables of multiple correlation coefficients may be obtained upon request from the authors at the Centre for Research on the Utilization of Scientific knowledge or the Institute for Social Research, University of Michigan.

also apparent that peer goal emphasis plays a central role in this analysis: it is either the best predictor, or a significant additive, in five of the twelve cases.

Relation of peer to managerial leadership

Before assessing the adequacy of leadership as a predictor of effectiveness, it seems advisable to answer the question posed earlier about the relationship between peer and managerial leadership. Table 6 presents the intercorrelation; all 16 coefficients

Table 6

Intercorrelation of Managerial and Peer Leadership Variables*

| Managerial variables | *Peer leadership characteristics* | | | |
	Support	Goal emphasis	Work facilitation	Interaction facilitation
Support	0·59	0·67	0·52	0·58
Goal emphasis	0·54	0·65	0·72	0·59
Work facilitation	0·49	0·63	0·82	0·66
Interaction facilitation	0·55	0·71	0·62	0·74

* All coefficients significant beyond 0·05 level of confidence, 2-tail.

in the table are statistically significant, indicating therefore that there is a close relationship between all managerial characteristics, on the one hand, and all peer characteristics on the other. Following the same method as that used for effectiveness, it appears that the best predictor of peer support is managerial support; of peer goal emphasis, managerial interaction facilitation; of peer work facilitation, managerial work facilitation, and of peer interaction facilitation, managerial interaction facilitation. With one exception, therefore, the best predictor of the peer characteristic is its managerial opposite number. Table 7 indicates that three predictions are improved by related managerial characteristics.

Assuming causation, one may say that if a manager wishes to increase the extent to which his subordinates support one another, he must increase his own support and his own emphasis upon goals. If he wishes to increase the extent to which his sub-

Table 7

Improvement of Prediction of Peer Leadership Characteristics
by Addition of Other Managerial Leadership Characteristics

Peer measure	Managerial best predictor	Other managerial measures improving prediction
Support	Support	Goal emphasis
Goal emphasis	Interaction facilitation	Goal emphasis
Work facilitation	Work facilitation	None
Interaction facilitation	Interaction facilitation	Work facilitation

ordinates emphasize goals to one another, he must first increase
his own facilitation of interaction and his emphasis upon goals.
By increasing his facilitation of the work, he will increase the
extent to which his subordinates do likewise, and if, in addition,
he increases his facilitation of interaction, his subordinates will in
turn facilitate interaction among themselves.

These data appear to confirm that there is in fact a significant
and strong relationship between managerial and peer leadership
characteristics. In general, the statement may be made that a fore-
runner of each peer variable is its managerial opposite number,
and that substantial improvement is in most cases made by combining with this another managerial characteristic.

Adequacy of prediction by leadership measures

Because this analysis has placed great emphasis on leadership
constructs as predictors of organizational outcomes, it seems
desirable to consider the extent to which prediction of these outcomes can be enhanced by the inclusion of nonleadership variables.[5] Table 8 summarizes the data on predictability of all
criteria by nonleadership measurements. It seems likely from
these data that some of the criteria may be much more successfully predicted using nonleadership variables than using leadership measures, that some others may be enhanced by using both,
and that the predictability of still others is not improved by
nonleadership characteristics.

5. Nonleadership variables comprised a large majority of the 214 items
in the questionnaire.

Table 8

Prediction of Criteria by Nonleadership Variables

Criterion	Total no. of significant relations (N = 214)	No. of significant nonleadership variables	No. of significant nonleadership variables exceeding best leadership predictor	No. of possible causal variables*
Satisfaction with				
Company	56	52	33	23
Job	39	36	11	8
Manager	66	44	1	1
Fellow agents	56	34	0	0
Income	60	43	2	2
Factors				
Factor I	22	15	1	1
Factor II	19	19	19	17
Factor III	50	39	9	6
Factor IV	26	23	12	6
Factor V	19	17	5	1
Factor VI	17	13	13	0
Factor VII	11	9	9	0

* Based upon the judgment of the research staff.

The analysis at this point becomes somewhat complex, since relationships exist not only between leadership or nonleadership variables and criteria, but also among leadership and among nonleadership variables. In effect, therefore, the search for the best predictive model turns into a rather complicated examination of various chains and arrangements of constructs. To simplify this procedure, each criterion is presented separately, diagramming for each a plausible and statistically optimal 'causal' schema.

Table 9(a) presents the relationships of leadership and nonleadership variables to satisfaction with the company and with income. This diagram indicates that supportive managers make more satisfactory arrangements about the office expenses of their agents, and that these arrangements, in part, lead to greater satisfaction with the company as a whole. In addition, as

Table 9

Relationships of Leadership and Nonleadership Variables to Satisfaction with the Company and with Income

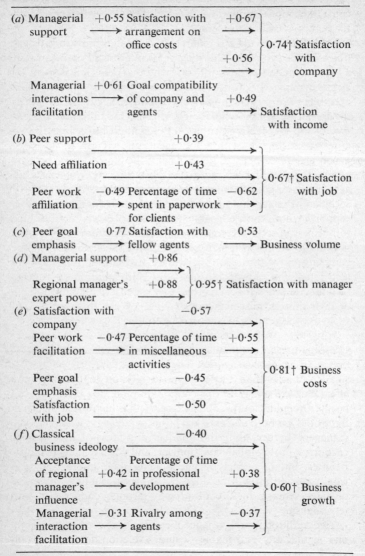

(a) Managerial support $\xrightarrow{+0.55}$ Satisfaction with arrangement on office costs $\left.\begin{array}{c} +0.67 \\ \\ +0.56 \end{array}\right\}$ 0.74† Satisfaction with company

Managerial interactions facilitation $\xrightarrow{+0.61}$ Goal compatibility of company and agents $\xrightarrow{+0.49}$ Satisfaction with income

(b) Peer support $\xrightarrow{+0.39}$

Need affiliation $\xrightarrow{+0.43}$

Peer work affiliation $\xrightarrow{-0.49}$ Percentage of time spent in paperwork for clients $\xrightarrow{-0.62}$ $\left.\right\}$ 0.67† Satisfaction with job

(c) Peer goal emphasis $\xrightarrow{0.77}$ Satisfaction with fellow agents $\xrightarrow{0.53}$ Business volume

(d) Managerial support $\xrightarrow{+0.86}$

Regional manager's expert power $\xrightarrow{+0.88}$ $\left.\right\}$ 0.95† Satisfaction with manager

(e) Satisfaction with company $\xrightarrow{-0.57}$

Peer work facilitation $\xrightarrow{-0.47}$ Percentage of time in miscellaneous activities $\xrightarrow{+0.55}$

Peer goal emphasis $\xrightarrow{-0.45}$

Satisfaction with job $\xrightarrow{-0.50}$ $\left.\right\}$ 0.81† Business costs

(f) Classical business ideology $\xrightarrow{-0.40}$

Acceptance of regional manager's influence $\xrightarrow{+0.42}$ Percentage of time in professional development $\xrightarrow{+0.38}$

Managerial interaction facilitation $\xrightarrow{-0.31}$ Rivalry among agents $\xrightarrow{-0.37}$ $\left.\right\}$ 0.60† Business growth

† Multiple correlation of variables listed against the effectiveness measure.

managers facilitate the interaction of their agents, the goals of the company and needs or aspirations of the people who work for it come to be more compatible, which also leads to satisfaction with the company and with income.

Table 9(b) presents a similar chain of relationships to satisfaction with the job itself. This diagram is interpreted to mean that as agents facilitate the work for each other, less time is spent by agents in paperwork for specific clients. When this happens, when agents behave more supportively toward each other, and when the agents are, on the whole, higher in need for affiliation, there is greater job satisfaction. Table 9(c) presents relationships to two criteria: satisfaction with fellow agents and volume of business. When agents emphasize goals among themselves, they become more satisfied with each other; and when this condition exists, an agency does a greater volume of business. Table 9(d) shows very succinctly that agents are satisfied with their manager if he is supportive and knowledgeable. Table 9(e) presents relationships to business costs in diagram form. Earlier diagrams showed the network of relationships associated with satisfaction with the company and with the job; here, these two satisfaction states are associated with lower business costs. In addition, as agents facilitate the work for each other, they spend a smaller proportion of their time in miscellaneous activities. When this occurs, and when agents emphasize goals to one another, costs are also lower.

Table 9(f) presents relationships to business growth. The relationships presented in this diagram are less reliable than those presented in earlier figures. They are, as a group, somewhat smaller in size than those found in relation to other criteria already described. With this caution in mind, however, they can be interpreted as follows: business growth is high when the agent force does *not* hold to a classical business ideology; when regional managers, by accepting the opinions and ideas of their agents, encourage professional development; and when managers reduce rivalries among agents by encouraging their interaction. Far from stressing growth attained by competitive effort, this paradigm presents a picture of growth through cooperative professionalism.

Two additional performance measures of effectiveness present one significant, reasonable 'causal' relationship each: staff-clientele maturity is greater when agents have a higher level of aspiration, and more advanced underwriting occurs when agents have a higher level of education. Although significant correlations were presented earlier in relation to these two factors, the reasonable interpretation of them is that the leadership measures are either effects or coordinates, not causes, of these descriptive rather than evaluative performance factors.

That no reasonable, significant relationships to manpower turnover are to be found is extremely puzzling. In most investigations of the effect of social-psychological variables upon organizational behavior, it is assumed that performance measures which are more 'person' than 'production' oriented will show the highest relationships to questionnaire measurements. In the present case this assumption is not supported. No variations of analysis that were attempted produced any noticeable change. An attempt was made to assess curvilinear correlations, but no improvement over linear correlation resulted. It was also thought that the factorial measure of turnover might be too complicated and that a simpler measure of proportion of terminations might be more productive. This also produced no noticeable effect. Apparently, manpower turnover in this particular company or industry is related to forces in the individual, the environment, or perhaps the organizational situation not tapped by the questionnaire measurement used.

It is not surprising that no correlations are found with the regional manager's personal performance. It is, as explained earlier, the weakest factor, and differs from the other factors in being descriptive of a single individual rather than of the agency as a whole. It may well be affected more by variables such as the regional manager's distance from retirement than by factors assessed here.

Discussion and Conclusions

To what extent have the data demonstrated the usefulness of the conceptualization presented at the beginning of this article? It seems reasonable to state the following:

1. Seven of the eight leadership characteristics outlined above in fact play some part in the predictive model generated from the

data; only peer interaction facilitation seems to play no unique role.

2. Both managerial and peer leadership characteristics seem important.

3. There are plausible relationships of managerial to peer leadership characteristics.

4. The model is not a simple one of managerial leadership leading to peer leadership, which in turn leads to outcomes separately; instead, different aspects of performance are associated with different leadership characteristics, and, in some cases, satisfaction outcomes seem related to performance outcomes.

5. Some effectiveness measures are related to causal factors other than those tapped in this instrument.

6. The ability to predict outcomes with the variables selected varies from 0·95 to 0·00.

7. The role of leadership characteristics in this prediction varies in importance from strong, direct relationships in some cases (e.g. satisfaction with manager) to indirect relationships (e.g. business volume) to no relationship (e.g. advanced underwriting).

8. Leadership, as conceived and operationalized here, is not adequate alone to predict effectiveness; instead, additional and, in some cases, intervening constructs must be included to improve prediction. These 'other' constructs are of several distinct types:

(a) *Leadership-related.* Regional manager's expert power, regional manager's influence acceptance, and rivalry among agents.

(b) *Work patterns.* Percentage of time in miscellaneous activities, in paperwork for clients, in professional development.

(c) *Personal and motivational.* Education, level of aspiration, need for affiliation, goal compatibility of individual and organization, and classical business ideology.

References

BASS, B. M. (1960), *Leadership, Psychology, and Organizational Behavior*, Harper.

CARTWRIGHT, D., and ZANDER, A. (1960), *Group Dynamics Research and Theory*, Row, Peterson.

GIBB, C. A. (1954), 'Leadership', in G. Lindzey (ed.), *Handbook of Social Psychology*, Addison–Wesley.

HALPIN, A. W., and WINER, B. J. (1957), 'A factorial study of the leader behavior description questionnaire', in R. M. Stogdill and A. E. Coons, eds., *Leader Behavior: Its Description and Management*, Bureau of Business Research, Ohio State University, pp. 39–51.

HEMPHILL, J. K., and COONS, A. E. (1957), 'Development of the leader behavior description questionnaire', in R. M. Stogdill and A. E. Coons (eds.), *Leader Behavior: Its Description and Management*, Bureau of Business Research, Ohio State University, pp. 6–38.

KAHN, R. L. (1956), 'The prediction of productivity', *Journal of Social Issues*, vol. 12, pp. 41–9.

KAHN, R. L. (1958), 'Human relations on the shop floor', in E. M. Hugh-Jones (ed.), *Human Relations and Modern Management*, North Holland Publishing Co., pp. 43–70.

KATZ, D., and KAHN, R. L. (1951), 'Human organization and worker motivation', in L. R. Tripp (ed.), *Industrial Productivity*, Industrial Relations Research Association, Wisconsin, pp. 146–71.

KATZ, D., MACCOBY, N., GURIN, G., and FLOOR, L. G. (1951), *Productivity, Supervision and Morale among Railroad Workers*, Survey Research Center, Michigan.

KATZ, D., MACCOBY, N., and MORSE, N. C. (1950), *Productivity, Supervision, and Morale in an Office Situation*, Darel Press.

LIKERT, R. (1961), *New Patterns of Management*, McGraw-Hill.

MANN, F. C. (1965), 'Toward an understanding of the leadership role in formal organization', in R. Dubin, G. C. Homans, F. C. Mann and D. C. Miller (eds.), *Leadership and Productivity*, Chandler, pp. 68–103.

SHERIF, M., and SHERIF, C. (1956), *An Outline of Social Psychology*, Harper.

STOGDILL, R. M. (1948), 'Personal factors associated with leadership: a summary of the literature', *Journal of Psychology*, vol. 25, pp. 35–71.

SUTTON, F. X., HARRIS, S. E., KAYSEN, C., and TOBIN, J. (1956), *American Business Creed*, Harvard University Press.

24 A. Etzioni

Dual Leadership in Complex Organizations

A. Etzioni, 'Dual leadership in complex organizations', *American Sociological Review*, vol. 30 (1965), pp. 688–98.

This paper attempts to integrate theoretically the Bales–Parsons model of small groups and a theory of complex organizations. The organizational positions of the instrumental and expressive leaders are seen as critical variables, affecting both the fulfilment of the functional needs of participant groups and the groups' commitment to organizational goals. Complex organizations are distinguished according to the nature of their goals, power employed, and the level of lower-echelon commitment they require. The relations between the small group and the complex organization are reviewed for each kind. These theoretical considerations are applied to the study and administration of prisons, the 'human relations' approach in industry, therapeutic mental hospitals, and schools.

The theory of complex organizations, like the theory of other social systems, alternates between periods of emphasis on new inputs and periods of consolidation. In one of the earlier consolidations the quality of the theory was considerably improved by combining the formal structural tradition with the insights and findings of small group studies in the Kurt Lewin and Elton Mayo traditions (see Likert, 1962, and Etzioni, 1964, pp. 32–47). The resulting product is symbolized by the pair concepts of formal and informal organization (and of formal and informal leadership). But the articulation of organizations with the groups in and around them is too vast a subject to have been exhausted by any one consolidation phase. The time may now be ripe for another effort to integrate small-group analysis with that of complex organizations.

One particularly promising approach seems to be a union of the Bales–Parsons structural-functional analysis of small groups with the main lines of analysis of complex organizations. Small group studies so far have obtained their data largely from groups created artificially in social science laboratories and from 'natural'[1] groups in 'natural' settings, mainly families in tribal and village communities (see Grusky, 1957; Cancian, 1964). Comparatively few data have been obtained, and few propositions formulated, for the structural-functional analysis of 'natural' small groups within complex organizations, i.e. in artificial settings (see Strodtbeck and Mann, 1956). A theoretical articulation of this kind is the task of this article. To carry it out, I shall draw on one other recent development: the comparative study of organizations. I shall then attempt to show that if the theory so extended is valid, it has policy implications for major spheres of applied sociology, illustrating once more that theoretical effort is but one step removed from well-founded applied work.

From a theoretical point of view, articulation between small groups functioning within complex organizations and their organizational setting is two-fold: first, the organization affects the fulfillment of the functional needs of these groups, and second, the way these functions are served in turn affects the operation of the organization itself. It is essential to keep these two systems of reference apart: that the same act, role, or leader has both group and organizational functions by no means implies that these functions are identical.

Dual Leadership in Non-Organizational Settings

Drawing liberally on the right of interpretation I shall briefly summarize the Bales–Parsons analysis of small groups, which is based largely on experimental studies (Bales, 1953; Bales and Slater, 1955). For my purposes here, by far the most important insight is that if small task-oriented groups are to operate efficiently, two kinds of leadership are required, and the two are to be mutually supportive.[2] Task-oriented groups tend to develop two kinds of leader: one, an expressive (or social-emotional) leader, who ranks higher than other actors in such interaction

1. 'Natural' groups are those whose culture and structure have evolved spontaneously. Since an element of artificiality (or self-consciousness and planning) characterizes most groups, 'naturalness' is a matter of degree.

2. Effectiveness is studied more directly by Shaw than in the Bales studies. See Shaw, 1959, and Mulder, 1959.

categories as 'showing solidarity' and 'asking for suggestions', the other, an instrumental (or task-oriented) leader, who ranks higher than other actors in such categories as 'giving suggestions' and 'showing disagreement'.

The distinction between expressive and instrumental orientations is not limited to a classification of leadership. All acts can be classified as expressive or instrumental. Roles can be classified according to the prevalence of one kind of act over the other. Moreover, the same analytical distinction can be applied to the functional needs of social systems. Here, *instrumental* refers to the need to acquire resources, or means, and to allocate them among the various role-clusters in the system, and *expressive*, to the need to maintain the integration of various parts of the system with each other as well as with its normative system.[3] Role clusters can then be classified as devoted primarily to the service of one or another functional need. Similarly, the same concepts are useful in classifying the elite roles of initiative and control, which direct the activities performed in various role-clusters by the respective followers (Etzioni, 1959).

Finally, actors in general and leaders in particular have instrumental or expressive psychological propensities. Of course, this is in part a situational distinction. Whether an actor becomes an expressive or instrumental leader depends in part on the psychological predispositions of the *other* members of his group, and a person may acquire some of the 'characteristics' of his kind of leadership (e.g. higher level of activity, ability to withstand hostility), once he has assumed the particular kind of leadership *position*, as he interacts with followers and with leaders of the complementary kind (Slater, 1955; Gardner, 1956). Still, one probably could predict, on the basis of a psychological test, the kind of leadership role a person is more likely to assume. Instrumental leadership seems to draw people who are more aggressive, more able to withstand hostility and more anxious to be respected, while expressive leadership attracts people who are more accommodative, less able to withstand hostility, and more anxious to be loved.

Drawing on these various levels of application of the twin con-

3. Here, my usage differs somewhat from that of the Parsonian tradition. See Parsons, 1951, pp. 145–7; Parsons, Bales, and Shils, 1953.

cepts, expressive and instrumental, the dual leadership theory suggests – though here data are particularly lacking – that task-oriented groups will be more effective in terms of task-achievement and members' satisfaction, when the group commands both instrumental and expressive leaders.[4] It suggests further that while these two kinds of leadership might be provided by a single actor ('great man'), they tend not to be. Finally, when two actors carry out the two leadership roles, mutual support is required for effective leadership of the group (Bales, 1953, pp. 148 ff.). This theory is contrasted with the approach prevalent in much of the psychological, administrative, and political science literature, which expects effective leadership to be provided by one man (Borgatta, Couch, and Bales, 1954).

Not all these statements are fully backed with empirical evidence, nor is the existing evidence immune to conflicting interpretation. Nevertheless, these statements may be used to develop additional propositions, which, of course, require validation in their own right.[5]

4. For a review of the research on this question and for references to earlier works, see Bales (1958).

5. Such validation should take into account that this is a functional theory. That is, it suggests that a group will be more effective *if* provided with both kinds of leadership, and *if* these kinds of leadership are mutually supportive. It also includes a non-functional statement that differentiated leadership is more common than 'great man' leadership, both because the psychological characteristics monoleadership requires are rare and because such leadership requires the same person to engage in opposing patterns of social behavior, e.g. to be assertive and accommodative simultaneously or at least in rapid succession.

On the other hand, the statement that the two kinds of leaders tend in fact to support each other is only an empirical finding (for the kinds of groups studied); it has neither a functional nor any other theoretical standing. Mutual support is a functional requirement of effective group action, but there is no reason, in theory, to state that most or even many small groups are effective. To refute this functional statement it would be necessary to show that when such support is lacking no dysfunction occurs, or that when provided, it does not increase effectiveness.

The functional model does not predict what pattern is common, but it does predict the *kinds* of pathologies that will occur if one of the two leadership roles is left vacant, or if mutual support is absent. Productivity will be low when the instrumental leader is missing, satisfaction when the expressive leader is missing; and both productivity and satisfaction will be reduced when the two leaders are in conflict rather than in coalition.

The dual leadership theory, briefly restated here, has been evolved largely in experimental, task-oriented groups and mainly applied to the study of 'natural' groups in the community (Parsons, 1955; Zelditch, 1955). But very little effort has been made so far to apply the dual-leadership theory to groups in complex organizations. In studies of committees, the theory has been used as though the participants constituted another 'natural' group, which is to disregard both the external organizational role-sets of the participants and the fact that they did not interact as individuals but as representatives of departments, services, agencies, or other organizations (Bales, 1954).

Before attempting to join the dual-leadership and complex organization lines of analysis, I must make one more preparatory comment. To deal with the articulation of groups and organizations, I focus on the concept of leadership. Leadership is the ability, based on the personal qualities of the leader, to elicit the followers' voluntary compliance in a broad range of matters.[6] Leadership is distinguished from the concept of power in that it entails influence, i.e. change of preferences, while power implies only that subject's preferences are held in abeyance.

For small groups, leadership guides the activities by which their expressive and instrumental functional needs are served. The question here is: what contributions is the small group to expect from organizationally supplied leaders in its efforts to answer these needs? For the organization, the single most important bridge to participants' motivational and normative orientations is its ability to provide leadership to the small groups to which they belong. (Such a bridge is often not available, but it rarely exists without leadership.) If the participants accept the organizationally provided leader (i.e. one who is committed to the organization's goal, structure, and personnel), their non-calculative commitment to the organization can be obtained. If they reject the organizational leadership, the organization effectiveness is restricted to maintaining law and order and to carrying out the more routinized kinds of production, i.e. to tasks that require relatively little emotional commitment from the large majority of

6. When only a narrow range is covered, referring to matters of little importance, influence rather than leadership is exercised.

the participants.[7] The study of leadership – the consequences of its being supplied from various organizational ranks, its orientation toward the organization, and the scope of its influence – hence provides a rewarding approach to the study of small groups in complex organizations.

Dual Leadership in Organizations

Organizations differ from other collectivities in that within them power is, comparatively, more deliberately distributed and institutionalized. Power is focused in the formally recognized elite positions in which status symbols, the right to give and withhold economic rewards, and control of means of violence are con-

	positional power +	positional power −
personal power +	formal leader	informal leader
personal power −	official	follower

Figure 1

centrated. In experimental task-groups leadership rests solely on the followers' attitudes and reciprocations, so that few discrepancies arise between leadership and power positions, but such discrepancies are common in complex organizations. An actor may have only positional power, in which case he might be referred to as an 'official'; only broad personal influence, in which case he might be called an 'informal leader'; or both, in which case he is best labeled a 'formal leader'. If he commands neither, he is probably a follower. (See Figure 1.) These concepts

7. This point is elaborated in Etzioni (1961) chs. 2 and 3. This is not to say that the independent commitment of personnel to the organizational goals is not an analytically separate factor. Some types of organization (e.g. universities) do attract personnel with a high degree of such independent commitment.

are not new, but defined in this way, they become part of a systematic conception.

When the dual leadership proposition is applied to small groups in complex organizations, the critical issues are not only whether both kinds of leadership are provided for, and whether they are mutually supportive, but also include the question of *how and to what extent the leadership is backed by organizational power*. A group in an organization where both types of leadership are exercised by informal leaders – persons without organizational positions – will be very different from a group where both types of leadership are exercised by formal leaders – persons in organizational positions – or a group where one type of leadership is provided by an occupant of an organizational power position while the other is not.

The organizational location of expressive and instrumental leadership affects (*a*) the degree of organizational control over the group; (*b*) the degree of collaboration between the two kinds of leaders; and (*c*) the power relations between the two kinds of leaders. Each of these points requires a brief elaboration.

Provision of leadership from organizational positions is a major source of organizational control over groups of participants. Holding an organizational position does not automatically assure the incumbent's loyalty to the organization's goal, its rules, or its higher-ranking leaders – nor does its lack necessarily imply alienation of the leader – but, all other things being equal, *informal leaders tend to be less loyal to the organization than formal ones*. Hence, by and large, an organization that provides both kinds of leadership (that is, its representatives are accepted by the small-group members as leaders), will have more control over the participants than one in which both kinds of activities are controlled by informal leaders.

The effectiveness of an organization that provides only one of the two kinds of leadership for the participants follows no definite pattern, for the effect of this configuration is contaminated by the nature of relations between the two leaders. This second variable, collaboration between instrumental and expressive leadership, is itself affected by the organizational positions of both leaders. All other things being equal, collaboration is more likely when both of the leaders hold organizational positions, or when neither does, than it is when only one of them does. (Exceptions are discussed below.) Where both leaders hold organizational positions, collaboration may be supported by various organizational mechanisms, such as rewards (e.g. more rapid promotions for leaders who 'get along' with others) and rules and institutionalized points (e.g. the next higher in command) for resolving conflicts, and by shared training experience, organizational perspectives, and ideology. Of course, when this is not the case, as when one of the two leaders has been recently recruited from the outside, or is more anxious to please his subordinates than to be rewarded by the organization (Sykes, 1956, and 1958), the likelihood of collaboration will decline; still, on the average such difference of background, perspective, and expectations should be less common between two formal leaders than between a formal and an informal leader.

Informal leaders are likely to be more similar to each other than to formal leaders because their income, prestige, interests, etc., are correlated with rank, and informal leaders of the same small group tend to be of similar rank. Being of similar rank, they may face a closed organizational level, into which they cannot be recruited (e.g. nurses facing the doctor's rank; enlisted men before the officer's rank); their organization may be slow to promote (e.g. young faculty at European universities); they may share the experience of having been left behind in an organization where rapid promotion is the rule, or of having refused on psychological or ideological grounds to accept a promotion into organizational leadership positions.

Finally, the relations between the expressive and instrumental leaders are much affected by their relative resources. These depend on their organizational positions, which in turn are influenced by the goals and compliance structure of the organization. In groups of four or five students meeting for four 45-minute discussion sessions, in a highly institutionalized situation, the only sources of power are personal; no member commands organizational power and hence it does not affect relations between the two leaders. But when the context is that of a complex organization, the question of their relative power is most important: which leader is superior in rank (or in other measures of organizational power) – the expressive or the instrumental ones?

Assuming all others things are equal, granting more organizational power to one kind of leader affects the goals to which the small group will be primarily devoted. That is, if the instrumental leader is superior, the group is more likely to be a task-oriented group, and if the expressive leader is superior, a socio-normative group. One might expect the goals of the organization to determine whether a group operating within it is predominantly instrumental or expressive. But the organizational goals must gain support; they do not translate themselves into appropriate action automatically. By recruiting personnel whose leadership potential is high, through leadership-training and by deliberately allocating superior rank to one kind of leadership, the organization can bring groups into line with its goals. If the leadership hierarchy contradicts the organizational goals, however, a predominantly expressive group is quite likely to appear in a producing organization (workers 'taking it easy', 'chumming it up with the foreman', playing cards on the job, etc.) and the other way around.

The critical observation linking the small group and organizational lines of analysis is that to maximize its effectiveness the organization must not merely gain control of the group via its leaders, but also must *allocate power so as to establish the superiority of the desired kind of leadership over the other*. Mechanisms for this purpose include giving one leader a higher rank, symbols of higher prestige, greater backing by the next higher in command, etc. One might think that a complex organization should always support the instrumental leader, since it is basically an instrumentally-oriented unit. But the answer differs from one type of organization to another, and is to be sought in a cross-institutional comparative perspective (as distinct from a cross-cultural one).

Contrary to an assumption widely held and perpetuated in many textbooks on administration and industrial management, organizations differ strikingly in the degree to which effective operation requires them to gain control and loyalty of the small groups that function in them. In some organizations – for example, prisons – such control is hardly possible, rarely attempted, and not essential for effective operation. In other organizations – for example, religious or political movements –

control is quite possible, often sought, and a prerequisite to effective operation. Organizational effects on relations between expressive and instrumental leaders should be examined against this comparative backdrop.

For our present purposes, it will suffice to classify organizations according to their goals and the corresponding needs to gain low, high, or medium commitment from the participants. Organizations whose goal is to segregate deviant members of the society – prisons, correctional institutions, and custodial mental hospitals – require relatively low commitment on the part of their inmates and most other personnel for satisfactory levels of operation. Their chances of gaining control of the small group within them by providing these groups with leadership are small in any case, since the participants, above all the inmates, are usually highly antagonistic to the organization and tend to reject any leadership it might attempt to provide, instrumental or expressive. Officials pursue their tasks by relying largely on power, not leadership.[8] Leadership in the small groups tends to be informal, and the expressive leader is likely to be superior, for alienated informal groups are primarily oriented not to tasks but to social and normative problems. These groups form the basis of social life in prison-type organizations and are the source of tension-management, aside from enforcing the special inmate code (Clemmer, 1958, pp. 111–34). Instrumental leaders, such as the traders in various scarce (cigarettes) or forbidden (narcotics) goods tend to be lower in status and power than the 'right guys', the expressive leaders of the inmates (Cloward, 1959). When the informal inmate groups are organized around escape efforts, and the instrumental leaders are in charge of the engineering and technical aspects of the escape, their status and power are higher, but they still tend to be subordinate to the expressive leaders. (This suggests that escape efforts are ritualistic and normative rather than rationally calculated operations.)

At the other extreme of the commitment continuum are organizations whose real goal is to socialize or re-socialize

8. The power of the inmate group is often sufficient to wring concessions from lower-echelon custodial officers in return for making their life bearable and not embarrassing them in the eyes of their superiors. In this sense the segregating type of organization can be said to work through the informal group to maintain its custodial control. See Rubenfeld and Stafford (1963).

members of the society; schools, rehabilitation centers, therapeutic mental hospitals, and religious organizations.[9] Religious
organizations belong in this category to the degree that one of
their major goals is to strengthen their members' commitment to
a set of values, a commitment that tends to be eroded in secular
life and, therefore, needs reinforcement. In this sense they are
resocializing agencies.

Effective socialization requires a high level of commitment on
the part of the participants, for without such commitment, without identification of the students, parents, parishioners with the
organizational leadership and its goals, and rules, the organization cannot deeply affect their personalities.[10] Hence, these
organizations must either provide the leadership of the small
groups or gain the leaders' support. If such efforts are unsuccessful and loyalties are locked in the group and not extended to the
organization, its failure is quite unavoidable. Conditions for
achieving leadership of these groups are much better here than in
the segregating type of organizations, however, for here participation is voluntary, and the means of control are largely symbolic
and not coercive. Participants' attitudes are much more likely to
be positive, and their groups more receptive to organizational
leadership. The organization, in turn, makes a much larger in-
vestment in leadership training and symbolic control of the
participants, and to the extent that it commands other kinds of
power, it is much more reluctant to use it.

The subordinate leader of small groups in socializing organizations had best be the expressive one. The organization's prime

9. The following discussion assumes that schools are organizations for
education and not just instruction; that successful therapy requires changes
in a patient's personality, not just his following the therapist's advice, and
that religious organizations are not just social clubs. This assumption is in
part the consequence of implicit theoretical premises to the effect that the
goals of these organizations cannot be served through instruction, advice,
or 'social' gatherings, but require deeper impact on the participants'
personalities. Furthermore, organizations ought to be classified according to
the business they are really in, however their licenses read. Thus, mental
hospitals that do not cure but only keep inmates off the streets should be
classified as segregating organizations, and so on.

10. The theoretical reasons for this assumption cannot be spelled out here;
they lie in the realm of psychology and their discussion would carry us far
afield from the subject of this article.

aim is to affect the participants deeply; its agents for this purpose are the expressive leaders – teachers, therapists, ministers – who either interact directly with the participants or at least affect them indirectly by influencing the small group in which the participants are involved (e.g. classes or therapeutic groups). Each organization (and each small group) of course also has instrumental needs. Buildings need to be attended to, funds must be allocated, and so on. Still, these considerations pertain to the acquisition and allocation of resources whose nature differs from that of the organizational goals. Unlike the profit goal, socialization goals are such that merely combining resources better, or giving superior status to instrumental role-clusters and to instrumental leadership, reduces the effectiveness of the organization. (These statements, it should be stressed, refer not to the overall head of the various organizations under discussion, such as school principals, hospital directors, or other administrative heads, but to those in the ranks immediately above the members, i.e. teachers, psychiatric social workers, and parish clergy.)

Organizations whose goal is to produce goods, or services, or to exchange them – such as factories, shops, and banks – require more commitment from their participants, including the lower-ranking ones, than do segregating organizations, but they can function quite effectively with considerably lower levels of commitment than socializing organizations. As a rule, producing organizations operate more effectively if their leadership is accepted by the small groups within them. If organizational leadership is rejected, however, producing organizations still can operate more effectively than much of the current literature suggests. The participants can 'trade' the organization a 'fair day's work' for a 'fair day's pay' without being committed to its goal (profit), to many of its rules, or to its management (treated as mere 'officials'). This is especially the case when the work is routine, requiring little initiative or responsibility. The latter qualities are difficult to supervise or measure, and they require internal commitment and rewards other than remunerative ones. It is easier for an organization to build a pyramid without its participants' commitment than to conduct research leading to a lunar landing. Producing organizations, hence, tend to rely on a mixture of 'official' power (especially remunerative) and leadership. What proportions are most effective depends on the kind of work carried out, according to the dimensions suggested above.

Apart from the amount of leadership an effective producing organization requires (and how much it actually commands), its maximum effectiveness is clearly served by making the instrumental superior to the expressive leadership. In this sense, producing organizations are in direct contrast to socializing organizations. Optimal combination of means is more directly relevant to the success of a producing organization than are its workers' moral and social lives. Production requires giving priority to calculations involving division of labor, assignment of personnel, and so on, and in fact, the interest of producing organizations in the expressive activities of participant groups is largely instrumental. Attention to expressive activities, including providing organizational leadership for them, is justified by the belief that it enhances organizational control of the *instrumental* activities. The need for expressive leaders is thus secondary. If expressive considerations were to prevail, production considerations would have to be significantly and regularly neglected to assure 'good' social relations between the workers and the foreman. While foremen not infrequently give precedence to expressive considerations, this clearly is not the intent of the producing organization, and not what effective service of its goals requires.

Thus, each type of organization has a different need to control its participants, according to its goals and the degree of participant commitment these goals require.[11] This suggests an optimal relation between the instrumental and expressive leaders for each type of organization. Segregating organizations do not require much commitment of the lower participants for effective operation, and in any case can rarely affect relations between instrumental and expressive leaders, who both tend to be informal.

11. Elsewhere I have proposed a typology of organizations: coercive, utilitarian, and normatives (See Etzioni, 1961). That typology provided a category for every complex organization. The present typology is not exclusive; it only provides for one or more examples of the most typical organizations in each of the three categories of the exhaustive typology. To note this difference, here the terms segregating, producing, and socializing are used.

Socializing organizations require deep commitment of the lower participants; the changed state of these participants is their main 'product'. This requires subordination of instrumental considerations to expressive ones, which in turn requires subordination of instrumental to expressive leaders. Producing organizations require a 'medium' degree of commitment. Their handling of lower participants is subordinated to other, wider considerations of combining means of which the work of participants is only one, for their product is not a state of the participants but goods or services. The participants' morale (in the broadest sense of the term) is but one consideration among many, and the expressive leader in charge of this category of means is hence subordinated to the instrumental one, who is in charge of the broader combination of means and more 'calculative' in his orientation to the workers. Thus a theoretical link exists between the kind of organization in question and the power relations between the two types of leaders.

Some Applications

The propositions I have advanced here are derived from two lines of analysis. Like all such theoretical derivations, they must stand the test of empirical research before they can be held valid. If validated, they would have significant implications for several seemingly unrelated areas of applied sociology; they would suggest revisions of the sociology of rehabilitation, therapy, labor relations, and education.

Much of the literature in these fields stresses interpersonal relations, leadership styles, and group atmosphere, as if the structural contexts in which these are introduced were immaterial. A 'sensitive' supervisor or 'democratic' foreman can achieve leadership of participants' groups, thereby enhancing organizational effectiveness. But the preceding analysis suggests that structural and cultural factors strictly limit the degree to which an organizational 'official', whatever his style, can gain the leadership of a group of participants, as well as the kind of leadership he can gain.

If the preceding analysis is valid, efforts to capture the expressive leadership of the inmate groups in segregating organizations by assigning a few professional workers (social workers, clinical psychologists, psychiatrists) must fail unless the basic nature of the organization (its security arrangements, restrictions of privileges, attitudes of guards or attendants, etc.) is changed. The inmates' groups in organizations tend to reject the organization's values (they feel the whole official conception of justice is distorted), its goals (they feel that their confinement is unjust), and its personnel (they feel that the guards or attendants are cruel and arbitrary). Anti-organization leaders and groups tend to prevail (Hayner and Ash, 1939), and though professional personnel in such a context may find isolated inmates who have not been assimilated and acculturated by the inmate community and who are amenable to their treatment, their efforts will largely be 'washed out' by counterforces in the inmate community (McCarkle and Korn, 1954; Wheeler, 1961).

The context changes when, instead of sending a few rehabilitation-oriented professionals into a segregating organization, their number and power in the organization is increased to a point where they can change some of its basic characteristics. But we are dealing then with a different type of organization, one that is, or is becoming, a socializing type. In segregating communities *per se*, isolated rehabilitation efforts, which require influencing inmates' expressive orientations and activities are liable to fail. A more effective approach would be to concentrate the available rehabilitation-oriented personnel in forces large enough to affect the basic structure of a few segregating organizations, and assign them to those most prone to change (as a result of favorable community interest, for example, or recent weakening of the coercive structure), rather than to distribute these scarce professionals among a large number of organizations on the assumption that they will convert other persons to their viewpoint, or in response to some sort of misplaced egalitarianism.

The preceding analysis implies that in producing organizations foremen trained in 'human relations' workshops are likely to be least effective! The human relations tradition calls upon the foreman to be a 'great man', which some might be and a few might become, but most are clearly not, nor are they capable of becoming, great men. A foreman is expected to hold two roles simultaneously, to be both an instrumental and an expressive leader. Under pressure from management, he is expected to set specific work loads and assignments, to supervise production, and maintenance of machinery, to encourage adherence to rules, etc. He might accomplish this, if the workers consider their pay adequate and their working conditions satisfactory, if they are not politically antagonistic to the particular production system, and if he understands the work process. Suppose that he now enters human relations training; he attends seminars, workshops, meetings with representatives of the Labor Relations Department and so on. He is encouraged to become the workers' expressive leader as well, to be not only respected, but also liked, popular, loved; to be concerned with workers' personal problems, participate in their social life, be a 'father' and a 'friend'.

To a limited degree an instrumental leader can exercise expressive leadership without commanding the rare talents of a 'great man'. A foreman can have a beer with his men or go bowling with them without corrupting his authority. But sooner or later the relation between his expressive and instrumental commitments will come into question. When management increases its demands, the foreman must decide whether he will seek to circumvent the new demands, thus keeping his 'popularity' with the workers, or impose them, which is likely to alienate the workers and undermines whatever expressive leadership he has attained (Whyte and Gardner, 1945). Attempts to do both things simultaneously produces a high level of tension for the foreman. This role-strain (Goode, 1960) is heightened rather than reduced by human relations training.

Another important consideration here is that the foreman returning from human relations workshop is likely to find the role of expressive leader filled, and the incumbent is likely to prevail in any conflict with the foreman over this position. The incumbent expressive leader may be an 'old hand', a union steward, or merely an influential worker (Sayles and Strauss, 1953); in any case, he has few, if any, instrumental demands to make of the workers and hence can be relatively 'purely' expressive in his relation with them. Such leaders are, as a rule, selected by the workers themselves; they tend to be spontaneous rather than imposed leaders. But the foreman is not selected by the workers and, compared to the informal expressive leader, he is farther from them in terms of income and rank. Since he must, at least occasionally, transmit pressures from management in his instrumental capacity, a foreman is likely to lose in such a competition for expressive leadership. And not only does he fail to secure the expressive leadership role, he also jeopardizes a possible coalition with the incumbent expressive leader. Although the producing organization's goals would be advanced by such a coalition, the human relations approach in effect renders it improbable by teaching foremen to challenge the indigenous expressive leadership.

The preceding analysis is also relevant to the management of therapeutic mental hospitals. One controversy in this field focuses on the question: Should treatment be largely in the hands of psychiatrists or can other professionals fully participate? This is a complex issue with many ramifications, but one point is closely related to the matters at hand. Psychiatric treatment, like other socialization and re-socialization processes, involves a supportive element to provide emotional security, and a demanding one to encourage growth, experimentation, and learning (Parsons, 1951 and 1951b). In the primary family, as it existed among the middle classes in the nineteenth-century Germany and France, the mother (or nurse) was probably the primary source of support; the father, of growth. This is not to assert that one actor cannot fill both roles. In a successful psychiatric relationship the therapist probably provides both, varying the amount of support relative to pressure to grow from session to session, and in particular over various phases of the relationship. But a division of labor between the psychiatrist and another agent of re-socialization – a psychiatric nurse, social worker, clinical psychologist or the like – would make more treatment hours available for each patient, reduce costs per hour, and hasten the patient's advance, for the psychiatrist would be free to specialize more in pressure to grow if another staff-member provided support.

The theory advanced here, though, should not be viewed as simply supporting the participation of other professionals in the treatment process. Sharing the treatment would be effective only if the psychiatrist (as the instrumental leader) collaborates with other professionals (as expressive leaders). One of the best ways to assure such a coalition is to give a clear power (and status) advantage to one of the two kinds of leaders, and since no member of the treatment team has as much prestige, or power, as the psychiatrist, in Western medicine at least, the psychiatrist is the obvious person to coordinate the efforts of the treatment team. It follows that the psychiatrist can never act as a purely instrumental leader, for at least he is also charged with guiding the expressive aspects of the treatment and articulating them with his own work.

In therapeutic mental hospitals two or more staff members often participate actively in the treatment process. This does not necessarily reduce the effectiveness of treatment, as the Bales–Parsons dual-leadership theory might suggest, because the expressive and instrumental leadership roles may be distributed among more than two actors, as in an extended family. Such a division is attained when several professionals work simultaneously with the same patient.[12] Needless to say, the need to harmonize the treatment efforts, and hence to institutionalize psychiatric coordination, grows with the number of professionals participating.

Other applications of the preceding analysis can be mentioned only briefly here. Mostly Army infantry units have two institutionally-provided leaders, the officer and the N.C.O., whose division of labor seems to follow the instrumental-expressive line. Armies differ greatly, though, as to which kind of leadership is given the superior rank, for reasons that have yet to be explored. All religious organizations provide for expressive leadership, but they differ in the degree to which they provide instrumental leaders (as against leaving this role to the laity), and in the degree formal or informal (Harrison, 1959) instrumental ones. Finally, for reasons that are far from clear, many American high schools provide no satisfactory formal expressive leadership. 'Home-room' teachers act as expressive leaders in some schools, but often they are 'officials' who possess some specialized knowledge or are in charge of discipline so that a home-room teacher typically attempts little and succeeds even less in securing the expressive leadership of the student groups. Actually the rotating system of classes, which regularly redistributes the students from

12. This approach is often practiced by rehabilition officers. For an illustration, see Benney (1960) and Black (1961).

hour to hour, undermines the sociological importance of this organizational unit, and by default increases the importance of the non-organizational peer-group and its informal expressive leaders. This might well account for the limited effect of high-school teachers on the deeper normative orientations of their students (Coleman, 1961). Any organization that requires a positive commitment from its participants must provide the leadership of participant groups, instrumental and expressive, or gain the collaboration of the informal leaders, if it is to be effective, but not all such organizations do so.

Behind these and many other applied problems lies one analytical issue: the role of dual leadership in linking organizations and groups of participants. The leadership of groups in organizations is a major mechanism by which groups and organizations are articulated, one that in part reflects and in part affects the degree to which groups and organizations, and their expressive and instrumental considerations, work hand in hand or at cross purposes.

References

BALES, R. F. (1953), 'The equilibrium problem in small groups', in T. Parsons, R. F. Bales and E. A. Shils (eds.), *Working Papers in the Theory of Action*, Free Press, pp. 111–61.

BALES, R. F. (1954), 'In conference', *Harvard Business Review*, vol. 32, pp. 44–50.

BALES, R. F. (1958), 'Roles in problem-solving groups', in E. E. Maccoby, T. W. Newcomb and E. L. Hartley (eds.), *Readings in Social Psychology*, Henry Holt, 3rd edn, pp. 437–47.

BALES, R. F., and SLATER, P. E. (1955), 'Role differentiation in small decision-making groups', in T. Parsons and R. F. Bales (eds.), *Family, Socialization and Interaction Process*, Free Press, pp. 259–306.

BENNEY, C. (1960), 'Casework and the sheltered workshop of the mentally ill', *Social Casework*, vol. 41, pp. 465–72.

BLACK, B. J. (1961), 'Rehabilitation of post-psychotic patients by industrial workshop', *Diseases of the Nervous System*, (Monograph Supplement), vol. 22, pp. 1–4.

BORGATTA, E. F., COUCH, A., and BALES, R. F. (1954), 'Some findings relevant to the great man theory of leadership', *American Sociological Review*, vol. 19, pp. 755–9.

CANCIAN, F. M. (1964), 'Interaction patterns in Zinacanteco families', *American Sociological Review*, vol. 29, pp. 540–50.

CLEMMER, D. (1958), *The Prison Community*, Holt, Rinehart and Winston.

CLOWARD, R. A. (1959), *Social Control and Anomie: A Study of a Prison Community*. Unpublished doctoral dissertation, Columbia University.

COLEMAN, J. A. (1961), *The Adolescent Society*, Free Press.

ETZIONI, A. (1959), 'The functional differentiation of elites in the kibbutz', *American Journal of Sociology*, vol. 64, pp. 476–87.

ETZIONI, A. (1961), *A Comparative Analysis of Complex Organizations*, Free Press.

ETZIONI, A. (1964), *Modern Organizations*, Prentice–Hall.

GARDNER, G. (1956), 'Functional leadership and popularity in small groups', *Human Relations*, vol. 9, pp. 491–504.

GOODE, W. J. (1960), 'A theory of the role strain', *American Sociological Review*, vol. 25, pp. 483–96.

GRUSKY, O. (1957), 'A case for the theory of familial role differentiation in small groups', *Social Forces*, vol. 35, pp. 209–17.

HARRISON, P. M. (1959), *Authority and Power in the Free Church Tradition*, Princeton University Press.

HAYNER, N. S., and ASH, E. (1939), 'The prisoner community as a social group', *American Sociological Review*, vol. 4, pp. 362–9.

LIKERT, R. (1962), *New Patterns of Management*, McGraw–Hill.

McCARKLE, L. W., and KORN, R. R. (1954), 'Resocialization within walls', *Annals of the American Academy of Political and Social Sciences*, vol. 293, pp. 89–98.

MULDER, M. (1959), 'Group structure and group performance', *Acta Psychologica*, vol. 16, pp. 356–402.

PARSONS, T. (1951), *The Social System*, Free Press.

PARSONS, T. (1951b), 'Illness and the role of the physician', *American Journal of Orthopsychiatry*, vol. 21, pp. 452–60.

PARSONS, T. (1955), 'Family structure in the socialization of the child', in T. Parsons and R. F. Bales (eds.), *Family, Socialization and Interaction Process*, Free Press, pp. 35–131.

PARSONS, T., BALES, R. F., and SHILS, E. A. (1953), 'Phase movement in relation to motivational symbol formation and role structure', in T. C. Parsons, R. F. Bales and E. A. Shils, eds., *Working Papers in the Theory of Action*, Free Press, pp. 163–269.

RUBENFELD, S., and STAFFORD, J. W. (1963), 'An adolescent inmate social system', *Psychiatry*, vol. 26, pp. 241–56.

SAYLES, L. R., and STRAUSS, G. (1953), *The Local Union*, Harper.

SHAW, M. E. (1959), 'Some effects of individual prominent behavior of group effectiveness and member satisfaction', *Journal of Abnormal and Social Psychology*, vol. 59, pp. 382–6.

SLATER, P. E. (1955), 'Role differentiation in small groups', *American Sociological Review*, vol. 20, pp. 300–310.

STODTBECK, F., and MANN, R. D. (1956), 'Sex role differentiation in jury deliberations', *Sociometry*, vol. 19, pp. 3–11.

SYKES, G. M. (1956), 'The corruption of authority rehabilitation', *Social Forces*, vol. 34, pp. 257–62.

SYKES, G. M. (1958), *Society of Captives*, Princeton University Press.

WHEELER, S. (1961), 'Role conflict in correctional communities', in D. R. Cressey (ed.), *The Prison*, Holt, Rinehart and Winston.

WHYTE, W. F., and GARDNER, B. B. (1945), 'The man in the middle: positions and problems of the foreman', *Applied Anthropology*, vol. 4, pp. 1–28.

ZELDITCH, M., Jnr (1955), 'Role differentiation in the nuclear family: a comparative study', in T. Parsons and R. F. Bales (eds.), *Family, Socialization and Interaction Process*, Free Press, pp. 307–51.

Part Nine A Question of Ethics

As psychological research has developed and as psychological knowledge has gained greater respect both from psychologists themselves and from other scientists, politicians and the public, there has been an increasing concern about the ways in which this knowledge may be used. Physicists have been both blamed and concerned about the use of atomic energy. They have found themselves wanting to disclaim responsibility for the ends to which it is used, but unable to free themselves of some feelings of guilt. Increasingly psychologists are coming to similar concerns.

In most recent times the topic of major interest, in the United States at least, has been the so-called 'invasion of privacy' issue raised by the use of personality tests in the selection and assessment of candidates for positions especially in the Civil Service. The slightly different rallying point, within the same general framework, a little earlier, had been the notion of 'manipulation' and this issue, which is inextricably interwoven with the psychology of leadership, cannot be said to be dead. It will probably remain a problem for psychologists, administrators, and educators for a long time to come.

The Democratic philosophy naturally poses the question: With what justification may one person, albeit more richly or appropriately endowed, influence the behaviour of others particularly when that influence affects the choice or setting of goals rather than simply their attainment? Where the right to direct others no longer depends upon an accident of birth nor upon physical might alone, it is natural for men to consider with care the processes by which support and following may be 'won'. To the extent that science can delineate the processes and prescribe the necessary action knowledge gives privilege, and ethical questions intrude.

Theodore Brameld is a respected philosopher of education well acquainted with the 'human relations movement' in the social sciences. His paper (Reading 25) points at least one path through a problem which indeed appears to admit of no unique solution.

25   T. Brameld

Ethics of Leadership

T. Brameld, 'Ethics of leadership', *Adult Leadership*, vol. 4 (1955), pp. 5–8.

Although group leaders are probably little different from other people in taking their ethics pretty much for granted, they would no doubt agree that the habit is not a defensible one. A responsibility as serious as that of affecting the interactions and decisions of any group of people is never to be taken lightly. The implicit or explicit judgments of good and bad, of right and wrong, that are held by every leader are bound in turn to influence his attitudes and conduct toward other members, and theirs toward him. Therefore, it is not too much to say that one of his highest, if also most neglected, obligations is to concern himself as honestly as possible with the character of the ethical standard that always and everywhere filters through his relations with fellow human beings.

The moment, however, that any of us begins to think carefully about this standard, he realizes there are few problems more difficult. The basic solutions that have been offered by the greatest thinkers of both East and West have differed profoundly. They continue to differ in our own day.

The task is made a little easier, to be sure, if we assume – as many of us certainly do – that the ethics we wish to practice must be in accord with *democratic* processes and goals. I say 'a little easier' because any fundamental interpretation of democracy is also very difficult. Here, too, most of us tend to take meanings for granted. We verbalize with cliches like 'dignity of personality' or 'liberty, equality, and fraternity', but oftener than not we fail to inject enough significance into them so that we behave differently as a result of our verbalizing. The more that group leaders crystallize their convictions about democracy and the more they try to incorporate these into their own actions, the closer they already find themselves to an ethical standard upon which they can depend, and for which they can act with some assurance of harmony in both their means and ends.

I shall not attempt to restate in any formal or systematic way the major values of democracy. I only insist that efforts at such delineation are not frequent enough in group experience, and that leaders might well consider how to achieve more of it than they usually encourage. The effort could prove not only fascinating, but perhaps much more practical in its long-range effects upon group achievement and morale than greater time devoted to superficially more 'pressing' tasks.

What I shall consider is the ethics of leadership from two more limited perspectives. Both of them proceed from the premise that democracy, rightly interpreted, is always a theory of ethics even though theories of ethics are by no means always democratic. The first perspective may be called 'attitudinal', the second 'operative'. Each is closely related to the other, so that the treatment is artificial to the extent that in on-going group experience they cannot in fact be separated.

Ethics as Attitudes

By the first perspective I mean primarily the attitudes of equality or inequality that the leader possesses as he associates with other group members. These attitudes are not always easy for him to identify because, as any student of psychiatry knows, they are rooted deep in the whole background of his life and thus in his personality. Even so, there is nothing to prevent him from asking himself as sharply as he can just how he reacts toward each of his associates.

If I am frank with myself, do I, for example, feel some secret disdain, perhaps plain contempt, toward one or another member? And if it happens that I do, can I detect the reasons in myself? Is it, after all, because Miss X is of a different color? (Of course, I condemn race prejudice, but the question I am asking now is: how do I *feel?*) Is it because Mr Y is Jewish? (I can't quite forget what my father used to say at the family dinner-table.) Is it because Mrs Z comes from a depressed area of town where people belong to the 'lower-lowers' or, at best, 'upper-lowers'? (And, after all, don't I belong to the 'upper-middles' by Warner's own criteria?)

Attitudes do not, certainly, manifest themselves always as disdain or superiority toward other participants. It is just as possible for leaders to respond in the opposite direction. The prestige of Mr A, a banker, may be so powerful as to tempt me to treat him with a certain deference. (I remember how much money he controls.) The knowledge and training of Dr B are greater than mine. (How, then, can I help but urge the group to follow his advice?) Mr C is my foreman. (He might resent it if I disagree with him too openly.)

I do not mean to imply that these are the only attitudes possible. Of course there are innumerable others. Nor do I imply that all leaders hold all of them, or even some of them, any more than all members hold them. I wish only to focus upon two ethical corollaries of these attitudes when they do exist.

One is the inconsistency that you or I as leader may detect between our abstract belief in the equality of members of a group and our underlying feelings about some or all of these members. Paradoxically, it is much more commendable to achieve awareness of this inconsistency than not to face up to it at all. By facing up to it we substitute, as it were, a kind of self-consciousness for self-hypocrisy. And while self-consciousness may not in itself be an ethical standard, it clears the ground for the creation of one.

Who is Equal to What?

The other corollary centers in the question of what constitutes a defensible measure of equality at all. Here our finest students of democratic ethics – A. D. Lindsay, say – help a great deal. Despite all the disputes that continue among them, on one proposition they seem wholly agreed: equality as a value cannot possibly mean identity among human individuals. It does not mean universalizing similarities and liquidating dissimilarities. To be sure, it does mean that people of all groups, races, cultures are alike in certain respects; hence, in part, equality is the ideal of increasing *some* similarities among them (especially satisfaction of basic wants like adequate food and health). But in part, also, it is the ideal of increasing by common consent some dissimilarities (esthetic talent is an instance). Democracy thereby generates another paradox: the more completely it is won, the more richly it provides equal opportunity for people to become unequal.

The right attitude of the leader toward his group and toward himself as well does not, therefore, condone mere likeness among its members. It is rather the expectation, on the one hand, that each member can and should invest his special experiences, interest, abilities in the welfare of the group; and, on the other hand, that as the welfare of the group is thereby enhanced it can, in turn, invest its resources in each member.

It follows also that the equalitarian attitude is not so much a matter of respect for the 'dignity of personality' (I have never been able to discover just what this phrase means), as it is a recognition of the small or large contributions that people of many types, if they are motivated to do so, can offer to the group as a whole as well as to themselves. Nor is it a question even of 'liking' everyone: leaders of this disposition are not always better than those who are not; on the contrary, they may simply be more romantic or insensitive. Of course, the more completely you and I can purge our irrational hostilities and prejudices the abler we shall be as leaders. Still, it is not impossible for us to have quite rational reasons for particular dislikes.

In a democratic society, we need to be receptive to the potentialities of every member of a group. Every member can and should be helped to share his resources, whatever they may be – to share them, moreover, not in the sense merely of rewarding them *to* others, but in the sense also of rewarding them more fully to himself through the stimulus and support *of* others. In a genuinely democratic group there is no conflict between vigorous self-interest and vigorous social-interest: each demands from and returns to the other, and thereby both are strengthened. Here the good leader is one who perceives emotionally as well as intellectually that such reciprocity is a ceaseless need. And each participant is regarded as a contributor to its satisfaction.

By the operative perspective, I refer to ethical problems that arise in the course of a leader's active conduct of a group. That his attitudes affect such conduct, just as the conduct affects his attitudes, is obvious enough. Nonetheless, the two perspectives are not at all identical.

Let me illustrate by one problem only: how the leader's own

convictions and preferences may operate in determining the ultimate outcomes and decisions of any group effort. To what extent,
if at all, is it ethical for him to lead the group to agree with these
convictions and preferences?

Suppose that a neighborhood group meets to consider what to
do about juvenile delinquency. The leader, deeply concerned over
the evil, has not only thought about it more than other members,
but is persuaded that the best solution is the construction of a
new youth center. Is it right or wrong for him to guide the group
into acceptance of his preference?

The same kind of problem arises in countless group discussions: shall the teacher of adults, for example, draw the group not
only *out* but also *toward* his own position that the United Nations
ought to be strengthened; that segregation should be abolished
without further delay; that communists ought to be prohibited
from teaching; that atomic energy for peaceful purposes should
be controlled by private enterprise; that the Chinese government
should never be recognized?

Not to Conceal, but to Reveal

No one, I suppose, would care to argue that a leader professing to
be democratic is justified in deliberate manipulation of a group
toward his own prejudgments. Manipulation implies, and correctly so, that the leader uses techniques that are morally repre-
hensible: refusing a full voice to opponents of his views; or
encouraging his sympathizers to speak oftener than their turn; or
stacking the cards by excluding unfavorable evidence; or heavily
stressing the favorable.

I am not speaking here, however, of the Machiavelli-type
leader, though he is common enough. I am speaking instead of
the leader who holds a position that he hopes, perhaps quite
earnestly and plausibly, the group will agree to accept, but who at
the same time is eager to conduct the process ethically and democratically. How then shall he function?

In the first place, he owes it to the group to indicate his own
preferences frankly and clearly, while yet making apparent in the
way he operates that these preferences are continually subject to
reconsideration, modification, or even disapproval. Whether such

indication should be made almost at the beginning of deliberations, or in the course of group interaction and growth, depends
both upon the nature of the group and upon the type of issue
under consideration. A group whose members are well acquainted, who know their leader, and have a fair degree of
maturity, is usually ready earlier in the process than one made up
chiefly of strangers or of persons relatively unfamiliar either with
group experience or with the issue itself. The principle that the
leader should be forthright is, however, the same regardless of
variation in the character of the group. And one of the chief
values of this principle is that members are alerted to and made
more critical of any weighted efforts the leader may make to
guide the process in his own preferred direction.

In the second place, the ethical leader does everything he can to
provide opportunity for expression of feeling and opinion by
those who differ with him. In part, this necessity stems from the
attitudinal perspective already considered: the leader whose
value of equality is sufficiently strong will encourage and respect
the contributions that all members are capable of making. In
part, also, it stems from recognition by the leader that his own
convictions may quite possibly be wrong. The point here is that a
conviction, properly defined, is radically different from a dogma
or prejudice: it is a reasoned-out judgment based upon evidence
and communication, and hence subject to correction by the same
process that originally formed it. No one is fit to be leader of a
democratic group who regards his judgments as infallible.

And in the third place, groups concerned with issues that involve the need of reliable evidence – and what issues do not? –
should be exposed at every opportunity to that evidence. Here
the leader's ethics are measured by the extent to which he makes
certain that ample facts, ample testimony, ample authority in
opposition to, as well as in favor of, his own position are introduced for utmost study and analysis. In educational terms, the
perils of conscious or unconscious indoctrination by the leader-
teacher are reduced in inverse ratio to the degree that such safe-
guards are increased.

The particular decisions emerging from this kind of leadership
cannot then be predicted beyond the assurance that they will be
democratically achieved. They may not be in accord with the

leader's hopes; they may even be quite at odds; but also, of course, they may approximate his original expectations. If, however, his preference for a youth center does become the considered preference of the group as a whole, or if the group does agree with his own convictions about China, it is not because he has manipulated the group toward such acceptance. It is because there has been authentic, uncoerced consensus. The ends of group process justify the means only if the means are as moral as the ends themselves.

It is scarcely necessary to emphasize that both the attitudinal and operative perspectives range far beyond the problems I have touched upon. Actually, both are grounded in a single conception of leadership – an ethical conception relevant not only to discussion or action groups as such, but to the whole structure and method of democratic institutions of every degree of complexity.

Much of the confusion over leadership results from failure to distinguish between three related roles. The first, exemplified by the attitude of equality, is the 'encourager'. A regard for the varied contributions of all participants is the essential value. The second role, exemplified by the operation of leading a group toward decisions or commitments, is that of the 'pointer' or 'suggester'. In this case the leader is not only required to disclose his own partialities, or to point to proposals that other members may have overlooked, but to guarantee that these will be exposed to the richest possible comparison with alternative partialities. The third role, which is also operative and adds a new dimension to our discussion thus far, I shall call the 'implementer'. It is the role of carrying through any decisions or policies that the group has affirmed. Here the administrator and engineer, both broadly defined, come into their own: they are members delegated with the task of translating general agreements into specific, workable acts and of seeing that performance takes place when the translation is done.

A Leader is Many Things

That there is an ethics of implementing as well as of encouraging and pointing is clear to anyone who has ever attempted it with conscience. The most important value it demands is clear

415

responsibility – responsibility to those who have entrusted the administrator or engineer to put their mandates, as expertly as possible, into operation. By the same token, the gravest danger, and one that requires constant vigilance, is that of taking arbitrary steps beyond and in violation of those that have been sanctioned. The engineer draws up plans for the youth center that conform strictly with group policy; he does not emasculate or distort the latter in favor of plans he happens to like better. The administrator formulates rules concerning communist teachers that are likewise strictly authorized; he does not make or enforce rules that reflect merely his own political opinions.

It does not, of course, follow that the same leader must, even at different times, play all three of these roles. Indeed, the more creative a democratic group the greater the likelihood that it will invite various members to play each of them. The encourager may or may not be an effective pointer. The implementer may be more skillful in turning an approved policy into concrete practice than in either of the other roles. Clearly, there is nothing unethical in the same leader performing all three roles within the limits of his energy or talent; on the contrary, there may be times when he definitely should. Yet the chances are that, in the degree that he is an effective leader, he will discover and encourage other members of his group who are able to perform one or more of them at least as well as he. Leadership that *distributes* leadership is, in the context of a democratic ethics, the strongest and most fertile of all.

Further Reading

There are many papers and studies of significance in the understanding of leadership which might have found a place in this volume but for limitations of space. These include:

BORG, W. R. (1957), 'The behavior of emergent and designated leaders in situational tests', *Sociometry*, vol. 20, pp. 95–104.

BORG, W. R. (1960), 'Prediction of small group role behavior from personality variables', *Journal of Abnormal and Social Psychology*, vol. 60, pp. 112–16.

CARTER, L. F., and NIXON, M. (1949), 'An investigation of the relationship between four criteria of leadership ability for three different tasks', *Journal of Psychology*, vol. 27, pp. 245–61.

CROCKETT, W. H. (1955), 'Emergent leadership in small decision making groups', *Journal of Abnormal and Social Psychology*, vol. 51, pp. 378–83.

FANELLI, A. A. (1955), 'A typology of community leadership based on influence and interaction within the leader sub-system', *Social Forces*, vol. 34, pp. 332–8.

HALPIN, A. W. (1955), 'The leader behavior and leadership ideology of educational administrators and aircraft commanders', *Harvard Educational Review*, Winter, pp. 18–32.

HAYTHORN, W., COUCH, A., HAEFNER, D., LANGHAM, P., and CARTER, L. (1956), 'The effects of varying combinations of authoritarian and equalitarian leaders and followers', *Journal of Abnormal and Social Psychology*, vol. 53, pp. 210–19.

HILLS, R. J. (1963), 'The representative function: neglected dimension of leadership behavior', *Administrative Science Quarterly*, vol. 8, pp. 83–101.

HOLLANDER, E. P. (1958), 'Conformity, status and idiosyncrasy credit', *Psychological Review*, vol. 65, pp. 117–27.

JENKINS, W. O. (1947), 'A review of leadership studies with particular reference to military problems', *Psychological Bulletin*, vol. 44, pp. 54–79.

LANGE, C. J. (1962), 'Leadership in small military units: Some recent research findings', in F. Geldard (ed.), *Defence Psychology*, Pergamon, pp. 286–301.

MORRIS, R. T., and SEEMAN, M. (1950), 'The problem of leadership: An interdisciplinary approach', *American Journal of Sociology*, vol. 56, pp. 149–55.

Further Reading

MULDER, M., and STEMERDING, A. (1963), 'Threat, attraction to group and need for strong leadership', *Human Relations*, vol. 16, pp. 317–34.

SHELLEY, H. P. (1960), 'Focused leadership and cohesiveness in small groups', *Sociometry*, vol. 23, pp. 209–16.

STEPHENSON, T. E. (1959), 'The leader–follower relationship', *Sociological Review*, vol. 7, pp. 179–95.

STEWART, J. C., and SCOTT, J. P. (1947), 'Lack of correlation between leadership and dominance relationships in a herd of goats', *Journal of Comparative and Physiological Psychology*, vol. 40, pp. 255–64.

TURK, H. (1961), 'Instrumental values and the popularity of instrumental leaders', *Social Forces*, vol. 39, pp. 252–60.

WAGER, L. W. (1964), 'Leadership style, hierarchical influence, and supervisory role obligations', *Administrative Science Quarterly*, vol. 9, pp. 391–420.

WOLMAN, B. (1956), 'Leadership and group dynamics', *Journal of Social Psychology*, vol. 43, pp. 11–25.

Other collections of readings and papers which help to round out the selection in this volume are:

BROWNE, C. G., and COHN, T. S. (eds.) (1958), *The Study of Leadership*, Interstate Printers and Publishers.

KEMP, C. G. (ed.) (1964), *Perspectives on the Group Process*, Houghton–Mifflin.

PETRULLO, L., and BASS, B. M. (eds.) (1961), *Leadership and Interpersonal Behavior*, Holt, Rinehart and Winston.

Recent integrative accounts by major contributors to the study of leadership include:

COLLINS, B. E., and GUETZKOW, H. (1964), *A Social Psychology of Group Processes for Decision-Making*, Wiley.

FIEDLER, F. E. (1967), *A Theory of Leadership Effectiveness*, McGraw–Hill.

HOLLANDER, E. P. (1964), *Leaders, Groups and Influence*, Oxford University Press.

KATZ, D., and KAHN, R. L. (1966), *The Social Psychology of Organizations*, Wiley.

STOGDILL, R. M. (1965), *Managers, Employees, Organizations*, Ohio State University, Bureau of Business Research.

A more popular but still excellent treatment of many aspects of leadership may be found in:

ROSS, M., and HENDRY, C. E. (1957), *New Understandings of Leadership*, Association Press.

Acknowledgements

Permission to use the Readings in this selection is acknowledged from the following sources:

Reading 1   *Administrative Science Quarterly*
Reading 2   Society for the Psychological Study of Social Issues and I. Knickerbocker
Reading 3   American Psychological Association and Professor R. M. Stogdill
Reading 4   The Journal Press and F. E. Terman
Reading 5   The Journal Press and Professor R. M. Stogdill
Reading 6   Plenum Publishing Company Limited
Reading 7   American Psychological Association and Dr R. D. Mann
Reading 8   The Journal Press and Dr T. S. Cohn
Reading 9   American Sociological Association and Dr A. M. Rose
Reading 10   American Psychological Association
Reading 11   *Australian Journal of Psychology*
Reading 12   College of Education, Ohio State University and Dr J. K. Hemphill
Reading 13   *Science Journal incorporating Discovery* and Dr F. E. Fiedler
Reading 14   Schenkman Publishing Company, Inc.
Reading 15   Free Press of Glencoe
Reading 16   American Psychological Association and Dr J. P. Kirscht
Reading 17   American Psychological Association and S. W. Becker
Reading 18   Holt, Rinehart and Winston, Oxford University Press and Professor E. P. Hollander
Reading 19   The Journal Press and Lt. P. D. Nelson
Reading 20   Holt, Rinehart and Winston
Reading 21   Society for the Psychological Study of Social Issues
Reading 22   *Personnel Psychology* and Dr E. A. Fleishman
Reading 23   *Administrative Science Quarterly*
Reading 24   American Sociological Association and Dr A. Etzioni
Reading 25   Adult Education Association of the U.S.A.

Author Index

Author Index

Subject Index

Subject Index

Subject Index